The Hispanic World and American Intellectual Life, 1820–1880

Iván Jaksić

Para mi querido Don Jorge, con la admiración, gratitud y respeto de su amigo de siempre.

Iván
Octubre 2007

THE HISPANIC WORLD AND AMERICAN INTELLECTUAL LIFE, 1820–1880
Copyright © Iván Jaksić, 2007.

First published in 2007 by
PALGRAVE MACMILLAN™
175 Fifth Avenue, New York, N.Y. 10010 and
Houndmills, Basingstoke, Hampshire, England RG21 6XS
Companies and representatives throughout the world.

PALGRAVE MACMILLAN is the global academic imprint of the Palgrave Macmillan division of St. Martin's Press, LLC and of Palgrave Macmillan Ltd. Macmillan® is a registered trademark in the United States, United Kingdom and other countries. Palgrave is a registered trademark in the European Union and other countries.

ISBN-13: 978–1–4039–8079–3
ISBN-10: 1–4039–8079–9

Library of Congress Cataloging-in-Publication Data

Jaksić, Iván, 1954–
    The Hispanic world and American intellectual life, 1820–1880 / Iván Jaksić.
        p. cm. — (The studies of the Americas)
    Includes bibliographical references and index.
    ISBN 1–4039–8079–9
        1. United States—Intellectual life—19th century. 2. Intellectuals—United States—Biography. 3. Scholars—United States—Biography. 4. Historians—United States—Biography. 5. Authors, American—19th century—Biography. 6. American literature—19th century—History and criticism. 7. United States—Civilization—Hispanic influences. 8. National characteristics, American. 9. Spain—Civilization. 10. Spain—Colonies—America. I. Title.

E166.J25 2007
9460072'02313—dc22   2007004613

A catalogue record for this book is available from the British Library.

Design by Newgen Imaging Systems (P) Ltd., Chennai, India.

First edition: October 2007

10 9 8 7 6 5 4 3 2 1

Printed in the United States of America.

To Juan Rivano, my mentor, who taught me how to question what we think we know.

Titus Septimius:

Follow me to distant Spain,
Let us plough the boist'rous main.
Soon in battle we'll o'erthrow
Th' ignorant Cantabrian foe,
O'er the Syrtte our banners wave
Where the Moorish billows lave.
I wish amid th' happy lands
Where the Grecian Tibur stands
I may find a rural seat,
In old age a safe retreat,
Far from toils and gloomy care
Far from all th' alarms of war.
Should the fates my will controll,
Where Galaesus's surges roll,
Where the flocks their shepards lead
Frisking on the flowery mead,
I'll beneath Phalantus's sway
Spend in peace my closing day.[1]

---

[1] William Hickling Prescott papers, Massachusetts Historical Society. This poem of approximately 1806 is identified simply as "Translation of Horace" but it is clearly a free translation of Ode VI, Book II.

Contents

Preface

This book is centrally concerned with those Americans who pioneered the serious study of Spain and Latin America in the early republic. Although some names such as those of Washington Irving, Henry Wadsworth Longfellow, and William H. Prescott remain familiar to this day, the reasons for their personal and scholarly Spanish interests, their reading of sources, and the literary, religious, and philosophical underpinnings informing their views constitute a lacuna in our knowledge of the intellectual history of the Americas and Spain. I seek to fill this gap by examining their writings, their contacts and, where appropriate, their visits to foreign nations. My contention is that these scholars were drawn into the history of the Spanish empire by their desire not only to examine the emergence of a once-vibrant national culture, but also to explain the causes of its demise, for reasons that resonated with their own concerns about the character and development of an emerging American national identity.

During the course of the nineteenth century, Spain lost most of its New World dominions, and as the former colonies struggled to define their respective boundaries and identities, questions were raised, in Spanish America and elsewhere, about the nature of nationhood in a postcolonial context. Did a truly American, or Spanish American, culture need be exceptional? Should these emerging nations maintain linkages to other countries, including their former imperial rulers? Could literature and scholarship in the humanities contribute to the shaping of new national identities? Intellectuals, both North and South, and across the Atlantic, generated a lively dialogue on these questions. This book is centrally concerned with the fluid nature of these contacts.

I was drawn to the subject while conducting research on Andrés Bello, the towering nineteenth-century Spanish American intellectual and statesman whose contributions to nation building remain as impressive today as they were in the immediate postindependence period. I noticed, at one point, that he devoted considerable attention to George Ticknor's *History of Spanish Literature* (1849), and consequently I ventured into the papers of the Boston-based literary historian. A whole new world of inter-American contacts opened up to me, and I decided to explore other contemporary figures. The papers of William H. Prescott, Henry Wadsworth Longfellow, and Mary Peabody Mann yielded similar results, and it occurred to me that an examination of these records might illuminate a significant aspect of the intellectual history of the United States, or at least do justice to the individuals who devoted their working lives to understanding the Hispanic world.

What follows is my attempt to document and explain the international origins, and national implications, of this intellectual tradition.

* * *

I am very indebted to the David Rockefeller Center for Latin American Studies (DRCLAS) at Harvard University, for it was there, as a Visiting Scholar in the Fall of 1997, that I encountered the records of George Ticknor that led me to pursue this current project. I could not do so immediately, but the completion of my work on Bello in 2001 allowed me to begin systematic research on the subject. I am also deeply indebted to the institutions that made it possible for me to find the time and the resources to devote to this study. The John Simon Guggenheim Memorial Foundation provided me with fellowship support in 2002–2003 that freed me from some of my usual academic obligations. The National Endowment for the Humanities and the Massachusetts Historical Society provided me with additional support that allowed me to spend half a year consulting the Society's magnificent collection, as well as various other repositories in the Boston-Cambridge area. DRCLAS provided me with a short-term library scholarship in July 2004, while the Friends of the Longfellow House awarded me a Stanley Paterson Research Fellowship in 2005. The Houghton Library at Harvard generously appointed me to the Stanley J. Kahrl Fellowship in Literary Manuscripts in 2005 as well. The University of Notre Dame provided me with travel funds to consult special collections in other parts of the country and abroad. Finally, a grant from the Ford Foundation (Southern Cone and Andean Regional Office) allowed me to finish the writing of this book. I am very grateful for the support of these institutions.

I also wish to thank the friends and colleagues who read various versions of the manuscript, or helped me in various ways: Peter Accardo, Alan Angell, Maria Ascher, the late Simon Collier, June Erlick, Pere Gifra-Adroher, Gary Hamburg, J. León Helguera, Richard Kagan, Gwen Kirkpatrick, Roberto López-Vela, Brian Loveman, Megan Marshall, John McGreevy, Joan Nordell, Gonzalo Palacios, Eduardo Posada-Carbó, Juan José Santos, William F. Sater, Doris Sommer, William B. Taylor, James Turner, Scott Van Jacob, Eric Van Young, Barry L. Velleman, and Conrad Wright. My wife Carolina endured my absences from home and my countless references to the project, while our daughter Ilse accompanied me to the archives when I was on the trail of Longfellow. I am grateful for their affectionate support.

Introduction

The venerable Boston Brahmin George Ticknor, Smith Professor of Modern Languages at Harvard and a founder of the Boston Public Library, was at the center of a little-known American intellectual tradition. Ticknor was the neighbor and friend of William H. Prescott, the celebrated historian whose first biography he would eventually write. Ticknor was also the mentor and friend of a young poet of unusual talent, Henry Wadsworth Longfellow, whom he recruited as his successor to the Smith professorship. Longfellow and Prescott became close friends and visited each other often in Cambridge, Boston, and their beloved seaside resort of Nahant. All three had at one time or another met or corresponded with Washington Irving, the expansive New Yorker who inspired and encouraged them and whose eulogy Longfellow would one day deliver at the Massachusetts Historical Society in Boston. All three also crossed paths with Mary Peabody Mann—novelist, translator, and tireless crusader for universal education and various charitable causes. Their now-silent voices, recorded in correspondence scattered over many distant archives, speak of strong ties of respect, admiration, and affection. They led very different lives, but something brought them together that made them very special: they were the pioneer American scholars and lifetime students of the Hispanic world.

Why did these gifted Americans devote their lives and talents to the study of the Hispanic world in the nineteenth century? The first and most obvious answer is that the breakdown of the Spanish empire in the Americas, and the resulting emergence of new nations in the Western Hemisphere, presented enormous challenges and opportunities for the United States: border issues, commerce, and diplomatic relations all moved to center stage when Spanish America won its independence from Spain in the 1820s. The reality of a new international order, and of a new hemispheric situation, was simply too hard to ignore and demanded immediate attention.

Yet the reasons why this group of pioneering Americans decided to concentrate on the Hispanic world had little to do with such compelling historical facts. It is the thesis of this book that they did so to contribute to the shaping of their own country's national identity during a crucial and very specific period in history. After achieving independence from the British empire, and especially after the War of 1812, Americans of the early republic deliberately engaged in an effort to define their culture, history, and uniqueness as a nation. Perhaps surprisingly, they did so by studying, and in some cases visiting, what may now appear as the most unlikely place in the world: the seat of the collapsing Spanish empire. Numerous other Americans traveled to many distant places during this period, but few parts of the globe beyond Great Britain attracted as much attention, or inspired as much writing, as Spain and its former possessions in the New World.

The majority of Americans who traveled to Spain and Latin America in the nineteenth century were engaged in diplomacy or business. What sets this group of writers apart is that although they may have had practical motivations for travel or study, they were or became *intellectually* engaged with the Hispanic world. Ticknor and Longfellow went to Spain in preparation for careers in higher education, but devoted themselves to the study of Spanish literary traditions. Washington Irving went to Spain to work on a translation, but quickly identified the romantic potential of Spanish history, particularly the clash between cultural and religious traditions. Prescott passed quickly through Iberia to London and Paris in search of a cure for his eye problems, yet he was captivated to such an extent that he devoted his entire working life to the study of Spanish history. Mary Mann went to Cuba as the companion of her ailing sister Sophia Peabody (the accomplished artist who later married Nathaniel Hawthorne), and as a result of this Caribbean experience she became not only a leading advocate for universal education in South America, but also the influential translator of a key Latin American text that did more than any other to shape American views of the Hispanic world.

When the varied, complex, and voluminous contributions of these intellectuals are considered together, a clear pattern emerges. First, these people were centrally concerned with understanding and defining the Spanish *national character*, whether from direct observation, study of Spanish history and literature, or a combination of the two. All of them viewed the Spanish character as consisting of two central elements: religion and chivalry. According to American observers, the glory days of Spain had been those of the *Reconquista*, the protracted struggle, lasting nearly eight centuries, which had eventually expelled the Muslim invaders from the Iberian Peninsula. During this time, the necessities of war had shaped the national character, fostering a martial temperament and a deep-seated belief in the sanctity of the Spanish cause. American observers agreed that these qualities had propelled Spain to an unparalleled position as a world power. But they concluded that once Spaniards were deprived of a common enemy after their astonishing victory, the positive elements of the national character had degenerated into a cruel tendency to fight and conquer. Moreover, Spain's initially pure religious motivations had now become blind fanaticism intent on imposing religious compliance and uniformity. This transformation from glorious nation builder to expansionist, corrupt, and fanatical empire had occurred under the Habsburg monarchs who, not coincidentally, had set in motion the forces that led to the European settlement of the Americas. In the collective view of American intellectuals, Spain had never recovered from the poisons of war and religious hatred. Slowly deteriorating into a sad version of its former self, it was now a country in ruins, a historical curiosity, an example of how low a culture could sink after losing its foundational values. All that survived, and all that was worthy, of the Spanish national character now resided in its common people. Their songs, their pride, their customs fascinated the Americans who are the subject of this book. The Spanish national character survived, but in a quaint version, a pale shadow of what it had been during the country's Golden Age.

This book's second major argument is that the story of the rise and fall of Spain contained *lessons* of great relevance to the fledgling United States. Its citizens still had vivid memories of the American Revolution, when Prescott's grandfather fought at Bunker Hill, and when George Washington, while in New York, met the wondering gaze of a child named Washington Irving, his future biographer. The values of liberty and union had created the new nation, much as religion and chivalry had done in Spain. Would such values weaken and degenerate as they had there, when the successors to Ferdinand and Isabella turned the Spanish nation into an empire? Such a decline was possible, Prescott and Longfellow believed when they observed with great anxiety the U.S. occupation of Mexico in the 1840s. Was not this the dreaded scenario in which a promising young republic unleashed the dogs of war, only to become mired in the domination of other countries and cultures? Here, in the history of Spain, they could point to the dire results of conquest. War for liberty against an oppressor led to independence, but war for conquest and expansion could lead only to weakness and decay, stifling in the process all aspirations for peaceful prosperity. The remarkable emphasis on the history of the Spanish empire, which is so characteristic of nineteenth-century America, was in the end a didactic reminder of what the United States should not become.

The third concern of this talented group of Americans was *religious*. All of them were proponents of liberal Christianity who wished not only to leave the dominant Calvinism of the past far behind, but also to contain the advance of other Christian denominations, which in their view were prone to sectarianism, superstition, and excessive "enthusiasm." The development of Spanish Catholicism, or at least their perceived version of it, provided them with the perfect example to underscore the superiority of liberal Christianity. The Spanish Catholic Church was seen as not only notoriously corrupt, abounding in examples of priestly excess, but also prone to use the forces of the State to impose religious orthodoxy within and beyond the boundaries of the country. In addition, the emphasis of the Church on the divinity of Christ, the Immaculate Conception of the Virgin, the celebration of saints' days, and the strict adherence to Vatican commands all served as examples to promote the higher spirituality and rationalist theology of liberal Christianity. But nothing could surpass the utility of the Inquisition as a cudgel in efforts to condemn all forms of religious intolerance and zealotry. None of the writers discussed in this book failed to describe the horrors of inquisitorial despotism and vengeance, in screeds ranging from Irving's "Student of Salamanca" in the 1820s, to Longfellow's "Torquemada" in the 1860s. In the end, however, their central concern was not exclusively religious bigotry in Spain, but rather the lingering fear that American toleration and democratic culture might provide fertile ground for religious sectarianism (especially Catholic) to prosper, and even become a major force in American government and politics. Perhaps their fears were exaggerated, but the Spanish Inquisition allowed them to deliver yet another didactic lesson about what the United States should never do in matters of belief.

Lacking any direct threats from Spain, or even a desire to emulate its development and history, why did American intellectuals devote such considerable time and energy to flogging the proverbial dead horse? Part of the answer might lie in the role played by romanticism in American letters in the nineteenth century. Romanticism served as the vehicle for building national traditions, even where few were to be found. Americans by and large, some notable exceptions notwithstanding, did not seek to anchor national traditions in the Native American past. They went elsewhere, to a Pan-European spectrum of sources, which not coincidentally the poet Longfellow studied and mastered in a remarkable way. They focused on Spain because, after all, it was Spain that had fought for liberty against foreign invaders to pave the way for one of the greatest accomplishments in world history: Columbus's discovery of the New World. Here were the true national origins of the United States. The enterprising, individualistic Columbus had done more than present a new world "to Castile and to Leon" (as the popular Spanish saying goes); he had established the foundations for the new republic. The American intellectuals discussed in this book deliberately set out to anchor American traditions in this foundational moment. It was Columbus—honored today in places such as the District of Columbia, Columbia University, Columbus Circle, and Columbus, Ohio—who helped to establish *American* national traditions. He came with baggage from imperialist Spain—heavy, problematic baggage, loaded with Catholic motives, and slavery—but this Spanish past was relevant and it had to be investigated.

This is the point where we see romantic interests turn into systematic historical research. The field of history was a prime instrument for nation building and for the promotion of specific values in the United States and elsewhere. In the nineteenth century, as new nations emerged around the world and old monarchies turned into fledgling republics, history helped Americans to shape the past in their effort to address the needs and aspirations of the present. The past, when properly presented, could show that a nation was destined for either greatness or failure. Thus, Prescott could argue that the Aztecs were doomed to defeat even before Columbus set sail across the ocean, or Hernán Cortés landed in Mexico. He could claim that Spain was doomed to fall because of its religious fanaticism and blind greed. The United States, because of its progressive values, had a chance for long-lasting success. History, in short, could reveal the most useful lessons and point the way to the future. In the process, American historians, of whom Prescott was a leading light, brought massive documentation to bear, in several languages, in order to give credibility to their claims. History had romantic origins, developed into a vehicle for the promotion of specific values, and left a legacy of research based on authentic documentary sources. Spain, because of the abundance of records (though many were still to be pinpointed for their relevance to the United States), became a surprising center of attention in nineteenth-century America. Columbus, Ferdinand and Isabella, Cortés, Francisco Pizarro, and even the dour Charles V, a religious fanatic to the end, became both popular names and enduring figures to characterize the Hispanic world. Spain was essential as a point of origin, as well as an example to be avoided, in the American search for a unique national identity.

As this book seeks to demonstrate, American intellectuals were more internationally oriented than is commonly assumed. They traveled abroad, read widely, received foreign visitors, and maintained an astonishing exchange of records and correspondence with counterparts across the Atlantic and in Latin America. They depended on their foreign colleagues to such an extent that Ticknor's monumental *History of Spanish Literature* could not have come into being, at least not in its present form, without the assistance of Pascual de Gayangos. Nor could Washington Irving's *Columbus* have been written without the massive research and generous guidance of Martín Fernández de Navarrete. Nor could Prescott's *Conquest of Mexico*, a book first published in 1843 and still in print, be what it is without the detailed comments of José Fernando Ramírez and Lucas Alamán. We read these sources and admire them, but until now have known little of the international conversations from which they emerged.

Hispanics had their own reasons for interacting with their American counterparts. They sensed that these intellectuals were engaged in the same endeavor they themselves were pursuing: the effort to define and build national identities and institutions. Both Spanish America and the United States had fought for independence and built republics. When the smoke cleared, they set about establishing national traditions, foundational myths, and appropriate histories to justify their actions. The challenge for Latin America, in contrast to that of the United States, was how to incorporate the Spanish colonial past. Its struggle for independence had been as vicious as all colonial wars, but more recent; the ashes of war were still smoldering. As a result, the national ideology that emerged was markedly anti-Spanish and was receptive, indeed grateful, for the American research that exposed the oppressiveness of the imperial system and the cruelty of the conquistadors. Anyone who read Prescott's *Conquest of Peru* with a nineteenth-century Latin American eye could not but cheer the struggle against the Pizarros of the world. Those Latin Americans who resented the still considerable role of the Catholic Church after independence had only to read Ticknor's *History*, in the marvelous translation by Pascual de Gayangos, to find an arsenal of arguments against the close relationship between Church and State. They read selectively, and found what they needed to condemn their own colonial past. American research and writing not only was well received, but played a crucial role in the construction of these new nations.

Back in old Spain, there were new stirrings as well. After the death of Ferdinand VII in 1833, Spain began a difficult journey toward a more liberal political system. They had their fill of despotic kings, and they liked the last the least. Spanish liberals looked with great anticipation at the relaxation of monarchical rule, as well as at the sharing of power with a reestablished parliament (*Cortes*). In this new political context, intellectuals were quick to seize an opportunity for reinventing the past, so they could show that the laws of history culminated naturally in the happy current state of affairs. For this, they needed to denounce the imperial absolutist past, from Charles V to Ferdinand VII, as a terrible parenthesis in the country's history. They thus returned to the glorious days of the *Reconquista* to recover the values that had led Spain to greatness in the first place. Washington Irving, with his *Columbus, Legends of Spain* and *Conquest of Granada*, provided them with a model of romantic literature that they could embrace. Ticknor, with his depiction of the decay of Spain in the sixteenth and seventeenth centuries, and especially Prescott, with his devastating presentation of the character and policies of Charles V and Philip II, provided liberal Spaniards with the ammunition they needed to condemn the old regime and strengthen the ideological foundations of their new political program.

But there were limits to the reception of American views, especially the views on Hispanic religion. Americans made little effort to hide their contempt for Catholicism in general, and for Spanish Catholic practices in particular. Proponents of Spanish liberalism, which was predicated on a marriage of convenience with the Church and the monarchy, resisted or openly rejected Protestant readings of Spain's dominant religion. Some reacted vociferously against condescending comments and the overall ridiculing of their faith. Likewise, in Spanish America, where tensions between Church and State were high in the postindependence period, the American condemnation of Catholicism was seen as a torch near a powder keg, and treated as such. Some anticlerical liberals applauded, but there was little they could do in a land where Catholicism was the official religion, supported by the State. The political environment recommended prudence, and prudence was exercised through creative translating and editing.

The American intellectuals discussed in this book decisively shaped their country's perceptions about the Hispanic world. On balance, their views were negative, and would provide the unfortunate foundation for even more negative views put forth by less talented observers in the future. Spain was firmly established as the antithesis of democratic, enterprising America. The country was corrupt beyond remedy, its former glories but a distant memory. The ultimate reason for such sorry decay was believed to be religious intolerance combined with government despotism: these were so thoroughly embedded in the country's soul that no reversal was possible. From this fundamental assumption, a number of stereotypes crystallized in the American imagination: Spanish people were not enterprising; they were lazy; they obeyed their priests blindly; they wasted their time in bloody bullfights; their music and dance were lovely, but unhelpful to their country or to themselves; they could not do anything on time; they did not plan ahead; they went to their graves having accomplished nothing in the way of improvement.

Latin America did not fare any better. All the negative characteristics ascribed to Spain were simply transferred across the Atlantic, where the element of race added even darker overtones. Prescott did not hesitate to label Mexicans a "degraded race," and feared during the Mexican War that the country would be annexed, to the detriment of the United States. But no stereotype could be more damning, or more difficult to overcome, than Mary Mann's importation of the concept of *Caudillismo* to define the essence of Latin American political culture. The *Caudillo* was the man on horseback—half bloodthirsty barbarian, half ruthless and unprincipled leader—commanding the suicidal loyalty of his followers in a campaign to destroy all societal order. This enduring trope dominated American views of the region in the nineteenth and twentieth centuries, and still surfaces in otherwise learned discussions about Latin American history and politics.

Yet, as this book shows, those gifted American intellectuals who devoted their lives to the study of the Hispanic world fostered an appreciation of its culture and history that has endured in the United States to this day. Their work engendered a now-solid tradition of scholarship about that world, and a more sophisticated understanding of the richness and diversity of Hispanic cultures. Their individual methods, styles, and motivations could be quite different: Washington Irving was essentially a fiction writer with a remarkable ability to build on historical subjects; George Ticknor applied the rigorous philological methods of his German mentors to the study of Spanish literary history; Henry W. Longfellow was just as knowledgeable in his command of languages, which he used to create lasting literary images of the Hispanic world; Mary Mann was a self-taught interpreter of the South American experience, committed to the abolition of slavery and the promotion of primary education, and William H. Prescott was a historian who lived through and contributed to the nineteenth-century transformation of the discipline from a romantic endeavor to an exercise in factual accuracy. But they all converged in their desire to make the Hispanic World known to an American audience. In the end, perhaps the ultimate contribution of this group was their willingness to see themselves in the mirror of Spain, to build their own sense of nationality on the basis of Hispanic traditions, and to celebrate the triumphs, as well as lament the sorrows, of a culture that they made a part of their own.

Chapter 1

"My King, My Country, and My Faith": Washington Irving's Writings on the Rise and Fall of Spain

Spain is virtually a land of poetry and romance, where every-day life partakes of adventure, and where the least agitation or excitement carries everything up into extravagant enterprise and daring exploit. The Spaniards, in all ages, have been of swelling and braggart spirit, soaring in thought, pompous in word, and valiant, though vainglorious, in deed.

Washington Irving, *Legends of the Conquest of Spain* (1835)

When Washington Irving's Rip Van Winkle awakes from his twenty-year slumber, thinking that it has been but a mere night, he can see that the Hudson River, the Catskill Mountains, and even his old village, are just as he remembers them. But how the people have changed! Not only has the portrait of George III at the entrance of the village Inn (now called the Union Hotel) mutated into that of someone named George Washington, but the talk among the residents is of elections, citizens' rights, Congress, liberty, and other words that are "a perfect Babylonish jargon to the bewildered Van Winkle." Literally overnight, Rip finds himself changed from a loyal subject of George III to a free citizen of the United States. However confused, he soon adjusts to the comings and goings of the village, reshaping his own story to accommodate present realities, and thus becomes a living proof that the colonial past can be made to fit the republican present. Irving, the creator of this tale, was himself a time traveler, although he chose another country, Spain, and journeyed into the past rather than to the future. He wanted to see how Spanish history now looked from the perspective of the American republican present. Yet the same bewilderment, skeptical outlook, and sarcastic commentary involved in comparing historical periods and values worked to produce the earliest and perhaps most influential American view of the history of Spain and its people.

Born in New York City in 1783, Washington Irving grew up absorbing the scant information that existed on Spanish topics, primarily from the little books published in the series entitled *The World Displayed, or, A Curious Collection of Voyages and Travels, Selected from the Writers of All Nations.*[1] As Rolena Adorno has shown, stories of Boabdil (last king of Granada), Columbus, and the Spanish conquest of

Mexico and Peru had a profound influence on Irving's subsequent literary and historical interests.[2] Cervantes had also become one of his favorite writers by the time he made his first trip to Europe (1804–1806).[3] But overall, he knew little of Spain and its history or traditions until he journeyed there as a forty-three-year-old man. But that time, his pen had run dry and he was struggling to revive a sinking reputation.

Washington Irving's *Sketch Book* had been enthusiastically received in England and the United States. Indeed, it had made him famous on both sides of the Atlantic, but his *Tales of a Traveler* (1824) was a complete disappointment. He was in Paris when he received the bad news about the response of English critics to the latter book, and it was there that he made the decision to study Spanish and eventually make a trip to that country. The idea had been planted by Alexander Hill Everett (1792–1849), whom Irving had met at The Hague in July 1822. Everett convinced him to travel to Spain when he became U.S. ambassador to the court of Ferdinand VII in 1825. By that time, Irving had taken Spanish lessons and was able to read Calderón and Lope de Vega with ease. He had also read some of the few standard histories of Spain.[4] Irving was in Bordeaux when he received a letter from Everett announcing that the great Spanish historian Martín Fernández de Navarrete was about to publish a series of documents on Christopher Columbus that might be well worth translating into English. Would he undertake the task?[5] Irving needed only three days to decide. Writing to his friend Thomas Storrow, he declared, "[I] shall set off immediately with my Brother for Madrid, to attack it tooth & nail." He added, on a more personal note,

> Thus we drive at the mercy of chance and circumstance. How little did I dream when I left Paris, of these squalls and cross purposes that were to produce such worry and perplexity. And how little did I dream a week since that Spain, the country I have been so long wishing to see, but into which I feared I should never get a peep, should be the very port into which the first whiff of good luck should blow me. I hope to come out of it stored with materials for future meditation and occupation.[6]

"Stored with materials" is something of an understatement, for he wrote, or took notes for, all his major works on Spain while in residence between 1826 and 1829. The first such book was *A History of the Life and Voyages of Christopher Columbus* (1828), which, in addition to providing a ponderous biography of the navigator, launched a number of themes relating to Spanish culture and history. Years of uncertainty and disappointment finally appeared to have ended. He was, in fact, beginning one of the most creative periods of his long career.

Irving arrived in Madrid with his brother Peter (who joined him as a research assistant) on February 16, 1826, and soon met the members of the small American community there. In addition to the Everett family, Irving's most important contact was Obadiah Rich (1777–1850), the U.S. consul who was also an avid book collector. The Irvings rented rooms in Rich's spacious house, and enjoyed free access to his impressive library, which contained many manuscripts, including Bartolomé de las Casas's copy of Columbus's journal.[7] Irving was soon at work examining Navarrete's documents, reading widely on Spanish history and literature, and taking Spanish lessons. He attended social events and was a frequent visitor to the theater, but his journal shows a grueling schedule of work on the Columbus materials. By

August 1826, he had made remarkable progress in what was obviously no longer a translation of Navarrete's compilation of documents, but rather a full-blown biography of the Italian navigator. His creative instincts also began to lead him toward the siege and fall of Granada, which was the historical preamble to the story of Columbus.[8] He was working on both projects through 1826 and 1827. In March of the latter year a twenty-year-old graduate of Bowdoin College in Maine saw Irving at work in Madrid. The young man was Henry Wadsworth Longfellow, who penned the following description of Irving in a letter to his father:

> . . . he is one of those men who put you at ease with them in a moment. He makes no ceremony whatever with one—and of course is a very fine man in society—all mirth and good humor. He has a most beautiful countenance—and at the same time a very intellectual one—but he has some halting and hesitating in his conversation—and says very pleasant, agreeable things in a husky—weak—peculiar voice. He has a dark complexion— dark hair—whiskers already a little gray.[9]

Irving noted the arrival of Longfellow in his own journal, and recorded several subsequent encounters and outings.[10] But he also continued his relentless schedule of work until, at last, he concluded an agreement with John Murray, the London publisher, to print his biography of Columbus. "As soon as the last manuscript is sent off to London," he wrote to Thomas Storrow, "we expect to start for Andalusia."[11] The decision to travel to the south of Spain was related to Irving's desire to incorporate fresh additional materials on Columbus, but also to visit the scenery of his new project on Granada. He lingered in Madrid, however, until February 1828, when he headed south, passing through Córdoba, Granada, Málaga, Gibraltar, and several other southern locations until he settled in Seville in April, hoping to gain access to the famed Archivo General de Indias.[12] At this time, he also made a most influential acquaintance with Johann Nikolas Böhl von Faber (1770–1836), a native of Hamburg who had settled in Spain in 1785, and who developed not only an interest, but also a considerable reputation as a scholar of Spanish literature.

Washington Irving was delighted to hear on July 9, 1828 that Böhl had invited him "to take a chamber in his house when I come there [to Puerto de Santa María]."[13] The two met in August, and over the next few months they took frequent walks together and shared meals to discuss literary matters.[14] Irving also borrowed books from Böhl's considerable library, including sources by Antonio de Herrera, Alvar Núñez Cabeza de Vaca, Gonzalo Fernández de Oviedo, and a book of *Volksmärchen*.[15] While at Seville, he also met Cecilia Böhl, Marchioness of Arco Hermoso, Johann's daughter and a writer who would later achieve literary prominence under the pen name of Fernán Caballero.[16] Thus was Irving introduced to the pioneers of Spanish Romanticism.

As scholar Carol Tully has shown, Böhl provided a bridge between German and Spanish Romanticism, applying the ideas of various German authors, including Augustus W. Schlegel, to his own studies of Spanish Golden Age literature.[17] German Romanticism viewed the Spanish literature of the period as a truly national one, representing an antidote to the universalist pretensions of the French Enlightenment. Böhl himself contributed important studies to highlight, and indeed celebrate, the works of Calderón de la Barca and Lope de Vega as embodying the purest national traditions.[18] At the time he met Irving, he had recently published the *Floresta de Rimas Antiguas Castellanas* (1821–1825), an impressive three-volume compilation of medieval and Spanish Golden Age verse.[19] Irving was delighted to meet a kindred soul, and was inspired, as he would later write to Böhl, to "doing more justice to old Spain."[20]

It is in the context of his contact with Böhl that Irving worked on the draft of his *A Chronicle of the Conquest of Granada*. He described this work to his agent in London, Thomas Aspinwall, as "an attempt, not at an historical romance, but a romantic history."[21] To Alexander Everett, who shared his interest in Muslim Spain, he explained that the book was "in the form of a Chronicle, made up from all the old Spanish historians I could lay my hands on, colored and tinted by the imagination so as to have a romantic air."[22] This was not an easy decision to make, for he knew that it would come at the expense of historical veracity. Indeed, one of the first skeptics was the perceptive Lucretia Orne Everett, who wrote to William Peabody that,

> [Irving] has also sent over another work or at least the first part of a work on the Conquest of Granada by Ferdinand [and] Isabella in the form of Chronicles. He was struck with the subject while making researches for Columbus [and] at the same time took notes for this work [and] as he has since visited Granada [and] visited all the old Moorish works there he will no doubt make a popular work [and] in order to render it more so he has purposely thrown an air of romance over it—which causes some of us to doubt whether the work will be improved by the latter quality.[23]

One might trace Irving's decision to throw "an air of romance" over his work to his contact with Böhl, or even with novelist Walter Scott, whom he had met in Abbotsford in 1817 and whom he greatly admired.[24] But he also knew that a dry history of a rather remote episode would not help him reach the wide audience that he wanted. And there were admirers such as Longfellow, who immediately understood the potential of the story: "I see by the papers that Mr. Irving has collected from old MSS in the archives of the Library of the Arch Bishop of Seville a series of Moorish Tales. I have no doubts they will be delightfully interesting. He is a fortunate man: and deserves to be so, for he is a good man."[25]

Religious Conflict in Irving's Work

The "Moorish tales" mentioned by young Longfellow, and the product of Irving's relentless toil, became *A Chronicle of the Conquest of Granada* (1829), and soon included *The Alhambra* (1832) and the *Legends of the Conquest of Spain* (1835).[26] The Granada book provided an elaborate romantic rendition of the increasingly dominant theme of the Spanish character and its relationship to religion. By focusing on the last campaign against the Muslims of Spain (1482–1492), Irving painted an epic picture of the triumph of Christianity (still untouched by the divisions precipitated by the Reformation) against the last stronghold of Islam on the Iberian Peninsula. Through his fictional chronicler, the Jesuit Fray Antonio Agapida, Irving told the story "of a pious crusade, waged by the most Catholic of sovereigns" (III, 9). The Muslims were often shown as a courageous, albeit doomed people (a romantic trope for describing American Indians, who might have been on Irving's mind), but mostly as a fickle population torn by internal political and dynastic disputes. Their religion was described as superstitious, prone to read too much into omens and predictions, and follow too blindly the dictates of their often deranged prophets. Although in Irving's account they fight for every inch of territory, their fall is imminent. As the beleaguered leader Cidi Yahye exclaims in despair "Fate is against our arms; our ruin is written in the heavens" (III, 350).

Christians, for their part, are depicted as having superior courage, but most importantly, as having a stronger and more consistent conviction about the holiness of their struggle. They also possess an unwavering loyalty to the Crown, approaching a near adoration of their flawless Queen Isabella. Few knights can surpass the Marquis of Cadiz, the ultimate example of chivalry and self-sacrifice. He is so highly regarded as to be compared by "contemporary historians to the immortal Cid" (III, 23, 200)—that is, Spain's ultimate national hero. He leads Christians to fight for "glory, for revenge, for the holy faith, and for the spoil of these wealthy infidels" (III, 29). Like the admirable Nestor of the *Iliad*, he was "as wise as he was valiant" (III, 52). King Ferdinand is shown in a favorable light also, although more often than not as impetuous, impatient, and having difficulty making up his mind without the aid of the queen. He is also "politic," calculating, and shrewd, conforming to Machiavelli's own treatment of the king in *The Prince*. Ferdinand, for instance, is cautious, "and fond of conquests gained by art rather than valor" (III, 386). He can be elaborately gracious, especially when grants and concessions are "in unison with his policy" (III, 264), or he can be a "master of dissimulation" when dealing with the international implications of his actions (III, 329). He is also relentless, for "the absolute conquest of Granada was the great object of this war, and he was resolved never to rest content without its complete fulfillment" (III, 140). Isabella, for her part, is all perfection, introducing a "lofty and chivalrous spirit" (III, 51) to the raw facts of war. She is also "the very soul, the vital principle, of this great enterprise" (III, 331). She has a "magnanimous spirit," that is often "filled with compassion," when dealing with defeated enemies (III, 99). Isabella is, after all, "zealous for the promotion of the faith, but not for the extermination of the Infidels" (III, 103). The queen is especially attentive to the needs of the many Christian captives who are released as the fortunes of war favor the Catholic monarchy. Not surprisingly, Isabella is "universally beloved by her subjects" (III, 201), and she is "venerated even by the Moors" (III, 341) because of her humanitarian gestures toward friend and foe. The queen rarely appears without Pedro González de Mendoza, the grand cardinal of Spain, and a "crowd" of priests who serve as her closest advisors. The influence of the former is made clear in a passage where Isabella has become despondent over the loss of Christians at Moclin: "The discreet words of the cardinal soothed the spirit of the queen, who always looked to him for consolation; and she soon recovered her usual equanimity" (III, 162). She is also assisted by her confessor, Hernando de Talavera, who is at hand during the siege of Málaga, along with "a great train of prelates" (III, 253).

The book on the surface amounts to an unquestionable celebration of the righteousness and inevitability of the Christian victory. At the same time, a closer reading reveals perhaps the exact opposite. Catholics have their own exaggerated beliefs, especially regarding the immaculate conception of the Blessed Virgin, a belief already subjected to withering ridicule by José María Blanco White in his influential *Letters from Spain* (1822).[27] Thus, the self-righteous Catholic knight Juan de Vera, who is sent to negotiate with the Muslims of Granada on behalf of the Catholic monarchs, breaks all protocol when he hits one of his hosts with a sheathed sword for "daring to question, with a sneer, the immaculate conception of the Blessed Virgin" (III, 14). When Vera returns to the Castilian court to report on his embassy he is "highly honored and rewarded" by King Ferdinand. Moreover, "the zeal he had shown in vindication of the sinless conception of the Blessed Virgin was not only applauded by that most Catholic of sovereigns, but gained him great favor and renown among all pious cavaliers and reverend prelates" (III, 16). Later, in the field of battle, Vera identifies the Muslim offender who has desecrated the Blessed Virgin and reacts instantly: "All his holy zeal and pious indignation rekindled at the sight; he put lance in rest, and spurred his steed to finish this doctrinal dispute" (III, 35). He slays the Moor gruesomely, perhaps in proportion to the magnitude of the offense; Irving quotes the fictional Agapida concluding that "thus was the immaculate conception miraculously vindicated" (III, 36). Irving's dwelling on this anecdote, clearly a legend more than a fact, is part of his effort to reveal the extreme religious motivations of the Spanish Christians. The valiant Hernando Pérez del Pulgar, in another instance, bursts into the besieged city of Granada, at the risk of his own life and that of his followers, for no other reason than to nail a tablet inscribed "Ave Maria" to the door of the city's Mosque. He "sprang from his horse, and, kneeling at the portal, took possession of the edifice as a Christian chapel, dedicating it to the blessed Virgin," and then made a daring escape (III, 389). Later in the struggle, the very same tablet was paraded by the Moor Yarfe, "tied to the tail of his steed, and dragged in the dust" in an obvious act of provocation. The Christian response is to be expected: "A burst of horror and indignation broke forth from the army" (III, 392–393). Consequently, the outraged Garcilasso [sic] de la Vega asked for permission from the Catholic monarchs to respond. In Irving's presentation, "the request was too pious to be refused," and thus a brutal hand-to-hand combat ensued, with royal approval, resulting in the slaying of the Moor:

> The laws of chivalry were observed throughout the combat—no one interfered on either side. Garcilasso now despoiled his adversary; then, rescuing the holy inscription of "AVE MARIA" from its degrading situation, he elevated it on the point of his sword, and bore it off as a signal of triumph, amid the rapturous shouts of the Christian army (III, 394).[28]

These references to the Virgin Mary can be easily missed in the larger account of the war, but there is no mistaking the intent of such descriptions, which were carefully embedded in the narrative, to give resonance to the Catholic worship of the Blessed Virgin. It became an often repeated reference in U.S. books on the Spanish empire, as will be seen in later chapters.

The darker side of Catholicism appears in the *Conquest of Granada* in the guise of the Holy Brotherhood, the greed of the Church, and various references that portend a future of intolerance and fanaticism. During one of the campaigns against the Muslims, a member of the Holy Brotherhood "attempted to roam [the enemy's land] in quest of booty," and had to be stopped by the Master of the military order of Santiago, who "rebuked him severely" (III, 69). The Count of Tendilla, Iñigo López de Mendoza, who was in charge of the fort of Alhama, is shown as mindful of the Church whenever he sallied to despoil the Moors: "The good friars were ever ready at the gate to hail him on his return, and receive the share allotted them"

(III, 133). Clergy, however, have a role far beyond collecting spoils. Both queen and king "are always surrounded, in court or camp, in the cabinet or in the field, by a crowd of ghostly advisers, inspiriting them to the prosecution of this most righteous war" (III, 160). These "ghostly men" provide specific advice even on military matters, and mobilize the range of resources needed for the campaign. They constitute a "cloud of bishops, friars, and other saintly men," eagerly providing assistance but also "garnering the first fruits of this Infidel land into the granaries of the church" (III, 208). Resorting to his fictive chronicler Antonio Agapida, Irving emphasizes that "as this was a holy war . . . and peculiarly redounded to the prosperity of the church, the clergy was full of zeal, and contributed vast sums of money and large bodies of troops. A pious fund was also produced, from the first fruits of that glorious institution, the Inquisition" (III, 296). Irving presents Ferdinand as eagerly using the Inquisition against "all kinds of heresy," but adding that Isabella was quite firm in preventing abuses (III, 297). Still, graver things to come regarding the power of the Inquisition are articulated by the valiant Muslim warrior Muza ben Abel Gazan, when the dwellers of Granada are about to capitulate:

> When Muza saw that they were about to sign the treaty of surrender, he rose in violent indignation: "Do not deceive yourselves," cried he, "nor think the Christians will be faithful to their promises, or their king as magnanimous in conquest as he has been victorious in war. Death is the least we have to fear. It is the plundering and sacking of our city, the profanation of our mosques, the ruin of our homes, the violation of our wives and daughters—cruel oppression, bigoted intolerance, whips and chains, the dungeon, the fagot, and the stake—such are the miseries and indignities we shall see and suffer; at least, those groveling souls will see them who now shrink from an honorable death. For my part, by Allah, I will never witness them!" (III, 407)

Thus, the account that appears to be a celebration of the Christian triumph over the Muslims is in effect a disturbing anticipation of what will become of Spain after the conquest of Granada. Irving maintained his focus on the war, but he made certain that some larger themes were addressed: he hoped that his readers would be entertained by his account, but he also expected to show how the very values that allowed Christians to triumph over the Moors eventually turned into a notorious system of religious intolerance and persecution. The use of such words as "whips and chains, the dungeon, the fagot, and the stake," was calculated to elicit dreadful images of the Inquisition. He had already done so in his "The Student of Salamanca," a tale included in *Bracebridge Hall* (1822). There, the Holy Office makes a mockery of justice by entertaining accusations but not listening to defense; indulges in intimidation, confinement, and torture; turns an auto da fé into a sickening public spectacle, and ultimately thrives on the population's fear and acquiescence. He wrote this horrific story even before he set foot on Spain, thereby clearly articulating a *view* of Spanish religious intolerance and persecution that appealed directly to his intended English-speaking audience. Irving's interpretation thus builds on tropes already in place, but also serves as a warning to the young republic about the dangers of religious intolerance.

Although religious themes abound in Irving's Spanish works, in the *Conquest of Granada* his main objective was to show Spain as a land where the religious and cultural struggles of the past, indeed the long history that culminated in the reign of

Ferdinand and Isabella, defined a peculiar national character.[29] And an important component of that character was Arabian, or "oriental."

Irving's Orientalism

While working on the Conquest of Granada, Irving became interested in the story of Roderick, the Visigothic king who suffered defeat at the hands of the Moors on the banks of the Guadalete River, a place that the writer could observe from the roof of his house in Puerto de Santa María. The subject had been treated by his revered Walter Scott ("The Vision of Don Roderick") in 1811, and by Robert Southey ("Roderick, The Last of the Goths") in 1814. Understandably, Irving had some qualms about competing with such giants. Scott had dwelt on Roderick briefly, tying this early defeat of Spain with the recent Napoleonic invasion. But Southey had written a long and nuanced poem emphasizing character, the debilitating Christian divisions of the period, and the emerging sense of Spanish nationhood. Irving asked Thomas Aspinwall in London for "a cheap edition of Southeys [sic] 'Roderick the Last of the Goths,'" adding that he wished to see what he may "have said about the Moors," obviously not wanting to be compared with his British counterpart. Expecting perhaps to surprise his potential critics, he summoned Aspinwall to "*say nothing on this subject to any one*," underscoring the sentence.[30] Anticipating negative comparisons, he steered clear of his predecessors by placing more emphasis on the Muslim side.

In the *Legends of the Conquest of Spain* (1835), Irving traced the origins of the eighth-century Muslim conquest of Spain as resulting from the indulgence of Roderick, whose worldly appetites generated rebellion and treachery, thus opening the door to the Muslim invasion, and soon the subjugation of the entire country. As the traitor Count Julian joins the Arabian Emir Muza ben Nosier, Irving describes the latter as "surrounded by somewhat of Oriental state and Splendor" (I, 441). Muza's main general is Taric ben Zeyad, whose "hot blood . . . was in ferment when he heard of a new country to invade" (I, 442). Muslims are presented as warlike, but they too have a tendency to worldly pleasures. The son of Muza, Abdalasis, who has become the Emir of Spain, sets the tone by pursuing the favors of Exilona, Roderick's widow, whom he soon marries. He neglects his obligations as the leader of an occupying force, and thus provokes implacable opposition. "The Moslems had already felt jealous of the ascendancy of this beautiful woman [Exilona], and it was now confidently asserted that Abdalasis, won by her persuasions, had secretly turned Christian" (I, 545). Roderick is overthrown and killed by his own people, a victim of his unrestrained passion. The Arab domination of Spain will be characterized by the combined elements of warlike impulses, fickleness, and a tendency to indulgence that will have a deep influence on the formation of the Spanish character.

At the other end of the Muslim occupation, in the midst of ruins of glories past, Irving examined what remained of the centuries of religious and cultural blending in Spain. In *The Alhambra* (1832), Irving writes that "the country, the habits, the very looks of the people, have something of the Arabian character" (II, 11). The Alhambra and its people concentrate most of what Irving advances as Spanish traits: the love of songs, legends of hidden treasure, and fascination with mystery and magic. The streets, alleys, buildings, and towers "retain their oriental character" (II, 27), and tales are constantly told that keep the Arabian past alive. Irving himself was transported when going about the place, "It is impossible to contemplate this once favorite abode of Oriental manners, without feeling the early associations of Arabian romance" (II, 32). Muslims in *The Alhambra*, in contrast to those of *Granada*, are presented under a more favorable light: Irving praises their heroism and moderation, explaining that "at length," they were "subdued by the obstinate and persevering valor of the Goth" (II, 41). The Alhambra ruins are "but an Oriental palace amid the Gothic edifices of the west; an elegant memento of a brave, intelligent and graceful people, who conquered, ruled, and passed away" (II, 42). In short, the triumphant Christian victory of the Granada volume is tempered by Irving's appreciation for the legacies of the Moors.

Having established the presence of the Arabian past, Irving then dissected the mix that now constituted the Spanish character. In various parts of the narrative, he identified "grandiloquence" (II, 15), "grave courtesy" (II, 18, 19), "poetical turn of thought and language" (II, 19), natural talent and wit (II, 45), "dignity of spirit" (II, 45), and idleness (II, 59), as central components of the Spanish character. But his most telling assessment is contained in the following passage:

> The common people of Spain have an Oriental passion for story-telling and are fond of the marvelous. They will gather round the doors of their cottages on summer evenings, or in the great cavernous chimney corners of their ventas [inns] in the winter, and listen with insatiable delight to miraculous legends of saints, perilous adventures of travelers, and daring exploits of robbers and contrabandists. The wild and solitary nature of a great part of Spain; the imperfect state of knowledge; the scantiness of general topics of conversation, and the romantic, adventurous life that every one leads in a land where traveling is yet in its primitive state, all contribute to cherish this love of oral narration, and to produce a strong expression of the extravagant and wonderful (II, 130).

Thus, the enchanting Moorish past is kept alive in the Spain of Irving's days because the national character itself is based on "oriental" characteristics.[31] That which is Christian has, under Catholic influence, achieved a strong cultural presence, but in the form of the outlandish exultation of the Blessed Virgin, the haughty presence of powerful prelates, and the exuberant recollection of the glorious conquest of Granada. Spain goes on to become one of the greatest empires in history, but in Irving's presentation, the seeds of its own demise are already germinating during this momentous event. All that now remained, in the 1820s, was ruins, charming traditions, and a lingering nostalgia for the time when Spain was all promise. The triumphant Catholic element of old has degenerated into inquisitorial persecution, massive greed and corruption, and ultimate inability to confront other (Protestant) powers. The Spanish common people are the heirs of a once mighty empire, but however fascinating they may be, they lead a listless life of little work, much idle conversation, and search for imaginary treasures. Thus does Irving address a number of important themes that resonate with issues in his own emerging nation: conquest and expansion can succeed, but there is no guarantee of stability and survival; religion, if allowed to become exclusionary, will lead to widespread fear and demoralization. The example of Spain, in short, is no antiquarian subject, but a warning to the new nation that the values of constant industrious activity, love of peace and moderation, and a humble, rational form of Christianity are the only hopes for the establishment of the nation on solid foundations.

The Spanish conquest of Granada, the fall of the Muslim empire, and the emergence of imperial Spain thus serve as the occasion for some political lessons to Irving's American readers. Muslims fall because they are *divided*; Christians win because they are *united*. But both share a warlike disposition and a dangerous reliance on clergy, prophets, and religious zeal. Armed conflict allows warriors to predominate, and they follow the logic of destruction some times to the bitter end. This is necessarily done at the cost of life and property, as one is often reminded in reading about each campaign in the *Conquest of Granada*. Irving thus teaches his readers that any society that relies too heavily on war will undermine its own prospects: nations that live by the sword will die by the sword. But perhaps the most lethal alliance is that of warriors and priests. Both Muslims and Christians in the story of Granada are at their destructive utmost when they unleash their forces in the name of religion. Beware, Irving implies, of this unhealthy union between Church and State. To the new nation he addresses a call for peaceful government, religious tolerance, and promotion of life, liberty, and security. That is why a Muslim merchant, and a Christian knight of the fifteenth century can sometimes speak the words of a nineteenth-century American.

New World, Old Vices

If the Conquest of Granada represents the high point of the reign of Ferdinand and Isabella, launching such great deeds as the discovery of the New World, the period that follows the death of the queen shows unmistakable signs of decay. In this sense, Irving's *A History of the Life and Voyages of Christopher Columbus*, and the related *Voyages and Discoveries of the Companions of Columbus*, contains both a celebration of the greatest moment in the history of kingdom, as well as a herald of ominous events to come. Scholars Claudia Bushman and Rolena Adorno have written persuasively about Irving's *Columbus* as a successful effort to provide a heroic character model for nineteenth-century Americans. Irving's Columbus, they argue, was presented in textbooks, essays, and poems as a visionary who, against considerable odds, bridged the old world and the new inspired by the values of enterprise, commerce, and genuine religious belief. My own view of this source builds on the work of Bushman and Adorno, but seeks to emphasize two themes that are related to Irving's larger corpus of Spanish works: his view of a rapidly decaying Spanish character, as exemplified by new extremes of chivalry and religious fanaticism, and the emerging theme of Spanish despotism, as exemplified by the cruel neglect and mistreatment of Columbus by King Ferdinand.

Chivalry was always a favorite subject for Irving, though it is quite apparent that in contrast to the *Conquest of Granada*, in the Columbus works he seeks to show it as increasingly out of touch, even ridiculous, during the conquest of the New World. In contrast to the Marquis of Cadiz, who was the ultimate chivalrous knight in the Granada campaigns, the most significant cavalier to appear in the Columbus story, Alonso de Ojeda, is quite nearly an irresponsible fool. Irving thus makes a Cervantine mockery of Spanish chivalry as it moves from the Muslim to the New World battlefields. Their expeditions, Irving states, "may be compared to the attempts of adventurous knights-errant to achieve the enterprise left unfinished by some illustrious predecessors . . . the spirit of chivalry entered largely into the early expeditions of the Spanish discoverers, giving them a character wholly distinct from similar enterprises undertaken by other nations" (V, 324). The end of the Granada wars had left the victorious cavaliers rather hungry for more: "The spirit of Spanish chivalry was thus suddenly deprived of its wonted sphere of action; but it had been too long fostered and excited to be as suddenly appeased" (V, 325). In Irving's presentation, the manifestations of this chivalry are often extravagant. Referring to the sighting of the Pacific by Vasco Núñez de Balboa and his followers, he describes the procedures for claiming the Ocean to conclude that "such was the singular medley of chivalrous and religious ceremonial with which these Spanish adventurers took possession of the vast Pacific Ocean, and all its lands—a scene strongly characteristic of the nation and the age" (V, 462). But chivalry can also have a disturbing edge. As Irving follows the career of Ojeda in the Caribbean, he pauses to describe him as "bigoted in his devotion, reckless in his life, fearless in his spirit, like many of the roving Spanish cavaliers of those days" (VI, 362). He is also, perhaps as Don Quixote, "a hot-headed man, with somewhat of a vaunting spirit," who "sets himself up for a redresser of grievances" against Columbus (VI, 526). The whole enterprise of discovery and conquest was fueled by the spirit of chivalry, "which led that nation to so high a pitch of power and glory." In a nod to the present, Irving states that this chivalry is not part of a remote past; it is in fact "still discernible in the great mass of that gallant people, by those who have an opportunity of judging them rightly" (V, 326).

On the religious aspects of the Spanish character, Irving dwells on images of bigoted priests (especially those close to authority), and the omnipresent subject of the Virgin. During the medieval ages, he writes, the study of geography suffered "during a long night of monkish bigotry and false learning" (VI, 17). Bishop Juan Rodríguez de Fonseca, the official in charge of New World affairs, comes close to serving the role of Irving's ultimate villain: he was "malignant and vindictive; and in the gratification of his private resentments not only heaped wrongs and sorrows upon the most illustrious of the early discoverers [Columbus], but frequently impeded the progress of their enterprises" (VI, 223). By the time of Columbus's third voyage, Fonseca had become his "cold-blooded enemy" (VI, 423). He is a man of "singular malevolence," whose "spirit appears to have been of that unhealthy kind which has none of the balm of forgiveness" (VII, 347). He was, in short, "an active and intrepid, but selfish, overbearing, and perfidious man" (VII, 348).

Alonso de Ojeda, who has already been identified as the quintessential representative of a degraded chivalry, is the main vehicle for Irving's commentary on the Spanish worship of the Virgin Mary. Ojeda, who always escapes injury, no matter how daring his exploits, attributes his safety to the "special protection of the Holy Virgin." He has been given a likeness—a small Flemish painting—of Mary by none other than Bishop Fonseca, and he carries it everywhere he goes, as a "protecting relic, invoking it at all times of peril" (V, 329). Ojeda finds himself so well protected that he throws himself into any trouble with cheerful confidence. "In a word, he swore by the Virgin, he invoked the Virgin whether in brawl or battle, and under the favor of the Virgin he was ready for any enterprise or adventure" (VI, 362). As he pursues the cacique Caonabo in Hispaniola, he invokes "the protection of his patroness the Virgin, whose images as usual he bore with him as a safeguard" (VI, 368). Not even the poisoned arrows of the Indians deter him, "Ojeda confided blindly in the protection of the Virgin. Putting up, as usual, a short prayer to his patroness, he drew his weapon, braced his buckler, and charged furiously upon the savages" (V, 372). After a particularly dangerous march through Cuba, Ojeda makes a vow to the Virgin that he will erect a chapel in her honor if taken to safety. He does, as one can only expect from a truly devout Spanish knight.

Columbus himself is not free, at times, of "a tinge of superstition," though it is usually of a "sublime and lofty kind" (VI, 41). On balance, however, "his piety was mingled with superstition, and darkened by the bigotry of the age" (VII, 196). He "considered himself under the immediate eye and guardianship of Heaven" (VI, 112), and attributed his survival from shipwrecks as providential events "mysteriously ordained by Heaven" (VI, 176). Most importantly, he "considered himself selected by Heaven as an agent" (VI, 214). His ultimate mission, in fact, was the recovery of the holy sepulcher from the hands of the heathen, a topic that allowed Irving to clinch his argument about the confluence of chivalry and religious zeal,

> The enterprise here suggested by Columbus [the recovery of the holy sepulcher], however idle and extravagant it may appear in the present day, was in unison with the temper of the times and of the court to which it was proposed. The vein of mystic erudition by which it was enforced, likewise, was suited to an age when the reveries of the cloister still controlled the operations of the cabinet and the camp. The spirit of the crusades had not yet passed away. In the cause of the church, and at the instigation of its dignitaries, every cavalier was ready to draw his sword; and religion mingled a glowing and devoted enthusiasm with the ordinary excitement of warfare. Ferdinand was a religious bigot; and the devotion of Isabella went as near to bigotry as her liberal mind and magnanimous spirit would permit. Both the sovereigns were under the influence of ecclesiastical politicians, constantly guiding their enterprises in a direction to redound to the temporal power and glory of the church. (VII, 40–41)

In addition to the themes of chivalry and religious bigotry, the story of the discovery of the New World allowed Irving to engage the enduring theme of Spanish despotism, to which he added significant force through clever word choices and powerful narration. Ferdinand becomes, in his account, the ultimate despot. The conflict between the daring individual Columbus and the dour, manipulating, and sinister Ferdinand serves the fundamental purpose of illustrating the tension between individual freedom and governmental despotism epitomized by Spain. The Crown under Ferdinand exercises a "despotic sway" over commerce, quite clearly an anathema for the nineteenth-century Americans Irving wanted to address (VI, 224). As Columbus exercises his rights of appointment in the lands discovered by him, Ferdinand looks upon this as "an undue assumption of power," which "gave great offense to that jealous monarch" (VI, 354). Ferdinand subordinates the requests of Columbus for needed assistance to his "ambition" in Italy (VI, 413). Soon, by 1497, on the eve of Columbus's third voyage, the king "began to look coldly on him" (VI, 416). He entertains all sorts of slander and permits every injustice against Columbus because of his "jealous mind" (VI, 538; VII, 14). He is "politic" in his dealings with the navigator, a calculating Machiavellian prince in Spanish dress. As the magnitude of the discovery becomes apparent to him, "His ambition, his avarice, and his jealousy were equally inflamed" (VII, 29). He moves to deprive Columbus of his rightful titles because the mariner "was no longer indispensable to him" (VII, 29). Columbus's pleas found "but a cold-hearted auditor in the king" (VII, 181), and thus "the cold ingratitude of his sovereign chilled his heart" (VII, 186). The purpose of such insistence on Ferdinand's attitude toward Columbus was made clear by Irving himself,

> Let the ingratitude of Ferdinand stand recorded in its full extent, and endure throughout all time. The dark shadow which it casts upon his brilliant renown will be a lesson to all rulers, teaching them what is important to their own fame in their treatment of illustrious men. (VII, 190)

Thus, by the 1820s and early 1830s, Irving had successfully created a highly readable and popular venue to convey a lasting view of Spain and the Spanish character. Irving's narrative, however charming at times, openly presented Spain as a country whose better days were now far behind. All that was left was a sad though picturesque legacy of ruins and widespread idleness. The causes were crystal clear: an exaggerated sense of honor and chivalry, combined with religious fanaticism, had brought the country to ruin. The dismal combination of religious persecution and governmental despotism had strengthened the hands of emperors, but poisoned the body politic to an irreversible situation of decay and near collapse. Irving intended this to be a lesson for the young American nation. Indeed, in what appeared to be a warning against repeating the cycle of imperialism initiated by Spain, he explained the cruelties of the Spanish conquest as the obvious result of imperial expansion:

> Such occurrences show the extremity to which human cruelty may extend, when stimulated by avidity of gain, by a thirst of vengeance, or even by a perverted zeal in the holy cause of religion. Every nation has in turn furnished proofs of this disgraceful truth. As in the present instance, they are commonly the crimes of individuals rather than of the nation. Yet it behooves governments to keep a vigilant eye upon those to whom they delegate power in remote and helpless colonies. It is the imperious duty of the historian to place these matters upon record, that they may serve as warning beacons to future generations. (VII, 161)

It was a warning indeed, as Americans spread far and wide in the 1830s.

Irving's Success

Irving had done his work quite well, because initially the contemporary reception of his books focused on anything but his highly opinionated views on Spain. By very nearly obliterating the omniscient narrative voice, turning it instead over to fictional narrators or old chronicles, Irving had managed to ascribe just about every negative stereotype about Spain to the Spaniards themselves or to their enemies. Thus, for instance, Alexander Hill Everett, reviewing the Columbus work in 1829 found little to criticize besides Irving's *historical* approach. Dividing historiography between "philosophical" and "narrative" in the eighteenth-century tradition, Everett thought that Irving had produced a charming example of the latter, but to the detriment of the far superior "philosophical" history. He had no objection to either the substance or the implications of Irving's seemingly accurate, but highly contrived, rendition of the Columbus story. Indeed, he argued that Irving's Columbus was much better than anything thus far produced, and identified its main virtues as "a judicious selection and disposition of the materials, a correct, striking, and discriminating picture of the different personages, a just and elevated tone of moral feeling, and above all, the charm of an elegant, perspicuous, and flowing style."[32]

Likewise, William H. Prescott, who would astonish the world within a decade with his groundbreaking *Ferdinand and Isabella* (1838), wrote in 1829 that Irving had composed a "narrative" history to which "he seems particularly suited by his genius." He celebrated the choice of subject, covering "one of the most brilliant achievements in the most brilliant period of Spanish history," saying little about Irving's tendentious descriptions. In fact, he indulged on a few of his own. Cardinal Jiménez, for instance, was described as "that most enlightened of bigots," while Ferdinand was without explanation called "crafty." Prescott seemed to have also fallen into Irving's clever trap, that of elevating Antonio Agapida to the status of a real chronicler, concluding that "we may honestly recommend [the *Conquest of Granada*] as substantially an authentic record of one of the most interesting and . . . one of the most untravelled portions of Spanish history."[33] As he started to study Spanish history seriously, and begin a lifelong engagement with historical documents, he became somewhat more critical of Irving. In his *Ferdinand and Isabella*, for instance, he criticized some of Irving's inaccuracies, but in the end concluded that he had portrayed the period "in the lucid and attractive form which engages the interest of every reader."[34] Moreover, he had done so in a manner which "few will care to follow."[35] Prescott elegantly criticized Irving for painting a picture of the Granada campaign "with dramatic brilliancy of coloring denied to sober history,"[36] but he did not challenge the underlying assumptions, or the implications about the presumed Spanish "character." He echoed, in some respects, George Bancroft's own assessment of Irving's work. Despite the magnitude of Columbus's achievements, the historian wrote in his *History of the United States* (1834), no one had come close to doing justice to the stature of the navigator, "till the genius of Irving, with candor, liberality, and original research, made a record of his eventful life, and in mild but enduring colors sketched his sombre inflexibility of purpose, his deep religious enthusiasm, and the disinterested magnanimity of his character."[37]

Irving's work received much more than scholarly acclaim: it was not only enormously popular, but it was also obligatory reading in large school systems such as those of the States of New York and Massachusetts. As a result, few dared to question the fundamental premises of his views on Spain. That is, until Severn T. Wallis launched a series of articles in the *Southern Literary Messenger* between 1841 and 1843. Wallis would go on to write two massive books about Spain in 1849 and 1853, but in these earlier essays the Baltimore lawyer charged Irving with failing to give proper recognition to the work of Spanish scholars, and to Martín Fernández de Navarrete in particular.[38] Navarrete had devoted over three decades of his life to the collection of archival records, under royal sponsorship, to document the history of the discovery of the New World. And yet, Irving had given him only perfunctory acknowledgment. "Mr. Irving," wrote Wallis, "is not quite explicit enough, in acquainting the American public, with the full extent of his indebtedness." Wallis was troubled by the claims of originality, which not only reflected badly on the American writer's judgment, but also gave a less than flattering portrayal of Spain as a backward country unable to identify and make available its own historical records. The Baltimore lawyer was particularly troubled that the State of New York should have recently adopted an abridgment of Irving's *Columbus* (1838) precisely on the grounds of his original research, thus again obscuring the contributions of Spanish scholars. He suspected that prejudice and misconception was at work: monarchical, despotic Spain, the "bigoted enemy of knowledge," could not be shown as supporting the massive research of Navarrete. Irving, in his view, was directly responsible for taking "from Spanish literature all the materials that he needed, and to publish them as his own," and for allowing the claims of originality to reverberate in the American scene, at the expense of Spain.[39]

Yet behind the specific charge of giving little credit where credit was due, Wallis confronted the larger issue about the views on Spain advanced by foreign authors. Without naming Irving directly, the reference to his work was unmistakable:

> Those who are disposed to think the best [of Spain], recall to mind the glorious romance of her past history; and suffering their imagination to roam through the deserted halls of the Alhambra, dwell only on the time when the peninsula was the battle-ground of Christendom and Paynimrie—forgetting all the while, that the same soil is trodden by a living, existing nation, modern, civilized and Christian.

Writers, especially travel writers, dwelled in addition on stereotypes such as the Inquisition and the bullfights as if nothing else mattered, or even existed. What can be expected, Wallis asked, "if we are taught to believe, that her [Spanish] citizens at large are ignorant, superstitious, cruel, filthy and contemptible? Can we love our neighbor, to who [sic] we give credit for such qualities?"[40]

Wallis finally received an indirect answer in the form of a counterattack from the *Knickerbocker*, a journal long associated with Washington Irving. Not only was the author of the *Southern Literary Messenger* articles charged with having some personal "prejudice or pique," but also clarified that Irving's use of Navarrete's work amounted to no more than "six of the twelve hundred pages," of the book. This response prompted Wallis to reiterate his case, and once again seek to demonstrate that the use was much more extensive than the *Knickerbocker*'s low statistics suggested. Moreover, he added, "Our attention was originally called to this subject, by conversations with several Spanish gentlemen of high attainments and position, from whom we learned that Mr. Irving had suffered much in Spain, from a supposed want of candor towards Navarrete."[41] Thus, Wallis raised the question about the reception of Irving's work in Spain. This was a pertinent question indeed.

Spanish Reactions

While in Madrid, Irving cultivated good relations with Martín Fernández de Navarrete, who was happy to oblige his new American friend with documents and expert opinion. He left clear evidence of the reasons for looking favorably upon Irving's endeavor. In the preface to the third volume of his documentary collection, Navarrete explained that he had not set out to write the history of Admiral Christopher Columbus, but rather "to publish the materials and evidence so that it might be written accurately." Fortunately, he added, Irving had made thorough use of the documents he had provided. Irving had one major advantage as an American, and that was to be free of the "rivalries that have thus far influenced European writing on Columbus and his discoveries." In addition, he praised Irving's "methodical arrangement and appropriate organization [of the contents]; his animated, clear, and elegant style." Navarrete hoped, however, that Irving would correct some errors and opinions in light of new evidence. In his view, they were the product of Irving's reliance on "less credible" sources.[42]

Clearly, Navarrete was willing to ignore Irving's most extreme opinions because he understood the value of a favorable view of Columbus and, by implication, Spanish history. He was in a strong position, as Director of the Royal Academy of History, to support Irving. As the records of the Academy show, Irving was nominated for corresponding membership on December 5, 1828, and duly elected on the December 12. After receiving his appointment letter, a delighted Irving wrote from Seville, in Spanish, to accept the honor and pledge his service.[43] He later sent Navarrete an advance copy of his *The Voyages and Discoveries of the Companions of Columbus*, stating in his letter that "you will find that I am largely indebted to your recent volume for many of my facts."[44] Navarrete and Irving respected and admired each other, and remained on good terms for the rest of the Spanish scholar's life.

Despite friendly scholarly support, there were procedures, both at the Academy and the government, that cast a more critical eye on Irving's publications. In 1830, the government required the Academy to issue a report on Irving's *Conquest of Granada* before giving permission to print. The Academy, however, refused on the grounds that "this is a historical novel, not a true history, and, therefore, beyond the purview and object of the institution." The government insisted, however, arguing that there was no other body better suited for the purpose.[45] At this point, the members decided that they could not delay, and commissioned a report to one of the members, Canon José Sabau y Blanco.[46]

Sabau, who had been a member of the Academy since 1817, was a prestigious cleric who rose to the position of Bishop of Osma. He was also the Antiquarian of the Academy and the Librarian of the institution until his death in 1833. A diligent, meticulous scholar, Sabau was baffled by three issues: first, he had been given only 22 chapters to read (up to the battle of Lopera) and thus only about a quarter of the entire work; second, the translation into Spanish had been made from a French edition of Irving's work, and, therefore, contained problems that could only be solved by comparing the text with the original English; and finally, he did not know quite what to make of the putative author of the Chronicle, Fray Antonio Agapida. Sabau contacted the librarians at the Escorial, who reported that there was no record of either the author or the manuscript. "I have well-founded doubts," Sabau explained to the Academy, "that such a chronicle ever existed, for it has never been cited by either modern or contemporary authors." Perhaps it was true that the document was lost during the War of Independence, he speculated, or that the French translator had added the opinionated chronicler to the English original to make the work seem more interesting. But none of these issues, he proceeded, should obscure his fundamental conclusion: the main story was accurate, as confirmed by the accounts of "our best historians," and it was written with such elegance that the reading was truly enjoyable. Moreover, "what is most worthy of praise is the author's identification of the [Catholic] faith as the fundamental basis for the valor and heroism of the Christian warriors." There was nothing, Sabau added, that could be construed as contrary to the dogmas of the Catholic Church, to morality, or to the rights of the king. The book, in short, deserved publication.[47]

Sabau read his report to the members of the Academy in February 1831. They not only listened with great interest, but also consigned his words into the minutes almost verbatim.[48] The Academy thus cleared the way for the dissemination of

Irving's work despite its negative undertones and subtle mockery of Spanish themes. This was not an isolated event, however, catching as it were the members of the Academy off their guard. They had another opportunity to review Irving's work when José Hevia y Noriega, the official in charge of press censorship (*Subdelegado General*), submitted two French editions of Irving's work, *Histoire de la vie et des voyages de Christophe Colomb*, and *Histoire de la Conquête de Grenade*, to the consideration of the institution.[49]

The assignment was given again to José Sabau, who reported in July that the French translation of the Granada book contained nothing objectionable and was in addition "a useful reading."[50] A week later, he reported in equally favorable terms on the Columbus work.[51] Later, Director Navarrete informed the members of Irving's gift of his *Voyages and Discoveries of the Companions of Columbus.*[52]

Such obvious receptivity to Irving's work coincided with the Academy's own desire to both cultivate better relations with foreign scholars, and switch to a more proactive role in the advancement of historical research. Just as the Academy was evaluating Irving's work, it was also entertaining proposals for the study of historical topics. "It would be most convenient," stated Director Navarrete at one of the meetings, "for the promotion of the study and development of the history of Spain, to grant awards to those who pursue subjects selected by the Academy, as it was once done, to shed light on matters that need and deserve particular attention."[53] The members were happy to oblige, and soon a number of topics reached the discussion table. "How were the bishops of Spain selected and who confirmed them in their posts before the fourteenth century?" was among the first topics proposed.[54] A veritable brainstorm produced four additional topics by Spring 1831: (1) a critical examination of the twelfth-century *Historia Compostelana*; (2) Castile's political and commercial relations with other countries prior to the discovery of the New World; (3) mining in Spanish history, and (4) the origin of the title "Admiral" of Castile. After much discussion, the members settled on topics one and two for a forthcoming competition.[55]

Concurrently, the government of Ferdinand VII, now approaching its demise and seeking reconciliation with its liberal enemies, advanced its own policy for historical development. A Royal Decree of March 18, 1833, signed by the Minister of Development (*Fomento General*), encouraged the Academy to publish papers on the Spanish economy, especially during the period of Arab domination; to resume publication of the *Historico-Geographical Dictionary of Spain*, and to state its space needs to maintain a proper research library.[56] The field of history was to lead the way in the liberalization of Spain.

It is in this context that the readable works of Washington Irving appeared on the scene. Members who may have conceivably objected to his exaggerations, inaccuracies, and stereotypes were willing to give him the benefit of the doubt for the sake of promoting research and other forms of historical activity. They said so explicitly in 1832, when they noted that Irving had "examined her [Spanish] antiquities and monuments with a zeal worthy of imitation by the Spaniards themselves."[57] Members also understood the political usefulness of Irving's work. Spanish liberalism was compatible with Catholicism, but liberals were interested in a different role for the Church and were, therefore, receptive to critiques of at least some aspects of the old relation between Church and State. Liberals, understandably, were also receptive to critiques of monarchical despotism. All in all, Irving and the Spanish

Academy enjoyed a prolonged honeymoon that ended only when the Wallis articles in the *Southern Literary Messenger* reached Spain. How this happened is worth examining.

The Academy was busy conducting its regular business for more than a decade after the publication of Irving's major works on Spain, on the assumption that there was little more to say about their corresponding member. In 1841, however, Pedro Sabau y Larroya took the floor to read his translation of the scathing Wallis article published in March of that year. One can only imagine their individual responses, but members were recorded in the minutes as expressing "the greatest satisfaction" (*suma satisfacción*) for an article that celebrated Navarrete's work on Columbus, while exposing Irving's inflated claims of originality.[58]

A second translation of Wallis's article also reached the Academy at this time. It was done by José Antonio Pizarro, a professor of Spanish at St. Mary's College in Baltimore, and apparently an acquaintance of Wallis. Although there was no editorial comment, the translation spoke for itself, not only in terms of its contents, but also in the desire to make it known to the members of the Academy.[59] Then the Spanish government, through its own channels, secured two additional articles by Wallis on the same subject, and forwarded them to the Academy for deliberation.[60] Pedro Sabau was asked to report on these articles, and when he did so he presented Wallis as "the defender of the work of our President [Navarrete]." The members agreed, and proceeded to nominate the Baltimore lawyer for corresponding membership.[61]

The Academy acted quickly, unanimously electing Severn T. Wallis on January 7, 1843, thus preempting the government's willingness to force the issue. Indeed, the Regency formally requested, just a day after the members' vote that Wallis be made a corresponding member on the strength of his "defense of Spanish literature from the attacks of Mr. Washington Irving in his book Life and Voyages of Christopher Columbus." The Academy's secretary, Justo José Banqueri, replied politely that the institution had already done so.[62]

The root of the problem, as identified by Wallis, was that Irving had not properly identified the extent of his debt to the massive work of Navarrete, and by doing so he had ignored the patronage of the Crown, as well as perpetuated the myths about the alleged Spanish disregard for the dissemination of knowledge. The members of the Academy were thus awakened from their benevolent complacency, but they chose not to manifest any overt animosity toward Irving. Making Wallis a corresponding member, implicitly endorsing his critique, was more than enough.

A somewhat bewildered Irving happened to be appointed U.S. minister to Spain at precisely that time, which accounts perhaps for his lack of contact with the Academy during the length of his assignment in the country (1842–1846).[63] Moreover, the portrayal of Irving's Columbus as derivative of Navarrete's substantial work had spilled over to the wider world of the press. Writing for the periodical *El Pensamiento* in 1841, just when the charges were revealed, the influential Enrique Gil y Carrasco coined the expression that would be forever associated with Irving: "*hábil colorista*" (skilful embellisher) explaining that anyone comparing Navarrete and Irving would reach the stark conclusion that in the latter's work on Columbus "there is nothing that belongs to him except the brilliance of his beautiful style."[64] There can be no doubt that Irving's reputation suffered as a result.

And yet the overall Spanish assessment of Irving's work shows that he survived the Wallis incident on account of two major developments. One was Navarrete's own view of Irving, and their cordial relations until the Spanish historian's death in 1844. As mentioned earlier, Navarrete had publicly acknowledged the work of Irving when he published the third volume of his *Colecciones de Viages* in 1829. When he wrote to Irving in 1831 to thank him for the *Companions of Columbus*, he praised "the method and charming color" with which he had described the history. Navarrete thus revealed a more liberal attitude toward literary borrowing than would be the case among subsequent generations of historians. He added that he was grateful that his own documentary work had found "such able hands" to shed light on these important historical events with discernment and grace.[65] There is no reason to doubt that Navarrete's feelings were sincere, and despite the Wallis incident, he never renounced them.

The most important development was Modesto Lafuente's treatment of Irving in his *Historia General de España*, the canonical work of Spanish history in the nineteenth century, and a major historiographical landmark to this day.[66] Lafuente (1806–1866) rescued Irving from the dangers of total dismissal as an important contributor to the historiography of Spain. Lafuente had a clear preference for well-documented history, but he also took seriously the evidence that could be gathered from legends and romances, not unlike Augustin Thierry's work in France. Moreover, he sought to avoid the positivist extremes of the emerging nineteenth-century historical criticism. Thus, for instance, he resisted the temptation to dismiss the story of Roderick, the king who lost Spain to the Arabs, as apocryphal, even though little hard evidence could be found to confirm it. Irving, of course, had made the most of that story, well beyond what Walter Scott and Robert Southey had done. Lafuente clearly had in mind Irving's ability to narrate the key episodes in the old history of Spain, but he also quoted him directly as an authority. This is particularly the case with Irving's work on Columbus, from which Lafuente drew information about the admiral's actions as governor of Hispaniola (VII, 165, 169). He also followed Irving's account of the Crown's decision to investigate Columbus (VII, 170), and the tensions that developed (VII, 173). He singled out Irving's discussion of the naming of the New World after Vespucci as "very lucid and impartial" (VII, 177). Not content with citing him in footnotes and appendices, Lafuente reproduced extensive quotes from Irving *in the text*, to illustrate the attitudes of King Ferdinand toward Columbus, and to endorse the writer's assessment of the character of the admiral (VII, 241, 246).

Lafuente was not free from political motivations. As a "progressive" liberal and member of parliament in the 1850s, he fully embraced the political aims of Isabella II's reign, that is, the conciliation of liberalism and Catholicism, as well as a balance of power between the Crown and parliament. An important ideological underpinning was the parallel established between the first Isabella, and the second: both were seen as unifiers of the "nation" who launched the country to glory and greatness.[67] Lafuente advanced this agenda by providing a most positive evaluation of Isabella the Catholic, while criticizing the role of Ferdinand, who was equated with the type of despotism that Isabella II was committed to eschew. These were of course central themes in Washington Irving's work, and hence Lafuente's endorsement.[68]

Lafuente's evaluation of Irving's work was quite positive, but not without qualifications. Referring to the *Conquest of Granada*, Lafuente addressed the concerns of his predecessors at the Academy by stating that Irving had "embellished the account of those important events by giving them a certain epic form, which foreigners call romance." He agreed with the conclusion that in the books "there is too much fact to call it a romance, but not enough to call it a chronicle" (VII, 23). He also addressed the crucial and highly problematic issue of the relation between the works of Navarrete and Irving, giving it a final formulation. There had been three major contemporary accounts of the history of Columbus, he noted, those of Navarrete, Irving, and Alphonse de Lamartine. Irving had "organized and embellished" the history, while Lamartine had given it poetic form. But his own preference as a historian was unequivocally in favor of Navarrete "because history must be principally based on documents" (VII, 34). The Spanish scholar, he added, had provided the richest source of evidence. "It was primarily on the basis of those documents that in our time the learned Washington Irving composed and arranged his *Vida y viajes de Cristóbal Colón*, which is the best summary [*resumen*] we know" (VII, 68).

Lafuente's assessment was destined to last, in part because it gave due credit to Spanish scholarship without disparaging the work of Irving. He provided an interpretation of the writer's best contributions while also paying him the compliment of direct quotation of the most felicitous passages, especially from his Columbus works. There was not a trace of animosity, or defensive nationalistic posturing in his coverage. The consummate historian was thus willing to engage the serious effort of another scholar, acknowledging his achievements, and in the process restoring Irving's credibility as an earnest student of Spanish traditions. Thus, the great Marcelino Menéndez y Pelayo, in 1895, could build on Lafuente's interpretation and give it its most eloquent expression. Irving's *Columbus*, in his view,

> . . . without ceasing to be one of the most agreeable, readable books which can be found, is at the same time a serious historical work, in which the author, holding back the luxuriance of his pen, has had the good taste not to add fabulous accessories to a reality which is through itself more poetic than any fiction. The novel was provided in the deeds themselves, and Washington Irving had only to tell them, which he did in a manner superior to all praise, extracting the juice from the documents published by Navarrete, reconciling them with published histories and with manuscripts, almost all of which he made use of, since Navarrete generally aided him with his counsel and with his books and since, moreover, he had free access to the [Juan Bautista] Muñoz papers and to other collections. Irving's erudition, then, deserves respect, the more so as he did not make a show of it, which would have been out of place in a popular book, in a work of art; and for this reason, as well as for its good judgment which he generally shows concerning doubtful questions, for the singular beauty of his descriptive and narrative style, for his great love of Spain, and for all that he did to make Spanish matters more attractive, we owe him a tender recollection and the justice of recognizing that, taken for all in all, his biography of Columbus has not yet been superseded . . .[69]

The question persists, however, on why most readers, with the exception of Severn Wallis, and to some extent Pedro Sabau, failed to see or ignored a consistent pattern of stereotyping Spain on the part of Irving. There might be at least three possible explanations: first, that Spaniards had seen it all when it came to coverage of their history. That is to say, that compared to British and French accounts of Spain, its history and its people, Irving was not only mild but actually full of admiration for the country.[70] Second, that Spanish scholars recognized in Irving's work a magnificent example of how history could be made popular and accessible at a time when they were themselves engaged in a great effort to expand the scope of historical scholarship in the nineteenth century. Irving's work *was* inspiring and popular in Spain, and his grateful readership saw the positive over the negative.

Third, and finally, that by deftly crossing the boundaries between romance and history, Irving never allowed himself to be pinned down on any particularly strong ideological agenda. If he produced a notoriously outrageous statement on Spain, he was careful to put it in the mouth of a fictional character, a foreign observer, or a recognized villain in Spanish history. With a wink of the eye, a knowing smile, and always an escape route, Irving succeeded in molding American perceptions of Spain in the nineteenth century and, perhaps most surprisingly, Spanish views of their own history, proving that satire, combined with serious engagement, could have a powerful transatlantic effect.

Chapter 2

Labor Ipse Voluptas: George Ticknor's History of Spanish Literature

The temples are fallen, the palaces overthrown, the ports filled up, the cities destroyed; and the earth, stripped of inhabitants, is become a place of sepulchers . . . Great God! Whence proceed these fatal revolutions? From what causes are changed the fortunes of these countries?

—Constantin Volney, *Les Ruines* (1791), Ch. II

We, too, are no doubt going on like the buried nations of antiquity, through the changes of youth and age.

—George Ticknor to George S. Hillard, July 17, 1848

On Tuesday afternoon, February 7, 1815, Thomas Jefferson bid farewell to the young George Ticknor, who had arrived at Monticello the previous Saturday from Boston to pay him a visit. Armed with a letter of introduction from John Adams, Ticknor had been eager to ask the former U.S. president about Europe, where he intended to go in the spring, and in preparation for which he wanted some letters of introduction. Jefferson was very impressed with the young man. He showed him his collection of antiquities, his gallery of paintings, and most importantly, his 7,000-volume library. The 24-year-old visitor was so poised and intelligent in conversation that he left a most favorable and lasting impression, which Jefferson conveyed to several correspondents. He assured Ticknor's father, Elisha, that George would most certainly profit from his visit to Europe, and would be "a sample to our youth of what they ought to be," predicting that he would become "a model for imitation in pursuits so honorable, so improving, and so friendly to good morals."[1] To young Ticknor Jefferson paid an extraordinary compliment two years later, while he was engaged in the foundation of the University of Virginia and was thinking about the recruitment of outstanding faculty: "Would to God we could have two or three duplicates of yourself, the original being above our means or hopes."[2] Something in the young man's comportment made him optimistic about the future of American letters.

George Ticknor had chosen a life of scholarship, and he intended to pursue advanced studies in classical literature at the University of Göttingen. There was no indication, at this point, that he would become the foremost scholar of Spanish literature in the United States and, for a time, in the world. Born in 1791, Ticknor had been educated at home, and then admitted as a junior at Dartmouth College, where he graduated in 1807. He was bound for a career in Law, but a combination of inspiring mentorship and parental support allowed him to pursue his true interests in literature and both classical and modern languages. At the age of 12, he received instruction in French from a recently arrived French immigrant, Francis Sales, who later became his colleague at Harvard. After graduation from college, young Ticknor was tutored by John Sylvester John Gardiner, Rector of Trinity Church in Boston, who in three years gave him not only a strong foundation in classical literature, but also introduced him to some of the most learned Bostonians of the period, including Joseph Stevens Buckminster, who became a close friend and supporter.[3] Before the age of 20, Ticknor had distinguished himself as a serious student, and an active participant in such circles as the Anthology Society, and smaller literary groups that gathered to read Latin poetry. One of those groups was named simply "The Club," and included Alexander H. Everett and his close friend Edmund Flagg. To the latter he reported, in 1808, the year of Napoleon's invasion of Spain, that he had been studying Spanish, and was about to start Italian.[4] He also apprenticed in law under William Sullivan, but his desire to pursue a literary career led to the decision to study abroad. Reading Madame de Staël's *De l'Allemagne* convinced him of the advantages of German universities, and especially the University of Göttingen. It was there that he headed, along with his friend Edward Everett, in April 1815.

The University of Göttingen was a vibrant place, and Ticknor and a few other pioneering Americans made the most of it.[5] English speakers more generally had long resorted to the university, due to its connections to the British Crown and its openness to foreigners. Arriving there in August 1815, the eager Bostonian submitted to a grueling schedule of lectures and language tutoring for the next two years, primarily in Greek, but also attended a variety of courses on historical and scientific subjects. He used some of the time to visit universities and libraries, and to call on such literary giants as Goethe, and respected scholars like Ferdinand Wolf. It was there that many of his long-standing views on the nature of national literatures were developed. As a letter to his friend Edward T. Channing of Boston shows, he had become certain that "German literature is a peculiar national literature, which, like the miraculous creation of Deucalion, has sprung directly from their own soil, and is so intimately connected with their character, that it is very difficult for a stranger to understand it."[6] This is precisely what he would later say about Spanish literature, although at the time he had no intention to examine it in any serious degree. He was preparing himself, at the moment, for a career in classical literature, while developing an appreciation for modern German letters.

Ticknor's decision to study Spanish (and French) literature was the result of a series of coincidences. In 1815, Abiel Smith of Taunton, Massachusetts, a 1764 graduate of Harvard, bequeathed the sum of 20,000 dollars for the establishment of a professorship in the French and Spanish Languages. John Kirkland, Harvard's president, had met Ticknor at the Anthology Society, and thought immediately of him for the position. The particulars of the appointment are well worth examining in some detail.

President Kirkland wrote to Ticknor in July 1816 to report that the Harvard Corporation (one of the two governing bodies of the College) had met on June 24 to offer him the position in French and Spanish, with a salary of $1,000, "from the legacy of the late Abiel Smith."[7] Ticknor received the letter in Göttingen in early November, and thought about it for five days before writing to his father. He had two major concerns, he said, one being the salary, which he thought would be insufficient to support a family if he were to marry upon his return. The second was the nature of the Chair:

> Here is at once a new subject of study [Spanish] proposed to me, to which I have paid no attention since I have been here, and which I have not taken into the plan of my studies and travels in Europe. If I am to be a professor in this literature, I must go to Spain; and this I cannot think of doing, without your full and free consent.

Specifically, he asked his father for additional income to supplement Harvard's salary, and for an extension of six months to visit Spain. He placed the burden of decision squarely on his parents by sending them two letters to Kirkland, one affirmative and one negative regarding the offer: "Choose, dear father and mother, whichever you please, and be assured your choice will make me happy."[8] Meanwhile, he wrote to Kirkland to give thanks and to say that in the event that he accepted, he would need time to learn the languages required by the professorship and also money to purchase books. He added that he wished to live with his parents in Boston, for as long as they lived, and thus wanted to be exempted from residence requirements at the College.[9]

Ticknor's conditions reveal that he understood the advantages of the position, but also that he was less than enthusiastic about its nature. He was excited about his classical studies, and eager to explore the richness of Göttingen. "I hope you mean to become the Smith Professor," William Tudor wrote to him from Boston, "I think Cambridge will in a short time be in a very brilliant condition."[10] Ticknor, however, was hesitant, and tried to secure the best possible terms for himself while he waited for the advice of his parents. Meanwhile, his friends Edward Everett and Joseph Green Cogswell urged Ticknor to accept the offer.[11] Kirkland, for his part, felt caught between his desire to fill the position and the limitations of the endowment. He responded to Ticknor that money was limited, and that there were no provisions for redirecting the bequest's income for the purchase of books.[12] Still, he promised to do what he could and, indeed, he succeeded. The minutes of the meeting of the Harvard Corporation on June 30, 1817, show that Ticknor's conditions were met: he could stay two years abroad, and use his salary, when he was not teaching, for the purchase of books. The revised offer reached Ticknor in Rome, and he communicated his formal acceptance on November 6, 1817.[13] No doubt, his decision was made easier by the response of his father, who had made up his mind to encourage his son to accept the appointment: "A seat at the University," Elisha wrote, "is much more congenial to your taste, genius, and habits, in my opinion, than to be employed on the boisterous and vexatious ocean of law and politics."[14]

While considering the offer, and perhaps as an indication that he would accept it, Ticknor threw himself into the study of European literary history. He was lucky that Friedrich Bouterwek, the foremost German scholar of European literature, was offering precisely that course in the spring of 1817. Ticknor also cancelled his planned trip to Greece, and instead headed for France, Italy, and Spain, both to collect books and to learn more of their languages and literatures. He also dispatched letters to London to inquire about "the best information on the subject of Spanish literature."[15] For most of 1817, he was also busy socializing with the leading lights of Europe. Thanks to Jefferson's letters of introduction, and others from Germany and England, Ticknor met the likes of Lafayette, Alexander von Humboldt, Madame de Staël, Augustus Schlegel, Benjamin Constant, Chateaubriand, and many others. In Italy he met members of many a European royal family, in addition to countless diplomats. Even the Vatican's doors were opened for him to meet Pope Pius VII. George Ticknor's social skills and language abilities, it appears, made him a welcome guest in the salons of Europe. This seems to have been an exhilarating time for him, and perhaps one of the reasons why he returned to Europe twice more during his lifetime. On April 5, however, he wrote in his journal, "I could stay in Florence no longer, for I must hasten to Spain with all the speed I can make."[16] His experience in Spain represented quite a contrast to all that he had seen and enjoyed thus far in Europe.

From Italy, Ticknor made his way to the Iberian Peninsula through the South of France in the spring of 1818. He left Perpignan on April 29, 1818, and entered Spain the following day. Ticknor's remarkable journal shows pendulum-like reactions at what he saw. The country struck him as "half-civilized" and its various sights produced in him a sadness he had not experienced during his entire absence from New England. His notes during the next six months show a gradual acceptance of some Spanish ways, but also a strong undercurrent of rejection. Some of the latter appeared so soon, and so vividly, that only a strong sense of duty to his newly accepted appointment appears to have made him persevere. At the same time, the journal reveals two other sources for his negative views: one was the obvious contrast between the European countries where he had been in the past three years, let alone his own, and Spain, barely emerging out of the devastations of the Peninsular War, where he could daily see evidence of the most wretched misery. The other was religious and cultural, coming from the assumptions of his milieu about Catholic Spain, whereby the influence of the clergy on all aspects of life was considered beyond question. On his second day in Spain, the town of Gerona gave him "my first glimpse of another less favourable side of the Spanish character,"

> I mean its religious slavery. When I walked through the streets and found every fourth or fifth person I met a solemn ecclesiastick with a long black cloak and a portentous hat curled up at the sides in a most characteristick and exclusive manner; when I found the lower class of people doing more reverence to them than a Pharisee ever exacted, and all around me indicating the preponderance of ecclesiastick influence over every other, it seemed as if I must be in a dream, and that it must have been the Pyrenees I passed last September and the Alps I had crossed the day before; for in Italy and in Rome I saw nothing like this influence on the one hand, and this servility on the other . . . I felt at once that I had never been in a Catholick country before.[17]

The 400-mile trip from Barcelona to Madrid, where Ticknor was headed, took 13 days in very uncomfortable conditions. It was on this trip that Ticknor provided evidence of his acquaintance with and love for Cervantes's *Don Quixote*. He made some allusions to Matthew Lewis's *The Monk*, and to Le Sage's *Gil Blas*, on several occasions during his stay in Spain, but it was Cervantes who provided the main points of reference for his descriptions of the country. "Whoever wishes," he wrote of the dismal inns along the way, "to have an idea of the squalid filth and rude manners of those who keep them has only to read *Don Quixote*, where the descriptions are still as faithful as nature."[18] He had brought a copy of the book with him, and entertained himself and his fellow travelers by reading it aloud, apparently with such theatrical effect as to have his listeners aching from uncontrollable laughter. He found it a pleasure "to witness the effect this extraordinary book produces on the people from whose very blood and character it is drawn."[19]

Ticknor already had some fairly developed notions about how a genuine literature reflected the national character of a people, and Cervantes's work served as the clearest demonstration. In the midst of discomforts and poverty, as in Don Quixote's day, there lived a sturdy Spanish people who ultimately won Ticknor's heart, both in a literary and in an actual sense. He had nothing but contempt for the king (Ferdinand VII), "a vulgar blackguard," for the nobility, "gross and unworthy," and only limited sympathy for the middling classes, "oppressed and unworthy." He found it astonishing that under the chaotic circumstances of Spain the government should work, unless one took into consideration the common folk, "for a more quiet, orderly people, a people more obedient and loyal, I have not seen in Europe." Moreover, they were "gay and lighthearted in their natural disposition," and possessed "a kind of instinctive uprightness, which prevents them from servility."[20] One might suspect that Ticknor tended to simplify, perhaps even romanticize, the division between rich and poor, or nobility and commoners in Spain, in order to make sense of a new and to some extent overwhelming experience. But a letter to Barbara Channing, written at this time, reveals that he was testing a larger theory (which he had picked up in Göttingen) about the relationship between the true sources of national character, and a genuine, worthwhile literature:

> Spain and the Spanish people amuse me more than anything I have met in Europe. There is more national character here, more originality and poetry in the popular manners and feelings, more force without barbarism, and civilization without corruption, than I have found anywhere else. Would you believe it?—I speak not at all of the highest class—what seems mere fiction and romance in other countries is matter of observation here, and, in all that relates to manners, Cervantes and Le Sage are historians. For, when you have crossed the Pyrenees, you have not only passed from one country and climate to another, but you have gone back a couple of centuries in your chronology, and find the people still in that kind of poetical existence which we have not only long since lost, but which we have long ceased to credit on the reports of our ancestors.[21]

Ticknor, to his credit, was not satisfied with sweeping generalizations that would render his understanding of Spanish culture and literature easier. Instead, he submitted himself to the same grueling schedule of study that he had followed in Germany. From six in the morning to four in the afternoon, he studied the language and took lessons in Spanish literature from the noted Spanish scholar José Antonio Conde. Dinners, *tertulias* (social gatherings), and theater attendances all served the same purpose of advancing his knowledge of country and culture. He shared the British disgust for bullfights, but that did not stop him from attending them. Ticknor thought that the events of the *toreo*, and the response of the audience, revealed some deeper political meanings than were apparent to many visitors to the country. But he was certainly horrified when a nearby spectator laughed, clapped, and yelled that a bull pierced by swords looked like a *mater dolorosa*.[22]

Traveling in southern Spain, he was particularly struck by the strong Muslim presence, especially in architecture. He joined newly acquired friends such as the duke of Rivas and his younger brother Ángel in rides off the beaten track. Ticknor embraced festivals, meals, and all sorts of social encounters, especially popular, with glee. He even joined a band of 28 smugglers in order to cross the boundary from Spain to Portugal, in an act that he rationalized as the most expedient way to reach his objective, but in which he discovered a "gay recklessness" that he did not know he possessed, whereby he could live on "a footing of perfect equality and good fellowship with people who are liable every day to be shot or hanged by the laws of their country." After a harrowing passage in which at points he took command of the group, he bade farewell to "the only country in the world where I could have led such a life."[23]

When he arrived in Lisbon in October of 1818, Ticknor was pleased to learn that he had been elected a corresponding member of the Royal Academy of History in Madrid. He and the German scholar Friedrich Bouterwek had been nominated by José Antonio Conde on September 18, and had been duly elected on September 25.[24] His visit to Spain had been, on balance, a rewarding and even exhilarating experience. By the time he reached England from Lisbon in November, however, he seemed to have undergone a rather abrupt change of mind, rapidly returning to his usual New England propriety. To his father he wrote,

> I cannot express to you how I have been struck by the contrast between Spain—which is now continually present to my imagination as a country dead in everything a nation ought to be—and England, where the smallest village and the humblest peasant bear some decisive mark of activity and improvement and vital strength and power; Spain, where all is so stagnant and lifeless.[25]

Though he affected intellectual rejection, the country had touched him deeply. This ambivalence would remain the defining element of his views on Spain.

George Ticknor spent another six months in Europe, mainly in London and Paris. He resumed his rounds of social activity, book collecting, and study. On this occasion, he met Walter Scott, Washington Irving (who was about to launch his *Sketch Book*), Simonde de Sismondi, and Leandro Fernández de Moratín. Indeed, it is in his journal entries covering the trip to Paris in December 1818, that we find him most focused on the tasks that awaited him back home. "I went there [Paris]," he wrote, "merely to see some books and manuscripts in the King's Library," and to seek titles that the Spanish scholar Juan Antonio Llorente had suggested to him.[26] Most importantly, he went there to seek guidance from the scholars François Raynouard (on Provençal literature); Moratín (on Spanish literature), "the best writer of Spanish comedy alive," and José María de Souza-Botelho (on Portuguese literature), "the generous editor of the *Lusiads*." He had every reason to be satisfied, for he worked under the direction of all three and, at the Royal Library, he found, "particularly in ancient Spanish literature, much that astonished me—much, indeed, not to be found at Madrid in the Escorial or at Seville."[27]

His spirits were high, and he knew he was now fully on track to launch his career as a scholar. Sadly, he received the news, while traveling in Scotland in February of 1819, that his mother had died the previous December. He had known that she was ill, but had received assurances from both parents that she was recovering. However, he received a very different impression from his friend Alexander Everett, who told him plainly that the situation was grave.[28] Another friend had the worst news to tell. "George is with me now," Joseph Cogswell wrote from Edinburgh, "and on Thursday [February 11] I had to perform the painful duty of communicating to him the death of his mother."[29] The impact was so severe that Ticknor could not bring himself to write about it for six months. But he did what he had come to do in Scotland, and that was to meet the revered Walter Scott, who received him well and did much to distract him. They discussed, among other literary subjects, the origins of Spanish national literature. "I have to return you my best thanks," Scott wrote on March 2, "for your most valuable information respecting the Spanish Romances."[30] Together they spent many a day walking about and talking, but Ticknor's thoughts had turned primarily to returning home and to starting his duties as the new Smith Professor of French and Spanish.

After Scotland, Ticknor went to London, but not without stopping first at Keswick to visit Robert Southey, to talk to him about Spain and Portugal, and look at his rich collection of books.[31] Once in London, Washington Irving did much to amuse him there, accompanying him to excursions, plays, and balls. A lasting friendship emerged from those otherwise sad days. "I recommend you to see as much of him as you can," the genuinely impressed Irving wrote to his friend Henry Breevort, "for your own sake."[32] Lord Holland and John Allen also tried to keep him engaged, but Ticknor was in a hurry to leave.[33] Soon after he finished his preparations, on April 26, he departed for Liverpool, where he awaited to embark on the *Albion*, a vessel bound for New York. There he registered his reflections,

> As I stood on the same stone steps by which I had landed in Europe four years before and on which I was now waiting for the boat that was to carry me from it forever, many a strange thought crossed through my mind. How different Europe was to me now from the fairy land it then seemed—and how my country now rose before me like a bright and blessed vision of peace and happiness.[34]

Indeed, the pace of life had quickened much of late, and, after four years abroad, he was prepared for a change. He was warmly received by his family in Boston, where he arrived on June 6, 1819, and where he soon resumed his relations with such friends as William H. Prescott, Daniel Webster, and Andrews Norton. He also joined William Ellery Channing's Church, and remained a Unitarian for the rest his life. He was formally inducted into the professorship at Cambridge on August 10, 1819, after he signed the following oath:

> I George Ticknor, elected Smith Professor of French and Spanish languages and literatures, and Professor of Belles Lettres, believe the Christian religion, and have a firm persuasion of its truth. I promise that I will discharge the duties of my offices with diligence and fidelity, that I will endeavor, as well by my example as otherwise, to encourage and promote true piety, and all the Christian virtues.[35]

He then delivered an address that reveals the extent to which he had formed his opinions about Spanish literature:

> In modern times no poetry has sprung so directly from the popular feelings, or exercised so great an influence on the national character, as that of the Peninsula, beyond the Pyrenees. This rich and admirable country, standing in some measure between Europe

and Africa, served, for above seven centuries, as the advanced guard of Christendom, against the attacks of the Arabs, who then threatened to overrun Europe, as they had already overrun the half of Asia. In these conflicts—where, during four hundred years, the Spaniards were uniformly beaten, without ever shrinking—*a national character was gradually formed, in which chivalry and religion were mingled and confounded by the cause in which they were alike engaged*; while, at the same time, the bitterness of an hereditary animosity, that tolerated neither compromise nor hesitation, was admirably softened by the generous virtues and higher refinement of their Moorish enemies.[36]

Ticknor went on to emphasize that Spanish literature "has never had but one tone, and that tone has been purely and exclusively Spanish, nourished by a high moral feeling, and a proud and prevalent sense of honor, loyalty, and religion." In the lecture he introduced the following four central themes: (1) history, especially the conflict with the Moors, made Spain different from any other country in Europe, indeed the world; (2) true Spanish literature was essentially popular, springing from the common people's struggles and daily lives; (3) the fundamental components of the Spanish national character were chivalry and religion; and (4) Arab elements influenced the Spanish character, especially the love of luxury and refinement. In his later writings he developed additional themes, such as the influence of the Inquisition and the government on the national character, but in this first public statement of his views, Ticknor launched the central elements of his long-standing interpretation of Spanish history and culture.

There were other day-to-day tasks associated with the Smith Professorship, and Ticknor did not shy from them, sometimes to the annoyance of President Kirkland and other members of the faculty. He told Kirkland that he intended to collaborate with Francis Sales, who had provided Spanish instruction at Harvard since 1816, and that he would work primarily with his students. By this Ticknor meant to emphasize that a degree of acquaintance with the Spanish language would be expected from his pupils.[37] He first concentrated on his French lectures, but in 1821 he informed the president that he was ready to begin those on Spanish literature. The following year, he requested university funds to print the syllabus for his Spanish course, which he obtained. This is a highly valuable document, for it provides clear evidence both of Ticknor's learning, and of his manner of teaching the literary history of Spain.[38]

The Smith Professor envisioned a course of 34 lectures, each an hour in length. As he explained in the opening statement, the subject was "quite untouched," for not even in Spain was there a comprehensive study of the country's literature. He gave due credit, however, to Friedrich Bouterwek's *Geschichte der Poesie und Beredsamkeit seit dem Ende des Dreizehnten Jahrhunderts* (1801–1819), partly devoted to Spanish and Portuguese literature, and Simonde de Sismondi's *De la Littérature du Midi de l'Europe* (1813), which was also partly devoted to the literature of the Iberian countries. But, he stated, these authors had little access to sources, whereas he had obtained "a collection of works in Spanish literature nearly complete for such purposes." He had, indeed, collected in earnest while in Europe after he accepted the Harvard appointment. In time, his library of Spanish and Portuguese books would become the best in the country, but for the moment his claim was legitimate, in that his syllabus reveals a command of sources far beyond those discussed by his European counterparts. Most importantly, he presented his materials not as a random selection of authors, with huge gaps between periods, but rather in a detailed and larger chronological context, and in divisions that included individual writers as well as literary genres, or "departments." It was a bold yet systematic arrangement that revealed how much he had reflected on the internal dialogue between authors and sources, and the relationship between literature and history.

Ticknor discerned three major periods in Spanish literature. The first spanned the years 1155 to 1555 or, roughly from its very beginnings through the end of the reign of Charles V. The second ranged from the era of Philip II to the ascent of the Bourbons, that is from 1556 to 1700. The third and last encompassed the year 1700 to "the present time," which meant up to the reign of Ferdinand VII, still in place at the time of his lectures. The division seemed natural enough, but there were some interesting choices. The starting date, for example, was justified as the time of "the first appearance of the present written language," and the following five centuries as a period when Spain was "essentially untouched by the influence of any foreign literature." Ticknor viewed the second period as a time that "comprehends the best literature of the country," but also a time that showed some signs of decay. The final period marked a transition from the Austrian to the Bourbon dynasties, when Spanish literature came, for better or worse, "under the influence of the court," and the influence of French literature.

What is remarkable about the syllabus is the range of coverage. For instance, the first "epoch," covers not only the most important sources and names of the period (the *Poem of the Cid*, writings by Gonzalo de Berceo, Alfonso the Tenth, Juan Manuel, and Juan Ruiz), but also a multitude of lesser-known authors writing ballads, chronicles, romances of chivalry, and drama. There was, in addition, a section discussing the influence of Provençal and Italian literature on Spanish letters. His coverage of the second epoch is by far the richest, in that it includes not only coverage of such authors as Cervantes, Diego Hurtado de Mendoza, Alonso de Ercilla, Lope de Vega, Calderón de la Barca, and Francisco de Quevedo, but also a discussion of authors in 12 distinct categories, namely, epic poetry, drama, lyric poetry, satirical poetry, didactic poetry, bucolic poetry, ballads, romantic fiction, eloquence, epistolary correspondence, history, and didactic prose. In contrast, the coverage of the third epoch is brief, and it proceeds by a simple division of reigns (those of Philip V, Ferdinand VI, Charles III, Charles IV, and Ferdinand VII). Although in this section Ticknor discussed some important authors (José Francisco de Isla, Leandro Fernández de Moratín, José Cadalso, Gaspar Melchor de Jovellanos, Juan Meléndez Valdés, and Manuel José Quintana), his handwritten notes show that he viewed this period as one characterized by "decay of intelligence, refinement and moral dignity." Still, even in discussing the worst moment in Spanish literary history, there had never been, in the United States, such a rich examination of Spanish sources.

How did he come to know what he seemed to know so well? An important part of the answer lies in the systematic way in which he collected, studied, and consulted with scholars in Europe once he accepted the Harvard position. But perhaps more important is the course of studies he pursued under Bouterwek at Göttingen. Fortunately, he took some 700 pages of notes that show precisely what he learned there, especially with regard to Spanish literature.[39] And it was a lot. A number of Spanish authors were examined, including many whom Ticknor had not known, under discernible categories such as chronological periods and genres. Ticknor borrowed heavily from Bouterwek's systematic organization, and also from his overriding theme in analyzing European literatures: what made them *national*.[40]

It is not possible to understand Ticknor's syllabus without considering his notes on Bouterwek's lectures, or his writings in a manuscript volume that he titled *Spanish*, which contains notes from his reading of sources at the royal libraries of Madrid and Paris between 1818 and 1819.[41] Together they provide the fundamental sources not only for the syllabus, but for his lifetime work, which grew more and more elaborate over time. In fact, he wrote hundreds of pages of lecture notes that closely followed both the European logs and the outline of the course. It was in these candid lecture notes, prepared between 1819 and 1822, that he fleshed out the central ideas of his inaugural lecture and his larger vision of the history of Spanish literature.[42] They stand as the earliest and most elaborate examination of any foreign literature in the United States, and as such they deserve close attention.

The Lectures on Spanish Literature

In his lectures to Harvard students, Ticknor was primarily concerned with the emergence of a "Spanish national character" under the peculiar historical conditions of the Iberian Peninsula. Christians having been driven to the mountains of the north by Muslim invaders, their literary efforts had been limited and had understandably centered on the theme of war against infidels. Thus, "the first notes of their wild, romantick and truly national poetry [have] come to us mingled with their war shouts, and breathing the very spirit of their victories" (I, 8). He viewed the *Poem of the Cid* as the best example of the genre, and proved to be far ahead of his time in considering this little known poem as a central source in Spanish literary history.[43] There had been precedents in other areas of the world, such as the eighteenth-century attention on Ossian and Homer, to develop a cult of "primitive" or "folk" poetry, and Ticknor was certainly familiar with how it influenced European romanticism. The story of the Cid, he wrote, is the story of "the most romantick achievements of the most romantick hero of Spanish poetry." He provided a detailed analysis of both the historical figure of the Cid (Rodrigo Díaz de Vivar), and the poem that celebrated his exploits. But he was also interested in the language of the poem, which he thought was "the language he himself spoke—still half formed yet breathing the bold, fresh, and original spirit of the times when it was struggling for an existence amidst the other wild elements of the national genius" (I, 14). Ticknor believed that the poem had been composed no later than 1150, and exemplified the "wide force of religious enthusiasm" (I, 19), a theme that would recur in his analysis of Spanish literary history. The literature that followed, for as long as Christians fought against their invaders, was characterized by the related themes of religion and chivalry, and also, by its *popular* roots. Ticknor thought that the large mass of historical ballads of medieval Spain demonstrated the following: "The early heroes of the Spanish history grew so directly out of the popular character . . . that they of course became the first, the chief and the favorite subject of that poetry which was so truly the very breathing of the popular feeling and character" (I, 60). On a larger scale, the literature of Spain during this first era took its inspiration from the historical conditions of the war against the Muslims, and reflected a Spanish popular character fired by a religious and chivalric spirit that, however unrefined, was truly national.

But the national circumstances had changed during the second epoch, and with them some important elements of the national character. The fundamental change, of course, was the emergence of Spain as an imperial power under Charles V. The sheer expansion of Spanish might was "something entirely new," and produced "a corresponding effect on the national character" (II, 3). It opened up the gates, as it were, to literary creativity, and constituted, "to this day the only genuine school of Spanish literature," lasting fully a century and a half until the advent of the French Bourbon dynasty (II, 4). Still under Charles V, "it seems as if the national genius had been suddenly inspired with a poetical ambition no less bold and extraordinary, than its military success had inspired into the masters of the Empire" (II, 157). Such an inspiration led to the unsurpassed glory of Cervantes, Lope de Vega and Diego Hurtado de Mendoza, to whom he devoted extensive attention. Their work, and sometimes even their persons, exemplified the originality and force of a Spanish character that was popular, romantic, and chivalrous, even if at times also roguish and fanatic. Ticknor could be critical of this very character, especially in its religious dimensions. Describing the work of Lope de Vega, for instance, he stated that it provided

> . . . a most extraordinary exhibition of the state of his feelings and of the character of Catholick Christianity in his time. Some of these pieces are written with a light, frivolous and festive air, as if they were songs for a common merrymaking, which, no doubt, many of the church holidays then were, even in the religious part of the ceremonies—others are marked with a gross, sensual fanaticism, which it fills us with horror to read and which show an alienation of mind from the purity of holy things, which educated as we are, we can hardly imagine to have been short of insanity. (II, 110)

Spain under the Philips provided numerous other examples of religious fanaticism and Ticknor did not spare his students some pointed commentary. Speaking of Lope de Vega's *Autos Sacramentales*, Ticknor stated that the Spanish author could mix "gallantry and buffoonery with the holiest feelings of religion" in a manner that was "perfectly revolting" (III, 9). But he was hardly alone, for "the *Autos* were the natural result of the coarse and vulgar fanaticism of the lower orders of society in Spain" (III, 14). As the glorious days of Charles V yielded to the declining years of his successors, the combination of religious fanaticism and a sense of decay and defeat would doom the national character and its literary manifestations. The "enthusiasm of the popular character," as it existed in medieval Spain and through the reign of Charles V, he stated, "was no longer possible." Instead, it "gradually faded away under the cold, close and cheerless tyranny of the Philips. The independence and dignity of the national feeling was broken down by an unrelenting despotism; and its poetical elevation was humbled and degraded by disaster abroad and disgrace at home" (III, 24). No branch of literature could flourish under the circumstances. Instead, by the end of the Austrian dynasty, "the whole body of the national literature [had] fallen into a premature, perhaps; but, probably a hopeless ruin" (III, 96). The question now became how to explain the causes of such a precipitous decay, from which "the country has never since recovered" (III, 97).

Ticknor identified two major causes. First and foremost was the influence of the Inquisition, "the most fearful tribunal that was ever set up for the restraint of the human mind and the most successful in the accomplishment of its purposes."

He wanted to clarify, however, what he considered to be a major mistake: that the Inquisition achieved its objectives purely through violence and against the nation's will. No institution could do that, and especially not against the courageous Spanish people. Instead, "the Spanish nation was subdued by its own fanaticism or the Inquisition could never have existed." He told his students that when the institution began its ghastly work, "no people in Europe was so bigoted." This explained the disastrous expulsion of the Moors and the Jews, despite the blow it delivered to the nation's well-being. After accomplishing this notorious deed, and lacking infidels to persecute, the Inquisition "became a cruel, secret police, whose great object was, to search into the opinions of men and punish their thoughts" (III, 99). The educated became special targets, so as to prevent the emergence of a critical spirit, but no one escaped its suspicions and severity,

> The thoughts and minds of men were subjected to its control. A standard of right and wrong suited to its purposes was fully established throughout the country, and the national character, though it did not for a long time, feel itself restrained and oppressed, was constantly losing its spirit, its energy and its dignity in this unnatural state of moral constraint, where the best faculties of the mind and the highest qualities of the character [were] prevented from their appropriate exercise and cut off from their natural support. The Inquisition, in fact, reigned triumphant throughout Spain, during the whole of this period because it kept the general opinion of the country on its side—because, perhaps, most of those who exercised its very cruelties believed them to be religious duties, and because most of those who suffered them, submitted to them as expiatory punishments. (III, 101)

In short, the Inquisition could only do what it did because of the "disease infecting the minds and character of the whole nation," namely, religious bigotry. Yet it could not ruin the Spanish character all by itself, and thus Ticknor introduced the second major cause of decay: "the political government of the country," which was "no less jealous and severe" than the Inquisition (III, 102). Philip II, in particular, was "unremitting in his efforts to repress the dangerous spirit of inquiry, which the progress of the Reformation had sent into all the departments of human knowledge." Persecution of individuals, additions of books to the *Index Expurgatorius*, and control of speech and publication characterized his somber reign. But his detrimental policies extended far beyond his actual years as monarch, due to the indolence and incapacity of his successors in the seventeenth century. Thus, "the long, silent and unresisted influence of the Government and Inquisition had made their spirit a part of the national character." Ironically, this was not incompatible with the sporadic emergence of great works of literature, such as those that characterized the seventeenth century, but the poisonous environment slowly undermined the national spirit,

> Such great moral contradictions between the different parts of the national character could not continue long without producing, in some way or other, disastrous consequences. The Spanish nation and writers might, for a time, remain light-hearted and happy because they were deluded, but the effects of the oppression they were suffering could not, on that account, be finally prevented. The less, in fact, they were conscious of the tyranny that was humbling them, the more surely it would be successful. And so it proved. Philip II, Philip III and Philip IV each left the country lower in the scale of nations and more degraded in power than they received it from their respecting

predecessors . . . [thus] the poetical genius of the nation, which had always depended more in Spain on the elevation and excitement of the popular character, than it ever did in any other country, disappeared, [and] we have no right to look for its restoration (III, 106–107).

Given such a conclusion for the end of the second epoch, students could rejoice that the final epoch was mercifully short: it consisted of a quick review of literary works under the five monarchs who followed Charles II. There were some major accomplishments during this period, especially the creation of national academies of language and history, and the emergence of a few very gifted writers, but Ticknor made no mistake about his overall assessment: "The last epoch of the literary history of Spain is one of the most melancholy in the literary history of any modern nation" (III, 108). Students probably wondered why they should go through such a futile exercise, but Ticknor insisted that they must know not just what Spaniards wrote during this period, but how they fared in the hands of incompetent governments and bigoted religious institutions. French influences, in addition, did "quite as much injury as benefit to the progress of letters in Spain" (III, 136). And if the last injury was not fatal, French troops finally inflicted it when Napoleon invaded the Iberian Peninsula, sending Spain into a vortex of chaos from which it had not recovered, and perhaps never would.

On the last day of class in 1823, Ticknor intuited that his subject was far from motivational, and thus urged his students to regard Spanish literature, not as a "perfected literature" like the French or Italian, but certainly of "more richness and originality than either." He also thanked students for their interest in the lectures, and expressed hope "that you will not hereafter neglect to pursue a literature so original, picturesque, and abundant."[44] This was hardly an enthusiastic call to embrace Spanish letters, but he had made his point, in excruciating detail, about the rise and fall of the Spanish empire, as seen through its literature.

It is pertinent to ask here whether Ticknor stood alone in his interpretation of Spanish literary history by briefly examining the surveys against which he competed, namely those of Bouterwek and Sismondi.[45] As mentioned earlier, Bouterwek (1766–1828) had devoted two volumes of his *Geschichte* to Iberian literature, one each to the Spanish and Portuguese. Many of his views were strikingly similar to those of Ticknor, especially those regarding how literature reflects national character, the damaging influence of both the Inquisition and the government, and the ultimate decay of Spanish letters. Bouterwek viewed the national character, which in its earliest origins stood out for its simplicity and moral gravity, sadly transformed under the Austrian dynasty into a fondness for "luxury and extravagance."[46] The Inquisition was characterized as a "terrible tribunal" which "to the disgrace of human reason" exercised "monstrous powers" (150). Religion became little more than an instrument for the exercise of royal despotism. Under Charles V and Philip II, "ecclesiastical and political despotism left no free scope for the exercise of the mental powers" (307). The national spirit, under the three Philips, "became at last like the national resources, completely exhausted" (540). By the eighteenth century, national literature was in "lamentable decline" (538). That is, in terms of tropes of Spanish character and its relationship to religion and government, the similarities between Bouterwek and Ticknor are strong. But there are differences, too, not only in terms of the number of sources examined, but also in the identification of certain periods as turning points in the larger history of Spanish literature. For Bouterwek, the story of decay began in earnest under Charles V, while for Ticknor there were nuances in all periods, thus giving more coherence to the entire history even within an overall narrative of decline.

Similarly, we find that Ticknor's themes are also present in Sismondi's work, although the language of the first, even at its most candid, appears moderate compared to that of the French-Swiss author (1773–1842), whom Ticknor had met in France and in England during his first trip to Europe. In addition, Sismondi made a much stronger case for Arabic influences on Spanish literature, though surely not because of any thorough research: "The literature of Spain," he said in contrast to the rest of Europe, "is decidedly oriental. Its spirit, its pomp, its object, all belong to another sphere of ideas— to another world."[47] He had little to say, however, about works other than the *Poem of the Cid*, and *Count Lucanor*, by Juan Manuel. Indeed, he stated, "In the course of four centuries the poetry of Castile made no perceptible progress" (139). What follows is a relentless story of decay, beginning with Ferdinand's use of the Inquisition for political purposes, and the ferocity of war during the reign of Charles V. Although Spanish literature achieved much during the time of the latter monarch, he still saw "the symptoms of its approaching decay" (172). Moreover,

> The drama, the romances, the poetry, and the history of Spain are all so deeply tinctured by religion, that I am constantly obliged to call the attention of the reader to this striking characteristic; to mingle, as it were, the Inquisition with their literature, and to exhibit the national character as well as the national taste perverted by superstition and fanaticism. (294)

Sismondi assured his readers that Spain had many qualities, including: "genius, imagination, depth of thought, constancy, dignity, and courage," but, he regretted, "her religion has almost at all times rendered these brilliant qualities unavailing" (364). Cervantes received some praise, but Lope de Vega and Calderón were sharply criticized for their religious bent, and in fact he called the latter "the true poet of the Inquisition" (338). Only the *Poem of the Cid* received unqualified praise, and so Sismondi concluded that "the literature of Spain has, strictly speaking, only one period, that of chivalry" (400).

When Ticknor's lecture notes are read in the context of the two major existing works on Spanish literature, they stand out as sharing the negative views of their predecessors yet without going to some of their extremes. Most importantly, however, Ticknor's coverage was far more extensive, discussing a wider array of sources, and neglecting no period in the country's history. He was determined to provide as full a discussion of Spanish literature as he could with the sources at his disposal. There was something in the nature of scholarship that he thought helped modify received wisdom, and invited even deeper historical research. But he still needed to communicate this conviction to a notoriously unruly undergraduate audience, in an academic environment that left much to be desired.

Teaching at Harvard

George Ticknor taught at Harvard for nearly fifteen years, many of which were quite unhappy. In fact, he expressed discontent with academic practices early on, and especially with the relaxed leadership of President Kirkland. There is, indeed, evidence of trouble as early as 1823. As he put it in a frank letter to Kirkland,

> My course on the history and criticism of Spanish literature is entirely ready, but as you granted permission to so many to keep school during the latter part of the Fall term as to break up my class for a month there is no time to deliver above four lectures even if it were worth the labor to lecture longer in the unprofitable way I have been compelled to lecture heretofore to this class. Of such a result, however, you were early aware . . . I can never go properly through my lectures while you continue to make this noxious enlargement of the winter vacation to three months.[48]

The problem, as Ticknor saw it, was the lack of rules about what was expected of both faculty and students. His own sense of his pedagogical obligations was to deliver at least thirty lectures per term, but such exemptions as those granted by Kirkland undermined his methodical plan.[49] The poet James Russell Lowell had a less formal interpretation of Kirkland's administrative style. In his "Cambridge Thirty Years Ago" (1854), he spoke of the amiable president as "a man of genius, but of genius that evaded utilization— a great water-power, but without rapids, and flowing with too smooth and gentle a current to be set turning wheels and whirling spindles."[50] That there was a problem, there can be no doubt. Students went on wild rampages about town that raised serious questions about discipline; faculty voiced grievances wherever they could be heard. Ticknor was distinctly unhappy, and issued frequent complaints about rules that compelled undergraduates to take his courses, which resulted in what he felt was militant student indifference. In, 1825, for instance, he responded to the required report on meritorious students by saying that beyond a handful of them, "it would be difficult to distinguish among the rest, except that a few took pleasure in seeming to know nothing."[51] In 1826, he delivered a report to the College, stating that he had delivered 54 French lectures during the year to about 60 students who were "generally present." By this he meant that only 3 had been excused at some point, while 62 others had been absent without any reason.[52]

Still, Ticknor seemed to attract some of the best students. He taught Emerson in 1821 and John Motley in 1828, among many others in between. He was apparently a terrific lecturer. Allowing for some family bias, it is worth considering his nephew's recollections: "He always, in my time, fixed and kept the attention of his class; indeed, there was never any movement or sound in the lecture-room that evinced an absence of attention. . . . He followed the very exact and methodical order of his syllabus, introducing discussions which were always animated and sometimes eloquent."[53] If he could take command of his class, he could also take command of his field. Indeed, he concentrated on strengthening instruction in order to counter the laxity of the College. In 1828, he issued a set of regulations for the Department of Modern Languages, whereby students would not be required to take its courses, but if they did, they would follow a strict schedule, with little room for absenteeism or disruptive behavior. Students were placed in courses according to proficiency rather than class, and could choose any of the languages offered by the department: French, Spanish, German, and Italian.[54] He received, as chaired professor, the full support of his colleagues. With over a 100 students in the 1820s, the department was not an inconsiderable part of the College.[55]

The largest number of students chose French, but a steady number took Spanish, usually in the range of 10 to 15 students in the 1820s. The Regulations of the Department spelled out the readings for each language, which in the case of Spanish included Augustin Louis Josse's *Grammar of the Spanish Language, with Practical exercises*; José Cadalso's *Cartas Marruecas*; Tomás de Iriarte's *Fábulas Literarias*; Cervantes's *Don Quixote*; *Comedias Españolas*, by various authors, and Voltaire's *Charles XII*, a work that students were expected to translate into Spanish. Most of these books were edited by Francis Sales, specifically for the purpose of teaching at Harvard.[56]

Despite success in his own field, Ticknor was not happy at the College. As he put it in a letter to his friend Charles Daveis of Portland, "I have been an active professor these fifteen years, and for thirteen years of the time I have been contending, against a constant opposition, to procure certain changes which should make the large means of the College more effectual for the education of the community . . . when I gave up hope, I determined to resign."[57] He communicated his decision to Harvard's President Josiah Quincy in November 1834. "I need not tell you," wrote a somewhat irritated Quincy, "how deeply I regret your intention of resigning, especially considering this determination of yours to be irrevocable."[58] He stepped down by the end of the academic year, in 1835, in part because of the wearisome and fruitless attempts at reform of the entire College, but principally because of a desire to devote himself to scholarship.[59] Francis Sales was devastated. "Permit me to express," he wrote upon learning the news, "the ineffable regret I feel at your leaving the post you have occupied for a series of years, with so much distinction, honour and advantage."[60] Ticknor was well liked by his immediate colleagues, but expressed no regret in leaving Harvard. After a long trip to Europe (1835–1838), he settled comfortably at his new home on Park Street overseeing the Boston Common, apparently devoted to reading and collecting old books and manuscripts. In fact, he had set out to revise his lectures and turn them into a book, which would in time become the monumental *History of Spanish Literature*.

Ticknor's Magnum Opus

During his second trip to Europe, Ticknor visited as many scholars and library collections specializing on Spain as he could, clearly an indication that the preparation of a book was his central purpose. Ticknor, his wife Anna, and their children arrived in England in June 1835, and then proceeded to the continent, but not without first contacting and then visiting Robert Southey.[61] They were in Dresden by November and Ticknor soon contacted Ludwig Tieck (1773–1853), the great German Romantic writer and scholar. "He seems past sixty," Ticknor wrote in his journal, and found him overall fine, "but somewhat whimsical and peculiar in his opinions and notions." He was particularly interested, indeed surprised, by Tieck's collection of Spanish books: "It is a great deal better than Lord Holland's; a great deal better than any collection in England; but still, on most points, not as good as mine." Ticknor could afford to be immodest, for he was a discriminating collector. But he was perhaps less charitable in referring to Tieck's knowledge of Spanish literature, "[It] goes no further than his books will carry him, and in some parts of it I remarked quite a striking ignorance."[62] That he had his own book in mind is also made clear in a letter to his friend Prescott in Boston, "I pick up, among other things, a good deal for my Spanish matters; but it is quite impossible to write out a book here," in reference to the many social distractions.[63]

Ticknor also visited Ferdinand Wolf at the Imperial Library in Vienna. He was there on June 24, 1836, to look over the collection of Spanish books, which had grown significantly when the Habsburgs ruled both Austria and Spain. Wolf, Ticknor wrote in his journal, "is a great amateur in this department, and I found much to interest and occupy me, though almost nothing of value that was *quite* new. The most curious parts were out of the collection of an old archbishop of the Valencia family, of the house of Cordova."[64] He found time to attend a performance of Agustín Moreto's *El desdén con el desdén* at Ischl (Upper Austria), which was apparently not very good. But, he wrote, "I enjoyed it a good deal, because the original, which I never saw represented, was quite familiar to me."[65] Indeed, he had taught that piece at Harvard. His appetite for things Spanish was insatiable; he would not be deterred by a bad staging of the play.

The Ticknor family proceeded from Austria to Italy, and in Rome they found or received many American friends, including Francis Gray, Joseph Cogswell, Samuel Ward, and the Rev. and Mrs. Ezra Stiles Gannett. It is obvious that he enjoyed their company enormously, but he did not fail to report on his multiple encounters with Simonde de Sismondi, who was coincidentally spending some time in Rome as well. Sismondi had grown a bit old and deaf, but they spent many hours together, no doubt going over their favorite subjects, literary history, and Spanish.[66]

The Ticknors left Rome in late April, 1837, and after stops in Austria, Germany, and Belgium, they approached Paris on September 11. There, he tracked down Claude Fauriel, whose work on the romances of the Provençal he wanted—and did—obtain. He found that the French scholar's knowledge of early Spanish literature exceeded that of Wolf, and found much pleasure in conversation with this quiet and unassuming scholar. He started to attend his lectures on Spanish literature at the Sorbonne on Mondays, but grew rather impatient at the professor's plodding pace. Fauriel was, he noted,

> much too minute on the antiquities that precede [the] appearance [of Spanish literature]. In fact, now, after an introductory lecture and two others, he has not completed his view of the state of things in Spain at the first dawning of tradition, seven hundred years before Christ. At this rate, he will not, by the time we leave Paris next Spring, have reached the Arabs.

He noted with admiration that Fauriel had an audience of 50 or 60 students, obviously undeterred by his thoroughness. "He is very learned and acute," Ticknor reflected, "but too minute and elaborate."[67] Still, he persevered. Once he received copies of Prescott's *Ferdinand and Isabella*, which had just been published in England and the United States, he did not fail to give one to the French *savant*. As he told his friend in Boston, Fauriel was "the very best scholar of Spanish literature and Spanish history alive, as I believe, and one of the ablest men, as a general scholar, I know of anywhere."[68]

Ticknor visited other scholars in Paris, but none impressed him as much as Fauriel. He did appreciate, however, their libraries. One in particular was Henri Ternaux-Compans', whom he met on December 25, 1837, and whose collection he found "curious in many respects, especially in old Spanish literature and in early

American history."[69] During this very cold winter in Paris, he also met the learned Portuguese Viscount Santarem. Ticknor pronounced him a "very extraordinary person," as well as a nobleman "of the rare scholarship which is sometimes, though very seldom, found in his nation."[70] His next stop was London, where he made some new and decisive acquaintances. As usual, he set out to meet those who had some knowledge of Spain and its literature, and also to visit some collections. He found that many in the London circles he frequented had already read Prescott's *Ferdinand and Isabella*, published in late 1837, and thus Ticknor's visit could not have been more timely.

At Holland House on April 1, 1838, he took great pleasure to hear both Lord Holland and John Allen give Prescott's book "high praise." Indeed, Allen pronounced the chapter on the constitutions of Castile and Aragon better than Henry Hallam's equivalent in his work on the Middle Ages. "This I regard as decisive," wrote Ticknor, "for no man alive is better authority on such a point than Allen."[71] Armed with that opinion, and with letters from Sydney Smith and Lord Holland, the persevering Ticknor convinced McVey Napier, editor of the *Edinburgh Review*, to publish a review of Prescott's book. It was in that context that the name of Pascual de Gayangos came up, as a young Spaniard of unusual talents, who did in fact review Prescott's book, and who became a central figure for both Boston scholars.[72] But Ticknor had to wait until June 3 to meet Gayangos personally at a dinner at Lord Holland's. As he wrote in his journal, he wanted to see him, and thus he "took pains to get between [Sir Francis] Head and Gayangos at dinner, because I wanted to know them both. The Spaniard—about thirty-two years old, and talking English like a native almost—I found quite pleasant, and full of pleasant knowledge in Spanish and Arabic, and with the kindliest good-will towards 'Ferdinand and Isabella.'"[73] Ticknor reached his immediate objective, but found also a lifetime friend who became indispensable to his own work.

Ticknor found plenty of other things to do in England, including some forays beyond learned circles in London. He wanted in particular to visit the famed Bodleian Library at Oxford, "I was curious for old Spanish books," he wrote in his journal, "but the Bodleian, vast as it is, and even with Douce's rare collection added to it, making in all nearly half a million volumes, is yet miserably deficient in Spanish literature . . . I was much disappointed, for I thought I should have found a great deal in odd corners."[74]

In early May, Ticknor and his family began the trip back to the United States. Just as they were preparing for embarkation, a letter reached Ticknor at the George Inn in Portsmouth: it was from the legendary Joseph Blanco White, the author of *Letters from Spain*, whose peripatetic geographical and religious life had taken him most recently to Liverpool and to Unitarianism. Ticknor had passed through that city in June, 1835, but did not know that Blanco White was there.[75] It was Lord Holland who told him in London of Blanco White's whereabouts. Now, on the occasion of the publication of Prescott's *Ferdinand and Isabella*, Ticknor had sent him a copy of the book with his greetings and those of his Boston friend. Blanco White replied,

> Within the parcel I had the pleasure to find a note from you, with both a most flattering message from that gentleman, and a most welcome assurance of esteem on your part, which, coming from one so well qualified to judge as well of English as Spanish literature, must be highly gratifying to a writer who, by an uncommon combination of

circumstances happens to have been a humble aspirant to usefulness in those two languages. Allow me therefore to request you that you will take the first opportunity to return my thanks to Mr. Prescott for the honor he has done me. Though I find myself in a deplorable state of health which prevents my reading in a very connected way, I have no doubt that the valuable work I have received from your friend will afford me considerable relief in the solitude to which my extreme weakness condemns me.

Blanco White was indeed very ill. But he was afflicted by ailments of a different nature: a sad and lonely existence, alienated from the land of his birth, and never quite fitting in his adoptive country. In addition, he told Ticknor, "One of the trials of my literary patience has been that of writing for many years, when I had no public to address." On a more optimistic note, he added, "I am therefore exceedingly pleased to hear that, as a Spanish writer, I have not yet [fallen] into utter oblivion."[76] Indeed, Ticknor and Prescott had him very much in mind, and often cited him as an authority on Spanish matters. Sadly, there was not much time left for their newly established contact to flourish, as Blanco White died in 1841. But the second European journey gave Ticknor this and other invaluable contacts.

Once back in Boston, Ticknor drew on Gayangos' expertise, and Obadiah Rich's efficiency as a book collector, to gather materials for his work. Gayangos, in particular, supplied Ticknor with books he purchased as well as with many from his private collection. Most importantly, his knowledge of medieval Spain was such that he was also able to clarify a number of scholarly questions. On June 16, 1841, for instance, Ticknor wrote to Gayangos to thank him for "having finally settled the etymology of *Mozarabes*, about which Covarrubias & all the rest had talked so much nonsense."[77] Over a hundred letters from Ticknor to Gayangos at the Hispanic Society of America in New York reveal an impressively learned exchange of views on sources and scholarly issues. Ticknor requested books and documents from Gayangos, but he also relied on other friends and scholars in France, Germany, and England who provided him with specialized opinion on specific subjects. To Washington Irving, recently appointed U.S. minister in Spain, he wrote in 1842: "I have been employed for some time on a 'History of Spanish Literature,' and need for it copies of a few manuscripts to be found in Madrid and in the Escorial."[78] He asked Irving to facilitate the work of Gayangos in coordinating what needed to be done. Progress on his writing could only be as fast as the copying and collecting, which required a great deal of travel, labor, and the efficiency of shipments across the ocean. Some times it was difficult to get materials from across the Charles River. "I find myself suddenly and unexpectedly in want of *these* books without delay," he wrote to his successor Henry Wadsworth Longfellow at Harvard, and listed the *Fuero Juzgo*, the *Siete Partidas*, and the *Coronica General* of Alonso XI. "I have no right to take out books at all, and, therefore must go to someone who has, by courtesy or law, an unlimited right." He told Longfellow that he had done that for others when he was a professor at Harvard, and asked whether the new Smith professor could now do it for him. Also, that he arranged for the books to be sent by the Baggage Wagon to his address in Boston.[79] Sources were obtained, with difficulty, from near and far.

But progress he made, and in 1846 Ticknor could tell Dr. Nicolaus Julius of Hamburg that "I work away constantly at my 'History of Spanish Literature,' after which you kindly inquire. It is now approaching 1700, after which there is not much, as you well know."[80] At long last, in early 1848, Ticknor informed Gayangos that "my manuscript of the Literary History of Spain will all be copied in the course of about a month."[81] Prescott, who knew about it, was delighted when he wrote to Mary Lyell,

> Have they [the Ticknors] told you [that] Ticknor himself is breaking ground as an author? His magnum opus—the history of Spanish Literature is actually finished and is now in the hands of an amanuensis, who is making a fair copy for the press. It will make, he thinks, three portly volumes; and from the specimens I have seen, from the richness of his materials, and the care he has bestowed on it, it will, I am confident, finally supply what has been so long a desideratum in literature. For all that Bouterwek and Sismondi have done, is merely to put together the bones of the skeleton. I am to have the manuscript in a few weeks, and before the summer is out, I trust it will be sent to press.[82]

He had reasons for doubting, he told Mary Lyell, for "a man who does not print before he is fifty six stands a good chance of never printing at all—and to say truth, I never thought he would." Yet print Ticknor did, but not before considering the comments of Prescott, who sent him detailed notes and a long letter in May 1848. Prescott was decidedly favorable, even if he had a few quibbles about matters of style and also about the overwhelming detail about obscure authors. "Even those superficially acquainted, as I am, with the Castilian literature," he wrote, "must be astonished to see how prolific the Spaniards have been in all kinds of composition known in civilized Europe, and in some kinds exclusively their own." He noticed the impressive scholarly apparatus, which rested on hundreds of original literary sources, and which provided many extracts from known and lesser known works. Most importantly, Prescott noted, "You have clearly developed the dominant national spirit, which is the peculiar and fascinating feature of the Castilian; and you have shown how completely this literature vindicates a place for itself apart from all other literatures of Christendom."[83] He had much to praise, and would soon write a long, positive review for the *North American Review*.[84]

When the publication came out in late 1849, it included over 1,600 pages of text divided into 3 volumes, thousands of notes, and several appendices. "You have produced three strapping volumes," wrote Washington Irving, "full of life and freshness and vigor, and that will live forever."[85] It was an impressive, thorough, unique piece of scholarship resulting from over 30 years of work. And yet, he made a most surprising statement in the preface. There, Ticknor explained that in the interval between his two trips to Europe he had delivered the lectures at Harvard discussed earlier, and that upon return from the second voyage,

> I endeavored to arrange these lectures for publication. But when I had already employed much labor and time on them, I found—or thought I found—that the tone of discussion which I had adopted for my academical audiences was not suited for the purposes of a regular history. *Destroying, therefore, what I had written*, I began afresh my never unwelcome task, and so have prepared the present work, as little connected with all I had previously done as it, perhaps, can be, and yet cover so much of the same ground.[86]

Professor Thomas R. Hart, first in a dissertation and later in an essay, has established that there is no such departure from the lecture notes to the published version of the

History. He has noted that the organization of the materials, the general principles of interpretation, and even the wording, are nearly identical. Therefore, he has concluded, "Ticknor may have felt that his apparent idleness after his resignation from Harvard in 1835 demanded some kind of explanation."[87] In the environment in which he lived and worked, Hart believes, it was important for Ticknor to show that he had been industrious. Thus, he claimed to have truly started his work only after 1838. This is a valuable insight, which places Ticknor in the context of the values of his milieu, but it is not sufficient to explain the truly astonishing statement of the preface. His correspondence after 1838, especially his letters to Pascual de Gayangos, demonstrates that the Boston writer felt no anxiety at all about idleness. Anxious he was at times, indeed, but about the length of time required to secure books and fill his numerous requests, to say nothing about lost or misdirected shipments and the wait for their replacements. Today, we are too far removed from the mid-nineteenth century to fully appreciate the time required to maintain communications across the ocean. And as the writing advanced, new sources were needed, and they meant yet another wait. In fact, it is rather remarkable that Ticknor would have completed the work in less than a decade since his return from Europe, especially for a work of that size and complexity.

Why, then, did Ticknor imply that his Harvard lecture notes had been destroyed and the book begun afresh? One is tempted to say that perhaps the remarks made at the lectures were too candid for publication. But we have seen that they were moderate compared to what was common in writings about Spain at the time. In addition, they were not substantially changed, except in minor stylistic ways. Not only the substance, but the main explanations for the decline of Spanish literature (and of Spain along with it), remained intact in the printed version. Thus one might consider another possible explanation, and that concerns the evolving standards of scholarship in nineteenth-century America. Ticknor, like Prescott, believed that no claim would or should be taken seriously without thorough, indeed massive, documentation. It was the *scholarly apparatus* that was developed in earnest after 1838, but basically to support the conclusions of 1823 and even before. There had been no destruction of the corpus of the lectures, but rather a shift in emphasis from conclusions to evidence, in ways that gave an entirely different tenor to the work.

Still, Ticknor wanted to make the book appealing and readable to a larger audience. As he put it in a letter to Sir Charles Lyell, accompanying a presentation copy of the book,

> You know our reading public in the United States, how large it is, as well as how craving and increasing; so that you will be less surprised than others, that I have prepared my book as much for general readers as for scholars. . . . Indeed, for a great many years I have been persuaded that literary history ought not to be confined, as it has been from the way in which it has been written, to persons of tasteful scholarship, but should be made, like civil history, to give a knowledge of the *character of the people* to which it relates. I have endeavored, therefore, so to write my account of the Spanish literature as to make the literature itself the exponent of the peculiar culture and civilization of the Spanish people. Whether I have succeeded or no remains to be seen. But *if I have*, my book, I think, will be read by my countryman, whose advance in a taste for reading on grave and thoughtful subjects increases so perceptibly that there is a plain difference since you were here.[88]

Anna Eliot, Anna Ticknor, and George Hillard noted that several thousand copies of the book were sold in the United States, but perhaps an even clearer indication of interest beyond the scholarly comes from the fact that three revised editions of the *History* appeared in Ticknor's lifetime (he died in 1871).[89] Appreciative reviews appeared both in Europe and the United States, and the book was also translated into Spanish, German, and French. There can be no doubt that the book became a resounding national and international success. To Gayangos he wrote, "I continue to receive much better accounts of my book from Europe than I think it deserves."[90] And yet Ticknor did not consider the work finished and proceeded collecting and working on the subject as if *labor ipse voluptas* was indeed his motto. As he put it in a letter to his British friend Sir Edmund Head, "So, you see, I go on, almost contrary to my principles, piling up old Spanish books on old Spanish books. *Cui bono?* Time will show." At the time, he was preparing the second edition of the *History*, which appeared in 1854. "Meantime," he told Head, "the old Spanish books do no harm; they amuse me, and they will be valuable in some public library hereafter."[91]

Nathaniel Hawthorne, who visited him in his house in May 1850 (to ask him about translations of Cervantes's works), noticed that "a volume of his book was open on a table, and apparently he had been engaged in revising or annotating it." His gifted eye registered many other things: the imposing marble hall, the magnificent library, the large portrait of Walter Scott that Ticknor had commissioned many years before. "You recognize in him at once," Hawthorne wrote, "the man who knows the world; the scholar, too, which probably is his most distinctive character, though a little more under the surface." He added,

> He is not, I apprehend, one of the highest or profoundest of men, but a man of great cultivation and refinement, and with quite substance enough to be polished and refined, without being worn too thin in the process. Fond of good dinners; appreciative of the quality of wine; a man of society. There is something peculiar in his manner, and odd and humorsome in his voice; as of one who knows his own advantages and eminent social position, and so superinduces a little oddity upon the manners of a gentleman.[92]

The scholarly inclinations may have been a little more under the surface, but in practice he worked obsessively on a book that many had considered definitive. His correspondence with Pascual de Gayangos continued uninterrupted, in part because of the Spanish translation of his work, but also because the subject had clearly not ended for him. When he went back to Europe in 1856, it was to collect more books, both for his own collection, and that of the Boston Public Library, in whose foundation he was closely involved, and to which he eventually donated his entire collection of Spanish and Portuguese books.

His last trip to Europe (1856–1858) was spent visiting scholars and collections in England and Italy. But he did not go to Spain, and gave no explanation for it. One might, however, surmise some of the reasons. A massive popular rebellion against the government exploded in 1854; a cholera epidemic afflicted the country in 1855, and civil unrest continued unabated until Queen Isabella II was deposed in 1868. Few would have visited Spain under the circumstances, but the aging Ticknor grew more and more wearisome of contemporary Spanish politics, even if he continued to love the literature, especially old literature, of that country. Upon returning to the United States, he also suffered some major blows, which soured his by now less than cheerful disposition. One of them was totally unexpected: the death of his younger friend Prescott in early 1859. "A cloud seems to have come over everything, since this disheartening sorrow has fallen on me," he wrote to Gayangos, "and much of the sunshine is taken from what little may remain to me to the path of life that I am yet to thread."[93] No one was as close to him as Prescott outside of his family. He barely managed his sorrow by writing a biography of his friend.[94]

The other major cloud was the Civil War. "I need not tell you," he wrote to Gayangos in 1861, "how badly our political affairs go in the United States, for all the world knows about it."[95] He had little doubt that the North would prevail, but that was no reason for rejoicing. "It is a terrible, insane contest, and it makes me very unhappy," he wrote to Gayangos two years later, "but I look beyond the immediate military contest and there I see only darkness. For whether we are to be two nations or one, we are to live on the same soil. And the North and the South are to hate each other as no two nations have ever hated each other before. Our great troubles, therefore, are to begin after our military questions are settled."[96] He revealed a more personal impact of the Civil War to his nephew, George Ticknor Curtis, a former Whig who served as defense counsel for Dred Scott in 1857, and who was about to publish his *Life of Webster*,

> On reading the proofs I am more and more struck with the fact, that the events you relate, most of which have happened in my time, seem to me to have occurred, much longer ago than they really did. The civil war of '61 has made a great gulf between what happened before it in our century and what has happened since, or what is likely to happen hereafter. It does not seem to me as if I were living in the country in which I was born, or in which I received whatever I ever got of political education or principles.[97]

George Ticknor had been describing the decay and collapse of Spain for his entire adult life. In his old age, he contemplated a dismal future for another country, his own, that he almost did not recognize. He could not, and would not, cut himself off from it, but Spain was another matter. After Isabella II was driven out of Spain in 1868, and his friend Gayangos moved back to England, he wrote to him, "The Spain that I visited and where I was so happy, half a century ago, has ceased to exist; and if it should ever be revived, it will not be in the life-time of a man now above seventy eight years old."[98] He asked, therefore, to cut all the connections he had maintained, through Gayangos, with that land.

George Ticknor died on January 26, 1871, leaving a monumental legacy to scholarship on Spanish literature and history, but anguished that the story of the emergence and collapse of Spain could be replicated in his own country.

Chapter 3

The Enlightened Foreigner:
The Reception of Ticknor's Work
in the Hispanic World

A Spaniard ought to feel a debt of gratitude to the enlightened scholar, who, though a foreigner, has been the first to carry the light of sound criticism into the dark places of the national literature.

—William H. Prescott to Pascual de Gayangos, Boston, June 1, 1853

When the *History of Spanish Literature* was finished and presentation copies were ready to be sent, George Ticknor remembered a friend who, many years before, had taken him on horseback through the hills of Andalucía. It was Don Ángel de Saavedra, a veteran of the Peninsular War, who after trading the sword for the pen had achieved considerable literary fame with the publication of *El Moro Expósito* (1834) and the popular play *Don Alvaro, o la Fuerza del Sino* (1835). Ticknor kept track of Saavedra, who upon the death of his brother Juan Remigio in 1834 had become the new duke of Rivas. He had been named minister to Naples in 1844, where Ticknor hoped to find him in 1850. The diligent Bostonian sent Don Ángel a copy of his work, along with a friendly letter. He had reasons to be worried when several years passed without an acknowledgment. But then, in 1856, he finally heard from his old friend:

> I am very flattered that you still remember me. Let me assure you that I myself have never forgotten that likable young American whom I had the pleasure to welcome in my native Córdoba, in the year 1818. Since that time, great and strange events have shaken Spain and the rest of Europe, and I have experienced many ups and downs.[1]

This was putting it mildly. In fact, the duke—a target of the vindictive and intolerant Ferdinand VII—had endured 11 years of exile, first in England, then in Italy, and finally in France. As many other exiles who had supported the Constitution of 1812, he had a new political chance after the demise of the king. Saavedra became a liberal *moderado*. This was the new political force that succeeded the old regime in 1833, only to be quickly overthrown during an outburst of popular unrest in 1836. Under the unstable period of the regency of María Cristina, and then the shaky reign of Isabella II, he experienced further ascents and falls, running for his life during the revolution of 1854, and then reemerging as ambassador to France in 1856. All along, he wrote poetry and plays, and found the time to read various works, including Ticknor's.[2] "I knew already about your excellent work," he wrote in his letter to the Bostonian, "which I read in the very good translation of [Pascual de] Gayangos. Reading the original now, I have had occasion to admire both the great knowledge you have of our literature, and the method, order, taste, as well as the exact and judicious criticism with which you have approached the history of our letters." The duke of Rivas was effusive yet sincere in his praise, but could not avoid expressing some regret about his own life. "You should be a happy man, Mr. Ticknor, to have enjoyed such a quiet and pleasant life to devote yourself, with so much advantage, to the cultivation of letters! I have not had such luck, nor do I expect it now, when old age demands of me rest, both physical and moral." He was to face further troubles, first resigning his ambassadorship in 1858, and then returning to Spain to die after a long illness.

The judgment of the duke of Rivas is particularly valuable because he could examine Ticknor's work from various perspectives: that of a scholar, creative writer, and statesman who had lived through every major event, and there were many, of Spanish history for two-thirds of the nineteenth century. He was, in many ways, representative of the appreciative Spanish reception of Ticknor's work although, as we will see in this chapter, there were also detractors. Much of the ground for this favorable reception had been prepared by the substantial contributions of Johann Nikolas Böhl von Faber, whom Ticknor had met during his journey through Andalucía in October 1818. Böhl von Faber, who introduced the views of Herder and, especially, Augustus Wilhelm Schlegel into Spain, had decisively shaped the major contours of Spanish Romanticism, with its emphasis on popular traditions, a search for Spanish national themes, and its positive evaluation of Catholicism.[3] Although Ticknor differed on the latter respect, he emphatically validated the other two. Ángel de Saavedra, who was very much a part of the evolution of Spanish Romanticism in the middle decades of the nineteenth century, could read and appreciate the book of his New England friend in the original, unlike most Spaniards at the time. But as he indicated in his letter, he read it also in the translation of Pascual de Gayangos.

As we know from chapter 2, Pascual de Gayangos had rendered invaluable assistance to Ticknor since 1838. He had provided him with books, original manuscripts, and expert advice. Although his own interests in Spanish literature and history were different (the Muslim presence in Spain), Gayangos felt that Ticknor had a unique perspective, as a foreigner, to provide an overview of Spanish literary history. He felt enough ownership of Ticknor's enterprise that he now endeavored to translate and publish his friend's magnum opus. For this purpose, he recruited the assistance of Enrique de Vedia, an emerging literary scholar, but the work was largely his own. The result was four volumes of translation and notes that appeared in Madrid between 1851 and 1856, that is, during one of the most unstable periods in nineteenth-century Spanish history. Even if judged solely on those grounds, Gayangos's work was little less than heroic. But his work stood out on other grounds as well. The translation, for one, was accurate, and indeed captured Ticknor's subtle ironies as well as damning critiques with unflinching faithfulness. There was none of Pedro Sabau y Larroya's wounded national pride or religious disagreement, as can be seen in his translation of Prescott's *Ferdinand and Isabella*. Gayangos rendered Ticknor's words as Ticknor himself would have wished: with imposing scholarly authority, critical spirit, and elegant Castilian. But Gayangos was more than a translator, and indeed he criticized his friend and colleague when he erred or when his information was shown to be insufficient. The result was 314 printed pages, virtually a monograph, of detailed notes—which accounts for the 4 volumes of the Spanish version vis-à-vis the English 3.[4] The erudition of the translator more than matched that of the author. Indeed, it added substantial new information.

Gayangos had no qualms in pointing out Ticknor's problematic attributions of authorship, dates, and erroneous citations. He enjoyed certain advantages, the main one being that during the 1850s he resided in Madrid. There, he could consult published and manuscript sources at the Spanish Biblioteca Nacional, the Real Academia de la Historia, and other repositories, something that Ticknor had not done since 1818. He also had access to the private libraries of his friends, including that of Bartolomé José Gallardo (himself a former Spanish exile in London) and that of the Marquis Pedro José Pidal. In addition, he had taken copious notes on sources available at the British Museum (he later published a catalog of Spanish manuscripts available there), and other British repositories. This accumulated knowledge allowed him to correct, confirm, or expand on the points made by the New England scholar. Gayangos filled various gaps in Ticknor's literary coverage with extensive transcriptions of unpublished poetry, added biographical information on authors, and provided detailed information on rare editions of books. And yet, he did it in the spirit of restoring and adding finishing touches to an edifice, elegantly confirming that the main foundation of the work was sound. His principal critiques of Ticknor were his reliance on dubious authorities, and, on occasion, a misreading of the etymology of some words. The translation was itself a triumph of scholarship, and helped Ticknor to revise subsequent editions of his work.[5] It also made the Bostonian's work available to a larger audience in the Spanish-speaking world, as some copies traveled across the Atlantic to the new nations of Latin America.

Gayangos's work was carried out with difficulty, in part because of the dearth of interest in scholarly topics, lack of official encouragement, and the reluctance of publishers. Severn Teackle Wallis, a Baltimore lawyer who arrived in Spain in 1849 to negotiate U.S. claims concerning Florida, registered the difficulties encountered by Gayangos. He had the highest opinion of Ticknor's *History*, and believed that there was strong Spanish scholarly support for his work: "The acuteness and profundity of its criticisms, and its perfect comprehension and appreciation of the Spanish mind and taste and spirit, were regarded by the most eminent writers and thinkers as all that a Spaniard could have been able to attain, and next to miraculous in a foreigner." And yet, he also observed Gayangos's trouble in finding a publisher, and pronounced that "their unwillingness to engage in the adventure was a conspicuous illustration of their want of liberality and taste,—as well, perhaps, as of a similar defect in the book-buying public."[6] The keen-eyed Lady Louisa Tenison, passing through Madrid in the early 1850s, confirmed this impression when she noted that though Ticknor had done justice to the literature of Spain, and Gayangos his best to make the work known, little could be expected "where so few read."[7]

How the publication came out at all was painfully revealed by Gayangos in a letter to William H. Prescott: he paid for the printing of the first two volumes with money from his own pocket. "Had not the author been Ticknor, whom I love and esteem, and had I not been persuaded that I do a service to the literature of my country by publishing in Spanish a work that I consider *so very good*, I would have abandoned the project already."[8] There was something in Ticknor's book, indeed, that was worth the effort. As the translator explained in the Prospectus, Ticknor's work not only filled an obvious gap, but it underscored the richness of the "national literature."[9] There was also an important additional motivation: for literary scholars who were struggling to navigate the storm of politics, the *History of Spanish Literature* legitimized their activities as not only relevant, but necessary. Gayangos and a few others understood that the Boston-based scholar had successfully turned literary scholarship into a resource for judging the past, current, and future course of their country's history. They felt that their work was important, and hoped that the larger society would eventually recognize their own endeavors as crucial to the nation's well-being.

Ticknor received a copy of the first volume of the translation on June 24, 1851, and was pleased. "I have had time to read only a part of the new notes and a few pages of the text—but all I have read has gratified me."[10] A few months later, with more time to read Gayangos's work, Ticknor stated, "Your notes to my book have given me much pleasure—and I shall use them freely when I print another edition of it either here or in England."[11] Readers unaccustomed to Ticknor's prose might justly consider such statements as lukewarm, considering Gayangos' Herculean task, but in fact he could barely hide his enthusiasm. Ticknor understood that this translation was his passport for reaching a discriminating Spanish audience—ultimately his toughest audience. He thought carefully about whom to send presentation copies. In addition to the duke of Rivas, Ticknor asked Gayangos to distribute copies to the poets Manuel José Quintana and Francisco Martínez de la Rosa, to the scholars Agustín Durán, Eugenio Tapia, Antonio Ferrer del Río, José Amador de los Ríos, José Gómez de la Cortina, José Joaquín de Mora, and Manuel Bretón de los Herreros. It would be hard to find a more representative list of Spanish scholars, many of whom were personally unknown to Ticknor.[12]

Spanish scholars were eager to read a history of their literature, for no comprehensive treatment by one of their own had appeared since Juan Andrés had published his *Origen, progresos y estado actual de toda la literatura* (1784–1806). But that unwieldy ten-volume work was not specifically on Spanish literature, but rather an ambitious comparative study.[13] Thus, the need for a focused study of the national literature was sorely felt. By 1828, the accomplished writer and scholar Alberto Lista lamented the fact that there was no modern study of Spanish literature, and pointed to the consequences: the neglect, and indeed ignorance, of Spanish contributions to European literature.

"Ignorance," he told the members of the Royal Academy of History, "that might be excused in foreigners, but which cannot be excused in us. How are they to value our good writers if they do not know them? And how are they to know them if we lack our own literary history, written philosophically, where we can show them how to appreciate our literature?"

He also asked,

Shall we wait until foreigners come to remove the dust in our archives and libraries, and find treasures which they cannot appreciate in their true value because they do not have a profound knowledge of either our language or our history, which is yet to be written? Will we be so unjust as to blame them for not doing the work that we ourselves are unwilling to do? I have seen learned foreigners who had no idea, upon arrival in Spain, that there was any literature in our country. At the same time, I have seen references, quite honorable to our writers, in books by foreigners, references that I would search for in vain in Spanish books.[14]

Despite the call, foreigners continued to provide the few available literary histories of Spain. Indeed, a year after Lista's address, José Gómez de la Cortina (1799–1860) and his collaborator Nicolás Hugalde answered the call for a work of this nature, but with a translation of Bouterwek's volume on Spain discussed in chapter 2. They submitted their translation to the judgment of the Royal Academy of History stating that "it is truly a shame that [Bouterwek's] History of Spanish Literature should be circulating for years in all the learned languages of Europe, while in Spain it has barely been known through one or two copies of the French translation."[15] They added that a study of this type was quite overdue, and that it was a pity that it should be neglected. Their argument, combined with Lista's, was compelling, and as a result the Academy named a commission to report on the translation. Members José de la Canal, Francisco de Paula Quadrado, and José Muso y Valiente had nothing but praise for the translation. "They do a great service to our literature," they stated, "by shedding new and brilliant light to that provided by the German author."[16] Indeed, Cortina and Hugalde had added a great deal of detail to Bouterwek's limited coverage. The Academy was pleased, and voted in favor of recommending publication.[17]

The translation by Cortina and Hugalde appeared under the title *Historia de la literatura española desde el siglo XIII hasta principios del XVI* in 1829.[18] It filled a major gap, but the work covered only one period, the earliest in Bouterwek's larger three-part history. The observant Caleb Cushing, who was in Madrid at the time, met Cortina ("Sparkling animated face, interesting & gentlemanly mannered), and noted that "the translation of Bouterwek will compose 4 vols. In the last one *aperçu* of the present state of Spanish literature."[19] The plan did not prosper, as Cortina left for Mexico in 1832, and no further volumes appeared. Thus, there was still space for a comprehensive history of Spanish literature, and Ticknor, who was well aware of the translation, rose to the occasion.

As mentioned earlier, the *History of Spanish Literature* was well received in Spain, but there were several negative reactions to Ticknor's work on account of his critique of specific authors, and the wounded national pride that some felt after seeing yet another book on the subject written by a foreigner. Among the reactions of the first kind, there was Adolfo de Castro's, whose edition of *El Buscapié* Ticknor subjected to close scrutiny, thereby inaugurating a series of rebuttals and debates. The Spanish scholar claimed, in 1848, that this rare source had been penned by Cervantes, but used superficially persuasive evidence to prove his point.[20] Ticknor thought that such a claim would be worth considering, given the potential importance of the finding, but he quickly discovered inconsistencies, both external and internal to the source, and dismissed the work as apocryphal.[21] Rather than accepting the evidence, Castro challenged Ticknor in a Madrid periodical, *El Heraldo*, in October 1850, and in a new edition of *El Buscapié* en 1851. "Forgive me, Mr. Ticknor," he stated, "but I do not recognize in a foreigner, however great his erudition might be, sufficient authority to judge as authentic or apocryphal any of our books." Ticknor responded, in Spanish, that national origin was not an issue in

the scholarly world, but rather the nature of the evidence, which, until Castro
submitted the manuscript to scholarly scrutiny, was suspect. This, he added,

> Don Adolfo de Castro has refused to do. But until he does obtain a scholarly verdict
> authenticating the work, he cannot claim exemptions from the examination to which I
> have believed my duty to subject his *Buscapié*. This can be done by either a Spaniard or
> a foreigner who is motivated, like me, only by a respectful admiration for Cervantes,
> and by a fondness for the literature of the country that gave him birth.[22]

This rebuttal may not have won Ticknor many friends, especially Castro, but it did
win the case. No such a claim was ever repeated, showing just how exacting the
standards of literary scholarship could be. False attributions of this sort would not
prosper for some time, though they sadly reappear from time to time, in fields well
beyond Spanish literature.

In a similar vein, Pedro José Pidal contested Ticknor's argument that another
source, the presumed fifteenth-century *Centón epistolario*, by a certain Fernán
Gómez de Cibdareal, was apocryphal. It had often been treated as a real source, but
Ticknor found inconsistencies in the language, factual errors, and insufficient evidence to determine exact dates in the extant editions. He followed, in this respect, a
long philological tradition, going back to the days of Lorenzo Valla, of exposing
forgeries (in this case, the presumed donation of Constantine). Pidal did not take it
too well, and responded that Ticknor's own arguments were insufficient evidence to
conclude that the book was apocryphal, but admitted that the proof would require
even more extensive research, and he did not provide it. In a moment of impatience,
Pidal argued, like Castro, that "no foreigner, however enlightened, is the best judge
to decide to what extent the letters of Cibdareal are inconsistent with the language
of fifteenth-century Castile." He added, candidly, that "I might be blinded by
passion and the love for our [literature]," but would not concede the point.[23] What
was apparently bothersome to him was that Ticknor's application of strict philological and literary criteria, in his view, diminished the stature and richness of the
national literature. In the event, when the translation of the *History* appeared,
Gayangos and Vedia accepted Ticknor's reasons, although they wisely praised the
erudite efforts of their compatriot.[24] It was, in the end, an elaborate hoax, plotted in
the seventeenth century by a nobleman seeking to enhance his reputation by extending
the age of his ancestry, and Ticknor had exposed it.[25]

A similar, although less tempered critique was issued by Francisco de Paula
Canalejas in the *Revista Española de Ambos Mundos*. The author set out to review
the third volume of the Gayangos translation in search for what he said he had not
seen in the previous two: a "system," or larger thesis that informed Ticknor's work.
He was once again disappointed, he stated, because there was little besides arbitrary
classifications and meaningless discussions of individual authors and sources.
Ticknor, in his view, had failed to grasp the true nature of Spanish civilization, and,
in particular, the role of religion in it. Rather than analyzing the true sentiments of
the Spanish people, the American author had imposed his own religious prejudices.
Indeed, the Spanish critic argued, Ticknor's "constant accusations of intolerance
and blindness against the Catholic Church" were tainted by "the intolerance and
blindness of some Protestant creeds." Thus, Ticknor was ill-prepared to judge the
greatness of Calderón, Lope de Vega, or any other writer because he did not understand the depth of their religiosity, or the religious context in which they lived.

Canalejas did not fail to identify Ticknor's standard Protestant emphasis on the extremes of Catholic intolerance, but he took particular offense at every instance where the author of the *History* judged a Spanish literary work to be of high or low quality. In short, the reviewer made it clear that this was a flawed, misguided, and nearly worthless piece of work.

Canalejas was no expert on Spanish literature. But he had an objective, which he made abundantly clear in the conclusion of his essay. "We wanted to find a Spanish soul in that book," he wrote, but could not find it and thus he thought about ending his review on a note of total disappointment. However, it had come to his attention that the distinguished literary scholar José Amador de los Ríos was about to launch his own history of Spanish literature. Canalejas stated that he had read parts of it in manuscript, and pronounced it far superior to anything—meaning especially Ticknor's *History*—available.

> "It is a philosophical work," he wrote, "that successfully brings together civil, political, religious and literary history. Written in a beautiful Castilian worthy of the best days of the Golden Age, Don José Amador de los Ríos' *Historia de la literatura española* exceeds all the expectations of even his most enthusiastic admirers, because of the author's talents, vast learning, and high qualities as a writer."[26]

With such an endorsement, one might be tempted to pronounce Ticknor's work obsolete even before the last volume was in print. It is perhaps not difficult, then, to surmise with what anticipation this new history, this time by a patriotic Spaniard, was expected in the learned circles of Madrid.

José Amador de los Ríos (1818–1878) published his lengthy *Historia crítica de la literatura española* between 1861 and 1866.[27] He had written an earlier review of the first volume of Ticknor's work, which he found lacking in terms of "plan" and "erudition." He thought of it as prejudiced and marred by errors and omissions, and regarded it not as a *History*, but rather as a "bibliographical memoir," jumping arbitrarily from book to book across centuries.[28] "Savage &Tartarly," wrote the horrified William H. Prescott when he read the review, echoing Lord Byron's verse "Who killed John Keats?/ 'I,' says the Quarterly/ So savage and Tartarly,/ 'Twas one of my feats." "What could have provoked the bile of the Spanish Aristarch to this degree?" asked the Boston historian in shock and disbelief at seeing his friend's opus thus mauled.[29] But there was much more; indeed, all seven volumes of Ríos's *Historia crítica* were written as a riposte to Ticknor's work.

Ríos's book was massive but incomplete, in that it did not go beyond the reign of Ferdinand and Isabella. It also had a nationalistic tone, as well as obvious official endorsement. The author dedicated his work to the Queen, and lavished extravagant praise on Isabella II: "Your enlightened patriotism and Spanish chivalry not only applauded my progress on such a difficult task, but also wanting to encourage it, you honored me with the magnanimity of royalty by listening to some chapters of this work." How much Isabella heard, and what she derived from it, is unclear, but what is beyond doubt is the official sanction that was bestowed upon the author. Ríos himself emphasized the nationalistic purpose of the *oeuvre*. Shall his work not measure up to the grandeur of the subject, he said, "Let us at least not forget that the *Historia crítica* has the merit of being the first [book of literary history] written by a Spaniard in our Castilian tongue."[30] Ticknor had clearly managed, albeit unintentionally, to excite some national sensibilities.

That patriotism was the major motivation of Ríos's otherwise seemingly learned and detailed work is clear in his comments on Ticknor's *History*. He claimed to have been encouraged by the American's interest in Spanish letters while he was writing his own work (a reminder that he had been writing on such subjects well before the New England scholar). Also, he pointed out that he was impressed by Ticknor's vast command of Spanish sources. But, despite the erudition of his American counterpart, Ríos identified the following major flaw,

> One cannot with justice say the same [good things] about the plan and method of [Ticknor's] work. There is no rich or transcendent principle to orient him, and one finds nothing of the majestic signs of that civilization which emerged out of patriotism and religion from the mountains of Asturias, Aragon, and Navarra; which developed and grew thanks to the sacred fire of faith and freedom, and which, overcoming all obstacles arrived triumphantly at the walls of Granada, to move on to Africa, Asia and America, to the great astonishment of Europe.[31]

Ríos set out to expand and highlight as important what Ticknor had treated economically, but at the cost of much celebratory prose and an abundance of glowing adjectives that added up to seven volumes. A clear example of the differences between these scholars can be noted in their respective treatments of the *Poem of the Cid*. Ticknor evaluated this poem most favorably in 12 pages of his *History*, regarding it as a significant reflection of the age in which it was written, and as an enduring testimony of the "national bearing" and "national character" of the emerging Spanish nation. But he noted that it was not a historical document, as some events described there would suggest. Its real value was as a poem, which Ticknor considered as "simple, heroic, and national."[32] He viewed it as an admirable rendition of the chivalric spirit of Spain, but was far from being uncritical about it on philological grounds, reflecting in many ways the critical approach to the history of individual European languages during the first three quarters of the nineteenth century:

> The very language in which it is told is the language he himself [the Cid] spoke, still only half developed; disencumbering itself with difficulty from the characteristics of the Latin; its new constructions by no means established; imperfect in its forms, and ill furnished with the connection particles in which resides so much of the power and grace of all languages; but still breathing the bold, sincere, and original spirit of its times, and showing plainly that it is struggling with success for a place among the other wild elements of the national genius.[33]

In contrast, Ríos devoted over 100 pages of unqualified praise to the poem. He agreed with Ticknor that the poem was national in character, though meaning more specifically Castilian. But it was much more, in his view, in that it reflected the true religious spirit of Spain, as well as the force, nobility, and determination that animated the historical figures of the time. Ríos paid short shrift to matters of versification, but asserted unequivocally that whatever deformity there might be in the poem was more the problem of bad transcriptions or the standards of pedantic critics.[34]

Beyond the *Poem of the Cid*, Ríos bestowed a heroic tone to his narrative of the emergence of Spain's national identity. His book, however, was fundamentally reactive, and without additional research, it insisted on such patent falsehoods as the authentic nature of Gómez de Cibdareal's *Centón Epistolario*. He provided a celebratory *Spanish* version of the country's literary history, but at such length that it was doomed from the start to remain incomplete. Ticknor himself grew impatient and disappointed that the work of his Spanish detractor would be so slow in coming and seemingly endless. "I am sorry that Amador de los Ríos," he wrote to Gayangos, "does not go on with his History of Spanish Literature, for he was just coming to the part I should care to read."[35] That is, in an effort to outdo Ticknor, the Spanish author managed to get mired in one period of his country's literary history, without adding much to it.

Still, there was more than wounded national pride in Ríos, for Ticknor's work was also celebratory, although perhaps more detached and analytical. Both recognized the resilience of the Spanish sense of nationality, and the impressive richness of the country's literature. But Ticknor saw the elements of decadence in the religious components of the national character, whereas Ríos saw clear indications of its continued vitality. The polemic was bound to remain unresolved, for Ticknor had provided extensive coverage of the period of decline, while Ríos had not. In fact, the latter avoided the theme of decline altogether. In the fluid political situation of the middle decades of the nineteenth century, he was perhaps representative of Spanish intellectuals who preferred to think that the best years of the country were still ahead.

Latin American Responses

Compared to the Spanish reactions to Ticknor's *History*, those from Latin America were less defensive, although they were fewer, in part because of the difficulty of obtaining books from Spain, in part because of the lack of venues to engage in scholarly criticism during the early period of nation building in the nineteenth century. But even so, there are important exceptions. Moreover, some Latin Americans read Ticknor's book in the original English, or were well acquainted with his work. Some, like the Cuban Domingo del Monte (1804–1853), had direct contact with him even before the publication of the book.

The largest concentration of contacts was in fact with Cuba, due to the country's proximity to the United States, and the complicated web of politics and economics that characterized the relations between them. Cuba had remained in the Spanish fold—along with Puerto Rico—even after most countries in the region had won their independence. As a result, there was a great deal more exchange between Cuba and Spain, and travel between the two countries often involved a stop in one of the major U.S. harbors on the Atlantic seaboard. One of Ticknor's early visitors was Ramón de la Sagra, the director of the Botanical Garden in Havana, who spent five months in the United States and later sent him a copy of his travel book.[36] Ticknor did not meet Domingo del Monte personally, but had the most contact with him

Domingo del Monte spent considerable time in both Spain and the United States, and both became places of residence until his death in Madrid in 1853. It was during his first visit to Madrid in 1827 that he met Alexander H. Everett, then serving as U.S. minister to the court of Ferdinand VII. This was precisely the time when Everett was aiding Washington Irving, George Ticknor, and William H. Prescott in their respective works. It was thanks to that contact, which evolved into a friendship, that Del Monte developed an appreciation for American letters and for Ticknor in particular.

Upon his return to Cuba in 1828 as a newly minted attorney, Del Monte became quite active in the field of letters. He participated in a number of cultural organizations, such as the Real Sociedad Patriótica, and the journal *Revista Bimestre Cubana*, founded by the Catalonian Mariano Cubí y Soler (1801–1875), and modeled after the *Edinburgh Review* and the *Quarterly Review*.[37] During the 1830s, there was a sizable number of Americans, especially from Boston, either residing in Cuba or visiting the island for health reasons. Thus, Del Monte and other Cubans had personal contacts with some of these Americans, and also access to American books and such journals as the *North American Review*. Writing from Matanzas in 1831, Francisco Guerra Bethencourt could tell Del Monte that "another very useful endeavor, and perhaps more amenable and appropriate to our country, where so many either possess or are learning English, would be to make known the greatest contemporary American authors such as Cooper, Chaning [*sic*], Irving & c."[38] Del Monte was determined to bridge the gulf between the two countries by writing directly to Ticknor, who was by this time widely known as a professor of Spanish literature at Harvard. He nominated Ticknor for corresponding membership to the Cuban Academy of Literature, an honor that Ticknor gratefully accepted.[39] Del Monte presented the Harvard professor with various published items, including an issue of the *Revista Bimestre Cubana*. Ticknor was impressed:

> I have been struck, ever since I first began to read the Revista Cubana [*sic*], with the amount of literary talent and accomplishment in your island. Nothing to be compared with it has, so far as I am informed, ever been exhibited in any of the Spanish colonies and even in some respects, nothing like it is to be seen in Spain proper. For instance a review of such spirit, variety and power, has never been attempted at Madrid.

Ticknor added, commenting on a volume of poems included in the parcel that "I have been much pleased, also, to see, that while your poets have preserved in a considerable degree the established forms of your [Spanish] literature, like the *Romance*, the coloring and tone are local and peculiar. This, it seems to me, is the right road and promises to lead you far."[40] By this time, Ticknor had already resigned his Harvard professorship, and was about to embark on a four-year trip to Europe, which necessarily limited the contact between the two. But Del Monte managed to find ways to remain informed, especially thanks to Alexander Everett, who in the 1840s was himself in Cuba, and stayed in touch while at Jefferson College (Louisiana) and then back in Boston.[41] For Del Monte and other Cubans the connection with American scholars became a needed source of moral and intellectual support once the political climate of the island turned tense under the government of Captain General Miguel Tacón (1834–1838). In a letter to Ticknor in 1837, Del Monte described how the country, deprived of political freedom, forced intellectuals to engage in themes that would not awaken government suspicion, "unless the poet chooses, like Dante, to be a fugitive from his own land because of his writings."[42] He did become a fugitive in 1843, although on account of his alleged participation in a British abolitionist scheme. Accused of conspiracy, he left Cuba never to return again.[43]

After a period of residence in the United States, and then France, Del Monte settled in Spain. It was there, in Madrid since 1846, that Del Monte developed a friendship with Pascual de Gayangos and was able to keep track of Ticknor, Prescott, and other admired American writers. He knew through Alexander Everett that the

New England scholar was engaged in writing a history of Spanish literature. "[George] Bancroft, Ticknor and Prescott are greatly obliged by your kind remembrance," Everett wrote to his Cuban friend, "Prescott's book on Mexico is ready for publication, and will appear in the autumn. Ticknor's is, I fear, postponed *ad graecas kalendas*" [i.e., indefinitely].[44] Everett added, later in the year, "Ticknor has in manuscript a course of lectures on Spanish literature, which he will one day publish, but probably not for many years to come."[45] It is probably due to these less than subtle references to Ticknor's fastidiousness that Del Monte eventually wrote, in a review of Prescott's book on the conquest of Peru, that

> this gentleman [Ticknor] of Boston was a professor of foreign literatures at Harvard College, where he taught his students to know and appreciate the best manifestations of the Spanish genius. His course [on Spanish literature] remains unpublished, to the great disappointment of those who have read his articles in the *American Quarterly* of Philadelphia, and the *North American Review* of Boston.[46]

Ticknor, as we will see momentarily, was not procrastinating but rather meticulously developing the scholarly apparatus of his work.

But then, at long last, Del Monte received a copy of the *History of Spanish Literature* in Madrid. He replied to Ticknor that he had already inserted an announcement of the book in *El Heraldo* of Madrid, but that he would wait for the publication of Gayangos's translation to prepare a full review. He intimated, however, that he would do it only if "my mind is free from the disquiet produced by the threats of invasions, wars and political calamities to my country." In that case, he wrote, "I will try to highlight the skills of the American writer who has so profoundly studied our letters, and who has been able to judge them with such equanimity."[47]

It was not to be. Domingo del Monte found peace neither at home nor in Madrid. It was clear by 1849 that he was in trouble with the Spanish government, probably on account of his Cuban political connections, for he was denied permission to consult the Archivo General de Indias in Seville for his project on the chronicles of Gonzalo Fernández de Oviedo.[48] Then, in 1852, he was driven out of Madrid.[49] On November 4, 1853, he died, widowed and heartbroken, at the age of 49. As Pascual de Gayangos put it in a laconic yet pained note to Prescott, "We have lost a most esteemed friend and enlightened literary scholar."[50] Ticknor himself lost a friend who had so promisingly brought his work to the attention of the Spanish-speaking New World.

Still, Ticknor continued to enjoy the attention of Cuban scholars who were obviously more aware of him than he was of them. The accomplished Pedro J. Guiteras sent him the two-volume set of his *Historia de la Isla de Cuba* (1865), adding in a letter that he would be most pleased to have his comments, due to "your knowledge of the art of composition and of the character of our language and literature."[51] Another Cuban, Nicolás Azcárate, passed through Boston on his way to Madrid in 1866, specifically to see him and to offer to translate anything he may write on Cuban literature. He also revealed that he was in possession of Domingo del Monte's papers, and that he would attempt to publish them in Spain.[52]

There is also evidence of contact between Ticknor and the Cuban poet José Agustín Quintero (1829–1885), the peripatetic patriot who lived in Cambridge in the 1840s, and who returned to Cuba in 1848 to face persecution, a death sentence, and ultimate escape to the United States.[53] It was perhaps at Ticknor's request that Quintero provided him with a manuscript essay on "Lyric Poetry in Cuba," a piece that confirmed the astonishing richness of poetry in that island.[54] After his escape from Cuba, Quintero sent him a presentation copy of another essay, this time on General John Anthony Quitman, a veteran of the Mexican American War and notorious filibuster, which he had published in Spanish in New Orleans.[55]

As a regular reader of the *North American Review*, Ticknor found additional information about Cuban letters in an essay by William Henry Hurlbert, which provided a more detailed coverage of many of the authors discussed by Quintero in his manuscript, including José María Heredia, José Jacinto Milanés, Gabriel de la Concepción Valdés (*Plácido*), and Rafael María de Mendive. Hurlbert echoed Ticknor's surprise when he revealed that "a Cuban gentleman of education and taste" had provided him with a list of 53 Cuban poets.[56] Such abundance was deceptive, however, as few were as well known as Heredia, whose ode "Niagara" was translated and frequently reprinted in American poetry collections.[57] But the Boston-based scholar was clearly better informed about literary developments in Cuba than in any other Spanish American country.

Ticknor's contacts with other Spanish American intellectuals were few, due in large part to the problems of communication with such a vast region, but visitors to the United States did not fail to contact him or pay him a visit. The purposes could be quite varied, and often caught Ticknor at awkward times. The Guatemalan-born scholar Antonio José Irisarri (1786–1868), who had represented the government of Chile in Great Britain during the independence period, and was now (1850) residing in New York, sent Ticknor presentation copies of his own books, and announced that he and a collaborator intended to translate the *History*. An alarmed Ticknor declared himself immediately against such a project, because Gayangos had already started his version in Spain. "I have written to them to discourage them from their undertaking," he wrote to Gayangos, "and told them of your translation, and how much I expect to have my work enriched and improved in your hands."[58] He did dissuade the would-be translators, but Irisarri found other opportunities to praise Ticknor's work. In his *Cuestiones filológicas* (1861), he stated that three Americans, Washington Irving, William H. Prescott, and Ticknor, were "among those who have done the most justice to Spain." Ticknor's *History* was simply "the best and most complete [work] I know on the subject."[59] As a scholar interested in philological issues himself, this was no ordinary praise. But as a Latin American, it is also clear that he did not react with the same wounded pride of his Spanish counterparts.

Many other Latin Americans visited Ticknor or sent him letters and books. The Chilean Pedro P. Ortiz saw him in Boston, "the Athens of the New World," as he enthusiastically but not very originally called it, in 1853. They talked about the great Venezuelan scholar Andrés Bello, who now resided in Chile, and to whom Ticknor sent a set of his *History*.[60] Another Chilean, the promising historian Diego Barros Arana, sent him two volumes of his *Historia jeneral de la independencia de Chile* (1854), with compliments "to the erudite author of the *Historia de la literatura española*," and offered his assistance in the collection of Spanish American books.[61] The Mexican Legation secretary in Paris, Andrés Oseguera, asked Matías Romero, the country's minister in Washington who was in contact with Ticknor, to present his pamphlet *Question Mexicaine*, to the Boston scholar, "as a bibliographical curiosity, and not because this first-rate literary historian should need to know anything new on Spanish literature."[62]

Perhaps the most famous of Ticknor's Latin American visitors was Domingo Faustino Sarmiento (1811–1888), the nemesis of dictator Juan Manuel de Rosas, pioneer educator, author of the famous *Civilization and Barbarism* (1845), and eventually president of his nation (1868–1874). He visited Boston in October 1865, during his tenure as Argentine minister in Washington. Sarmiento, who was not known for his modesty, told his correspondent Aurelia Vélez, that during the week he spent there, his visit was a resounding success. To illustrate it, he said that "the celebrated literary scholar Ticknor has been looking for me for three days, and today he has again asked me for an appointment [*audiencia*]."[63] When they met, Sarmiento realized that it was not his fame that Ticknor was after, bur rather information about intellectual activity in the region. A somewhat humbled Sarmiento wrote two days later to José Mármol, the author of *Amalia* (1851) and one of the greatest Spanish American writers of the nineteenth century, who was then serving as Argentine minister in Brazil, to send copies of his books to Ticknor so that he would have a chance to comment on Argentine literature. The Boston scholar, who in Sarmiento's view was "today the only true Spanish critic and erudite, even though he is an American," had apparently lamented, along with Henry W. Longfellow, "not knowing a single verse from our country."[64] Speaking before the Rhode Island Historical Society on October 27, Sarmiento had occasion to make another reference to Ticknor, this time publicly. The erudite New England scholar had written his *History of Spanish Literature* with the aid of "five thousand volumes," showing a most rare expertise in Spanish, "like the British, who study the Sanskrit forgotten by the Hindus themselves."[65] He made certain that Ticknor would have at least some of his books, but wrote nothing about Ticknor's main work, perhaps in line with his view that there was nothing worth pursuing in the dead literature of Spain.[66]

It is clear from these various contacts that Ticknor was widely known in Latin America, highly respected as a scholar, and considered an obligatory visit while in the United States. Latin Americans, in addition, were more likely to be in contact with their American colleague, than with each other. This gave Ticknor a much wider sense of the state of intellectual activity in the region, but he did not seek, as many would have wanted, to extend his coverage of Spanish literature to Latin America.

One important reason for this omission, as he admitted to another Spanish American correspondent, the Argentine Juan María Gutiérrez (1809–1878), was the difficulty of obtaining books published in the region. Gutiérrez, a gifted writer, scholar, and Rector of the University of Buenos Aires, tried to remedy this by sending Ticknor two of his own books.[67] Referring to one of them, the first volume of the *Estudios biográficos y críticos sobre algunos poetas Sud-Americanos anteriores al siglo XIX* (1865), Ticknor expressed "the earnest hope that you will continue them," and added,

They are interesting contributions to Spanish literature on this side of the Atlantic, such as have long been wanted and such as I have often sought in vain. From Mexico, from Peru and from Cuba, I have received a moderate number of books, chiefly from their authors, but this is the first time that I have received anything from Buenos Aires. This last is peculiarly valuable to me, especially your *Estudios*, which contain notices that I do not know where else to find and one in relation to [Sor Juana] Inés de la Cruz of which

I shall gladly avail myself in the next edition of my History of Spanish Literature. At one time I hoped that it would be possible to add a notice of American Spanish literature to the last edition published [1863]. But I was entirely unable to collect the necessary materials.[68]

It was through Gutiérrez that he gathered information about a Spanish American he had known in the early 1820s: the Argentine-born José Antonio Miralla (1790–1825), who lived in Cuba between 1816 and 1822, and who spent nearly a year in the United States promoting the cause of Cuban independence (unsuccessfully), before seeking support for it in Simón Bolívar's Colombia (also unsuccessfully), and dying an untimely death in Mexico.[69] He made quite an impression on Ticknor and his friend Charles F. Bradford, during the brief time they spent together in Boston. "He was occasionally at my house," Ticknor told Gutiérrez, "and, as I well remember improvisate [sic] there with extraordinary facility and success." Ticknor went on to relate how Miralla had fallen desperately in love with a woman from Virginia, apparently with considerable less success than with his poetic improvisations. Ticknor added that people who knew Miralla in New England would be eager to read Gutiérrez's account. "In short, your Life of Miralla finds more of his friends here than you could have anticipated when you wrote it." He urged Gutiérrez to send copies of his biographical essay, and a portrait of Miralla.[70] When he received them, he commented on how he and others, "after so long a period, still retain an interest in this singular and gifted man."[71]

It appears that Miralla had made quite an impression among Americans with his command of poetry and his remarkable translation of Thomas Gray's "Elegy Written in a Country Church-Yard." Charles Bradford related how Miralla, while he was in Philadelphia in 1823, had responded to doubts about whether the poem could be translated into Spanish by producing his version of it. Bradford offered additional recollections,

> During the years 1822 and 1823, [Miralla] visited the country, and the writer of this article knew him well. He was in terms of intimacy with several persons here in Roxbury, some of whom still remember him, he also visited Cambridge and received attentions from the faculty there. The distinguished professor of Modern Languages of that time [George Ticknor] was said to have expressed great desire to be made acquainted with the translator of Gray's Elegy into Spanish; and one of his successors [Henry W. Longfellow] said of the translation, "of all the versions into modern tongues the Spanish one of Miralla seems to me to be the best."[72]

Miralla did not linger long in Longfellow's memory, but he did in Ticknor's. The former had an ear for poetry, but Ticknor had an eye for texts, in the sense that he could compare originals and their various translations. Miralla was one of those who seemed to him to have done what no one else had in Spanish. After receiving many visitors such as him (and corresponding with many others) from Spanish America over the decades, the historian of Spanish literature reached the end of his long engagement with the region by remembering the tragic Miralla of his own younger days. He could derive much pleasure, and perhaps some nostalgic memories, from these contacts. But no one had challenged, or otherwise engaged, his lifetime work with the depth and knowledge of Andrés Bello (1781–1865), the most towering intellectual figure in nineteenth-century Latin America.

Born in Caracas, Bello was a promising young scholar when the events of independence took him, as member of a diplomatic mission, to Great Britain. There, he remained for 19 years, until he moved to Chile in 1829 to work for the government and launch the works for which he is famous to this day, the *Principios de derecho internacional*; the *Gramática de la lengua castellana*, and the *Código Civil de la República de Chile*.[73] Few of his contemporaries in Chile, however, knew of the extent of his knowledge of Spanish literature. Occupied with other tasks, he had published little on the subject. But the appearance of Ticknor's work gave him an opportunity to make a number of points on the origins of the Spanish language, the character of Castilian versification, the nature of the romances of chivalry, and the larger relationship between literature and national identity. These were issues that he considered central to nation building in nineteenth-century Latin America, and Bello understood at once that a commentary on Ticknor's work was an excellent venue to establish how the medieval Spanish past fit into the new realities of Latin American independence. He was responding to widespread calls to completely sever the ties, especially cultural ties, between the New World and an allegedly backward and decadent Spain. In this radicalized environment, Bello argued that the nations of Latin America would abandon the language, culture, and institutions of Spain at their peril, and proposed instead that they preserve them while also developing new cultural traditions anchored in the Spanish past. The recent struggle for independence, bloody as it was, should not get in the way of building bridges to the Iberian past, an argument that proved persuasive enough to be embraced by every nation in the region.

Ticknor's work was valuable to Bello because it showed precisely how the relationship between history and culture provided the key for the emergence of unique national traditions. Aesthetic worth was not excluded from the consideration of literary pieces, but in Bello's view Ticknor demonstrated how every poem, chronicle, and popular song, fit into a larger historical process that culminated in the crystallization of a Spanish national identity. New nations could certainly benefit from a similar inquiry into their origins. Therefore, Bello's reception of the New England scholar's work was quite positive. "Readers will find in Ticknor," he told his audience of academics at the University of Chile in 1852, "an intelligent judge who is capable of appreciating the beautiful and the great in the peculiar productions of every country and every century." He added that perhaps the most important element of Ticknor's work was his historical approach to literary history, meaning his willingness to accept that no age should impose its own standards on the evaluation of past literary contributions. He celebrated, in particular, "the philosophical thread that helps him bring together events, the sagacious manner in which he tracks his sources, and the lucidity with which he presents the development of the national character in the various branches of literature."[74]

Bello was not without some criticisms, mainly differences on very erudite points. But one major critique stands out: it concerns the origins of the Spanish language, where Bello felt that Ticknor, perhaps by following Pascual de Gayangos too closely, had failed to explain how the Castilian language had managed to thrive despite the power and influence of the Arabs in the Iberian Peninsula. He agreed with both his counterparts that Castilian had absorbed many words and idioms from Arabic, but that the strongest antecedents came from Latin sources, as transformed over the centuries of contact with other European peoples, but especially from France.

Ticknor had argued, consistent with his view of the emergence of national literatures, including Spanish, that they owed little to foreign influences, be they Arabic
or Provençal. Bello, for his part, argued that the influence of French sources was too
strong to ignore, especially in the *Poem of the Cid*, which Ticknor had treated only
briefly in his *History*. Bello deployed massive documentation to prove his points,
mostly from manuscript sources he had consulted at the British Museum in the
1810s and 1820s, revealing a close acquaintance with medieval European poetry.
But it is apparent that there was more involved than pedantic erudition in Bello's
rebuttal: what was at stake was the larger question of whether the "national character" needed to be entirely free of external influences to be considered truly national.
By seeking to demonstrate that even such a foundational poem as that of the Cid was
indebted to a tradition of European versification, he sought to address the fundamental question of Latin American cultural independence. The new nations needed
not to agonize over how to create an exclusively autochthonous culture, sprouting,
as it were, from its own soil, but to acknowledge instead its larger reservoir of
Iberian origins. Political independence would not be threatened, but rather be
enhanced, by such recognition.

George Ticknor was impressed by Bello's critique, and showed how much he
cared about his colleague to the South on the sad occasion of the death of Juan
Bello, Andrés's son, in New York in 1860.[75] But Ticknor did not change his mind
on the fundamental point about the nature of national literatures. Spain was too
fixed in his mind as an exemplary case of uniqueness in literature and character.
Without it, there could be no narrative of decline, and it was decline that obsessed
him. And this is perhaps the major difference between scholars of Spanish literature
North and South. Spanish Americans such as Bello felt that independence opened
new opportunities of contact with the larger world, and for them Spain was simply a
part of the past—or living present—yet to be incorporated into an evolving national
program. But for Ticknor the country was a living reminder of the life cycle of
empires, with decadence reaching ever new lows. The dark years of the Civil War
seemed to him an unmistakable symptom, a frightening reminder that whatever
unity Americans had achieved during their own emergence as a nation had reached
a point of dissolution, from which it might never recover.

Chapter 4

The Spanish Student: Henry Wadsworth Longfellow

We Americans have yet to really learn our own antecedents, and sort them, to unify them. They will be found ampler than has been supposed, and in widely different sources.
—Walt Whitman, "The Spanish Element in our Nationality" (1883)

Carry me Caravan take me away
Take me to Portugal, take me to Spain.
—The Doors, "Spanish Caravan" (1968)

It was a lovely September day in Brunswick when Josiah Stover Little rose to make his speech to the Bowdoin Class of 1825. His subject was "The Influence of Government on Literature." With valedictorian confidence, he established the main parameters of the interaction between political institutions and literary activity. He told the assembled crowd that monarchical institutions had a corrupting effect on literature, producing, with some few notable exceptions, only subservient, adulatory, unworthy works. On the whole, he said, "free institutions are better adapted" to the advancement of literature. "Not all the rewards and honors that monarchs can bestow," he stated, "will excite that energy and strength of conception which result not from a desire of pleasing but of influencing others." The achievement of public recognition, and the ability to both influence and represent popular feelings, were powerful aims for the Class of 1825. The speaker then turned to the president of the College, the governor of the State, the trustees, the overseers, and his fellow classmates. "It was this spirit," he told them, meaning that of free institutions, "that gave rise to the bold and lofty style that characterizes the writings of the present day; writings of which we have recently in our country had such noble examples."[1] Nathaniel Hawthorne was one of Little's classmates in the audience, somewhat forlorn but happy to have completed his degree requirements after a lackluster college performance. Henry Wadsworth Longfellow was also in the audience. He had graduated fourth in his class, but was third in the line of speakers. He, too, had something to say about the promise of American literature.

As he stepped up to the podium, Longfellow knew from inner conviction what many in the audience could only suspect, namely, that he was determined to follow through on the substance of his speech. "Whatever is noble and attractive in our national character," the self-assured Longfellow predicted, "will one day be associated with the sweet magic of Poetry." He admitted that "as of yet we can boast of nothing farther than a first beginning of a national literature: a literature associated and linked in with the grand and beautiful scenery of our country—with our institutions, our manners, our customs, in a word, with all that has helped to form whatever there is peculiar to us, and to the land in which we live."[2] But the future was bright, for "no people are richer than we are in the treasures of nature." An appreciation for the gifts of the land, and confidence in the power of free institutions, provided the solid foundations from which a truly great national literature would emerge.

Longfellow was true to his convictions. After graduation from college, he went on to achieve an unparalleled reputation as the foremost *American* poet of his time.[3] He became the beloved poet of *The Song of Hiawatha* and *Evangeline*, the bard whose memorable lines resonated in every classroom in the nation during his lifetime and far beyond. And yet, his literary reputation was built on substantial mastery of the literatures of other parts of the world. As a well-traveled American of his time, he was able to absorb the literary gifts of the major languages and nations of Europe. In doing so, he was motivated by a desire to know more about his own country. He wanted to know, in particular, how national traditions emerged, and what made them unique. It is in this context that Longfellow's interest in Hispanic culture developed, and was sustained over time.[4] Such is the subject of this chapter.

The Early Years

As in the case of George Ticknor, Longfellow's interest in Spanish subjects developed as a result of accident and opportunity. There was no clear path leading him in that direction, but when the prospect of a professorship in modern languages opened at his alma mater, Longfellow visited Spain, achieved remarkable fluency in the language, and devoted significant attention to Spanish topics for the rest of his long life. In the early 1820s, he had received some instruction in French at Portland, but his exposure to Spanish only began when he traveled to Europe in 1826. His path to the Hispanic world was primarily through the study of literature, a precocious gift for poetry, and a youthful interest in other societies and cultures.

Longfellow was born in Portland, Maine, in 1807, the son of a lawyer who served as a federalist representative to the Eighteenth Congress. Stephen Longfellow was a somewhat overbearing parent, but had enough flexibility and care for his child to let him follow his intellectual inclinations, and even support him morally and financially in his endeavors. Still, young Longfellow had to assert himself regarding his future on more than a few occasions. While a junior at Bowdoin, he asked his father, "I am curious to know what you do intend to make of me! Whether I am to study a profession or not? and if so, what profession?" Before an answer could arrive, however, he stated "I hope your ideas upon this subject will agree with mine, for I have a particular and strong predilection for one course of life, to which you I fear will not agree."[5] He was not mistaken, for his father insisted that he should learn a profession, meaning most decidedly the law, but giving him the option of a religious career. There was much back and forth until father and son eventually worked out a compromise, but not before young Longfellow declared, "The fact is, I most eagerly aspire after future eminence in literature, my whole soul burns most ardently for it, and every earthly thought centers in it."[6] When his father persisted, Longfellow indicated that his heart would not be in any profession, and exclaimed in frustration, "Ought I not then to choose another path in which I can go on with better hope of success?" That path was of course literature, and he thought he had a good chance to succeed due to the number of poems he had already managed to get into print.[7] By late January 1825, however, his father had prevailed. A disheartened Longfellow wrote then that "it seems to be your fixed desire, that I should choose the profession of the Law for the business of my life." But he did secure his permission to study languages and literature at Cambridge for one year.[8]

Unexpected developments came to Longfellow's aid. The trustees of Bowdoin College voted to establish a professorship in modern languages in 1825, the year of Henry's graduation. Having shown a gift for literary work, he was considered as a primary candidate for, though not immediately offered, the position. The fact that Stephen Longfellow was one of the trustees of the College shows not only that he exercised his influence to secure Henry a position in a related area, but also that he was open enough to accommodate his son's wishes. To qualify for the formal aspects of the professorship, it was understood that young Longfellow needed to travel to Europe to study the languages at their source.[9] Thus a plan was conceived to visit France, Spain, and Italy. Henry was then 18 years of age.

It was in this context that Longfellow first met George Ticknor in Boston in early May 1826, as the person who could be most instrumental in shepherding the young scholar through the grand academic tour of Europe. Ticknor struck him as "a little Spanish-looking man, but exceedingly kind and affable."[10] It made sense to visit Ticknor, for he was a well-established professor of modern languages at Harvard, and had himself traveled to Europe to acquire several languages and pursue a course of literary studies. What Longfellow did not expect, but was persuaded about it nonetheless, was Ticknor's insistence that he should study in Germany. The point was reinforced when, on his way to Albany, Henry visited Joseph Cogswell and George Bancroft (who had studied at Göttingen) at their Round Hill School establishment. Soon after this last visit, Longfellow told his father that he was convinced of the importance of a German sojourn.[11] Ticknor supplied him with a letter of introduction to the great Old Testament historian Johann Gottfried Eichhorn, who was his teacher in Göttingen. The Harvard professor also supplied him with letters to Longfellow's idol, Washington Irving, and the British poet and scholar, Robert Southey.

Stephen Longfellow was not pleased to hear about the proposed change of plans, especially after his son reached Europe and was having second thoughts about going to Spain. Henry had written to his father that "you either over-rate my abilities and my advantages, if you think that I am already master of the French," in order to delay or possibly cancel his trip to Spain. Moreover, "the German language is infinitely more important than the Spanish, being infinitely more rich in literary resources." To drive the point to a more vulnerable spot in a parent's heart, he added that he had met a young gentleman, recently arrived from Spain, who told him that the country was "very dangerous, on account of the dissentions which distract the country and the frequent assassinations which take place there."[12] The senior Longfellow was apparently unimpressed, because his son felt he had to insist, "I think indeed that I must give up the Spanish; at all events I must give up the idea of visiting Spain. That country is filled with all the horrors of a civil war." He added a more pathetic statement, "I never desired to come to my end by the dagger of an assassin or the pistol of a robber."[13] Stephen seemed unmoved by his son's pleas, and at last issued an ultimatum,

> Your ulterior object [acquiring the languages necessary for the Bowdoin professorship] cannot be accomplished unless you obtain an accurate knowledge of the French and Spanish languages. Such are the relations now existing between this country and South America that a knowledge of the Spanish is quite as important as of the French. If you neglect either of these languages you may be sure of not obtaining the station which you have in view. And I should never have consented to your visiting Europe had it not been to secure that station.[14]

Young Longfellow was probably not in the best frame of mind going into Spain after this exchange with his father, but he made the best of it. "Thus you see me on my way to Spain," he wrote from Bordeaux, "and I cannot say that I leave France with much regret." Interestingly, one of the reasons he cited for leaving so easily was the French ministry's recent assault against freedom of the press. "It is the dark and dangerous policy of the priesthood that is doing this," he wrote to his father. "The Jesuits rule the mind of a weak-hearted king—and you know it is a point with them, to keep the people in utter darkness."[15]

What were Longfellow's religious beliefs? He came from a solidly Unitarian family, and he himself remained one for the rest of his life. His father had been a classmate and friend of William Ellery Channing at Harvard, and young Longfellow became a decided admirer of the Boston-based minister. At Bowdoin, he was secretary of the Unitarian Society, and promoted the circulation of Channing's 1819 tract, *Objections to Unitarian Christianity Considered*. Young Longfellow gave a great deal of thought to religious matters. An early indication of his commitment to the liberal Christianity promoted by the Unitarians can be found in a letter to his cousin George Wadsworth Wells, in which he admitted that "I conceive that if religion is ever to benefit us, it must be incorporated with our feelings, and become in every degree identified with our happiness. And hence I love that view of Christianity which sets it in the light of a cheerful, kind-hearted friend, and which gives its thoughts a noble and a liberal turn."[16] Thus, on entering Spain, he was faced with religious views and practices that challenged his values and, as in other cases of Americans visiting the country, cemented his own.

Longfellow knew little about Spain before he actually visited the country. He had access to William Robertson's books in his father's library and, of course, to the ubiquitous *Don Quixote* by Cervantes. He also held certain views that were as common as they were unquestioned among Americans of his era. Writing to his mother about life in out-of-the-way Bowdoin, the young student had declared, "we have nothing here but what is old. Like the Spaniards, we are a century behind the rest of the world."[17] This was not much of a background on the country, and thus Longfellow's first impressions were quite strong and simple. He told his father that, "One of the first things which attracts the attention of the traveler on entering the northern provinces of Spain, is the poverty stricken appearance of everything around him. The country seems deserted . . . the people have nothing left them but rags and religion. Of these—such as they are—they have enough." He added, in a more literary vein, that "it is like going back two centuries in this old world, this visit to Spain. There is so little change in the Spanish character, that you find everything as it is said to have been two hundred years ago. You see the same dresses and the same equipages, that are represented in the old plates of Gil Blas and Don Quixote."[18]

Longfellow crossed the French-Spanish border in early March 1827 and arrived in Madrid on March 6. "I have reached the very heart of the empire," he wrote to Stephen, "without falling among thieves or becoming such a melancholy illustration of Spanish blood-guiltiness, as some of my friends anticipated."[19] Longfellow thus arrived during what is known in Spanish history as the "ominous decade" (1823–1833). After a liberal interregnum (1820–1823), Ferdinand VII had restored the absolutist rule for which he was notorious and that was to last until his death in 1833. The combination of devastation resulting from the Peninsular War, plus the political crisis that followed, serves as a background for Longfellow's low expectations about the country. But once in Madrid, he found that he liked the city. The young traveler soon met the small American community residing there, including Alexander Hill Everett, the U.S. Minister; Obadiah Rich, the Consul and book-collector, and Lieutenant Alexander Slidell (later Slidell-Mackenzie) of the U.S. Navy. Longfellow and Slidell got along quite well, and in fact decided to travel together to Segovia soon after Longfellow's arrival in Madrid. Slidell later described the visitor as

> . . . a young countryman, who had come to Spain in search of instruction. He was just from college, full of all the ardent feeling excited by classical pursuits, with health unbroken, hope that was a stranger to disappointment, curiosity which had never yet been fed to satiety. Then he had sunny locks, a fresh complexion, and a clear blue eye, all indications of a joyous temperament.[20]

Longfellow was also thrilled to meet Washington Irving, who was already settled in Spain, and who lived at Rich's house. Irving reciprocated by taking an immediate liking to the seemingly likable young man, and introduced him to his own acquaintances. "We have now quite a circle of Americans [in Madrid]," wrote Lucretia Everett to her family, "lately increased by the arrival of Mr. Longfellow of Portland, a young man of considerable promise & Louisa says the handsomest man she ever saw."[21] Lucretia also mentioned that Irving had taken the young man to an evening party at the house of the Marchioness of Casa Irujo (Sally McKean), the American-born widow of a former Spanish Ambassador to the United States.[22]

Longfellow visited Irving and other Americans in Madrid often, but his main purpose was to observe the country and learn the language. Clearly, he knew little of either on his arrival, but was soon able to converse at least colloquially and gain a more thorough understanding of Spanish society. According to Caleb Cushing, one of the few but growing numbers of Americans traveling in Spain in the 1820s, Longfellow learned to speak Spanish perfectly well within four months, thanks to the expert instruction of a Spanish teacher, Diego Díaz Cuenca.[23] Young Longfellow warmed up to the country, perhaps in proportion to his ability to communicate. Yet either in an effort to please his stern father, or as a reflection of his own distance from the religious aspects of Spanish culture, his early impressions of Spain were mingled with a clear rejection of the ubiquitous Catholic presence. Among the most vivid scenes of Spain for him, and the most recurrent, were

> . . . the religious ceremonies of the Catholic Church, which in Spain are still celebrated with all the pomp and circumstance of darker ages. The Spaniards in their faith are the

most obedient people in the world: they will believe everything a priest tells them to, without asking why or wherefore: but at the same time, as you may readily infer from this, they have as little pure religion as can be found upon the face of the earth. In fact their religion may very justly be compared to one of those little grocery stores in the purlieus of Green street, which has its whole stock of sugar hats and gingerbread images stuck up at the windows.[24]

The people's reverence for the passage of the Host, the humility shown by the king and queen ("eaten up by the effects of a most gloomy and melancholy religious frenzy"), and the observance of saints' days, were all dutifully noted by Longfellow, though often in a detached or even sarcastic tone. Otherwise, he was captivated by the country, especially as he gained confidence speaking the language and traveled to southern Spain. A clear indication of his increasing fluency can be seen in a portion of his journal which he wrote in Spanish, covering the thirteen-day journey from Madrid to Seville.[25] He also kept an English-language record, which reveals how much he had assimilated from his reading of *Don Quixote*. Crossing the mountains of the Sierra Morena, for instance, he came to a narrow pass called *Despeñaperros*, where he recalled that

It was there that the "Knight of the Woeful Countenance" performed his solitary penance whilst Sancho carried the ill-fated letter to Dulcinea. Just at the entrance of the pass, stands the "Venta de Cadenas"—the inn at which the poor knight-errant suffered so many and so sad misfortunes. It is a long low house, with a paved cart-road passing through the center, and a ruined out-house in the rear. The kitchen was a mere nook in the wall: and within it a strapping wench was busy amongst pots and kettles. She was the very counterpart of the faithful Maritornes, whose midnight assignation with the muleteer began the melancholy history of Don Quixote's adventures at the inn. But I sought in vain for the window, at which the maiden left him hanging in her garters, when faithful to the laws of chivalry, he guarded at midnight the gates of what he deemed an enchanted castle, and listened with easy credulity to the lament of the captive princess!

This level of detail must have certainly come from a recent reading of the book. The colorful rendition also shows Longfellow's obvious thrill at being at the very place described by Cervantes two centuries before. But there was something else, and that was the traveler's inclination to look at prosaic reality through romantic literary lenses. "I confess," he wrote, "that to beguile one tedious hour, I would believe a fairy tale!"[26] As he continued his journey into southern Spain, however, his impressions and feelings revealed a deeper impact. This was particularly the case in Granada, where he arrived on November 11, 1827, after visiting Seville, Cádiz, and Gibraltar.

When he arrived into the walled city, he looked out the window of his lodgings, and caught his first glimpse of the Alhambra. "It seems a dream to me," he exclaimed, "How my spirit is stirred within me! How my heart is lifted up! How my thoughts are rapt away in visions of other times! Is it not a dream?"[27] Longfellow could not sit still; he returned time and again to the sites that Washington Irving would later immortalize in *The Alhambra* (1832). Toward the end of his stay, he pronounced that "No portion of my life has ever been so much like a dream."[28] Though he never returned to Spain in person, he never forgot the place. According to his younger brother and biographer Samuel, he never returned because "he was unwilling to break the spell of that early time."[29] After lingering a few days longer in Málaga, Longfellow proceeded to Italy, only to realize that some remarkable transformation had taken place. He confessed to his mother that he was traveling through Italy without enthusiasm. "The fact is," he told her, "I am homesick for Spain, I want to go back there again. The recollections of it completely ruin Italy for me: and next to going home—let me go to Spain."[30] It was in Italy, in fact, that the seeds of *Outre-Mer*, containing his nostalgic remembrances of Spain, were planted.

From Italy, Longfellow proceeded to Germany, armed with the letters of Ticknor and Bancroft, plus newly acquired ones from Washington Irving.[31] An important dimension of his travel was the consultation of rare books, and his journal shows how discriminating he had become. While at Dresden, he wrote that he had found at the Royal Library "a very curious old Spanish book treating of the troubadour poetry of Spain, entitled the *Cancionero General*."[32] This source provided the basis for his work of dissemination of Spanish literature in the United States, long before Ticknor's *History of Spanish Literature* came out in 1849. While in Germany, he told his father, he had started writing a book, "a kind of Sketch Book of scenes in France, Spain, and Italy."[33] He seemed to be quite content in Germany, but then, just like Ticknor a decade before, he had to hurry back to the United States upon learning of the fatal illness of a member of the family, in this case his younger sister Elizabeth. His cherished hope of studying at Göttingen was thus cut short, and while at Paris on his way back to the States, he learned of his sister's death. An anxious Longfellow arrived in New York on August 11. Nine days later, he was in Portland. He had been gone three years and three months.

Professor Longfellow

Longfellow assumed the duties of his position at Bowdoin in September 1829, but not after an unpleasant dispute with the College was settled in his favor, namely, that he was to be appointed professor, not tutor.[34] This incident delayed his delivery of the customary inaugural address, which took place at commencement of the following year. On this solemn occasion (September 2, 1830), Longfellow provided a cogent summary of the emergence of the Romance languages in Europe. The new professor paid particular attention to poetry, because poetry provided both the first manifestations of vernacular European literature, and also a unique window into the "manners and character" of the various nations. Indeed, "poetry is but the expression of the thoughts and feelings of a people, and we give it the appellation of national, only when the character of a nation shines visibly and clearly through it."[35] As far as Spain was concerned, the *Poem of the Cid* occupied a central place in Longfellow's rendition of the emergence of the national literature. The poem bore a rude, martial character, he said, in keeping with the conditions of occupied Spain. It was also rudimentary in its versification, and yet "its antiquity, the noble spirit it breathes, and the simple, unaffected dignity which animates it, places [the poem] among the most curious and remarkable works of modern literature." In this, and subsequent Spanish ballads, "a high and peculiar tone of national feeling sounds through every line; and the majestic lineaments of the ancient Spanish character stand in clear and bold relief upon their face."[36] As illustrated by the following key passage in Longfellow's address, the development of an authentic national Spanish

literature was a direct reflection of the history of Spain during the times of the
Muslim occupation:

> There is no page in the history of the warlike ages, which to my eyes presents a portrait
> of more signal moral beauty, than that in which are portrayed the outlines of the
> Moorish sovereignty in Spain. As the eye glances over the records of those days, even at
> this distant period, we catch glimpses of something like a golden age. It is true that the
> heart of Castile still throbbed with the pulsations of liberty, and the iron tempest of war
> beat against the northern frontier of their realm. But in the quiet bosom of the coun-
> try all was peace. No terrors had followed the footsteps of the Moslem conqueror: no
> captive chained to his chariot wheels adorned his triumph: no iron sceptre smote the
> land and blasted the fruitful field. The husbandman sowed his seed and gathered his
> harvest in security: and the spires of the Christian Church arose amid the domes of the
> Saracen Mosque. The conquerors and conquered seem to have had common interests
> and common pleasures: and they sat together beneath the shadow of the palm-tree and
> the olive, and sang their common loves and jealousies. There was nothing but the dif-
> ference of religious creeds, which prevented these people from uniting together and
> blending into one. The tolerance that prevailed in this is every way remarkable: for in
> the zeal of the Moorish Government to spread their learning and arts through the
> country, Colleges and Libraries were established in all the principal cities of the south
> of Spain, and thrown open alike to Mohammedans, Jews, and Christians. . . . These
> genial influences gave a softer tone to national feeling, and though the spirit of the
> warrior is visible in a great portion of the Spanish romances, in others the knight throws
> his spear and unclasps his helmet. The sound of the Moorish flute mingles with the
> brazen voice of the trumpet; and the rough feelings of the chieftain give way to gentler
> affections and more peaceful dreams.[37]

Clearly, Longfellow's view of Spain had become more nuanced. The passage cited
amounts to a very positive view of Islamic Spain, in which *convivencia* (the harmo-
nious relationship between different religions and ethnicities) prevailed. Longfellow
paid more—and more positive—attention to Islamic Spain than was the case among
other scholars of Spanish history. Irving, Ticknor, and Prescott all emphasized the
superiority of Christianity over Islam, especially after they had carefully distinguished Christianity from Catholicism. Longfellow himself had no doubts about his
own Christian convictions, but he drew a useful lesson from Muslim Spain: in any
society, perhaps pointedly in his own, tolerance of religious difference was good.

At Bowdoin, Longfellow settled into a teaching routine that soon made him
restless. His days were consumed by language instruction, recitations, and preparation of didactic materials. He wrote to his friend James Berdan, whom he had met
in Paris in 1826, that "I feel as if I were living in exile here: and it will be a deed of
charity in you to come and make a long visit as soon as you can find leisure."[38] He
was clearly eager to receive friends, and some did make it to Brunswick, like José
Cortés y Sesti, whom he had met in Madrid, and who stayed with him at Bowdoin
after his arrival in the United States in October 1832. Cortés delighted Longfellow
by reading him portions of *Don Quixote*. "Es un placer oir el Quijote leido por un
Español," he wrote in Spanish in his journal, "pues el mismo tono de la voz da una
gracia particular a lo que se dice, y casi nos hace creer que el Caballero de la Triste
Figura y su Escudero Sancho nos están entreteniendo con sus pláticas" [It is a pleasure to hear a native Spaniard read Don Quixote, for the very intonation of the voice
adds humor to what is being said, and it makes us almost believe that the Knight of

the Rueful Countenance and his Squire Sancho are entertaining us with their talk].[39] Such pleasures could not last long, however, for Cortés soon left to try to make a living in Portland, and eventually returned to Spain. Other visits included those of Alexander Hill Everett, whom he had also met in Madrid, and who spoke at Commencement in 1834. Earlier, in the Fall of 1830, George Ticknor and his wife Anna visited Longfellow and later kept in touch with the young professor. Ticknor's friendship was crucial to him, not only because of a shared expertise in Spanish literature, but also because the older scholar was in a position to help him advance in his career. When Longfellow pursued a job prospect in New York, Ticknor was happy to provide him with a letter of recommendation.[40] Few could assess Longfellow's capabilities as he could,

> Soon after he was graduated at Brunswick—wrote Ticknor—he became known to me by an interest, quite remarkable at his age, and still more so, perhaps, from the circumstances in which he was placed; an interest I mean, in the early Provençal literature and in the literature of Spain and Italy. This interest, in no length of time, led him to the continent of Europe. He passed time in France and still more in Italy and in Spain; and his knowledge of the language and literature of each of these countries, has, for several years past, seemed to me quite extraordinary. He writes and speaks Spanish with a degree of fluency and exactness, which I have known in no other American born of parents speaking English as their vernacular. His knowledge of Spanish literature is extensive and to be relied upon, and several publications he has made on the subject have been accompanied with poetical translations of much spirit and fidelity. Besides this, he is, for his years [twenty-eight], an accomplished general scholar, particularly in modern literature; and full of activity and eagerness in the pursuit of knowledge. His general appearance, address and manners are very prepossessing; his temper amiable, and his character without blemish from his earliest years to the present time.[41]

The appointment did not materialize, but Ticknor was soon able to help recruit young Longfellow for Harvard. He had sincere admiration for the younger scholar who, finding it hard to secure the time needed to write in a creative vein, was eager to try a new position. Up to that point, he had only published textbooks and a few articles on Spanish scholarly subjects for the *North American Review*.[42] He did, however, publish a much admired translation of the poems of Jorge Manrique (1440–1478).[43] Ticknor immediately pronounced his translation abilities "more faithful and valuable than either [John] Bowring, [John Gibson] Lockhart, or Lord Holland, to say nothing of [Thomas] Rodd and the earlier versifiers which do not deserve to be, in any way, compared with them."[44] Longfellow's first major work, however, was *Outre-Mer*, which he had conceived in Europe, but had written mostly in the United States. In March 1833, he told his friend George Washington Greene that, "I am writing a book—a kind of Sketch Book of France, Spain, Germany, and Italy—composed of descriptions—sketches of character—tales, illustrating manners and customs, and tales illustrating nothing in particular."[45] He proceeded quite rapidly, because the book was in print before the year was out.

The Spanish Sketch Book

Longfellow's *Outre-Mer* was intentionally structured as homage to Washington Irving's enormously successful *Sketch Book*. Indeed, he so admired Irving's work that he not only paid it the compliment of imitation, but declared, in a memorial service at the Massachusetts Historical Society in 1859, that "every reader has his first book. I mean to say, one book among all others, which in early youth first fascinates his imagination, and at once excites and satisfies the desires of his mind. To me this first book was the *Sketch Book* of Washington Irving." In *Outre-Mer*, he sought to convey the same qualities that so attracted him to Irving's work, "its pleasant humor, its melancholy tenderness, [and] its atmosphere of reverie."[46] Longfellow also conveyed more reflective views on Spain and its culture. As he had previously announced, he was to provide a series of vignettes about his various travels, but he also wanted to emphasize some particular themes. They included the relevance of literature for the description of scenery and manners; the identification of the Spanish national character and its major components, and the role of Catholicism in Spanish culture and society.

Regarding the first, literary theme, it is perhaps not surprising that those models included *Don Quixote* and *Gil Blas*. The barren looks of the countryside, the dilapidation of buildings, and the hand-to-mouth existence of the peasantry naturally lent itself to evocations of those literary sources. A village barber, thus, would be shaving his client not over a plain basin, but over the helmet of Mambrino (134). Adjusting nicely to the practice of the *siesta*, Longfellow exclaimed, "from my heart I can say with honest Sancho, 'blessed be the man that first invented sleep!'" (151). Traveling through La Mancha, Longfellow's enthusiasm was evident, "Here are the windmills, as of old; every village has its Master Nicholas—every *venta* its Maritornes." Moreover, "to the peasantry of Spain, Don Quixote and his squire are historic personages" (206–207). Meeting a muleteer, he wondered whether he might be descended from the character portrayed in the second chapter of *Gil Blas*. Finding lodgings in Madrid's Calle de la Montera, Longfellow wrote that he followed the example of Gil Blas in wanting to be close to the famed Puerta del Sol (144).[47] There are also references to a larger literary genre, as when Longfellow summarized the country's history as "resembling more the fables of romance than the solemn chronicle of events" (139). In a romantic vein, he wrote about the contrast between past glories and present decadence, with an emphasis on ruins.

> What hand shall now wield the sword of the Campeador [Rodrigo Díaz de Vivar], or lift up the banner of Leon and Castile? The ruins of Christian castle and Moorish alcazar still look forth from the hills of Spain; but where, oh where is the spirit of freedom that once fired the children of the Goth? Where is the spirit of Bernardo del Carpio, and Perez de Vargas, and Alonzo de Aguilar? Shall it forever sleep? Shall it never again beat high in the hearts of their sons? Shall the descendants of Pelayo bow forever beneath an iron yoke, "like cattle whose despair is dumb?" (140).

Likewise, his visit to Granada and the Alhambra elicited reflections far more elaborate than those of his travel journals. "Majestic spirit of the past, I recognize thee!" he wrote, "Thou has taught me to see in thee the principle that unfolds itself from century to century in the progress of our race," meaning that "generations perish, like the leaves of the forest, passing away when their mission is completed" (224). A hidden wisdom lay in those ruins, and Longfellow hoped to convey how fragile the foundations of all civilizations could be.

The second central theme in *Outre-Mer* is that of the Spanish national character. Longfellow defined it as follows: "Its prominent traits are a generous pride of birth, a superstitious devotion to the dogmas of the Church, and an innate dignity, which exhibits itself even in the common and every-day employment of life" (140). He found evidence of these traits everywhere he went, and added that there was "a tinge of sadness in the Spanish character" (141), as shown by Spanish music and festivals. Even the bullfights (which he refused to describe, as an already trite subject) had "the same serious, sombre character" (142). Looking for examples of the national character, Longfellow went far back into the history of ballads, producing in the process an interesting classification of the ancient ballads: Historic, Romantic, and "Moorish."[48] In the Historic, which recounted the deeds of such heroes as Bernardo del Carpio, the Cid, and Alonso de Aguilar, he identified "the spirit of Castilian pride, with the high and dauntless spirit of liberty that burned so fiercely of old in the heart of the brave hidalgo" (159). The Romantic ballads, for their part, included the many fictitious heroes of the age of chivalry. "There is an exaggeration in the prowess of these heroes of romance which is in accordance with the warmth of the Spanish imagination" (161). Lest readers conclude that this was a mere antiquarian speculation, Longfellow added "the ballads which celebrate their achievements still go from mouth to mouth among the peasantry of Spain." Finally, referring to the Moorish ballads, he announced that "here we enter a new world, more gorgeous and more dazzling than that of Gothic chronicle and tradition" (166). Like Washington Irving, he wanted to emphasize the centrality of the Muslim tradition in Spain:

> Among the Moorish ballads are included not only those which were originally composed in Arabic, but all that relate to the manners, customs, and history of the Moors in Spain. In most of them the influence of an Oriental taste is clearly visible; their spirit is more refined and effeminate than that of the historic and romantic ballads, in which no trace of such an influence is perceptible. (167)[49]

The Spanish character, as reflected in the literature of Spain, included an important Muslim component.

Catholicism, finally, received its share of attention in *Outre-Mer*.[50] He reported on a visit to the village of Villanueva del Pardillo, where he saw a priest instructing children on the mystery of the Holy Trinity. He transcribed an exchange in which the children mechanically responded to the priest's questions with set, memorized answers, and then concluded,

> I did not quarrel with the priest for having been born and educated in a different faith from mine; but as I left the church and sauntered slowly homeward, I could not help asking myself, in a whisper, "Why perplex the spirit of a child with these metaphysical subtilties, these dark, mysterious speculations, which man in all his pride of intellect cannot fathom or explain?" (179)

Clergymen appeared everywhere in the book, and ranged from an ascetic Carmelite friar to a frivolous village priest. But in addition to the picturesque description of these figures, Longfellow engaged in a more involved discussion concerning the relationship between religion and literature. He devoted a section on the moral and devotional poetry of Spain, a version of which had appeared earlier in the *North American Review*. The essence of Christian values might be universal, he stated, but different national traditions render the manifestations of divinity differently. "Thus,

Catholic nations sing the praises of the Virgin Mary in language in which nations of the Protestant faith do not unite" (185). Spaniards had been celebrating "the lives and miracles of the saints and the Virgin" (187) ever since the times of Gonzalo de Berceo (the thirteenth-century poet). In these miracles, the Virgin and the saints appear physically, in a way that "tends to strip religion of its peculiar sanctity," because such "earthly and material character" detract from "the more spiritualized perceptions of the internal sense" (190–191). Beautiful though some of this poetry might be, corporeal representations of divinity have "a very unfavorable influence upon an unenlightened and superstitious [mind]" (192), because of their tendency "to sensualize and desecrate the character of holy things" (194). These representations, Longfellow argued, were not confined to medieval times, and to prove it he provided a variety of Spanish Golden Age examples, especially the *Autos Sacramentales* and *Vidas de Santos*, including some by Calderón de la Barca. But he stopped short of condemning them altogether,

> Thus far I have spoken of the devotional poetry of Spain as modified by the peculiarities of religious faith and practice. Considered apart from the dogmas of a creed, and as the expression of those pure and elevated feelings of religion which are not the prerogative of any sect or denomination, but the common privilege of all, it possesses strong claims to our admiration and praise. I know of nothing in any modern tongue so beautiful as some of its finest passages. The thought springs heavenward from the soul—the language comes burning from the lip. The imagination of the poet seems spiritualized; with nothing of earth, and all of heaven—a heaven like that of his own native clime, without a cloud, or a vapor of earth, to obscure its brightness. (201–202)

Such appreciation was rare in the American publications of the early republic, and was made more compelling by Longfellow's knowledge of the language in which this literature was written. *Outre-Mer* thus provided one of the earliest treatments of Spanish topics that went beyond the merely sarcastic or picturesque. Surely, there was some of that in Longfellow's work, but the tone, and especially the depth, of his literary discussions was fresh. The book captured the attention of a wide readership, but it resonated particularly strongly with the smaller community of Hispanists, most notably George Ticknor, who was at the time contemplating his resignation from Harvard, and was thinking about a possible successor.

Longfellow at Harvard

Ticknor resigned the Smith Professorship in December 1834, hoping that a replacement would be found before the end of the academic year. Harvard's President Josiah Quincy had obviously discussed the succession with Ticknor when he contacted Longfellow and offered him the position. Longfellow was quite prepared to leave Brunswick, and agreed to the terms, which included a visit to Europe, at his own expense, "for the purpose of a more perfect attainment of the German."[51] Quincy was here acting on the recommendation of Ticknor, who had earlier advised Longfellow to acquire German skills, which he personally favored, but which were also essential for the job. Thus, Longfellow set out for Europe, where he stayed between May 1835 and November 1836, spending several months at Heidelberg. Soon after his return to the States, on November 17, he was formally elected Smith

Professor. His actual teaching at Harvard, however, did not begin until May of 1837. Except for two leaves of absence, he remained in the College for 18 years.

Longfellow's experience as Smith Professor at Harvard was mixed. It was a pleasure for him to teach Dante, Goethe, Cervantes, and Molière regularly, as well as topical courses on modern literature or Spanish drama, but teaching such subjects was not the only, or indeed the primary demand on his time, which was occupied rather by administrative matters and basic language instruction.[52] He soon grew weary of the constant modifications in College regulations, which often encroached upon his field. Though large in terms of students, the "department" of Modern Languages had only one professor, himself, and, therefore, limited influence on the College as a whole. In addition, he soon confronted serious problems with two of the four instructors (those of German and French) and was compelled to force their resignations in 1838.[53] To his surprise, rather than supplying a replacement for the French instructor, the Harvard Corporation demanded that he take on the obligations himself. He did, and eventually managed to get a replacement in 1840, but when the Italian instructor, Pietro Bachi (1787–1853), was forced to resign in 1846 by the new Harvard President Edward Everett,[54] Longfellow was again asked to assume the duties of language teaching to cover for the recent loss. Only this time, his "temporary" assignment lasted seven years.

There was also pressure to force his Spanish (and French) instructor, Francis Sales, to resign, on the questionable grounds of his advanced age. A furious Longfellow wrote in his journal that "they [Harvard College] are talking about cutting poor Sales adrift, because he is old and almost useless." He ended with a dark reflection: "Thus, one of these days, if I grow old in the service of these men, shall I likewise be remorselessly set free."[55] Longfellow managed to retain Sales for several years after this attempt, but then in 1846, President Everett put pressure on him to force the resignation of the Spanish instructor on the new grounds— however true enough—that he was barely able to maintain classroom discipline. Again Longfellow succeeded in keeping Sales, who was a pillar of his Department, but the balance of 18 years at Harvard was one of internal struggles, changing College rules that he could not control, weariness at the drill of language instruction, and constant attempts at redefining the duties of his professorship. But the reason for his ultimate resignation from Harvard in 1854 was his earnest aspiration, which had never died, to devote himself exclusively to imaginative literature.

The Harvard years were not entirely unproductive, for it was during this time that he published the prose works *Hyperion* (1839) and *Kavanagh* (1849); the poetic works *Voices of the Night* (1839), *Ballads and Other Poems* (1841), *Poems on Slavery* (1842), *The Belfry of Bruges and Other Poems* (1845), *Evangeline* (1847), *The Seaside and the Fireside* (1849), *The Golden Legend* (1851), and the play *The Spanish Student* (1843). For the purposes of this chapter, we may now turn to this last work, which was centrally concerned with a Spanish subject.

In the early Fall of 1840, the normally sedentary Longfellow ventured into Boston to watch a performance by the famed Austrian dancer Fanny Elssler. "Her Spanish dances are exquisite," he wrote to his father, "and remind me strongly of days gone by."[56] He was seized, indeed, by nostalgia, at precisely the same time when he was systematically reading pieces of Spanish drama. He determined, therefore, to carry out an idea that had occurred to him earlier in the year. "A good idea! Yes, I will write a comedy."[57] Thus was born *The Spanish Student*. He confided this idea to his friend Samuel Ward, who responded enthusiastically: "I know it will be eloquent for it will be a true one."[58] They discussed various aspects of the play during the remainder of the year, and while doing so, they addressed each other as "Hypolito" (Ward) and "Victoriano" (Longfellow) after the student figures in the poem. In their correspondence, the poet also mentioned the name of the protagonist, Preciosa, who happened, like Fanny Elssler, to be a dancer.[59] By the end of the year, he told his father that "I have also written a much longer and more difficult poem, called 'The Spanish Student'—a Drama in Five Acts."[60] For reasons unexplained, he asked him to keep this as "a great secret," and indeed he did not publish the work until two years later, in installments, in *Graham's Magazine*. His procrastination was a matter of much vexation to his friend Ward who, by 1842, was clamoring for the poet to finish. "I want you to lose no time in taking up the *Spanish Student*. Purify it and publish it as a dramatic poem."[61] The poem finally appeared in book form in the late Spring of 1843.[62]

In *The Spanish Student*, Longfellow took the name of its principal female character from Cervantes's *La Gitanilla*. Preciosa is a gypsy dancer who turns out to be not a gypsy at all, but a noblewoman who had been stolen as a child. Longfellow borrowed from other sources, mainly Calderón and Lope de Vega, to write his story in the tradition of the *comedias de capa y espada* (cloak and sword tales). The play is, therefore, full of meandering plots and subplots, action, suspense, and misunderstandings, but the basic outline is as follows: Victorian, a student at the University of Alcalá falls in love with Preciosa, who is in turn accosted by two other pretenders, one a gypsy, the other a Castilian nobleman. There is much jealousy, and painful separations, but in the end Victorian prevails; he rescues Preciosa, after the king of Spain has decreed the expulsion of the gypsies from the land. The couple manages to get free from the other bothersome suitors, both of whom conveniently die. The lovers also unexpectedly learn of Preciosa's noble origin and wealth when her father, Don Carlos, reveals the truth about her life. Although the ending is not entirely explicit, it is certainly a happy one.

What is remarkable about *The Spanish Student* is Longfellow's mastery of Spanish literary tropes. Subtly embedded in the play are numerous references to a larger Spanish literary tradition, and also proverbs and characters extracted from specific literary sources. Perhaps the most frequently used is *Don Quixote*, for the majority of proverbs—and much of the dialogue depends on them—comes from that book, as does the character of Chispa, who is modeled after Sancho Panza. In addition, Longfellow put his own knowledge of the country to use, as he did in the impressively vivid description of Segovia,

> 'T is a notable old town,
> Boasting an ancient Roman aqueduct,
> And an Alcázar, builded by the Moors,
> Wherein, you may remember, poor Gil Blas
> Was fed on *Pan del Rey*. Oh, many a time
> Out if its grated windows have I looked
> Hundreds of feet plumb down to the Eresma.
> That, like a serpent through the valley creeping,
> Glides at its foot.

Besides picturesque scenery and classic literary references, Longfellow did not miss the opportunity to use clergymen as comic relief or to issue strong critiques of

Catholic duplicity and ignorance. Preciosa explains in Act I, Scene 3, that she must perform before the Cardinal and the Archbishop of Toledo, because "Thou knowest the Pope has sent [directives] here into Spain/ To put a stop to dances on the stage." When the private performance takes place, the stern Church officials reveal what they seek: "By seasonable stop put here in Spain / To bullfights and lewd dances on the stage." As Preciosa begins to dance, they "look on with gravity and an occasional frown." But as she proceeds, they become "more and more pleased and excited." Ultimately, they "rise from their seats, throw their caps in the air, and applaud vehemently." The real threat to her and the gypsies, then, is not from Vatican vigilance, or priestly voyeurism, but rather from the Crown's view of them as "vagabonds and beggars." Priests appear indeed as weak and vain. At Guadarrama, the village priest puts on some airs when he receives Hypolito and Victorian, the students. "It is not often that I have occasion / To speak with scholars; and *Emollit mores, / Nec sinit esse feros*, Cicero says." Hypolito protests that the line is from Ovid (as indeed it is, from *Epistulae ex Ponto*, II, 9, 47: "Softens the heart, and curbs the wild desires"), not Cicero, but the priest insists, and then fully exposes his vanity and ignorance as the student begins a game of name-dropping to tease him. The priest's relevance goes no further than organizing supper for his visitors.

Longfellow's *The Spanish Student* circulated widely, as most of his works did, but it was not a critical success or even considered a major work in his larger literary corpus.[63] Edgar Allan Poe was particularly blunt about it: "Its thesis is unoriginal; its incidents are antique; its plot is no plot; its characters have no character." Poe charged that Longfellow had taken much more from Cervantes than he acknowledged, but without replicating his artistry, especially in the "stupid imitation of Sancho Panza." Contrary to the rules of drama, the various scenes had no connection and its incidents were entirely arbitrary. Readers might "with a very decided *chance* of improvement, put the scenes in a bag, give them a shake or two by way of shuffle, and tumble them out." The twists and turns of the plot were entirely un-original, forming "the staple material of every Hop O'My Thumb tragedy since the flood." Given ten minutes, he would locate every incident of the poem in the comedies of Calderón and Lope de Vega.[64]

Poe was somewhat ill-tempered in his review, but he had a point. Judged as drama, *The Spanish Student* suffered from inconsistencies, and read better as a poem than as a play. But Poe's standard was even higher, in that he was looking for *originality* in the American drama, and could not find it in the derivative work of Longfellow. And yet, that was precisely the intention of the poet: to compress numerous Spanish literary tropes into one representative play. *The Spanish Student* also captured well what was then expected of Spanish motifs: honor, chivalry, popular wit, government despotism, and Catholic mischief. It represented a significant step forward in the dissemination—and acceptance—of Spanish literature, especially at a time when most of the sources embedded in the play were not available in English. Ultimately, however, it was a minor literary work, written when Longfellow felt the need to go back to his memories of Spain in order to reconcile himself to the drudgery of teaching, and perhaps even to his own personal situation.[65]

That the dissemination of Spanish poetry—as well as other modern languages, including Portuguese—was indeed a major concern of Longfellow is demonstrated by his edition of *The Poets and Poetry of Europe* (1845). He included hundreds of poems and ballads from the twelfth to the nineteenth centuries, in translations by himself or by others. No such wealth of international poetry had ever been published in the United States, and thus the compilation represents an important development in the reception of foreign literature.[66] The book placed Spanish poetry in the larger context of European literature. Longfellow sought to emphasize the richness and uniqueness of national poetry, but in the company of compositions representing all the main languages of Western Europe. This catholicity of poetic interests was also reflected in the various meters he used in his own works.[67] With the publication of this volume, Longfellow effectively expanded the poetic reservoir of American literature.[68] This would not be his last effort, for in the 1870s he produced 31 volumes featuring poems from and on places around the world, including of course Spain. The *Poems of Places* (1876–1879) consisted of a selection of works celebrating cities, villages, geographical landmarks, by poets both native and foreign, mostly in translation. This was yet another way of making Spain—and other parts of the world—known to an American audience.[69] Longfellow added some of his own poems on Spanish subjects, such as "The Challenge" and "Castles in Spain" (from *Birds of Passage*), and "Guadarrama Pass" (from *The Spanish Student*). He also translated several poems concerning Spanish places by Teresa de Jesús (on Avila), Dante ("Saint Dominic," on Calahorra), Jorge Manrique (on Ocaña), and Gonzalo de Berceo (on both the convent of San Miguel and Simancas), thus revealing a preference for the moral and devotional poetry that had attracted him since his younger days.

Longfellow's Political Concerns

Longfellow had a natural inclination for literary work, and though he disliked personal involvement in politics, he nevertheless combined the two and followed the main political events of his time. He was, for instance, quite aware of the growing tensions between the United States and Mexico over Texas. To his father he mentioned the occupation of San Antonio by Mexican forces led by General Rafael Vásquez on March 5, 1842, a minor incident that lasted only two days, but which underscored the volatile nature of border issues.[70] As war loomed ever larger, Longfellow allowed himself some wishful thinking, "I do not fear that [the war] will take place," he wrote in his journal, "Deliberately to embrace Slavery and War with Mexico, is too much. The Southerners cannot be so mad."[71] Once the Polk administration declared war against Mexico, Longfellow was highly approving of his brother Samuel, then attending Harvard Divinity School, when he delivered a sermon in which he prayed for "the country in her hour of shame."[72] He similarly condemned American proslavery attempts, through the filibustering expeditions of Narciso López, to annex Cuba between 1849 and 1851.[73] Part of his rejection of armed confrontation reflected his agreement with Charles Sumner that, at least in the context of the United States at this time, slavery and expansionism were intimately related. Sumner had in addition rejected President Ulysses Grant's proposal to annex the island of Santo Domingo, in ways that "stirred me like the sound of a trumpet!"[74] Then, in 1873, Longfellow fully endorsed Sumner's call for restraint after Spanish authorities in Cuba seized the *Virginius*, and executed several Americans who were supplying weapons to Cuban insurgents. Both felt that the fledgling Spanish republic, which had just recently overthrown the monarchy, and was about to be overthrown itself, deserved some consideration.[75] But while Longfellow was clearly against war, his views about slavery were far more complex.

Slavery

Henry Wadsworth Longfellow was present at the Senate when Henry Clay pronounced his famous speech on the petitions for abolition (February 7, 1839). It was a most Whiggish speech, proclaiming state rights, sanctity of property, and an African colonization plan. It was also strongly critical of "the real ultra" abolitionists "who are resolved to persevere in the pursuit of their object at all hazards, and without regard to any consequences, however calamitous they may be."[76] Longfellow, who was in Washington to meet family and friends, recorded his impressions in a letter to his father, "Yesterday Mr. Clay made a great speech on Abolition, which I shall not report, as you will see it reported in the papers. It was highly interesting. Some tears were shed; a part of which, came from his own eyes. His voice reminded me of Dr. Channing."[77] This was not a ringing endorsement of mainstream Whig views on slavery, or those of Clay, but neither was it a condemnation. Longfellow, in fact, did not initially take strong positions on the issue. But when he did, he made a surprising choice, namely, to associate the themes of slavery, Spain, and Catholicism.

One of the poet's earliest, though private, reflections on the subject of slavery was his intention to write a tragedy based on the Haitian emancipation leader Toussaint L'Ouverture (1743–1803). "As soon as I can find or make leisure," he wrote in his journal, "I intend to write one upon that topic: thereby doing what my feeble talent enables me in the cause of slave emancipation."[78] Alas, he never undertook the project. It was only through the influence of his intimate friend Charles Sumner that he eventually made a more public pronouncement. It was indeed under his direct suggestion that Longfellow wrote his *Poems on Slavery* in 1842. He was leaving for Germany when Sumner told him: "I long for those verses on slavery," and challenged him to "write some stirring words that shall move the whole land."[79] The somewhat reluctant poet agreed, and wrote his verses on board the *Great Western* during his journey back from Europe in late 1842. Despite his diffidence, the poems were compelling. Longfellow dedicated his work to William E. Channing, who had died the same year, and presented the slaves' suffering in compassionate, not denunciatory ways. And yet, there was a very strong warning that the institution of slavery threatened the very life of the Republic. Using a biblical reference, he closed his volume as follows,

> There is a poor, blind Samson in this land,
>   Shorn of his strength and bound in bonds of steel,
> Who may, in some grim revel, raise his hand,
>   And shake the pillars of this Commonweal,
> Till the vast Temple of our liberties
> A shapeless mass of wreck and rubbish lies.[80]

Longfellow showed little enthusiasm for this work. He called it "a small affair" and feared that his poems would be misinterpreted by those who read them from a political perspective. When he wrote to his friend Henry Russell Cleveland, who was then convalescing in Cuba, he said of his verses, "I shall not dare to send them to you in

Cuba, for fear of having you seized as an Abolitionist."[81] He did, however, send them, "thinking they may furnish you with agreeable topics of conversation with the planters of Matanzas, Habana, and the neighborhood."[82] Still, he demonstrated how little he thought about slavery when he envisioned a visit to his friend in Cuba, "I wish I were away; enjoying with you the gay South; strolling under palm-trees and towering *ceibas*, or journeying on the banks of the Canimar [River] in a *Volante*, whose huge wheels, like the wheel of Fortune, should take us over the rough roads safely."[83]

The *Poems on Slavery* provide a unique window into Longfellow's political attitudes regarding slavery in the 1840s. He told William Plumer that "the spirit in which they are written is that of kindness—not denunciation—at all events not violence," and reiterated to John Forster that "they are written in a kindly—not a vindictive spirit. Humanity is the chord to be touched. Denunciation of Slave-holders would do more harm than good; besides, that is not my vein. I leave that to more ferocious natures."[84] But he grew impatient as letters came in expressing strong disagreement with his position. To George Lunt, he replied with a terse summation of his views on the matter:

1. I believe Slavery to be an unrighteous institution, based on the false maxim that Might makes Right.
2. I have great faith in doing what is righteous, and fear no evil consequences.
3. I believe that everyone has a perfect right to express his opinion on the subject of Slavery as on every other; nay, that every one ought so to do; until the Public Opinion of all Christendom shall penetrate into and change the hearts of the Southerners on this subject.
4. I would have no other *interference* than what is sanctioned by law.
5. I believe that when there is a *Will* there is a *Way*. When the whole country sincerely wishes to get rid of Slavery it will readily find the means.
6. Let us therefore do all we can to bring about this *Will*, in all gentleness and Christian charity. And God Speed the time.[85]

Whether he wanted it or not, the *Poems on Slavery* placed him among the enemies of the institution, and as such he made friends and foes. But he did not regret being in that position, especially because it was loyalty to Charles Sumner, not a determined plan of attack, that prompted his choice. On occasion, he had to assert his independence, as when he wrote that "though a strong anti-Slavery man, I am not a member of any society, and fight under no single banner."[86] He actually grew to dislike some of the Abolitionist positions, especially after he endured a barrage of criticism for what he thought was a minor issue: "The abolitionist papers are abusing me for publishing the Illustrated Edition [of his works] without the Slavery poems. What a nest of vipers these abolitionists are! One thing is certain, they shall never have me under their control."[87]

Longfellow separated the politics of Abolition from its human dimensions. In 1846, he met a former slave, Josiah Henson (1789–1877), who was now a preacher collecting funds for a school for emancipated blacks. Longfellow was very impressed by Henson's frank demeanor, but could not help notice that the man's right arm was "crooked and stiff," and later wrote in his journal that "it had been broken by a savage blow with a stake from a fence."[88] That was all the evidence he needed, and was distraught that the larger, more politicized issues on slavery would obscure this human side. He was also distressed that Slavery divided some of his closest friends. Anguished to do something, he contributed money to purchase the freedom of slaves. He also registered his bitterness about such events as passage of the Kansas-Nebraska bill (March 3–4, 1854), which he called, using a Prescottian theme, "that *noche triste* of our history,"[89] or the implementation of the Fugitive Slave Act in Boston, when a runaway slave was arrested in June 1854 and returned to his owner. In this latter occasion, he wrote bitterly in his journal that "I am sick and sorrowful with this infamous business. . . . Dirty work for a government, that is so loud about freedom as ours is, to be engaged in hunting fugitive slaves!"[90] But nothing prepared him for the brutal beating of Charles Sumner, which very nearly disabled the Senator, after he pronounced his speech "The Crime Against Kansas" (May 19–20, 1856). Longfellow was beside himself when he wrote to his friend, "I have no words to write you about this savage atrocity, only enough to express our sorrow and sympathy for yourself."[91] More reflection on the event did not abate his anger. He told the Senator,

> I have just been reading again your speech. It is the greatest voice, on the greatest subject, that has been uttered since we became a nation. No matter for insults,—we feel them with you; no matter for wounds,—we also bleed in them! You have torn the mask off the faces of traitors; and at last the spirit of the North is aroused.[92]

The attack brought the two friends closer than ever, but it did something else as well. Longfellow had only slowly embraced the cause of antislavery; now he was as determined against it as he was clear in its condemnation. Shortly before the incident, he had quoted a passage from Dante's *Purgatorio*: "For he who waits to be asked, and the need seeith, / Malignly already is leaning toward denial." He told Sumner that he found the verses applicable to those who recognized the evils of slavery, but would do nothing about it. He was perhaps reflecting on his own trek from mild to determined opposition, a trajectory and timing that was indeed common among Northerners. After the incident, he showed little doubt when he wrote to the convalescing Senator, "At length Freedom and Slavery stand face to face in the field as never before."[93] He saw no alternative to the Civil War, and supported the North strongly when it broke out. His own son, Charles, fought for the Union Army and was seriously wounded in the battle of New Hope Church.

Longfellow had many reasons to look intently into the subject of slavery. Few Americans, either for or against it, could ignore the issue and its escalating conflicts. But there were other reasons as well, and they pertained to the reflection on the origins of African slavery in the hemisphere. Spain had introduced it, and naturally became a subject of inquiry. Few had done as much as William H. Prescott to popularize the study of the Spanish monarchy in books from *Ferdinand and Isabella* to his unfinished *Philip the Second*. Moreover, in the 1850s, British historian Arthur Helps made the connection between Spanish imperialism and slavery even more explicitly. In the preface of his *The Spanish Conquest in America* (1855), Helps explained, "Some years ago, being much interested in the general subject of slavery, and engaged in writing upon it, I began to investigate the origin of modern slavery."[94] Thus he was led to the study of the Spanish conquest, and to the events and policies that introduced African slavery into the New World. He argued that the Catholic Church was centrally responsible for it, although for an apparently worthy cause: the protection of the Indians. Therefore, "bishops and monks [were] slow to perceive the mischief of any measure which might tend to save or favor large communities of docile converts." As a result, "the evil of negro importation must have appeared . . . comparatively a small evil."[95] Three centuries later, however, it was clear that the evil had acquired mammoth proportions, and was yet to be confronted. "An interesting, valuable book, I should say," Longfellow wrote to Charles Sumner, "[Helps] has looked deeply into the subject of Slavery."[96] So had he, but now wanted to look into Spanish history more closely. It is no coincidence, then, that his chilling poem "Torquemada" (*Tales of a Wayside Inn*), which contains his darkest reflections on Spain, was written in 1862, just as Union General Ambrose Burnside was leading his troops to the disastrous battle of Fredericksburg. I examine it more closely below.

Catholicism and Slavery

Already by the time of his inaugural address at Bowdoin, Longfellow had denounced the tendency of the Roman Catholic Church to become corrupt and oppressive. In the Middle Ages, he told his audience, "Europe groaned beneath the triple tyranny of her Kings, her feudal lords, and her licentious priesthood."[97] "The human mind," he added, "had become hoodwinked and *enslaved*."[98] Priests became warlike and greedy, and thus "the priesthood was enabled to set its foot so completely on the neck of people."[99] An even more direct connection between religious and chattel slavery appeared in a letter to his sisters, written while he was visiting Rome. People in "the Pope's dominions," he said, were so wretchedly poor on account of their religious observance that "the negro slaves within the precincts of the Southern States are their equals in liberty, and infinitely their superiors in every comfort."[100] Similar descriptions appeared later, as mentioned earlier, in Longfellow's *Outre-Mer* and in his private correspondence. But in the context of the Civil War, his portrayal of an oppressive Church acquired a more sinister character, in the form of the shocking story told in the *Tales of a Wayside Inn*.

The tale "Torquemada" takes place during the times of Ferdinand and Isabella, when "An old Hidalgo proud and taciturn" was so consumed by religious fanaticism that he became suspicious of the orthodoxy of his own daughters: "Jealous, suspicious, with no sense of shame, / A spy upon his daughters he became." Having overheard in their conversation something that seemed to confirm his fear of heterodoxy, he cried, "Heresy!" and denounced his daughters to the Grand Inquisitor. "To him the Hidalgo went, and at the gate / Demanded audience on affairs of state." As Torquemada listened approvingly and thanked him for his zeal, "A sacred frenzy seized the father's brain, / And mercy from that hour implored in vain." Thus the Hidalgo's children were arrested, imprisoned and sentenced to death by fire. Not satisfied with this, the father asked Torquemada, "Grant me one more request, one last desire, / With my own hand to light the funeral fire!" To this, the Grand Inquisitor replied, "'Son of the Church! Thine offering is complete; / Her servants through all ages shall not cease / To magnify thy deed. Depart in peace!'" The Hidalgo then proceeded with his ghastly deed.

In his journal, Longfellow noted upon finishing "Torquemada," that the poem was about "a dismal story of fanaticism; but in its main points historic."[101] He clarified that he had taken the story from Adolfo de Castro's *Historia de los protestantes españoles y de su persecución por Felipe II* (1851),[102] an author who, as we have seen in the controversy over the authenticity of *El Centón Epistolario* and *El Buscapié* (chapter 3), was less than careful about evidence. Moreover, the story mentioned by Castro was supposed to have happened in 1581 under Philip II, not during the reign of Ferdinand and Isabella, as Longfellow presented it. Thus the significance of the poem is not to be found in whether it was historical or not, but rather in the implication that Catholic fanaticism could so enslave the mind as to make a father the murderer of his own children. Castro himself said so directly: "The inquisitors saw in their man [the father] a model of a slave."[103] Such were the consequences of slavery, religious or otherwise, that reduced human beings to fuel for the running of a cruel machine. In Longfellow's poem, the Hidalgo himself died in a blaze of fire, consumed by flames as much as by his own fanaticism. As the poem suggests, the taciturn Hidalgo might now be dead and forgotten, "But Torquemada's name, with clouds o'ercast / Looms in the distant landscape of the Past, / Like a burnt tower upon a blackened hearth, / Lit by the fire of burning woods beneath!"

The great fire of nineteenth-century America, the Civil War, had burned too close to the poet's own home. His eldest child had been dangerously wounded, and when discharged, embarked on a listless life until his premature death at the age of 49. Some of his closest friends had been bitterly divided over the issue of slavery, and the Civil War separated them forever. Death, destruction, division, had all passed before the poet's increasingly weary eyes. To give expression to such horrors, the Spanish topic of Torquemada's deeds gave him the unspeakable words, the dismal thoughts, and the bitter reflections that war at home had provoked. When the dust settled, Longfellow slowly returned to the more benign side of the Spanish literary and artistic reservoir that he so much treasured. In "Castles in Spain"(1877), he could write that "The softer Andalusian skies / Dispelled the sadness and the gloom / . . . Making the land a paradise / Of beauty and of bloom."[104] He continued to read the major pieces of Spanish drama, and rejoiced at meeting his Spanish and Spanish American visitors (to be discussed presently). But in the end, it was Torquemada, who in the poem "Looms in the distant landscape of the past," that lingered as Longfellow's most lasting image of Spain.

Chapter 5

Outre-Mer: Longfellow's Hispanic Ties

We, as Catholics and of Spanish origin, must publicly thank you for the generous and sympathetic spirit with which you have treated our religion, our history, and our language.
—Rafael Pombo to Henry W. Longfellow, Bogotá, July 8, 1880

These comments by the noted Colombian poet Rafael Pombo may seem unusual, especially given Longfellow's "Torquemada" and his other statements about Catholicism and the Hispanic world. And yet, to many Spaniards and Spanish Americans increasingly weary of the demeaning rhetoric of "Manifest Destiny," Longfellow's work was welcome as sympathetic and even celebratory of Hispanic traditions. As such, he was unusually appreciated, becoming perhaps the most beloved American poet of the nineteenth century, and certainly among the most frequently translated.

Longfellow did not seek this influence. In fact he was surprised and flattered by it. As is discussed in this chapter, much of Longfellow's popularity came as a result of his willingness to engage in correspondence with Spaniards and Spanish Americans, and in his obliging hospitality when visitors from all parts of the Hispanic world knocked at the door of his Brattle Street home in Cambridge. Also, many of his themes, his calm and sympathetic tone, and his poetic expertise became a model for Hispanic counterparts who sought to shape national traditions in ways that he had obviously accomplished for the United States. Although Longfellow was perhaps the most influential American in this regard, he was in fact part of a larger, yet closely knit, community of Hispanists in the United States. It is also important to consider, especially in light of new evidence, Longfellow's emotional connection to Spain, which grounded his scholarship and poetry in a deeply personal framework.

The New England Network of Hispanists

After teaching at Bowdoin, Longfellow moved to Harvard College, where his closest collaborator was Francis Sales, the congenial Frenchman who had dutifully drilled Spanish language skills into generation upon generation of students. Longfellow knew little about his biography, as well might anyone born a whole generation later. But there was much history behind this man, whose original name was François Sala.

In April 1793, while living in Cádiz, the 20-year-old Sala was forced to make a quick decision. The Spanish government had ordered French subjects to leave Spain within three days if by sea, or eight days if by land across the Pyrenees, in retaliation for the execution of Louis XVI and in response to the outbreak of the French Revolutionary Wars. Sala learned that French nationals leaving by land had been brutally murdered by angry mobs. So he determined to leave by sea. Neutral vessels, however, were insufficient for the evacuation, even though passengers were packed "as thick as bales of cotton." Fortunately, a young American gentleman, William Foster, offered him passage on the American ship *Bald Eagle*, bound for Boston. The anguished Sala understood at once that this might be his only chance to survive, even if it meant to never see his homeland again. After a harrowing passage of 73 days across the Atlantic, due to bad weather and inexperienced sailors, he arrived in Boston on July 3. The following day he attended the Independence Day celebrations in town. John Quincy Adams, he recalled, was the speaker that year.

François Sala decided to weather the European political storm in Boston while using the time to learn English. Within three years, however, he had married and was making a modest living as a teacher of romance languages and occasional court translator. It looked as if his stay might be prolonged indefinitely. But then, in 1798, with war between the United States and France seemingly imminent, the Congress gave President John Adams extraordinary powers to deport or otherwise confine foreigners as needed. Sala decided, at that moment, to acquire U.S. citizenship in order to preempt yet another traumatic displacement. He also decided to change his name because he was tired of being asked how it should be pronounced; "it bothered and annoyed me tremendously," he said. Sala became Mr. Francis Sales, and lived for the rest of his long life in the Boston-Cambridge area. He seemed to have assumed an entirely new identity, for no one knew the particulars of his life until, nearing death, he penned a short autobiography.[1]

Sales was also the tireless editor of the main Spanish books adapted to language instruction during the antebellum period, including José Cadalso's *Cartas marruecas* (1827), *Selección de obras maestras dramáticas por Calderón de la Barca, Lope de Vega, y Moreto* (1828), *Colmena española* (1832), *Fábulas literarias de Tomás de Iriarte* (1832), and perhaps his greatest accomplishment, Cervantes's *Don Quixote* (1836).[2] Despite his knowledge and eagerness, Sales had trouble maintaining discipline among the students, not a rare difficulty at Harvard, but he compensated for it with his enormous patience and good humor. Longfellow protected Sales from the administration's attempts to oust him, but he could not control the dynamics of the College, or Sales's deteriorating health. One of Sales's students in the 1840s, Andrew Peabody, recalled how his classmates "put him to his wit's end in the vain endeavor to preserve some show of discipline." In vain indeed, because as Peabody put it, "two or three times [Sales] invited my aid in restoring, or to speak more correctly, in establishing, order, which lasted while I staid."[3] The likeable teacher was vulnerable in this regard, and when Edward Everett assumed the presidency of Harvard in 1846, he tried to fire Sales and get Longfellow to assume his duties. "I will consent to nothing that shall harm a hair of Old Sales's venerable head," an upset Longfellow wrote in his journal.[4] But then, in late 1846, Sales suffered a grievous accident from which he never fully recovered. Still, Longfellow stood by his colleague, undoubtedly out of compassion, but also out of respect for the man's knowledge and experience.

When Francis Sales became seriously ill in January 1851, Longfellow was there to aid and comfort him. By May, as the illness lingered, the poet began to raise money to assist his colleague. "Poor old man!" he wrote in his journal, "how the clouds gather, cold and gray, round his last days."[5] Longfellow wanted to help tactfully, and thus contrived a scheme that he knew would charm the Spanish instructor. He put money into a paper box, writing on it the Spanish inscription "Aquí está enterrada el alma del Licenciado Pedro García" [here lies the soul of the graduate Pedro García], a reference taken from the preface of *Gil Blas*. He attached a note stating that Sales's friends were eager to help because, "sabiendo que de cuantos ladrones en el mundo hay, no hay peor ni más molesto que la enfermedad, pues quiere quitarnos al mismo tiempo la vida y el bolsillo" [knowing that among the world's many thieves, there is no one worse or more annoying than illness, because it tries to rob us of both life and purse]. Longfellow then added a clever line, from Francisco de Quevedo's *Letrilla*, to conclude that in such cases, "Poderoso señor es Don Dinero" [Mr. Money is indeed a powerful master].[6] Sales was delighted and replied with a polite letter, also in Spanish, in the same playful tone.[7] The charitable deed clearly lifted the man's spirits, and he rallied. By August, he was happy to report that he was ready to resume his duties "as Instructor in Spanish."[8] Later, he found out that the poet had arranged for the payment of his medical expenses.

> I am amazed at the number of unexpected noble and generous deeds which have been conferred on me by neighbors, friends and pupils since I had the misfortune of being overthrown a few years ago by a powerful steed attached to a sleigh, and from which I escaped as it were by a miracle, being crushed to death, and the afflictive disease which has tormented me since December 1850.[9]

Longfellow was quite moved by the man's modesty and gratitude, and was only sorry that there would be further occasions to aid the rapidly declining colleague. He chose, however, to remain anonymous, and represented himself as merely the conveyor of financial support. "I cannot imagine," wrote Sales, "what merits or services can bring on me such generous tokens of friendship and regard."[10] The grateful man did not last long. He was ill enough to resign in December 1853, and was bedridden by February 1854, when Longfellow paid him his last visit. "Good old man," he wrote in his journal, "He is dying. There he lay, emaciated and sharp, and sometimes panting for breath. He clasped both my hands and said, in a feeble voice 'Kiss me'; and then 'Don't forget me!' and I took leave of him forever."[11] He died on February 16, 1854. His old friend William Foster, who had rescued him in Spain more than 60 years before, attended the funeral.

Thus passed the man whom Charles Sumner recalled as "unique elegant [*sic*] in appearance, kind in manner and bountiful in efforts to teach."[12] Longfellow was devastated by the loss of Sales. Although he had already decided that he would not continue at Harvard, it is perhaps not coincidental that he formally resigned his professorship on the day Sales died. He could not conceive of continuing without the good-natured assistance of his Spanish instructor.

Among the Hispanists, Longfellow was also close to William H. Prescott, perhaps closer on account of age. The historian, who was nine years Longfellow's senior,

occasionally served as member of the examining committee in the Modern
Languages department at Harvard, giving them several opportunities to interact as
colleagues.[13] Longfellow grew to admire Prescott, and made frequent notes of their
multiple social encounters. He also noted, read carefully, and gave away copies or
recommended some of the historian's major publications. Longfellow did not fail to
tell his friends, or write in his journal, about the multiple occasions when he met
Prescott, either fortuitously or at social events. He gave the following portrait of
Prescott upon the publication of *Ferdinand and Isabella*,

> This morning as I was sitting at breakfast, a gentleman on horseback sent up word that
> I should come down to him. It was Prescott, author of *Ferdinand*. He is an early riser,
> and rides about the country. There on his horse sat the *great author*. He is one of the
> best fellows in the world, and much my friend;—handsome, gay, and forty:—a great
> diner-out;—and fond of good wine—gentle, companionable, and modest, and quite
> astonished to find himself so famous all of a sudden.[14]

A few years later, Longfellow told his father of the publication of the *History of the
Conquest of Mexico*: "We have just commenced it, and it promises to be exceedingly
well-written and interesting."[15] In some cases, he complemented his own work
with readings from Prescott's books. While he was writing *The Song of Hiawatha*,
for example, he was concurrently reading the historian's *Conquest of Peru*.[16] He was
also delighted to receive the first two volumes of Prescott's unfinished *Philip the
Second*, "the Overture of your grand Opera."[17] He was particularly impressed by
some episodes, like the death of Don Carlos, Philip II's son, which had attracted
much attention on both sides of the Atlantic since Schiller's work was first published
in 1785.[18]

Prescott was somewhat of a social magnet, and his friends, including Longfellow,
visited him in Nahant, his summer seaside residence, and later when he moved to
nearby Lynn. In the summer of 1841, for instance, Longfellow reported seeing
Prescott, Jared Sparks, George Bancroft, and Hugh Legaré.[19] Thus, a closely knit
network of scholars and friends, many of whom shared a strong interest in Hispanic
literature and history, developed during these years. He also visited Frances (Fanny)
Calderón de la Barca as often as he could, or as often as the peripatetic Scot and her
Spanish husband Ángel were in town. These visits almost invariably included
Prescott, perhaps the closest friend of the couple.[20] The historian was famous for his
conversational skills, but the reserved poet occasionally grew impatient with
Prescott's studied social persona, as when he noted "It is curious how Prescott
always says the same things over and over. His conversation seems stereotyped: one
could think he had got it by heart."[21] And yet, there can be no doubt of his esteem
for Prescott, and especially his sense of loss when the historian passed away in 1859.
"Yes, he is dead," he wrote to Charles Sumner, "We shall see that cheerful, sunny
face no more! Ah me! What a loss this is to us all, and how much sunshine it will take
out of the social life of Boston!"[22]

The poet could still count on George Ticknor, whom he had known for many
years and whom he saw frequently after his return from his second trip to Europe.
Longfellow was able to observe how intensely Ticknor worked on his *History of
Spanish Literature*, and would on occasion spend several days at his home in Boston.
There was also a lighter side to their relationship, as Ticknor often invited him for
dinners and social events involving visits of literary figures. Sometimes he spent

Christmas at the Ticknors's imposing house on Park Street, by the edge of the Common. Their relationship cooled significantly when Charles Sumner, who was becoming increasingly vocal about slavery, was cast out of Ticknor's circle in 1843.[23] Longfellow continued to visit Park Street, but scaled down his visits after that year. Later, George Ticknor's support for Secretary of State Daniel Webster's conciliatory position on the Fugitive Slave Act further deepened their differences. But if slavery divided them, other issues brought them together, such as their Spanish interests, which ranged from the sharing of books and other sources, to the vexing matter of international copyright. They extended to the most erudite exchanges, as when Ticknor commented in exquisite detail some fine points of Longfellow's translation of Jorge Manrique's *Coplas*.[24] Sadly, the early closeness of Longfellow and Ticknor could not survive the political storms of the 1850s and 1860s concerning slavery. Even in intellectual matters, the differences grew sharper. Longfellow found much to criticize when Ticknor published his *Life of William Hickling Prescott* in 1864. The poet registered no emotion when he recorded Ticknor's death in his journal in 1871.[25]

Another close friend was James Russell Lowell, his successor as the Smith Professor at Harvard, with whom he shared the same passion for Spanish subjects, and especially for Spanish proverbs and witticisms. They enjoyed each other's company until Lowell eventually left for Spain as U.S. minister in 1877, never to meet again. While there, Lowell served as a conduit for the communication between the poet and the Royal Spanish Academy, which had elected him corresponding member of the Institution in 1877. Longfellow missed the lively exchanges with Lowell, but he could still converse on Spanish subjects with Charles Frederick Bradford, the author of a remarkably erudite annotation of Diego Clemencín's *Don Quixote* (1833–1839). They often exchanged translations and scholarly works concerning Spanish and Portuguese languages and literature.[26]

This cluster of experts on Spanish subjects was essential for Longfellow's sustained interest in Hispanic culture. He consulted with them on the fine points of literary history, exchanged sources, and ascertained the meaning of arcane words essential for his research and translations. Most importantly, they constituted a support network of like-minded scholars and friends who were determined to establish Hispanic studies in the United States. Occasionally, they would come together to receive visitors from abroad. But it was Longfellow who most frequently greeted these visitors, and who left the most detailed record of their contacts.

The Spanish Connection

As well as in Latin America, where he became a beloved poet, Longfellow was greatly admired in Spain, especially in the last quarter of the century. His relationship with Spain was also intensely personal. He maintained his long friendship with José Cortés y Sesti, the young member of the Spanish Royal Guard (born 1810), whom he met in Madrid in 1827. Their correspondence speaks of strong feelings of friendship, lasting nearly thirty years despite differences in careers and the enormous distance that separated them. Cortés actually moved to the United States in 1832, lived with Longfellow in Brunswick, and then tried—unsuccessfully—to establish himself in Portland, Boston, and New York before returning to Spain in July 1834. It is thanks to Cortés, in addition to unpublished portions of his journal, that we learn some important facts about Longfellow's Hispanic ties that are not covered in his biographies.

Longfellow's first love affair took place in Spain, thus perhaps cementing his emotional relationship with the Iberian land. While in Madrid, Longfellow took rooms at the house of Mr. Valentín González at 16 Calle de la Montera, and fell in love with his daughter Florencia. Longfellow mentioned her in his journal with Victorian economy and prudery, but the references speak of a strong intimacy and attachment.[27] There is also an extant letter from Florencia to Longfellow, but it is a polite addendum to her father's own letter to the poet. Even so, she managed to write such sentimental expressions as "I will never forget you, no matter how many years pass," and the hopeful "If we ever have the joy of meeting again."[28] Cortés intervened as a go-between, and in his letters to Longfellow, Florencia added post-scripts where her sentiments were more direct: "My dear Enrique," she wrote in one, "I learn from your letter to Cortés that you are not feeling well. This causes me great concern . . . you must relieve me from this anxiety."[29] When Longfellow left Spain, he felt emotionally deprived, very nearly losing interest in the world around him. While waiting for passage home in 1829, he took the time to write a poem in Spanish, with perhaps more feeling than skill, thinking about "someone I know in Spain:" "Linda alaja! tus ojos bellos / Dos claras estrellas son: / y cuando me miro en ellos / me palpita el corazón." [Your beautiful eyes, oh lovely jewel / like two clear stars glow / And when I look into them / I feel my heart flutter].[30]

As time passed and it became clear that Longfellow would not return to Spain any time soon, Cortés had the duty to tell his friend that Florencia was engaged to someone else, a Cuban by the name Ambrosio de Meza. He told him that Don Valentín had said that he would be much happier if Florencia had married Longfellow, and that he himself had asked her directly about her feelings. She replied to Cortés that "I cannot love anyone as much as Enrique."[31] The marriage to Meza did not take place, in the end, but the chances for Longfellow and Florencia dissipated as well, as the poet became established and assumed the responsibilities of a professor and a proper New Englander.

Once again a part of a tightly knit community in Portland, Longfellow became engaged to the young and frail Mary Storer Potter in 1830. Little is known about her and their courtship, but a marriage soon followed (September 14, 1831) that seemed to have pleased their respective parents more than the couple itself. Sadly, Mary did not survive long, the victim of two miscarriages.[32] For the time being, as a married man and a responsible professor, Longfellow saw the intense recollections of Florencia and of Spain recede. All that was left of her was the lingering memory that can only be traced through Cortés's letters. "You will take pity on me," wrote Cortés on one occasion, referring to the leave he had himself taken from a loved one, "remembering your own experience."[33] When Cortés insinuated that Longfellow was better off not having married Florencia, and said something nega-tive about her, Longfellow was furious. "Alright," responded the chastised Cortés, who almost cancelled his planned trip to the United States as a result, "I will not say anything else about a matter that so touches your heart [*que tanto te llega al corazón*]."[34] Neither mentioned Florencia again, at least not in writing.

Longfellow continued to be on very close terms with Cortés after his wife Mary died in 1835. The normally reserved Longfellow told him of his growing love for Fanny Appleton, whom he had met in Europe and whose acquaintance he renewed in Boston. He was soon in love with her. Unaware of the ups and downs of that courtship, Cortés wrote from Spain in 1838 to say that "you are probably married by now, for you seemed quite excited about the woman in Boston."[35] Longfellow wrote to Cortés on April 18, 1838, to tell him more about Fanny. "You seem to be much in love," Cortés replied, "with such a rich and beautiful woman."[36] The Spaniard seemed to recall having met Fanny at a party in George Ticknor's home, but preserved no clear memory. When he finally learned the good news of the marriage, the irreverent Cortés congratulated Longfellow for marrying the "Señorita Tonelada de Manzanas," a playful mistranslation of the name Appleton.[37] As Cortés settled into the routine of life in Spain, he grew nostalgic about his youthful experience in the United States, and pleaded for a visit from Longfellow and Fanny. That never happened, but the strength of their friendship provides a clear demonstration that the poet's relationship to the country, which he would later recall so beautifully in "Castles in Spain" (1877), was firmly rooted in intense personal experiences.

Despite his personal involvement, and in contrast to Prescott and Ticknor, Longfellow's work did not have an immediate impact in Spain. While the historians wrote prose on known events, Longfellow's more evocative poetry found fewer translators. Indeed, it was not until the 1870s that his poems began to be included in anthologies and periodicals in Spain. Longfellow's *Evangeline* enjoyed the widest circulation, in translations by either Spaniards or Latin Americans. In fact, the first translation of this poem was published in 1871 by Carlos Morla Vicuña, a Chilean diplomat residing in New York. In Spain itself, Vicente de Arana translated and included *Evangeline* in his collection *Oro y Oropel* (*Gold and Tinsel*) in 1876. There was an important difference in the two translations, in that Morla rendered Longfellow's hexameters in *Ottava rima*, while Arana did it in less demanding prose. Still, none of the compelling force of the poem was lost in translation, and others would try their hand at it as well.[38] By the 1870s, Longfellow was widely known and appreciated in Spain. Fermín de la Puente Apezechea of the Spanish Royal Academy said so explicitly in 1875, intimating to a colleague that the Academy would be honored to count Longfellow among its members.[39]

The institution was at the time cultivating relations with Latin America, and also with Hispanists in the United States. The Academy formed a committee, the *Comisión de Academias Correspondientes Americanas*, in charge of promoting closer relations with New World scholars. As a member of this commission, De la Puente eagerly sought contacts across the Atlantic. One of these contacts was Antonio Flores, the Ecuadorian minister to the United States, who knew Longfellow personally and respected him both as a poet and as a Hispanist. De la Puente himself had translated Longfellow's "Sand of the Desert in an Hour-Glass," and could, therefore, appreciate his merits. In short, the interest was part of a larger effort to build cultural bridges across the Atlantic.

The appointment materialized after three members of the Academy, Patricio de la Escosura, Manuel Cañete, and Juan Valera formally nominated Longfellow for corresponding membership in November 1877. James Russell Lowell was delighted to tell Longfellow that there was a bit of a dispute about who would second the nomination (Juan Valera did) for, as the Permanent Secretary Manuel Tamayo y Baus put it, "tiene muchos apasionados aquí el señor Longfellow [because Mr. Longfellow has so many passionate admirers here]."[40] The American bard was formally and unanimously elected by the full body of the Academy on December 13, 1877, after pronouncing him "a poet of universal fame, and a fine lover [*fino amante*] of our language and literature."[41] That the enthusiasm was genuine can be seen in an informal letter from Tamayo y Baus to Charles F. Bradford (who was also elected to the Academy): "It is with intimate jubilation that I write to tell you that, last night, Mr. Longfellow was unanimously elected corresponding member of this corporation."[42] When he learned about it, Longfellow was a bit puzzled by the formalities, but clearly pleased.

Despite the recognition of the Academy, and the enthusiasm of others who read or translated his work, there was not much in the way of serious literary criticism of Longfellow's work in Spain. Indeed, it was not until 1883 that the librarian, linguist, and amateur historian Víctor Suárez Capalleja (1845–1903) articulated some of the reasons for the importance of Longfellow's poetry in Spain. His *Estudios sobre Longfellow (vida y obras)* (Studies on Longfellow [Life and Works])[43] provided a favorable, indeed celebratory coverage of the American poet's work. His assessment, however, was based on the fundamentally wrong assumption that Longfellow was Catholic, an assumption Suárez derived from the reading of selected poems, some vague and secondhand biographical information, and some invented touches such as the poet's death in the faith (13–14). Still, and however partial, Suárez provided an impressive array of poems in translation by various Spaniards (in addition to Vicente de Arana, by Miguel Gutiérrez, Baquero Almansa, Juan de Izaguirre, and Teodoro Llorente), which suggests that Longfellow appealed to a wide segment of the Spanish intellectual milieu. Suárez included translations of many of the poet's most famous early lyrics. But he made no mistake about his assessment that the most important poetry—and relevant for Spain—was Longfellow's religious poetry. Suárez devoted extensive treatment to "The Psalm of Life," "The Ladder of St. Augustine," and "Excelsior," a trilogy that he considered a "true gem," not only of American poetry, but also "*de todos los pueblos*" [of all peoples]. These poems provided an antidote, in his view, to the "epicurean philosophy of pleasure, and the insensitive and contemptuous philosophy of the Stoics." The mysticism of "The Ladder of St. Augustine," in particular, was genuine because it was Catholic, "in contrast to the egotistic, inert, and infirm," mysticism of other unnamed religions (37). Suárez saved his most florid praise, perhaps not surprisingly, for Longfellow's *Evangeline*, which he regarded as an "immortal" work (69). The Spanish critic was particularly attracted to this poem because it exposed the very cruelties that the British ascribed to the Spaniards in the New World, thus anticipating by three decades the fuller treatment of the subject in Julián Juderías's *La Leyenda Negra* (1914). It was the religious message, however, that he emphasized the most. "This admirable poem," he wrote, "is not only moral and religious; it is also Catholic." It was a Catholic poem, he added, "because only Catholicism, that great pyramid of light and truth, can offer such splendid beauties, and so many marvels, as those that enrich *Evangeline*" (93).

Suárez found evidence of Catholic religiosity everywhere in Longfellow's work, in some obvious places, such as "The Golden Legend," and in others less so, like *The Song of Hiawatha*, where he construed the arrival of the Jesuits in the closing stanzas of the poem as demonstration of Longfellow's Catholic inclinations. Such single-minded search for confirming evidence led him to ignore the damning passages about clergy in *The Spanish Student*,[44] or dismiss the devastating critique of Catholicism contained in "Torquemada" (*Tales of a Wayside Inn*). Suárez knew perfectly well about the latter, but regretted that Longfellow should have used a Spanish story to illustrate religious fanaticism, when "he would have made a better choice by looking at the fagots lit by Calvin in Geneva" (26). Such a selective reading is perhaps to be expected from the theology-trained, ultra-Catholic Suárez, but his book reveals a desire to address an even larger issue, not entirely unconnected to Catholicism. In his discussion of *The Song of Hiawatha*, Suárez celebrated the poem as a sensitive rejection of the "noisy utilitarian progress, the dazzling conquests by the 'modern idea,' and the arrogant insolences of success [*éxito*]" (107). Here lies perhaps the key to his agenda: he embraced and promoted the poetry of the American author because he believed it to be the best antidote against a creeping modernity, whose components he listed as "pessimism," "socialism," "radicalism," and "naturalism or realism" (51). Suárez was not the only Spanish enemy of modernity, let alone the only Catholic European critic of it, but he was unique in marshaling the poetry of Longfellow to invoke a higher realm, and a Catholic sensitivity, to deal with the vexing problems of the age.[45]

In light of Suárez's assumptions about Longfellow's beliefs, a note of clarification is necessary. Although he was celebrated for his sensitivity toward religious difference, Longfellow was quite sure about his own Protestant beliefs. When he thanked the Irish writer Aubrey Thomas de Vere for the gift of his *May Carols* (1857), for example, Longfellow told him that he had read his poems, "not with such complete sympathy, perhaps, as if I were of your faith, instead of being a Protestant; but still with sympathy enough to give me an understanding heart."[46] It was sympathy for the different versions of Christianity, indeed, that transpired in his *Christus: A Mystery*. To Karl Keck, a German translator and correspondent, he stated that "I have striven to exhibit the simplicity of Christianity in its origin; some of its Medieval aspects, and some of the shapes it assumed under Protestantism."[47]

Like his friend Prescott, Longfellow equated Protestantism with being an American. He turned down an Order of Knighthood from the government of Italy because "as an American, a Protestant and Republican" he could not consistently accept it from a Catholic monarchy.[48] He turned down another such offer, in 1868, on the same grounds.[49] During a visit to Rome later in the year, he felt the urge to write to Louis Agassiz that "you may be sure that I grow every day more Protestant, more Republican and more American, if possible."[50]

Because Longfellow never returned to Spain after his youthful sojourn in 1827, and never visited a country in the New World other than Canada, most of the Spaniards and Latin Americans he met came to his home, or corresponded with him from various locations. Intellectuals as well as individuals holding the highest offices of the land, or suffering the rigors of political exile, sought his correspondence and his company. These acquaintances were numerous and quite important. For example, he met and corresponded with Mariano Cubí y Soler (1801–1875), the author of an important Spanish grammar widely used in the United States.[51] He identified Cubí to his father as "a Spanish gentleman from Ma[h]on," who had come to visit him in Cambridge in 1840.[52] A year later, Longfellow reviewed the sixth edition of Cubí's grammar for the *North American Review*, which he praised as "one of the best Spanish grammars in use; and is alike remarkable for correctness, perspicuity, and completeness."[53] Visitors such as Cubí often registered the gracious welcome and hospitality offered by Longfellow. Writing from Jackson, Louisiana, where he had gone to study the creole language in 1840, Cubí wrote "en el corazón español jamás se borran los favores recibidos [kindness is never forgotten in the Spanish heart]."[54] Longfellow made time to discuss matters well beyond grammar, as when he met Spanish Admiral Bernabé de Polo, who came accompanied by Antonio Flores, the Ecuadorian minister and future president of the country, or to have dinner with the Secretary of the Spanish legation, Miguel de los Santos Bañuelos.[55] A good example of New England hospitality, Longfellow rarely refused a social call, be it from a well-known visitor, or anyone simply attracted to his reputation.

Latin American Contacts

Latin Americans received Longfellow's work even earlier than Spain and with more consistent enthusiasm. From the very start of the poet's career, Latin Americans saw his work as addressing the fundamental challenges facing the newly independent region as it struggled to build modern nations: the place of slavery in those countries that retained it; the relationship between the expansion of the State and the impact on Indian lands and peoples, and the harnessing of nature to satisfy the economic needs of developing nations. Longfellow's work provided the best literary vehicles for the promotion of some civic projects such as love of country, the place of tradition, and the advancement of national aims. It was seen as having enough content and richness to respond to all of these concerns.

It is not surprising, then, that Latin Americans read, translated, or visited Longfellow as they wrestled with their own questions about the nature and direction of nationhood—varied as it was—in Latin America. One of Longfellow's most notable contacts was Pedro de Alcántara, better known as Dom Pedro II, the emperor of Brazil. When Dom Pedro visited the United States in 1876, Longfellow was quite pleased to receive a friendly letter from him announcing his visit to Cambridge.[56] "I need not tell you," the poet replied in French, "how glad we will be to welcome you in Cambridge." He apologized for perhaps contravening etiquette, but said that his informality was due to writing "to the man rather than to the emperor" [*C'est à l'Homme plutôt qu'à l'Empereur que j'écris*].[57] When Dom Pedro did come to visit on June 10, 1876, Longfellow treated him with to a dinner that included Ralph Waldo Emerson, Louis Agassiz, Thomas Gold Appleton, and Oliver Wendell Holmes. He noted in his journal that Dom Pedro was "a hearty, genial, noble personage, and very liberal in his views."[58] He reported with glee to his friend George Washington Greene that "The dinner was very jovial and pleasant."[59] Longfellow developed a sincere affection for the emperor, even though he could not have approved of his presiding over a slave society. "I wish you could know the pleasant and grateful memories you have left behind you in this country," he wrote to Dom Pedro after his return to Brazil in 1877, "particularly under this roof are these memories prized and cherished."[60] Again in 1879, in response to a letter from the emperor, Longfellow replied, "Need I say with how much gratification I recall your visit here; our conversation in this room [Longfellow's study], our walk on the veranda?"[61] Dom Pedro had written fondly of the conversations with him in that same veranda, recalling his "passion for poetry," and paying homage to "the author of Hiawatha and Evangeline."[62] The emperor invited the poet to visit Rio de Janeiro in 1880, but Longfellow was by this time too ill to travel. He was probably spared the sights of a Brazil in the throes of civil confrontation. By 1888, slavery was gone from the land—and so, soon, would be his friend, the enlightened Dom Pedro II.

What is remarkable about the Longfellow-Dom Pedro relationship is their poetic dialogue. Dom Pedro reminded Longfellow of a "modern Haroun Al Raschid,"[63] the Abassid caliph on whom the poet would write the verses of that name included in *Kéramos* (1877): "Haroun Al Raschid bowed his head: / Tears fell upon the page he read." Indeed, Dom Pedro had struck Longfellow as a humble man skeptical of the real power of kings. The monarch, for his part, had followed the poet's career closely and even translated his poem "King Robert of Sicily" (*Tales of a Wayside Inn*) as "O Canto do Siciliano. El Rei Roberto da Sicilia" in July 1864. "The translation is very faithful and very successful," Longfellow wrote in response, "The double rhymes give a new grace to the narrative, and the old Legend sounds very musical in the soft accents of the Portuguese."[64] Indeed, Dom Pedro had rendered Longfellow's poem with impressive fidelity, not only in terms of its tone and intent, but also in terms of the almost equal number of lines, a remarkable accomplishment in translations from English to the Romance languages.[65]

Longfellow enjoyed his personal relationship with the emperor, but his contacts and interests also embraced the larger field of Portuguese literature. For instance, he appreciated the work of James E. Hewitt, who sent the poet his translation of the first canto of Camões's *Os Lusiadas*, which elicited warm, favorable comments from Longfellow.[66] Present in his library was the author Miguel Maria Lisbôa's second edition of his *Romances históricos* (1866), which included a translation of "Robert of Sicily," inscribed to the poet.[67] The Portuguese Miguel Street de Arriaga, of Fayal in the Azores, sent him his own translation of *Evangeline* with the inscription "como testemunho de sua admiração e respeito" [as proof of my admiration and respect], rendering Longfellow's hexameters into Portuguese verse.[68] Franklin Doria of Brazil also translated *Evangeline* and inscribed the published copy he sent him "em homenagem a seu genio" [in homage to your genius].[69] Clearly, Longfellow had a significant presence in the Luso-Brazilian world.

In Spanish America, Longfellow had even more contacts. He met Domingo Faustino Sarmiento (1811–1888), the flamboyant writer and statesman who played a large role in the politics of two countries, Chile and his native Argentina, and who had an even larger role in Latin American culture.[70] Sarmiento was keenly aware of the utility of literature for advancing the goals of nation building in nineteenth-century Latin America. While in exile in Chile from the repressive regime of Juan Manuel de Rosas in the 1840s, he composed his famous *Facundo* (1845), a book that drew a contrast between "civilization" and "barbarism," which soon became one of the most enduring metaphors for understanding the predicament of the region after independence. Unlike many other writers during the period, sadly driven into exile, or killed, Sarmiento returned triumphantly to his homeland and had a unique opportunity to implement his views on education, culture, and politics. In the 1860s, he became Argentine ambassador to the United States, and in that capacity he traveled extensively around the country. He was in Cambridge and Boston in October 1865, meeting Longfellow at the house of Benjamin A. Gould. The American poet recorded how excited he was to try his Spanish, "the first time for six years or more," with Sarmiento.[71] He apparently made an excellent impression, for Sarmiento later wrote to compliment him, "I recall hearing you pronounce Spanish better than we do it in this part of America."[72] In *Las Escuelas* (1866), Sarmiento printed his recollections of Longfellow by referring to him as "the most notable poet in the English language, who also commands Spanish admirably."[73]

When they met, they spoke mostly of literary matters, especially the dearth of books from Spanish America, which prompted Sarmiento to send him several Argentine books over the years. He also sent him a copy of the French edition of his *Facundo* (1853), which Longfellow acknowledged as "full of interest and information." The poet added that "the 'Ruban Rouge' [the red ribbon used to proclaim loyalty to the dictator Juan Manuel de Rosas] would be a good theme for a romance or an opera."[74] Longfellow was perfectly acquainted with Sarmiento and his writings, and when Mary Peabody Mann (1806–1887) tried to recruit his help to get the Argentine ambassador an honorary degree from Harvard, he responded "I know him personally," and as "I have great regard for him," he would be pleased to see him receive the distinction.[75] The honorary degree, however, was not offered, as Harvard intended to bestow it upon academics. Mary Mann later approached him for help translating portions of Sarmiento's *Facundo*, which was titled in English as *Life in the Argentine Republic in the Days of the Tyrants*, but the poet was too busy and politely declined.[76] He did, however, stay in touch, either through correspondence or through common friends. There was a gap of communication when Sarmiento became president of Argentina (1868–1874), but the contact was soon resumed. Sarmiento thought of Longfellow while celebrating the first centennial of U.S. independence at the American legation in Buenos Aires, and wrote a warm letter of remembrance to the poet. He also kept a bust of Longfellow on his desk, which is today at the Museo Histórico Sarmiento in Argentina.[77] Longfellow, for his part, did not forget his Argentine friend. A letter from scientist Benjamin Gould, who was in Córdoba at the time, shows that the poet sent Sarmiento an inscribed copy of his *Ultima Thule*.[78] Sadly, by the time the book was in the former Argentine president's hands, Longfellow was dead. Sarmiento wrote an obituary for the press, outlining the main events of the poet's life, and recording his own cherished memories.[79] Longfellow, he wrote, was enthusiastic about the scenery of the Argentine plains as depicted in his *Facundo*, and he duly recorded the poet's reaction to the story of the red ribbon. Sarmiento also mentioned some of Longfellow's works, including *The Spanish Student*, but concentrated on *Evangeline*, which he described as "*su triunfo como poeta*" [his triumph as a poet]. This poem was "a modern Odyssey memorializing the colonization, indeed the foundation of the United States." It was that aspect of the poet's activity that resonated with Sarmiento: his remarkable ability to define the poetics of nationhood.[80]

The Cuban "Nightingales"

Among Longfellow's frequent Latin American visitors there was an unusual concentration of Cubans, in part because many New Englanders spent time there, in part because there was enough commercial traffic to ensure that a number of islanders would come to the major ports on the U.S. Atlantic seaboard. As one writer for the Brook Farm paper *The Harbinger* put it in 1847, "Every day brings to our ports vessels laden with the luxuries of this delicious clime [Cuba], and every day of this inclement season takes some drooping invalid to breath in new life with its balmy air."[81] Sophia Willard Dana Ripley taught several Cubans at Brook Farm, and it was she who first introduced one of them, Nicolás Vinageras, to Longfellow. She had developed an interest in Cuba while reading Sophia Peabody's (later Hawthorne) manuscript *Cuba Journal*, and her interest grew to include Cuban literature.[82] On

April 20, 1847, Longfellow wrote in his Journal,

> Had a visit from Mrs. George Ripley of Brook Farm. She has several young West Indians with her at school, and through them has discovered that Cuba is "a nest of human nightingales" namely poets. She has written a poem on the subject, and is very enthusiastic about her new discovery. The principal bards are [José Jacinto] Milanés, [Francisco] Orgaz, Rodan [*sic*], Plácido [Gabriel de la Concepción Valdés, and] Heredia. The last two I knew before. Plácido was a mulatto, condemned and hanged for a slave revolt. Heredia was long in this country; and published his poems in New York.[83]

A few days later, Vinageras brought Longfellow copies of works by Milanés, Plácido, and a collection of poems titled *Aguinaldo Matanzero*. Longfellow read them with interest, but confessed that he knew quite little about their authors, with the exception (apparently forgetting Plácido) of Heredia.[84] Vinageras was more than willing to enlighten the somewhat overwhelmed Longfellow. In a long letter from Brook Farm, he called the poet's attention to the works of Milanés, Rafael María Mendive, and Francisco Javier Blanchie.[85] He also offered to send more works from Cuba. Although the letters by Longfellow to Vinageras are not extant, it is obvious that the poet gave the young man several of his poems for distribution in Cuba. From Havana, Matanzas, and later Charleston, Vinageras literally showered Longfellow with a tropical storm of poetic names, including Leopoldo de Turla, Narciso de Foxá, Ramón Herrera, José Betancourt, Gertrudis Gómez de Avellaneda, Juan and Francisco Orgaz, Ramón Vélez, and Mercedes de Mendoza. Some, he felt, had been unjustly omitted in William Henry Hurlbert's 1849 article on Spanish American poetry in the *North American Review*.[86]

Vinageras was not alone in alerting Longfellow to the richness of Cuban poetry. The brothers Antonio (1819–1901) and Eusebio (1823–1893) Guiteras from Matanzas sent him Cuban books and then visited him in June 1849. Longfellow was a bit startled when the visitors appeared, having just woken up from "a long *siesta*," but soon warmed up to the company: "Don Eusebio is a very handsome fellow; and both are very agreeable and are Cuban Anti-Slavery Men!"[87] This comment, perhaps better than any other, provides a key to Longfellow's appeal to Cubans who were well aware of his position regarding slavery, as articulated most clearly in his *Poems on Slavery* (1842). As poets and literary scholars, they saw Longfellow's quiet condemnation of the institution as representative of their own feelings. The Guiteras brothers followed up with another shower of books, some of which now became duplicates in his library, like the poems of José Jacinto Milanés, clearly a beloved poet among his compatriots. "The poems of this unfortunate author," wrote Eusebio Guiteras referring to the sad fall of Milanés into insanity, "whom the youth of Cuba has proclaimed their most eminent poet, are the best [present] I can offer to the illustrious American writer who has shown an interest in our emerging letters."[88] Longfellow gave his favorable impressions about Milanés to Guiteras from Portland, where he had gone to be with his father during his dying days (he passed away August 3, 1849). Guiteras acknowledged Longfellow's loss but was delighted to hear the poet's opinion about Milanés, and was certain that "it will have great influence when his works are judged in our country."[89] Longfellow had become an arbiter for judging the merits of poets in Cuba, and well beyond it.

Poets worked under appalling constraints in nineteenth-century Cuba, and were liable to persecution, exile, and censorship. Therefore, they had to find ways to express patriotic feelings, or simply a form of expression, under some safe guise. Longfellow's poems provided an excellent vehicle and thus found their way into print in various journals and newspapers. During the second half of the century, translations (or "imitations") of "Three Friends of Mine," by Antonio Sellén, "The Arrow and the Song," by José Agustín Quintero, "Two Locks of Hair" (in turn a translation from the German by Longfellow), by Juan Clemente Zenea appeared in the press.[90] Quintero was particularly active in translating. Writing from New Orleans in 1855, he told Longfellow of his translations of "Excelsior," "The Arrow and the Song," "The Rainy Day," and "The Psalm of Life."[91] He was thrilled to hear that Longfellow liked them, but lamented the difficulties in the island that impeded the dissemination of the poems. "We need to take many precautions," he wrote, "to escape a despotic government that routinely violates the sanctity of correspondence, and even proscribes our names!"[92] Even so, he managed to get some of Longfellow's poems into print.[93]

The realities of Cuba were never far from Longfellow's sight. Some Cubans, like Santiago Cancio Bello, were simply desperate for help. Cancio Bello had been driven out of the island and found himself penniless in Boston, with no one to turn to other than Longfellow.[94] He and others usually wanted a reference or an intervention to secure them a job at Harvard or elsewhere teaching Spanish. Longfellow was perfectly aware that some of his Spanish or Spanish American visitors came with a baggage, and occasionally he would have a chance to regret it. None of these could surpass the imagination, or boldness, of Pedro Luján de Moretto, a Peruvian refugee with a long and improbable story of transatlantic love, intrigue, and complicated international politics. He asked the poet for money, which he gave but which never seemed to have been quite enough. Luján "lays hold like a leech," Longfellow wrote in his journal, "If one could only be sure of people! One may entertain angels unawares—and also devils, for aught I know."[95] The poet did his best to support Luján, albeit with some doubts, but then, on September 7, 1854, Longfellow read in the Boston papers that Luján had been arrested in Maine during the summer on charges of larceny.[96] Although he was acquitted on a technicality, the news was apparently enough for Longfellow, who appears to have expressed his displeasure clearly enough to the Peruvian. Having lost this last source of support, Luján left Boston in a hurry a few days later, protesting the "calumnies" leveled against him.[97] Probably somewhat poorer because of this incident, Longfellow could be now sure about where Luján de Moretto stood among angels and devils.

Poetic Affinities

Fortunately for Longfellow, the great majority of his correspondents were genuine admirers who sought his advice, or simply wanted to offer him their books, as did the Venezuelan poet Juan Antonio Pérez Bonalde.[98] A resident of New York for nearly two decades, Pérez Bonalde (1846–1892) sent Longfellow a volume of his poems, *Estrofas* (1877), which the American poet acknowledged and promised to read with "great interest and sympathy."[99] He certainly did, for he could see the affectionate inscription in the Venezuelan poet's handwriting, "to the distinguished American poet Henry W. Longfellow, I offer you this humble volume, as an author who admires and venerates you." Longfellow could also see that one of the poems in *Estrofas* was about him because of the reference to "A Gleam of Sunshine" (from *The Belfry of Bruges*) in the title: "*Al autor de El rayo de luz.*" The poem celebrated Longfellow's inspiration and genius while avoiding flattery, and indeed gave little indication of the poet's identity.[100] Pérez Bonalde clearly admired Longfellow and followed in his footsteps, becoming a beloved poet for schoolchildren in his native country.[101] But their contact was brief, as Longfellow died soon after their exchanges began, in 1882.

Although the Cuban exile and revered martyr of Cuban independence José Martí (1853–1895) arrived in New York too late to establish contact with Longfellow, he left a clear record of his esteem for the American poet, whose "It is not Always May," and *The Song of Hiawatha*, he translated in whole or in part.[102] When Martí became aware of Longfellow's terminal illness, he wrote a long article for the Caracas newspaper *La Opinión Nacional*, noting the enormous outpouring of sympathy across the United States. Children in Atlanta, he reported, recited Longfellow's "Excelsior," while those of Cambridge brought him flowers and other tokens of care.[103] Two days after the article was published, Longfellow died. Martí prepared a long obituary, reviewing the poet's main works and contributions. He also noted approvingly that Longfellow was not the poet of dismay, or inner turmoil, but rather the bard of hope and active toil.[104] It is perhaps not surprising that Martí would include a positive reflection on "Excelsior" in his novel *Amistad funesta* (1885). Just months before he died in battle in Cuba, he recorded in his diary what he thought made Longfellow a great poet: "Even though he was both extremely sensitive, and a bold reformer, he still embodied the spirit of his people."[105] Martí is chiefly remembered because of his untimely death and his political legacy, but in literary matters, the Cuban author revealed a strong affinity for the work of Longfellow, especially in the American's writing for children.

Much farther to the south of the hemisphere, in Uruguay, José Enrique Rodó (1872–1917), celebrated Longfellow's "Excelsior," and "The Psalm of Life." In his influential *Ariel* (1900), a work that would inspire an entire generation of Latin American intellectual and political leaders, Rodó stated that these poems offered an "infallible balm against all [forms of] bitterness."[106] By this he meant to acknowledge the American poet's usefulness in promoting a more spiritual and humanistic approach to life than that of the predominant, allegedly materialistic, Positivistic school, which had taken Latin America by storm in the last quarter of the nineteenth century. In Perú, Longfellow's poetry had a significant impact on the romantic generation of the second half of the nineteenth century, which included Ricardo Palma, Juan de Arana, and José Arnaldo Márquez. The latter had spent several years in the United States, and could thus appreciate the fame of Longfellow.[107]

As mentioned earlier, the Chilean Carlos Morla Vicuña, a career diplomat, had translated *Evangeline* and published it in two editions in 1871 and 1905. While in Paris in 1875, he also translated Longfellow's "Mask of Pandora" and provided extensive commentary on various poetic renditions of the Prometheus story.[108] But in Chile itself, it was the great historian José Toribio Medina who provided an admirable prose translation of *Evangeline*.[109] Medina is better known as an erudite historian of the Spanish empire in America than as a translator of poetry.[110] But his work in this area is quite significant, for it reveals how the Chilean historian, famous for his document-driven history, had his origins in romantic literature. In addition, like his Spanish counterparts, Medina responded positively to the religious message embedded in *Evangeline*. Indeed, for him the very essence of the poem was religious, and thus he pointed to various characters and symbols of Catholic religiosity.[111] The inescapable religious element of the poem was also captured by Medina's friend, the Mexican poet and prominent *científico* (positivist) Joaquín Demetrio Casasus (1858–1916). But when he translated and published *Evangeline* first in 1884 and then in 1901, he and his mentor Ignacio Altamirano, who provided an extensive prologue, put more emphasis on the national components of the poem, as well as its vibrant celebration of New World nature.[112]

Longfellow sustained a long and meaningful relationship with his admirers and translators, although many of them he never got the chance to meet. The most significant example was his exchange with Rafael Pombo (1833–1912), the gifted Colombian poet whose work encompassed sentimental poetry, children's stories, and poems of social and political content.[113] It was Pombo who initiated contact with Longfellow from New York, where he was serving as the Colombian legation secretary (1855–1872). He sent the poet translations, compositions by himself and others, books, and letters over the span of more than a decade until the poet's death. Longfellow was usually gracious with his correspondents, but it seems that he made an extra effort to recognize Pombo, who had indeed engaged his poetry as few others had, and who also made an effort to describe literary developments in his own country.

Rafael Pombo arrived in New York in the summer of 1855. He soon became aware of the leading United States writers of the period, and of Longfellow in particular.[114] It would be some time, however, before he decided to write to the Cambridge poet directly. He finally did so in 1868, when he sent Longfellow his unpublished (1864) translation of "The Psalm of Life." Much of the accompanying letter was concerned with technical matters of versification, but the Colombian poet provided crucial information on the impact of the American's poetry in his homeland. Members of his generation, he said, had admired Longfellow's translation of the *Coplas de Manrique* and had been inspired to prepare compositions of their own after reading them. Unfortunately, poetry and politics conflicted, and had ended many a promising career.[115] Longfellow did not answer this first contact immediately, but other missives and poems from Pombo prompted him to respond and pronounce his translations as "excellent." "They are at once faithful and glowing," he said, "in particular I like that of 'The Psalm of Life.'"[116] Pombo was immensely encouraged and sent him other original compositions such as "Cadena" [Chain]. "I do not dare to call it a poem," he wrote, "as I only intended to make a kind of metrical synopsis of social evils." Meter, he added, was "the best vehicle for ideas to turn the public mind and heart to something serious."[117] Longfellow considered the poem "vigorous," and helped Pombo with the translation. "I have read the original over again, and like it much. It is a very striking lyric," he assured his counterpart.[118] Longfellow also acknowledged Pombo's "Fonda Libre," a poem celebrating freedom through the imagery of birds, but also bemoaning the human experience of expatriation and worldly constraints. "It is a charming poem," Longfellow assured his correspondent, "very melodious, and as good as anything in [sixteenth-century Spanish poets] Montemayor or Gil Polo."[119] Longfellow also considered Pombo's *En el Niágara* as "a very fervid and striking ode," and his *El hombre de ley*, as "full of true and noble sentiments."[120]

All indications are that Longfellow and Pombo were destined for a warm friend-ship based on mutual poetic admiration. But they never met. Before he left for Colombia in 1872, Pombo made one attempt to find the poet in Cambridge, but unsuccessfully. His daughters Alice, Edith, and Anne, however, invited him into the house and showed Pombo the poet's study, his books, and his paintings. From Bogotá some years later, he told Longfellow of a recent dream concerning that visit. "I dreamt I was in your house and that I spoke with your daughters in Spanish. Then you came in and told me 'you look very much like a jeweler.'" The Colombian poet then added with glee, "Indeed, I am very much inclined to mount foreign diamonds on Spanish materials."[121] Pombo had found in the translation of Longfellow's poems a way to sustain both a dialogue with his counterpart in the United States, and also to promote a useful model for Spanish American poetry.

Pombo translated and published several poems by Longfellow, including (in addition to the already mentioned "The Psalm of Life"), "In the Shadow," "Santa Filomena," "The Village Blacksmith," "The Arrow and the Song," "Excelsior," "Weariness," "The Arsenal at Springfield," "The Open Window," "Daybreak," "Gaspar Becerra," "The Builders," as well as portions of *Evangeline* and *The Divine Tragedy*.[122] Pombo also composed an original poem about Longfellow, which reveals the impact of the American poet's verses on him in particular, and on Spanish America more generally. Using the images of arrows carrying the poems of Longfellow across the land, Pombo wrote that "Even in these mountains / in more than one palm / your arrows now rest."[123] The lines speak of fecundity, perma-nence, and poetic inspiration. Indeed, Pombo could demonstrate the extent of Longfellow's influence by sending him the translations done by Miguel Antonio Caro, Temístocles Tejada, David Guarín, César Conto, Rafael Torres Mariño, and Samuel F. Bond. The father of the last, also named Samuel, translated "The Village Blacksmith" into Latin (*Faber Rusticus*), and gave it to Pombo for transmittal to Longfellow.[124] Pombo also mentioned that Santiago Pérez, the nation's former president, and Supreme Court Justice José María Garrido had both translated "The Village Blacksmith" into Spanish.[125] One of the translators, Rafael Torres Mariño, later orchestrated the most important collection of Longfellow's poems in transla-tion anywhere in Latin America.[126] As scholar John E. Englekirk noted in the 1940s, Longfellow was the most widely translated American poet until World War II, engaging the largest number of translators in Spanish America. Perhaps not surpris-ingly, the upbeat "The Psalm of Life," with its message of hope, and disinterested toil, was both the most frequently translated and reprinted.[127] It is perhaps no coin-cidence that Bartolomé Mitre, one of the architects of modern Argentina, and pres-ident of the country, was among the translators.[128]

It is thanks to Pombo that we can gain insight into why Longfellow was so influ-ential in Spanish America. In preparation for a speech he intended to deliver on Longfellow at the recently created Colombian Academy, Pombo went through a detailed list of what made the American poet so important for the Hispanic world. He indicated that, first and foremost, Longfellow's work was marked by "a cosmo-politan spirit and heart, without limitations of race, nationality, language, time, and creed." Colombia had by this time become the first country in Spanish America to join the Spanish Royal Academy (1871), taking a substantial step in the direction of restoring cultural ties with the former empire. Spanish America in general had advanced significantly in the process of consolidating its independent nationhood, and was thereby more amenable to exploring the venues for expanding relations with other countries and cultures. Longfellow's literary cosmopolitanism resonated quite well in that context.

Pombo also highlighted values embedded in Longfellow's work, which he thought would be quite helpful in Spanish America, and these included "a constant and perfect morality and spirituality," as well as "love and respect for tradition," which he thought was particularly important "to make us whole by uniting the past and the future." To illustrate his point, Pombo recalled the lines from *Voices of the Night*, "And, loving still these quaint old themes, / Even in the city's throng / I feel the freshness of the streams, / that, crossed by shades and sunny gleams, / Water the green land of dreams, / The holy land of song." He interpreted these lines as an invitation to anchor national culture on ancient traditions.[129] Pombo also believed that Longfellow's work inspired those who felt that "poetry should be at once progressive and conservative," meaning that poets had an important role to play in fostering balance, advancing just social causes, and enriching daily life. Moreover, Longfellow inspired those who felt that much was yet to be done to sing the beauties of nature in the continent, despite the pioneering contributions of Andrés Bello, as well as the virtues of home life, "nearly absent in Spanish verse." He singled out *The Song of Hiawatha*, *Evangeline*, and *The Divine Tragedy* to illustrate what in his view was needed, and doable, in the Spanish American context: the poetry on Indian themes, songs to inspire love and spirituality, and biblical themes. He did not neglect to mention translations, so successfully done by Longfellow, which could be so helpful in enriching individual national cultures.[130]

In essence, Longfellow appealed to those Spanish American intellectuals who understood the potential of poetry as a vehicle for national identity formation beyond the structures of the State. That is, an accessible vehicle that could acknowledge human aspirations and sentiments, as well as inspire republican virtues among the citizenry. When the days of struggle against Spain were long gone, and when Spanish American nations could pay more attention to the development of unifying national myths, Longfellow became the first American poet to show how it could be done, bringing together old traditions, modern poetic techniques, social content, and wide appeal. Longfellow could not have suspected it, but he became the bard of an emerging Spanish American sense of distinct nationality.

Chapter 6

Mary Peabody Mann
and the Translation of
South American Politics

The vast plains of Buenos Aires are populated solely by Christian savages, known by the name of guachos [sic] whose principal furnishings are horses' skulls, whose food is raw meat and water, and whose favorite pastime is racing horses until they burst. Unfortunately, they preferred national independence over our cottons and muslins.
—Walter Scott, *Life of Napoleon Buonaparte* (1827)

The name of Mary Mann has resonated more than once in sympathetic Argentine ears, because the prestige of her husband, the apostle of primary education, and her translation of Civilización y Barbarie *under the title* Life in the Argentine Republic, *make her a patroness of our educational institutions and our literature.*
—Domingo Faustino Sarmiento to Samuel Alberú, 1887[1]

Standing on the Central Wharf of Boston harbor in early December, 1833, Mary Tyler Peabody contemplated the vast ocean that was about to take her and her sickly sister Sophia to a faraway island. It was a cool day, and the spirits of the accompanying family were dampened by the realization that they might never see Mary or—more likely—Sophia again. Their destination was Cuba, increasingly the haven for New Englanders suffering from the North American maladies of both climate and century. The sisters had been preparing for this trip, reading about Cuba and learning Spanish, but their main objective was to find a cure for Sophia's ailments. Mary would assist her and also teach the children of their hosts. Little did Mary know that this trip, and the eighteen months that she spent on the island with her sister, would establish the foundations of one of the most remarkable cultural bridges ever built between the United States and Spanish America.

While in Cuba between 1833 and 1835, Sophia and Mary together wrote what came to be known as the *Cuba Journal*, a collection of their letters home compiled by their mother, though most of the missives were written by Sophia.[2] They represent a valuable record of what these New England women saw in Cuba during the time they spent on the island. They lived in an isolated coffee plantation named "La Recompensa," about a day away from Havana, and thus their opportunities for observation were necessarily limited. In addition, they socialized mostly with either the international or Spanish-Cuban community. Still, they had some painful encounters with the realities of slavery. Sophia, who most assiduously recorded their stay, was an artist who predictably wrote about the wealth of colors and the exotic character of the nature around her. She also assured her family often about progress in her recovery. Occasionally she would make comments of a different kind. The Spanish "dons," she wrote, were "a proud, lazy, ignorant race," with only rare exceptions.[3] One of those exceptions was Andrés de Layas, "just what one would imagine a true Castilian, noble, yet withal unprincipled, a refined Epicure."[4] She liked to write about her social encounters, but slavery was another issue, "I do not allow myself to dwell upon slavery for two reasons," Sophia told her mother, "one is, it would certainly counter the beneficent influences, which I have left home and country to court, and another is, that my faith in GOD makes me sure that he makes up to every being the measure of happiness which he loses thro' the instrumentality of others." She would rather, she explained, "lose myself in other subjects of thought."[5]

Mary, for her part, proved to be more alert to the situation of the colony. Even from the isolation of "La Recompensa," she followed the succession struggles in Spain after the death of Ferdinand VII, which resulted in the appointment of a new governor for the island (Miguel Tacón), the official who was to exacerbate political tensions between Cubans and Spaniards in the years that followed.[6] She also observed how slaves were treated, both inside and outside the plantation, in a way that caused her both shock and dismay. Mary did not write as prolifically as Sophia, and was in addition constrained by the instructions of her concerned elder sister Elizabeth Palmer Peabody. "Drive slavery from your thoughts," Elizabeth wrote to Mary, worried about her distress and perhaps thinking that the subject might upset readers of the journal back home. She told Mary that it was not "prudent to trust its scenes to paper," and suggested that she should "try to think about slavery as little as possible."[7] Mary managed to convey some of what she saw in her letters home, but saved her condemnations for a remarkable novel, *Juanita: A Romance of Real Life in Cuba Fifty Years Ago*.

Mary Mann's *Juanita* was published posthumously in 1887.[8] According to an explanatory note by Elizabeth, the book remained unpublished for so long because Mann wished to avoid embarrassing any member of the family that had hosted her and Sophia in the Cuban plantation. What she had seen there and beyond, scathingly told, could be read as quite damning to the host family. When this was no longer an issue, 50 years later, Mary chose the abolition of slavery in Cuba (1886) to release the book. Although death prevented her from seeing it between covers, the version she delivered to the publisher was her own.

The book indeed has a retrospective flavor, in that the confident and uncompromising condemnation of slavery bears the mark of having been issued from the perspective of its abolition in the United States. There is in fact a certain anachronism in the story, which takes place in the 1830s, when slavery was still extant in the United States, and there was not yet consensus, or even a clear path toward abolition. No agony torments the protagonist regarding the status of the peculiar institution. Slavery, indeed, is simply "the sum of all villanies," as Helen Wentworth, the self-righteous New Englander who is the protagonist, endlessly repeats John Wesley's words to herself. While abolition might still be in the future for the United States, Mann, the omniscient narrator, could add moral force to Helen's condemnations because she knew the outcome. Helen is confident that slavery will be abolished, "not because I see any steps taken toward that end by our government, but because it must fade before the advancing light of truth" (214).

Helen Wentworth has gone to Cuba to visit Isabella, an old friend and classmate from their school days in Philadelphia, who is now married to a slave owner, the Marquis Hernando Rodríguez. Helen is immediately shocked to witness the realities of slavery, the rationalizations and denials of the slave owners, and the cruelties of the vicious *mayorales*, or overseers. Unfortunately for the otherwise kind hosts, everything that can go wrong in a plantation does go wrong. In breathtaking succession, Helen is paraded with constant scenes of human suffering that determine her to lift the veil that covers her friend's eyes and expose slavery for what it is. She does her work only too well, for Isabella begins to look at slavery from Helen's perspective, and is horrified. So much so that she undergoes a withering physical and emotional decline that precipitates her death. Once the fundamental unity of the family has been broken, based as it was on the denial of the realities of slavery, there is no escape but death or exile for the remaining members of the family.

The book is quite obviously an abolitionist text, but there are some complexities, and perhaps some alternative readings. By the time of publication in 1887, slavery in the United States had long been abolished, and had just happened in Cuba. In this regard, *Juanita* was not a part of the process of abolition, as *Uncle Tom's Cabin* and other novels were. It was, however, to its aftermath, in that the novel enshrines education as a means to contribute to the independence and dignity of the former slaves. There is also another agenda: the depiction of Spanish society and culture, in ways that resonate with the themes developed by her fellow Hispanists in the United States during the century. Her account was perhaps the most direct, and devastating.

Seen through the eyes of the austere, morally inflexible, and opinionated Helen Wentworth, Cuba does indeed look like a tropical version of hell. First and foremost, this is a corrupt land. The highest authority in the island, the Captain General, openly violates the treaty with England regarding the slave trade by protecting the slave merchants, while profiting personally from it (7). In the words of Marchioness Rodríguez, "The Captain General has his royalty upon every slave's head, and he is too powerful to be thwarted" (77). Corruption is pervasive, and it compromises the judicial system as well. Assassinations and other forms of violence go unpunished because the judicial system is "so corrupt that legal action would soon impoverish the richest man" (15). Debts are routinely ignored by the wealthy, "and such is the corruption of the judiciary in the Spanish colonies, that a moneyed man can act with impunity as long as he can offer bribes of sufficient magnitude" (115).

The Spanish "character" and "customs" do not fare much better. Perhaps the nicest thing that can be said about the Spaniards (who are often indistinct from Cubans) is that they love music, although this is often a backhanded compliment. "Music is in the air in Cuba," Mann writes, "Spaniards are musical, negroes are musical, and the very air is musical" (54). Dancing is so important that "the Spaniards of the colonies would have felt it to be an indignity to be called upon to pay for the privilege of dancing, until they were in danger of losing that pleasure" (109). From an early age, Spaniards partake in "low and degrading pleasures," such as hunting, card-playing, cock-fighting, "idle visiting," and dancing (54). The "pleasure-loving Spaniards," one learns, "make a holiday of every saint's day in the calendar, and intensify the feast whenever there is an apology for so doing" (191).

They seldom read, "but are never tired of playing cards or billiards" (57). Perhaps the only book that can reliably be found in households is the ubiquitous *Don Quixote*, because of tradition and necessity rather than for any love of literature. Indeed. "no one can understand every-day Spanish conversation who is not familiar with this work, for a proverb from it finishes off nearly every remark that is made" (54). "It is the only literature people here know," summarizes Ludovico, the eldest son of the Rodríguez family (169). They care little for education, especially the education of women (178). Islanders are in perennial need of "entertaining company" because "Spaniards have few resources within themselves" (57). This conclusion applies also to practical matters such as the use of technology and labor, which could be substantially improved "if the Spaniards could conceive of such a thing as innovation" (157). Innovation, indeed, is nearly impossible "among a people so nationally ignorant as the inhabitants of the Spanish colonies. No hope of such a change exists, except in the possibility of annexation to the United States" (201). They are, in short, "idle and good-for nothing," (106) and "standstill Spaniards" (202).

Spanish despotism gets its share of coverage in the form of the actions of Governor Miguel Tacón (1834–1838), who violently puts down any form of insurrection, and brutally punishes the slightest challenges to his authority. Readers learn that he "exercised his despotic power without regard even to the remonstrances of his nobility, which had hitherto been lawless" (16). Even dogs, by decree, must be silent while music plays in the public squares. Such absurd extremes are of course not confined to the governor, because Spain itself is "despotic" (17). Tacón is eventually removed in 1838, "which was due partly to the despotism he showed, and partly because he threatened to overhaul the slave-trade" (208). Despotism meets its match in Cuba, not through aspirations for liberty, but through the defense of crass interests. Despotism is simply an inherent element of the Spanish character.

Catholicism is also a target of ridicule, and it is presented as complicit with the rationalizations of slavery. As the notorious slave trader Miguel Arbrides explains to his son Carlito, the African "savages" are lucky to be brought under the tutelage of Christians, for after they are baptized by the Franciscan friar Padre Jean, who is Irish, they "can be good Catholics, and be buried in holy ground when they die" (21). The practice of Catholicism, for Africans and Spaniards alike, does not go beyond mere ritual. As Helen rhetorically asks of a fellow countrywoman, "What idea have they about the baptism, do you think?" Her interlocutor Ms. Warwick answers assuredly that "Oh, none whatever, except that if they die they can then be buried in holy ground, and that is everything to a Catholic" (188). Helen Wentworth looks admiringly at the imposing Havana Cathedral, but "she did not know then that the convent beneath it was filled with the friars and their families, or that the very semblance of celibacy was dispensed with by the colonial priesthood" (22). Morals are so degraded that "not even with a priest would a careful mother leave her daughter for an hour" (55). The Church does not interfere with the widespread practice of setting up "Holy Families," or unions not sanctioned by marriage. More troublingly, a virtuous woman must take extraordinary precautions "in a society so utterly corrupt as that of the Spanish colonies" (107). Helen cannot help but draw a contrast between the United States (especially the northern and middle states), where the "general elevation of society can only be rightly estimated when compared with an opposite state of things [like Cuba], where public morals are so corrupt that no one can be trusted" (127). She cannot help make these contrasts, which lead her to the conclusion that "I have often thought that we Americans do not live up to the theory of our society as we ought, but since I have looked back to my own country from this [Cuba], I appreciate, as I never could before, its advanced position" (164). Mann was referring to the northern states, for in many ways her critique of Cuba was also a critique of southern slaveholders and religious hypocrisy more generally.

The character of Juanita requires mention here, for Mann describes her as a "Moorish beauty, which bore no trace of the negro" (66). Slavery, therefore, is not exclusively associated with black chattel slavery, but rather with its African and religious origins, much as Washington Irving and George Bancroft had suggested in their writings: Spaniards had been enslaving Muslims from North Africa long before the West African traffic began. Juanita's grandmother had been purchased as a slave, a status that had passed down to Juanita's generation. Marchioness Rodríguez explains to Helen that his father-in-law had purchased Juanita's grandmother "in a coffle of slaves, of which she was the only Moor" (76). "They are not often enslaved," she adds, and sets them apart form other slaves. "They have little resemblance to other negroes;" she says, "indeed they are not negroes" (76). This tortuous reasoning apparently serves to justify the attraction that Juanita and Ludovico feel for each other, an attraction that Helen views with approval. But Spanish society could never sanction the legal union between a nobleman and a slave, and thus Juanita must die. Valiantly so, but die she must in order to solve a socially unacceptable situation. Thus, Juanita's case allows Mary Mann to underscore not only the evils of slavery, but the extraordinary rigidity of the Spanish class system as well.

Mary Mann's sojourn in Cuba was limited to her stay in "La Recompensa" for eighteen months, except for visits to nearby plantations (the longest of which was two weeks), and the necessary passage through Havana. Mary had been engaged as the tutor of the children of the Morell family, but what she saw about slavery was quite enough. She witnessed some of the horrors that are so graphically depicted in *Juanita*,[9] but some material appears to be borrowed, primarily from Abiel Abbot's *Letters Written in the Interior of Cuba* (1829). Abbot spent several months on the island in 1828, describing in rich detail what he saw, including the same plantation where the Peabody sisters stayed. Megan Marshall has indicated that Abbot's book "served as Mary and Sophia's guide to the island."[10] The book certainly helped Mary to learn about Catholic practices and liturgy far beyond what she was able to observe directly, in addition to much detail about the conditions of slavery in several plantations.[11]

Juanita, in many substantial ways, builds on Mary's Cuban experience, but the novel achieved its characteristic tenor through subsequent revisions. It *became* a gothic tale of slavery's horrors after a much longer and retrospective reflection on the American journey through abolition, Civil War, and Reconstruction. Scholars have indicated that Nathaniel Hawthorne, Mary's brother-in-law, may have had an influence on the literary conventions utilized in the novel. This is indeed plausible, just as there is concrete evidence of how Hawthorne was influenced by the "Cuba Journal" once he read it.[12] But there is also the influence of the intervening years. That is, between Mary's Cuban experience, and the actual publication of *Juanita*, there is an important development: Mary Mann's engagement with Spanish American affairs, especially through her contact with the Argentine Domingo Faustino Sarmiento.

Gauchos and the Threat to Civilization

Domingo Faustino Sarmiento was one of the most remarkable figures of nineteenth-century Latin America, and he remains conspicuous and controversial to this day. He was born in 1811 in a remote province of today's Argentina, and soon became a casualty of the tumultuous politics of the postindependence period. As an exile in neighboring Chile in the 1840s, Sarmiento made a name for himself as a journalist and eventually as author of the classic *Facundo* (1845), a clever political statement that posited a contrast between civilization and barbarism as a key to understanding Spanish American politics, and which became a powerful weapon against the dictatorship of Juan Manuel de Rosas (1829–1852). This book made Sarmiento famous, though it would only be through the translation of Mary Mann that he became widely known in the United States beginning in 1868. In between, Sarmiento had traveled around Europe, returned to Argentina, served as governor of his native province, achieved prominence as an educator, represented his government in the United States, and crowned his career as president of Argentina. He was a formidable figure who raised himself from provincial obscurity to international fame.

Mary Mann met Sarmiento personally when he first visited the United States in 1847, 12 years after her experience in Cuba. There is no extensive record of that meeting, which would prove to be so crucial for the subsequent collaboration between them, and also for the closer cultural contact between the United States and Spanish America. The Argentine visitor was a man in a hurry, collecting as much information as he could to write a report commissioned by the Government of Chile on the state of popular education in Europe and the United States.[13] It was just natural that he would immediately seek an interview with Horace Mann, the great educator and founder of educational institutions. Mann did not understand Spanish, and Sarmiento spoke not a word of English. They communicated through Mary's French, for she apparently was not confident enough in her Spanish,[14] or felt that Sarmiento's French was somewhat more discernible than his heavily idiomatic Spanish. But the link was made, and it would prove to be a fateful one.

It was Sarmiento who took the initiative to reestablish contact after a hiatus of 18 years, when he arrived in the United States as Argentine ambassador in 1865. During that time, Mary had gone from New England to Ohio, founded Antioch College with her husband Horace, given birth to three children, continued to write on educational matters, and endured Horace's death one summer day in 1859 (that terrible year also saw the death of Washington Irving and William H. Prescott). Back in Concord, Massachusetts, Mary raised the children, collected materials for a biography of her late husband, and supported various Civil War activities on behalf of the Union. As opposed to many who confronted the horrors of the war with shock and denial, she appeared to be cautiously confident about the future. She told Dorothea Dix, the superintendent of army nurses, that "I think we are improving as a nation which is the only consolation for this frightful war. I have of late been reading [and] copying letters from my dear husband upon the causes of all this trouble—he predicted all of this, but not *so soon*. I shall publish them before long."[15] The *Life of Horace Mann* appeared in 1865, while she was devoting her considerable energies to the cause of education, which she considered a key element of Reconstruction.

From New York, and trying his charming best, Sarmiento contacted Mary Mann to congratulate her upon the unveiling of Horace Mann's statue on the Massachusetts

Statehouse lawn (July 4, 1865). He told her that he had used Horace's writings and implemented his ideas in South America, and now asked for permission to translate Mary's *Life of Horace Mann* into Spanish, in order to "open the eyes of my compatriots to the treasures contained in its pages." He then added,

> The education of the people is South America's primary necessity and there are countries among us that have made great progress in spreading education among the classes. The Life of Horace Mann, the tale of his triumphs in Massachusetts and of his dedication and sacrifice, made available to everyone and enhanced by that eloquent testimony to the gratitude of the people, the statute erected in honor of their benefactor— such a work will not fail to find imitators everywhere, just as Plutarch's Lives has inspired heroic deeds and noble thoughts in the hearts of youth and just as the life of Washington illuminated the dark path Lincoln traversed through the forest and that of Franklin served as an example to so many of his illustrious compatriots during the awkward, early stages of their careers.[16]

Few could resist such a paean, and Mary was not about to. "I hasten to respond," she wrote, "as an expression of the gratification which so earnest a tribute to my beloved and lamented husband must necessarily give me."[17] She immediately offered all the help she could give to the Argentine ambassador, including papers, State and government documents, and contacts. She also offered to welcome him in Concord. Thus a lasting relationship began, with respectful but increasingly affectionate expressions on both sides. There was little indication of what Sarmiento expected in return for his professed desire to enlighten the world about Horace Mann. Indeed, his letters returned to this self-appointed task time and again. He told Mary how he had translated and distributed letters and speeches concerning her late husband. Moreover, "I shall publish in a short while a book on Education addressed to Spanish American Countries, the greater portion of which is made up with the life of your honored husband, including everything to his glory."[18] The book in question was *Las Escuelas*, which was indeed devoted to Horace Mann's ideas.[19] Sarmiento placed copies everywhere he could, in the United States, in Argentina, Brazil, Venezuela, Italy, and France, thus presenting himself credibly to Mann's widow as the tireless promoter of Horace's views.

Few could resist such a paean, and Mary was not about to.

However, Sarmiento clearly wanted something from Mary Mann. "I send you a little book entitled: Civilization & Barbarie," he announced, "that I wrote some twenty years ago, in order to explain the causes of the civil wars we have been subjected to during nearly half a century."[20] He did not wait long to come to his real purpose: "Are you blessed with an abundance of spare time and good will to undertake the translation of Civilization of Barbarism?," he asked, "Were you disposed to do it, I would feel particularly proud to see on the title page of a book written by Mr. Sarmiento the name of Mrs. Mary Mann."[21] Mary thought about it, and concluded that though her Spanish was not fluent, she could do the translation with his son Benjamin's help.[22] Sarmiento did not hide his pleasure, or his sense of entitlement. "I jumped with joy," he wrote to her, "God sent you to me as a guardian angel, and you must accept with Christian resignation this holy mission."[23]

Mary Mann needed both Christian resignation and the patience of a saint, for the task of translation presented her with formidable challenges, especially as Sarmiento grew more demanding and threw other translations and requests on her lap. "Whenever I sit down to write anything about your country & yourself," she wrote ruefully, "I am arrested by *want of knowledge*."[24] Indeed, Sarmiento's writings, addressed to a South American audience, assumed local knowledge that was not available to Mary or most people in New England at the time. She found herself, therefore, doing not just the translations, but researching Spanish American geography, history, and politics. And still she had plenty of questions to ask. At other times, she was completely befuddled by Sarmiento's writing and felt compelled to ask, "If you can find a dictionary in N.Y. which spells as you do, I will be very much obliged if you will purchase it for me" (at her expense).[25] Sarmiento, indeed, used the spelling system introduced by Andrés Bello and himself in Chile in the 1840s, which had its merits but was not widely adopted in the Spanish-speaking world, least of all in Spain, and thus made reading cumbersome. But she persevered, and asked for help whenever she needed it, and wherever she could find it. It was the work of two full years.

Translation was not the only challenge, for Mary Mann understood that, despite Sarmiento's robust self-image, he was little known in the United Sates. Therefore, she felt that for the book to succeed she needed to provide a lengthy portrait of the man. And for this she relied nearly exclusively on Sarmiento's own information. It was not an easy process, and Mary's frustration was quite apparent when she told him, "Please not to forget that *I* am writing your biography, not you! & I must be able to clearly explain my sentences!"[26] Determined as she was to promote the man who promoted the legacy of her husband, Mary Mann accepted Sarmiento's claims without objection. The result was a panegyric on a man who was unabashedly manufacturing his image to advance his own political agenda.

The "Biographical Sketch" that follows the translation of *Facundo, o civilización y barbarie* is a 120-page equivalent of a modern political campaign biography. Mary Mann tried her best to extract information from published sources, but most of the information came from the letters of Sarmiento himself. Thus, readers learned of Sarmiento's "brilliance" as a boy growing up in the isolated slopes of the Andes in Western Argentina.

> "One can conceive of no circumstances more adverse to the growth of fine character," editorialized Mary Mann, "than the isolated, provincial life of a Spanish colony, ruled by ecclesiastical domination, exercised over an uneducated mass like the remote descendants of Spaniards who have been cut off for two or three generations from means of improvement, and even from the knowledge of the world's progress."[27]

Still, the young man, with "determination and pluck" pulled himself up by his bootstraps to become a major intellectual and political figure. He taught himself various languages, and while working in the mines of Copiapó (Northern Chile) "he *translated* a volume a day of the sixty volumes of Sir Walter Scott's works, beside some other books."[28] While in Chilean exile in the 1840s, "he endeavored to organize primary instruction for the people—an idea that had never dawned upon the Chilian mind" (346). Sarmiento had indeed been the director of the first Normal School established in Santiago in 1842, but those who established it, funded it, and engineered the public education system, would have been surprised by the claim. Likewise, in another passage, Mary Mann asserted that "in 1843, [Sarmiento] founded and edited the periodical called 'El Progreso,' the first paper that had ever been printed in Santiago de Chili, the residence of learned Chilians" (349), yet another surprising claim for a country that was flooded with over a 100 papers at the time of Sarmiento's residence. Clearly, there was a purpose to such exaggerations, which included single-handedly establishing freedom of worship in Buenos Aires, launching major public works in the province of San Juan, putting down insurrections from turbulent gauchos, developing mining enterprises, and promoting education across the land. Mary Mann came to the point,

> A man who has contended with barbarism in South America, and has studied the sources of the development of other nations, during residence therein, must have acquired by practice and by comparison, rich materials for thought, and a fund of ideas of no common order. That of diffusing education among the people, from which nothing has distracted him for thirty years, neither war nor exile, the poverty of his private life, nor the seductions of exalted position, has given a special character to his life. (394)

Who could better lead South America? "It is evident that there are everywhere," Mary Mann concluded, "some who appreciate the true value of his labors, and there is a party there that understands how much it might be benefited by putting the reins of government into such able and experienced hands" (395). If Sarmiento had not yet been elected president, he surely ought to be.

Sarmiento was neither a shy nor a humble man. When he read the biographical sketch he was quite pleased. "On the mantle lie the pages of the biography. I've read it, it is excellent, and it only awaits the more important judgment of the public." Clearly he was not bothered by the inaccuracies and exaggerations that he had himself conveyed to Mann, and which he could now see quite close to publication. But he did take issue with Mary's version of his visit to Algeria, where she had him galloping in Byronesque fashion toward the pyramids. "I am not sure what is meant," he wrote, "because in Algiers there are no pyramids."[29] Moving on to more important things, he suggested that Mann include the news about his recent Michigan honorary doctorate in either the preface or the biographical sketch. No mention was made of the most egregious exaggerations. Perhaps he concluded that those who might call him to account were either dead or did not read English.

Mary Mann navigated the difficulties of translation, and Sarmiento's vast ego, but she still faced the challenge of getting the book published. To Henry W. Longfellow she confided thus:

> The whole publication is a work of love, for no publisher will take any risk about it that will not insure a return—so Hurd and Houghton have consented to publish it directly from the types, and without giving me *any* percentage for my trouble. I am very glad to get it done even so, for I am very sure it will prove interesting [and] give the public at least a good geography and history lesson.[30]

Longfellow was sympathetic: "I congratulate you on the completion of your work," he wrote, "and hope its success with the public will in some measure compensate you for your labor."[31] He was not far off the mark. Indeed, there was sufficient interest to sell the entire first printing within a year, thanks to the end of the Triple Alliance War (between the allies Argentina, Brazil and Uruguay against Paraguay, 1865–1870), and the rise of Sarmiento to the presidency of Argentina. A bit of extra help was also important, as William Dean Howells, with an unerring editorial eye, suggested a better title than the indifferent *Facundo*. The final title was *Life in the*

Argentine Republic in the Days of the Tyrants; or, Civilization and Barbarism, a catchy title for a book that continues to be in print to this day.[32]

The English *Facundo*

The translation of *Facundo*, despite the awkwardness of some passages, was indeed remarkably lively and suggestive. Ostensibly telling the story of a provincial warlord, Juan Facundo Quiroga, the book was both a powerful political statement, and a captivating metaphor about the essence of Latin American postindependence political culture. Mary Mann captured quite well Sarmiento's deliberate style: in part scientific travelogue, in part Ovidian lament of exile, and in part a compelling call for struggle against dictatorship. Scholars who have scrutinized Sarmiento's sources and rhetorical devices by and large agree that *Facundo* is indeed a classic, a foundational text that has stood the test of time and that continues to elicit rich yet conflicting readings.[33] Mary Mann's translation did full justice to the work, even if she missed some of the nuance of Sarmiento's writing. The book became a classic *English*-language text as well, dominating the field until a new translation appeared 135 years later, in 2003.[34]

The key to the success of the translation lies in the fundamental agreement between Sarmiento and Mann to make the text intelligible to a U.S readership. This meant catering to established views about the Hispanic world, especially with regards to religion and the Iberian heritage. Perhaps the clearest demonstration of this is the deliberate addendum of a piece *not* included in the original Spanish version, "Friar José Félix Aldao, Brigadier-General and Governor," as the conclusion of the book.[35] The text appeared originally in the Chilean press in 1845 (the same year of *Facundo*) and told the story of a Dominican priest who took up arms in the fight for independence, thus "increasing the number of the dead instead of comforting the dying." Training for the priesthood reinforced habits of "violence and immorality" that made Aldao thrive in the carnage of war, and look for a compensating excitement after it was over: "The monk henceforth became famous for his disorderly habits; his private life being devoted to intoxication, cards, and women." As Argentina struggled to build an independent nation in the 1820s, Friar Aldao happily joined the provincial *caudillos* who would prevent any such efforts from succeeding, thus beginning "the long series of crimes which brought the Republic to its present condition of barbarism." Just to emphasize what that condition was, Sarmiento explained,

> The caudillos of the interior rid their provinces of all lawyers, doctors, and men of letters; and Rosas pursued them even within the walls of the university and private schools. Those who were allowed to remain were such persons as could be useful in getting up a repetition of the government of Philip II of Spain, and of the Inquisition.

Aldao in Sarmiento's version naturally became an ally of Facundo, and a client of Rosas, but he was simply a petty warlord elevated to a position of power by the sorry conditions of the country. He ended his life in sickening debauchery, dissipation, and disease, a mere tool of the designs of the ultimate caudillo who dominated the land. Sarmiento chose to replace the original conclusion of his *Facundo* (which contained his program for nation building after Rosas) in an obvious effort to show just how bad the caudillos were, and how well he understood—and could deal with—them as a product of a Spanish heritage that permitted such political and religious corruption. It was an ending designed for a U.S. audience, and Mary Mann skillfully guided his hand, sharing wholeheartedly the view of what was wrong with Latin America.

The book succeeded spectacularly well in making the mix of fiction and politics appear as an objective account of Latin American conditions. The *New York Times* reported favorably on the book's "fresh and lively pictures of Spanish-American life, its descriptions of natural scenery, and its *résumés* and sketches of Argentine history and those who played their parts in it in [Sarmiento's] time." The review also commended Mary Mann for having done "her part well and faithfully."[36] Writing for the *Atlantic Monthly*, William Deans Howells, who already had a part in the publication of the book, followed Mary Mann's panegyric on Sarmiento, and added some more: the great man had "founded the first normal school in America," and substituted "such books as the 'Life of Franklin' for the monkish legends from which the children once learned to read." Sarmiento's book had finally made Latin America comprehensible when it explained the "character" of such tyrants as Juan Manuel de Rosas and Francisco Solano López "as gaucho chiefs, the heirs of Quiroga's system and ideas." The book, in short, had the virtue of "making us know the political and social life of Spanish America as it has never appeared before in literature."[37] Another reviewer went further in underscoring the relevance of Sarmiento's work for the United States:

> An intelligent American can hardly read the life of this Republic and its prominent representative, without seeing in it again and again the broken image of his own country, and a new illustration of the vital energy existing in Republicanism. Our fathers laid the foundations of our nation upon an existing society, whose bases were town government and the free schools. We have seen how the absence of one of these elements, in connection with a system closely allied to ignorance, has constituted a barbarism which it was the gigantic task of the purer civilization to exterminate. . . . How fast can we transmute ignorant freedmen and ignorant poor whites into intelligent citizens?—this is a question which is the condition of national growth and true prosperity. Far away, at the southern extremity of the continent, a society accepting the same instruments of government which we have had, has likewise had to pass through a conflict, more open, and lasting for a longer period than our own, but alike with ours, the conflict of civilization and barbarism.[38]

Sarmiento had not drawn such parallels in the original *Facundo*, but they were certainly present in the English translation, and in Mary Mann's biography, so as to draw the interest and sympathy of the U.S. readership. But Mary was not content with simply translating Sarmiento's work. She also tried to promote her Argentine friend in any way she could. He accepted such support gratefully, but considered it his due. "It will be an historic fact of great influence in South America," he wrote self-assuredly, "that the woman who aided Horace Mann in his great work in North America, also lent her fervent support to his followers in South America."[39] But Sarmiento wanted more, and requested Mary Mann's assistance in obtaining an honorary doctorate from Harvard. "If Mr [Thomas] Hill or someone else were to offer me one in Law," he wrote, "you cannot imagine the effect it would produce in my country where everything related to the United States is considered prestigious and Harvard College is well known. This honorary degree, coming from a renowned university, would undermine my opposition."[40] Mary Mann agreed and set out to work at once. "I have a request to make," she wrote to Longfellow, "I know from Mr. Sarmiento's history, which is a very interesting one, that it would be of incalculable advantage to his influence at home if he could have a complimentary degree of laws from Harvard University." She explained that the autodidact Sarmiento was barred from such a recognition in Argentina for lack of a regular college education. Sarmiento, she argued "knows more about legislation than any one in any of those republics." Not a master of the understatement when it came to promoting her friend, she asserted that "his works and acts in the educational field are surpassed by those of no man in the world." After asking Longfellow to validate Sarmiento's credentials, she stated candidly that,

> I can draw up a statement, but is best that it should be presented to the corporation by gentlemen. If he has this degree from Harvard, he will perhaps have one from Chili. The Buenos Ayres university is hostile to him because he has made strenuous efforts to get this law abrogated [i.e., on the granting of degrees]—besides which, Buenos Ayres is jealous of his influence. He is a prophet that is not fully estimated in his own country, or at least discredited because he puts them all to shame.[41]

Longfellow was receptive but noncommittal, not so much because he did not appreciate the accomplishments of Sarmiento, but because he was no longer a Harvard professor and did not want to influence the university's decisions. "If you could see President [Thomas] Hill upon the subject," he wrote, "it would do more to further the matter than anything else."[42] She did follow the poet's suggestion, and spoke directly with Harvard President Hill, who was mildly encouraging. But she was not entirely sanguine about either the prospects or the nature of the distinction. "In our country every college compliments the men it likes, whether for political reasons or otherwise, so easily, that the Dr's degree is a common subject of ridicule." She understood, however, that it might be "useful" to Sarmiento, and kept trying.[43] In the end, however, Harvard granted no degree to the Argentine ambassador. Sarmiento did, however, get his wish, although from an unexpected source. As Mary Mann told Juana Manso on the eve of Sarmiento's departure, "He has endeared himself to many here, besides commanding the respect [and] honor of all. Michigan University which is the best, though not the oldest in this country, has just done itself the honor to give him the degree of L.L.D."[44]

Mary Mann felt justifiable pride in having done all she could on behalf of Sarmiento. It had been a titanic task to complete the publication of *Life in the Argentine Republic*, but she felt vindicated as Sarmiento was at the time winning, vote by vote, and province by province, the race that took him to the presidency of Argentina in 1868. That he was able to parlay his U.S. successes, mostly thanks to the labor of Mary Mann, seem to have been of no concern to the self-effacing New Englander. In a gracious letter of farewell, just as Sarmiento was about to embark on what appeared to be his imminent election as president, she offered the following thoughts:

> You will sail, probably, the day after tomorrow. I must say the word—good-bye at last. It is a hard word to say when one feels that it is probably final—but although this interesting episode in my life closes to the sight, it does not end but with your life or mine,

for my interest will still be fresh in all you do, and are, suffer or enjoy. You do not seem to be one man, but a great nation of men. For you carry them all in your heart, and make them as one individual in the eyes of the public.[45]

Mary Mann's Educational Crusade

After Sarmiento's departure, Mary Mann remained in touch with his successor in Washington, Manuel R. García, a career diplomat recently arrived from France. There were several outstanding issues that required attention, such as a report commissioned by Sarmiento to Mann's son George, on the state of American higher education; the recruitment of elementary schoolteachers; the establishment of an astronomical observatory in Córdoba involving the Cambridge-based scientist Benjamin Gould, and the ongoing Triple Alliance War, which had claimed the life of Sarmiento's own son, Dominguito. García also kept Mary Mann informed about Sarmiento's challenges as president. "Our friend," he wrote, "is fighting a civil war that is waged against him by the reactionary party. I hope he will triumph, and soon. The prosperity of our country under his administration, his character, background, and *strong will*, will lead him to victory *au depit de toutes resistances*."[46] García availed himself of the opportunity to celebrate Sarmiento's intervention in the provinces: "He breaks with the tradition of our governments," he reported, "that by failing to assert themselves they become the toy of the *Condottieri*, perpetual and arbitrary governors of our poor provinces."[47]

Despite such confidence in Sarmiento, not all was well in Argentina, for the Triple Alliance War continued to take its toll. To meet expenses, deep cuts had been made necessary, and parts of it came from the educational budget. Insurrections lingered even as external war debilitated the country. According to Sarmiento's own assessment, recently elected and eager to impose martial law, "six years of convulsions [and] of executive inaction have created a feeling of repulsion to every means that might tend to secure tranquility."[48] From the perspective of Washington, Manuel García lamented an additional woe: the Paraguayan government of Francisco Solano López had found some defenders in the American press, and the Argentine legation had trouble finding ways to counterattack.[49] "Is this the product of ignorance?" he asked rhetorically, "I cannot believe it. If it is not because of ignorance, how does one explain presenting as hero the most repugnant monster of the present age?"[50] Part of the problem, as he understood it, was that the alliance with Brazil, the sole remaining slave society in South America, and a monarchy to boot, hurt Argentina's image in the United States.[51] Without asking her directly, García hoped to persuade Mann to write an article on the war that was favorable to the Alliance.

Much of Mary Mann's exposure to Argentine conditions came through her efforts to promote primary education in the country. But identifying and dispatching U.S. teachers was a complicated affair. Her correspondence with the Argentine educator Juana Manso is particularly telling in this regard, and some of it did not reflect well on Sarmiento's presidency, or personality. Manso told Mann unequivocally that the conditions of the country were far from ideal, even under the newly inaugurated (since October 12, 1868) administration. Sarmiento, she said, was unhappy with his own ministers, had chosen some unpopular ones, and turned his back on old friends. "I don't see him," she wrote in hesitant English to Mary Mann, "it is about four months and he never remember me in this lapse of time I loved him as a brother and I am been a first of his friends. But we must wait for a while God's Justice."[52] American teachers went into Argentina anyway, thanks to Mary Mann's tireless efforts, but Manso remained skeptical. "The plans of Mr. Sarmiento have failed," she pronounced, "because we really are not yet in a situation whereby young women can travel the desert *pampas* [plains] to towns lacking in civilization."[53]

The purpose of hiring American teachers had been to bring primary education to the provinces.[54] But some of the otherwise enthusiastic teachers identified by Mann and recruited by the Argentine government balked at the idea once they understood the conditions of the country. Some of them refused to proceed to the distant interior provinces and Sarmiento, in desperation, appealed to Manso for help. "The President called me after a year and a half," she wrote to Mary Mann, "just to intercede on his behalf." Manso tried but soon realized that there had been a disastrous meeting between the American teachers and the president. They told Manso that when they refused to go to the province of San Juan, Sarmiento "summoned them and did what a gentleman must *never* do to a lady: scold them, blind with fury, speaking half in English and half in Spanish." Naturally the American women were in a great state of agitation; Manso withdrew without further attempts at persuasion, although she managed to convince them to stay in Buenos Aires. Manso ruefully concluded that "the truth is that, though we are not Cuba, our interior provinces are like the villages around Cairo: in the heart of the desert, and barbarism. Each provincial capital [in Argentina] is a small village governed in the middle of nothing."[55] To bring American teachers to the provinces was equivalent to sending "religious missions to the Orient."[56] In essence, the end of the Triple Alliance War had presented no panacea to the country. Factionalism was rampant, the old struggle between Buenos Aires and the interior continued unabated, and "Roman fanaticism becomes every day more robust."[57] Manso was particularly upset by the latter. "Our city has fallen into the hands of the Jesuits," she wrote with dramatic flair, "it has been seven years since women have been regimented in secret religious associations. For a heretic like myself, there is nothing but hatred and war without a truce."[58] Perhaps not surprisingly, she wished to leave the country. All of this was allegedly but poignantly happening under Sarmiento's watch.

Mary Mann remained steadfast in her loyalty to the project and to Sarmiento. "I do not believe a word of the stories that have frightened [the teachers] from going to San Juan," she assured Sarmiento.[59] Indeed, she suspected that Manso herself may have had something to do with the refusal of the American educators to go to the provinces due to her own unhappiness about the country in general, and Sarmiento in particular. Clearly, Mary Mann was determined that the project should succeed, and was willing to look past the difficulties and even the warnings of correspondents such as Manso.

Perhaps the key to Mary Mann's convictions lies in the belief, shared by her husband and to some extent by Sarmiento himself, in the power of education, especially children's education, to improve the world. She had devoted her entire life to teaching, and was truly sympathetic to Sarmiento's plans for educational development in Argentina. Had she not perceived some sincerity in his commitment, she may have well balked at the time and energy that he demanded from her. But there were larger political convictions as well, which are particularly relevant in this context. And that involves the similarities she perceived between the conditions of the United States and Spanish America (but particularly Argentina) in the nineteenth century.

Mary Mann believed that both regions had been deeply hurt by the "pernicious doctrine of state sovereignty."[60] In the United States, she knew the consequences well enough, but now that she had an opportunity to look closely at the Río de la Plata region, however filtered by Sarmiento, she understood with singular clarity the fundamental issue of nineteenth-century Argentina: the damaging tension between Buenos Aires and the provinces and the difficulty, as a result, of building strong national institutions. In a key passage in her preface to Sarmiento's *Life in the Argentine Republic*, she traced the root of the problem to *caudillismo* (although referring to it as *caudillage*), or predominance of charismatic rural military leaders. She thereby provided perhaps the earliest manifestation of an enduring theme in U.S. historiography concerning Spanish America, as the words *caudillo* and *caudillismo* continue to be common currency to this day. She described how the efforts of the early patriots to build an independent national government were thwarted by rural indifference:

> The rural districts never made a movement which revealed a political idea, and they never misunderstood any government. It is true that the gauchos, a peculiar race of men that is seen in the pampas, and holds a middle place between the European and the aboriginal inhabitant, followed certain partisans of that epoch, but it was because those partisans were the immediate authority which they recognized; they followed them from personal affection and from the habit of obedience, but from no political conviction, nor from any desire to make any system prevail for their interest as a class. The chieftainship (*caudillage*) did not appear till 1829. The rural districts, passively obedient, knew neither "Unitarianism" nor "Federalism." If the Congress of 1826 had proclaimed a federation, the chiefs that then represented the federation would have cried *unity*; the opposition was against men, not against things, which were but a pretext.[61]

Mary Mann's understanding of *caudillismo* owed much to Sarmiento's own interpretation, but it reflected her desire to understand the peculiar nature of Argentine "federalism" during the Rosas period (and beyond), when it came to mean provincial autonomy at the expense of the national government. "It has been very difficult for me to picture to my imagination exactly what the word *Unitario* meant," she told Sarmiento. If she understood correctly, the *Unitarios* were opposed to the federalists but had come to embrace some of the basic tenets of federalism?[62] Indeed, she wondered, in what way was Sarmiento himself a *Unitario*? "Your question about the word 'Unitario' is most appropriate," he responded somewhat uneasily, "since it does offer difficulties." The old Unitarios such as Bernardino Rivadavia, he wrote, had attempted to build a central government, but had only managed to antagonize the provinces and unleash a "federalist" reaction. "I belonged to the Unitario persuasion," he explained, "because of my education and my antagonism to everything Rosas and the caudillos stood for." But then he had gone to the United States (in 1847) and experienced a revelation about "how federal institutions worked." Since then, he "had championed a federal government as a means of constituting the republic according to the system and constitution of the United States." When he wrote these words, in 1868, Sarmiento knew that he was a frontrunner in the Argentine presidential election, and wished to secure the support of the United States. In addition, he admitted that he wanted "to attract partisans from the various provinces because we were in effect advocating what already existed."[63] In short, he was trying to justify his transition from an anti-federalist liberal *Unitario*, to a conveniently committed federalist wielding *Unitario* powers, for solid political reasons. Mary Mann got the point and related this aspect of Sarmiento's conversion as follows: "The Foundations of [the] federal system were thus unconsciously laid by the Unitarios themselves, though at the time they opposed federation."[64] The Unitarios, in the end, were the true federalists. Sarmiento had a way with words, but only Mann could make them intelligible and acceptable to an American audience.

But there was one more compelling reason that made Mary Mann promote Sarmiento through thick and thin: the notion that the challenges of Reconstruction were similar to those of Argentina.

> "Such is the composition of our country," she wrote to President Sarmiento, "that we can sympathize with your difficulties far better than we could in those days of northern apathy when we winked at the evils of our southern country for the sake of the money they made for us—In the southern people with their millions of uneducated freedmen we have almost as great a difficulty as you have with your gauchos. This is saying too much, & is leaving out of the question the priest-ridden society that lies like an incubus upon the breast of your country."[65]

For Mary Mann the solution to all problems resided in education, and she felt that as a powerful national leader Sarmiento was in a position to demonstrate what could be done with elementary instruction for citizenship. She had every stake in his success, if indeed education was Sarmiento's central concern. The man who could implement her husband's program on a national scale would provide a wonderful example for the United States. It would be the fulfillment of her dream, a final act of loyalty to her beliefs and to the memory of Horace Mann. In the process, she did much more: she conjured the image of the untamed, "barbaric" gauchos to promote educational reform in the southern states, while at the same time providing the country with a view of Spanish America as uncivilized, yet improving; priest-ridden, but making significant strides to achieve freedom; and, ultimately, as a region of hope where American values could find fertile ground.

Chapter 7

The "Annals of Barbarians": William H. Prescott and the Conquest of the New World

The whole story has the air of fable, rather than of history! A legend of romance—a tale of the genii!

—William H. Prescott, *History of the Conquest of Mexico*, Book V, Ch. 7

It is a tale of destiny; a bloody tale, which reflects more credit on the heroism, than the humanity of the old conquerors.

—William H. Prescott to Pascual de Gayangos, April 4, 1840

On June 13, 1836, William Hickling Prescott wrote the last note of the last chapter of his *History of the Reign of Ferdinand and Isabella, the Catholic*. Despite a serious disability to his eyes, Prescott finished this book, seven and a half years in the making, and numerous other titles in the next two decades. After the publication of *Ferdinand and Isabella* (1838), the Boston-based, Salem-born historian authored the *History of the Conquest of Mexico* (1843) and the *History of the Conquest of Peru* (1847); wrote an addendum to William Robertson's *The History of the Reign of the Emperor Charles the Fifth* (1857); and penned three volumes of his unfinished *History of the Reign of Philip the Second, King of Spain* (1855–1858). Never at a loss for words, Prescott also wrote numerous reviews, which he compiled and published as a revised volume of *Biographical and Critical Miscellanies* (1845 and 1850). Due to his prolific writing and enormously successful record as a historian, Prescott became an international celebrity, and one of the most widely read American historians in the nineteenth century. Because of his near blindness, Prescott was also admired for the determination with which he overcame his disability, working long hours, writing in the dark, risking what little eyesight was left to him to read documents, and listening to his various readers when he could not bear the strain on his only working eye. Such a man invited well-deserved praise and compassion. He was a legend in his own lifetime.[1]

The recognition of Prescott's success, productivity, single-mindedness of purpose and well-defined intellectual agenda has tended to obscure a number of significant issues in his undeniably impressive trajectory. First, it is not often acknowledged that

Prescott doubted, procrastinated, and agonized over his decision to study Spanish history. Second, the view of the heroic, nearly blind historian writing alone and against considerable odds, has overlooked the considerable assistance he received from an international network of friends, paid assistants, and volunteers who furnished him with hard-to-find documents, ideas, and books. Especially neglected in the published correspondence and biographies are the contributions of Spanish American scholars, who provided pointed critiques and corrected many of the historian's errors. Third, Prescott's choice of subject appeared to be so novel and yet so familiar, his writing so attractive and yet so credible as history, that most of his underlying assumptions were seldom questioned. To what extent, for instance, did Prescott's interest in Spain and Spanish America rest on long-held views about the Hispanic world? Did his emphasis on the decline of Spain serve as a warning to his own country, now aggressively expanding at the expense of Mexico and the native inhabitants to the west? Did Prescott's Unitarian background influence his view of pre-Columbian religions as well as of Iberian Catholicism? Why were some historical actors and themes, such as the kingdom of Ferdinand and Isabella, Hernán Cortés, Francisco Pizarro, and the clashes of Christian and indigenous peoples more emphasized than others? These are some of the questions that are examined in this chapter.

William Hickling Prescott decided to study Spanish history after considerable doubts in 1826—that is, at the age of 30 and long after he graduated from Harvard in 1814. As a college undergraduate he lost the vision of his left eye due to an unfortunate accident (a classmate threw a piece of hard bread directly into his eye, causing irreversible damage). Shortly thereafter, his right eye began to suffer from unrelated but disabling inflammations that essentially ended a career intended for the law (his successful father's profession), and forced him to seek constant treatment as well as search for an alternative occupation. The Prescott family was sufficiently wealthy to send young William to Europe for medical treatment in 1815, and also to support him well past the point when he could have supported himself thanks to the extraordinary sale of his books (which only happened when he was in his forties). Prescott's talents pointed clearly in the direction of literary pursuits, and he decided relatively early that writing would be the career of his choice. But which specific sort of "literary pursuits"? He had little inclination for teaching, nor was there much demand for it, in the Boston-Cambridge area of the 1820s. Review writing was still an amateurish endeavor, not likely to secure anyone a respectable position in society. Still, he practiced it, writing some articles for the *North American Review*, the leading American journal of letters in Prescott's time. He also searched for a subject in which he could specialize as well as satisfy his own intellectual interests. One such subject was Italian literature, something of a favorite among his literary friends, especially the works of Dante. In the early 1820s, Prescott's journal entries are dominated by references to Italian works, especially epic poetry.

By 1824, however, certain references to Spanish literature began to appear. On April 18, for instance, he made a brief reference to Miguel de Cervantes y Saavedra. By November 20, he had determined to study a number of Spanish authors,[2] and by February 13, 1825 he could report that he had begun the systematic study of the Spanish language and had read José Cadalso's *Cartas Marruecas*, Cervantes's *Don Quixote*, and Alonso de Ercilla's *La Araucana*. This last work received detailed comment, as a particularly attractive, but not flawless, piece of epic literature. Between

July 3 and 10, 1825, he had read José María Blanco White's *Letters from Spain* (1822), a source that has been entirely missed by Prescott's biographers, and whose significance is discussed in chapter 8. By December he had narrowed his choice of topics to two, and stated a strong inclination to pursue a Spanish subject.

There was not much in Prescott's background to lead him naturally to such a choice. Growing up in New England, he had heard the usual negative references to Spain that crystallized after centuries of Anglo-Spanish antagonisms in the form of the so-called Black Legend. He had read *Amadis de Gaula* as a youth, and probably parts of *Don Quixote*, one of the few works of Spanish literature widely available in English. He had certainly heard of the Inquisition. Reporting to his father on his entrance exam at Harvard in 1811, the 15-year old Prescott spoke of his examiners as follows: "When we were first ushered into their presence, they looked like so many judges of the Inquisition. We were ordered down into the parlor, almost frightened out of our wits, to be examined by each separately."[3] The Inquisition, as part of the Roman Catholic Church, had been, and continued to be, the most recurring reference in discussions of Spain, Portugal, and their dominions. Writing to his parents from the Azores in 1815, where he visited his maternal grandfather on his way to London, Prescott felt informed enough to remark on the poverty and lack of industry that characterized Catholic countries.[4] Writing to his friend William H. Gardiner, he was even more sweeping: "It is an interesting employment for the inhabitants of a free country, flourishing under the influence of a benign religion, to contemplate the degradation to which human nature may be reduced when oppressed by arbitrary power and papal superstition."[5] In this, Prescott showed little divergence from the predominant American view of a backward, priest-ridden, and inquisitorial Iberian culture. His own father, one of the most enlightened men in early nineteenth-century Boston, asked his son in 1817, "What will become of Spain? Will bigoted priests continue to govern the king and persecute the best men in the nation?"[6] Given such automatic assumptions, the question about Prescott's strong inclination to study the Hispanic world becomes all the more important to answer.

The Age of Ferdinand and Isabella

It was George Ticknor who introduced Prescott to the serious study of Spanish subjects. Five years his senior, Ticknor met young William in Boston prior to his departure for study in Germany, but renewed his acquaintance in Paris in April 1817, when they lodged together and Ticknor looked after Prescott during a particularly severe bout of eye inflammation. "It was in that dark room," Ticknor wrote later, "that I first learned to know him as I have never known any other person beyond the limits of my immediate family."[7] When they were both back in Boston, they renewed what was now a strong and lasting friendship. Ticknor had become the first Smith Professor of Modern Languages at Harvard, and, having put his lectures in writing, he read them to Prescott. This is how Ticknor described what proved to be a turning point in Prescott's life:

> Thinking simply to amuse and occupy my friend at a time when he seemed much to need it, I proposed to read him these lectures in the autumn of 1824. For this purpose he came to my house in the early part of a succession of evenings, until the whole was

completed; and in November he determined, as a substitute for the German, to
undertake the Spanish, which had not previously constituted any part of his plan of
study.[8]

Prescott had clearly meditated much while listening to his friend's reading. By the
end of that year and throughout 1825, he read widely and systematically enough to
tax the resources available in Ticknor's library. During that period, he also formed
an idea of what he intended to study. He leaned heavily toward a topic in Spanish
history, "from the invasion of the Arabs to the consolidation of the Monarchy under
Charles V," but he also considered a study of "the revolution of Ancient Rome
which converted the republic into the Empire," a choice that is indicative of his
fledgling historical concerns.[9] He expressed a preference for the former on the
grounds of its novelty, and also because he thought it would be more "entertaining"
than the alternative topic. During January 1826, after much arguing with himself
about the pros and cons, he made up his mind to study Spanish history, in large
measure because "The age of Ferdinand is most important as containing the germs
of the modern system of European politics," and because "it is in every aspect an
interesting and momentous period of history."[10] He made his final decision on
January 19 and, three days later, he wrote to Alexander Hill Everett, then in Spain
as U.S. minister, to ask for his assistance in the collection of books and documents
relating to Spanish history. The correspondence between the two during the next
18 months provides a unique window into Prescott's earliest activities as a historian.

Everett insisted that Prescott should go to Spain, a suggestion that the latter
repeatedly declined. In December of 1826, for instance, Prescott wrote "I fear that
you will prefer I should visit Spain in person, than thus to persecute you with letters
and postscripts about my own concerns. But as my situation makes this impractica-
ble, I know no other way of accomplishing what I have very much at heart than
through your good offices."[11] A few days later, he felt that he had to make the point
more strongly: "The state of my eyes, or rather eye, for I have the use of only one
half of this valuable apparatus, precludes the possibility of it." How could he then
pursue his historical endeavors? "An intelligent reader," he told Everett, "who is
well acquainted with French, Spanish and Latin, will enable me to effect with my
ears what other people do with eyes." As a sign of his determination, and with a
certain anxiety, he concluded that he would look upon "literary pursuits as the
principal and permanent source of future enjoyment."[12]

Everett complied with Prescott's mounting requests as best he could, and relied
increasingly on the great book collector and dealer Obadiah Rich, with whom
Prescott soon established a direct correspondence. But it was to Everett that he first
revealed, in a detailed letter of 1827, the nature and scope of his current interests,
the reign of Ferdinand and Isabella in Spain:

> The more nearly I view my subject, the more I am struck with its importance and inter-
> est. The conquest of Granada, which would lead me to a general retrospect[ive] of the
> antique glories of the Spanish Arabs, the establishment of the Inquisition, the discovery
> of America, and the brilliant conquests of Italy . . . are doubtless the most imposing and
> captivating incidents of the drama. But the theory of government as it existed in the
> time of the Catholic kings, which I take to be the final epoch of the exercise of anything
> like popular rights, and which appears, much more than I was aware, to have presented
> an important era in the legislative history of the country . . . will have a deeper interest

for thinking minds than a chronological series of battles and treaties, and as such should claim a large share of the labors of the historian.[13]

It is certainly noteworthy that Prescott should now identify himself as a historian, and that he should also view history as not entirely divorced from literary forms, as evidenced by his references to the subject's "interest," and the period in question as a "drama." But he also had an additional motivation: "If I could accomplish such a work as I desire, it should exhibit not merely a historical record of transactions, but a lively veracious picture of the peculiar character of the Spanish nation, of that period, and of that of their civil institutions."[14] What he set out to capture, in this and in all subsequent works, was precisely that "peculiar character." In the nascent American historical tradition, the preoccupation with the ultimate essence of nationality (as illustrated by the work of George Bancroft), and especially that of Spain, was firmly established by Prescott.

In the process, Prescott also established a number of other themes and methodologies. History, in his view, had to be written on the basis of original records of the period under examination. Such emphasis on documentation, however, should not detract from the intrinsic interest of the story, or from an attractive narrative. His model, in this respect, was Amable Guillaume Prosper Brugière de Barante, whose *Histoire des Ducs de Bourgogne de la Maison de Valois* (1824) combined "all the interest of Romance with the solid instruction of history." He also considered the historian Gabriel Bonnet de Mably, of whom he wrote, "I like particularly his notion of the necessity of giving an interest as well as utility to History by letting events tend to some obvious point or moral." Prescott certainly admired, and to some extent followed, Augustin Thierry's use of popular romances as well as poetry in his own historical works.[15] The key to his success, in fact, was in the highly developed literary aspect of his writings. He also paid particular attention to issues of organization and chronological sequence. Prescott broke down historical topics into discrete segments, with clearly defined beginnings and ends. For instance, in his first work, the reign of the Catholic kings was seen as "an epoch lying between the anarchy of the preceding period and the despotism and extravagant schemes of the succeeding."[16] *Ferdinand and Isabella* was ultimately a story of triumphant reconquest and nation building, inspiring accomplishments in politics, exploration, and trade, and the highest manifestation of the Spanish national character. But it was also a story of impending trouble and decay, as the Inquisition gained ground and Spain was propelled to the status of a world power.

The Annals of Barbarians

Ferdinand and Isabella was received with wide acclaim in both the United States and Europe when it came out in late 1837. George Ticknor was in Europe at the time and promoted the book personally, placing presentation copies to individuals and magazines until he managed to secure substantial coverage in leading journals, most notably the *Edinburgh Review*.[17] Prescott was uncommonly enthused by the reception of his book in England, and reflected on his own personal reaction. He had feared the critique of unfriendly British reviewers, who had been consistently rude and condescending toward American authors. And yet, Prescott made it clear that he wanted their approval. "Independent in every other respect," he wrote, "we are still a colony in letters."[18] Writing to James Rich (Obadiah's son) he admitted that "we defer, I fear too much for our literary independence, to foreign criticism."[19] So important was the reception, especially British, of his work, that he had begun collecting materials for a life of Molière, in case his first major historical work should not succeed. But the accolades now persuaded him to undertake a history of the conquest of Mexico and Peru. Writing to the Spanish historian Martín Fernández de Navarrete in 1838, he described his new interests as follows:

> My history of the Catholic Kings has met with so favorable a reception from my countrymen that I feel stimulated to pursue the subject of Spanish history further, and no portion of it has greater interest for us than that connected with our own country, and which in itself is singularly romantic, like the Conquest of Mexico and Peru. The story has often been told, however, and it would not be worth while to attempt it anew without the use of such original documents as will give it the highest authenticity.[20]

As he put it in his private journal, the new project was a "natural continuation" of the first book, and in addition had "the superior advantage of relating to my own quarter of the globe." There was a potential problem, however, in that Washington Irving, perhaps the most popular writer at the time, was also contemplating a history of the conquest of Mexico. Both Prescott and Irving were initially alarmed, but in the end the issue was amicably resolved, with Irving yielding the topic to his younger colleague.[21] Once this hurdle was cleared, Prescott could begin the considerable arrangements for a work of such scope, and promise. He was made somewhat uneasy, however, by the prospect of writing "the annals of the conquests of barbarians."[22]

Besides commercial and critical success, *Ferdinand and Isabella* introduced him to many individuals in the Hispanic world who became devoted admirers and friends. Among the earliest are the Spanish-born, Oxford-educated Pascual de Gayangos, who wrote a favorable notice for the *Edinburgh Review*, and Ángel Calderón de la Barca, a Spanish diplomat who provided him with documents and information from his various posts, but most importantly with his own knowledge of people and scholarly subjects. Prescott met Calderón in 1837, when he was serving as Spanish minister in the United States. The ambassador was so impressed by Prescott that he wrote to the Royal Academy of History in Madrid to seek his appointment as corresponding member of the institution.[23] To Gayangos he introduced himself in a letter in 1839, thanking him for his review and asking for any manuscripts he might have concerning the conquistadors Hernán Cortés and Francisco Pizarro. Once Gayangos responded, their correspondence would only end with Prescott's death.[24] It was to him that the Boston historian intimated that his present subject was "a tale of destiny; a bloody tale, which reflects more credit on the heroism, than the humanity of the old conquerors."[25]

The Boston historian, now determined to begin with the Spanish conquest of the Aztec empire, also contacted Joel Roberts Poinsett, the former U.S. envoy to Mexico who had made himself notorious by meddling in the country's politics in the 1820s, and who was currently (1839) secretary of war in the Martin Van Buren administration. Prescott explained that he had obtained some letters of introduction from Ángel Calderón to the literary scholars José Gómez, Count of Cortina, and Manuel Eduardo de Gorostiza. However, due to the country's "state of bouleversement," he was not sure that he would find them, and asked, therefore, for additional contacts and for a secure way to convey mail.[26]

Poinsett was glad to help, and told Prescott that he would provide letters and any other assistance. He recommended that the historian also contact Lucas Alamán (1792–1853), the leading statesman and towering intellectual figure of nineteenth-century Mexico, although "I regret that from political differences I cannot offer you a letter to him." This was one of the first indications that research on Mexico would be greatly more complicated than research on his earlier subject. Poinsett, however, was encouraging:

"The work you contemplate is one of great interest and I think it still a hiatus in American history, especially the portion of it that relates to Mexico." The subject, he added "has been treated, but never fully, and the author of the *History of Ferdinand and Isabella* cannot fail to impart to it the charm both of novelty and of style."[27]

Perhaps sensing the potential difficulties, political and practical, Prescott contacted the commercial firm of Manning and Marshall, which had offices in Mexico City and the port of Veracruz, to handle correspondence and funds for the acquisition of documents and research assistance.[28] He also decided to limit the scope of his research. In response to Poinsett, he made the following admission:

. . . as my inquiries relate to the Conquest and its immediate period, I do not think there will be a large mass of materials to collect, though I know there are some. If I were to go deep into the antiquities of Mexico I should, doubtless, find an ocean of manuscripts. But I shall content myself, for these, with the accounts I can gather from printed works; my design, in this respect, being, to give such a view of the previous civilization of the Mexicans, as will interest the reader in their fortunes; and not involve myself in the mesh of speculation which has bewildered so many wiser and more learned heads than mine. But I do wish to place the Conquest both of Mexico and Peru on a perfectly authentic basis.[29]

What followed confirmed his concerns. He managed to get letters and packages containing presentation copies of his *Ferdinand and Isabella* to Mexico. Manning and Marshall acknowledged receipt of the first batch of letters on March 27, 1839, but within a month they reported that it would be difficult to secure research assistance. Apparently, Cortina was neither particularly diligent, nor responsive. In addition, "the archives of the various monasteries in this city have been suffered to fall into great confusion." The problem, as Manning and Marshall saw it, was securing a person "possessing not only intelligence but also a taste and inclination for research of the kind—any person whose labours are not incited by a higher motive than a disposition to oblige, or a pecuniary consideration, is not likely to devote to the subject the requisite assiduity." By the end of the year, the weary agents reported that they had been able to extract some books from Cortina, but that they had not been able to obtain a portrait, requested by Prescott, of the Aztec Emperor Moctezuma.[30]

Prescott's fortunes changed when his friend Ángel Calderón de la Barca was appointed Spanish minister to Mexico in 1839, and arrived there in February 1840. Calderón and his Scottish wife Frances Erskine Inglis, better known as Fanny Calderón, were happy to aid the historian, who had become a close friend during their stay in the United States. Calderón contacted Cortina, but quickly realized that not much could be obtained from the amiable but procrastinating aristocrat.

However, he had better luck with Lucas Alamán, who provided him with considerable information about the life of Hernán Cortés, and placed himself at the disposal of Prescott. Calderón was pleased with him and his offer, but he also described the frustrations of obtaining research materials in Mexico,

> As everything here is disorder and procrastination, it is necessary to seek these papers where they are, and keep the day and the season, because so-and-so is in the field or in the council, and the clerk who is to do the copying is ill or busy, and will come tomorrow; and tomorrow never comes. So I am occupied and shall be occupied without losing sight of it, with what you want and with whatever relates to your work; and whenever I may find a printed book that I think bears on your object or that you ask me to send to you. I only ask the indulgence that I must myself grant in the highest degree—patience and more patience.[31]

Both Alamán and Calderón urged Prescott to go to Mexico himself, but the historian declined. He had considered it, he told Fanny Calderón, but was dissuaded by the discomforts and perils of the trip.[32] He thought he had enough documents, and preferred to fill any gaps by literary means. The disadvantages of this approach would be quickly identified by Mexican historians, as we shall see later.

In many ways, Prescott's friends and self-appointed aides were more diligent than the Boston historian in securing documents and conveying information they thought he needed. Alamán, for instance, took Calderón to the Hospital of Jesus, founded by Cortés, where the conqueror's remains were buried for a time. There, on his own initiative, Calderón examined the archives and ordered copies of documents. He also conveyed whatever interesting gossip he encountered, such as the story that Mexican liberals had attempted to destroy the remains of Cortés in a fit of anti-Spanish frenzy, or that historian Carlos María Bustamante had taken materials from the library of the convent of San Francisco and never returned them.[33] Calderón obviously did not think too highly of Mexico after independence ("of the Mexican people almost nothing can be said in their praise"), and found enough eager individuals to confirm the worst stories about their personal or political opponents.[34] Prescott was generally careful about documentary evidence, but some of these unconfirmed rumors made it into the pages of his *History of the Conquest of Mexico*.

Prescott also enjoyed, and made much use of, Fanny Calderón's rich and detailed letters. The Scotswoman had an extraordinary power of observation, and wrote in an easy and pleasant style. Most importantly for Prescott, she wrote lengthy letters, and was happy to oblige her friend when he asked specific questions about the climate and the flora of Mexico. But she also indulged in the sort of condescending commentary about the country and its people that, if it did not inform Prescott's own views, at least he chose not to contest. Her lengthy descriptions of Mexican haplessness, laziness, lack of effective government, religious bigotry, were all told in picturesque prose, and invited equally lengthy responses from Prescott.[35] Her more sympathetic observations about the country were soon published under the title *Life in Mexico*, a book that enjoyed tremendous popularity in its day, and which is still in print. Prescott, who appreciated her letters very much, was instrumental in getting the book published, with his preface, and also wrote an encomiastic commentary for the *North American Review*.[36]

When the Calderóns left Mexico for Cuba in late 1841, Prescott continued a correspondence with Alamán, and soon established it with a few others.[37] This correspondence was of an altogether different character compared to that of the Calderóns. Alamán, for instance, was not only well informed about the history of his country, but he also had important records of his own. One issue of particular interest to Prescott was the fate of the remains of Cortés. Alamán told him that he knew about their whereabouts but that it might be best to keep the information confidential, for he feared acts of vandalism stemming from anti-Spanish sentiment. Alamán had previously told Calderón about an attempt to desecrate the remains of the conquistador in 1823, and Prescott had been informed about it. The American historian said that he regretted not to be able to provide a location for the remains, but understood Alamán's reasons. What he could not understand was the anger against the Spaniards coming mostly from their own progeny. "One would think that the Mexicans considered themselves as descended from the Indians and not from the Spaniards."[38] Preoccupied with the epic components of his history of the conquest, that is, a seamless narrative filled with literary ornaments, Prescott was exposed for the first time to the political realities of independent Mexico, where competing interpretations of the past elicited scorn, anger, and confrontation.

Alamán was unusually well read, and could be quite blunt in criticizing the works of others, especially when he detected tendentious political interpretations (of which he himself was by no means free). He criticized, for instance, José María Luis Mora's interpretation of the conspiracy of the sons of Cortés in 1566: "The liberal tone that he gives to the conspiracy is neither in accord with historical truth, nor with the ideas of the time, for their only purpose was to separate Mexico from the Spanish government in order to keep their allocations of Indians (*repartimiento de indios*)." He also criticized Carlos María Bustamante for propagating the "fiction" (*especie*) that Cortés had murdered his wife with his own hands, a charge without foundation that came from anti-Spanish propaganda. When Prescott asked him about the origins and authenticity of the picture of Moctezuma, which he had secured through the good offices of Cortina and Ángel Calderón, Alamán responded with a slight tone of impatience: "It is entirely apocryphal, because it was never taken from the original." The Spaniards who accompanied Cortés, he said, could hardly write, much less draw, "and it is only they who actually met the Mexican emperor." Moreover, and not without a touch of humor, Alamán indicated that Moctezuma looked "more Roman than Aztec" in this picture. Of Doña Marina, the legendary Indian mistress and interpreter of Cortés, there was not even an apocryphal image, and thus all depictions of her must be false. In short, Alamán was willing to help Prescott, but was not about to validate all his assumptions or sources of information.[39]

It is also very significant that Alamán was one of the few who, like the Calderóns, supplied Prescott with information, ideas, and even disagreements, while the Boston historian was in the process of writing. The latter, by 1842, was proceeding quite rapidly and successfully. George Ticknor told Henry Wadsworth Longfellow in the summer of that year that,

> I hear frequently from Prescott. He is well and has been working hard this summer. I have just been reading his manuscript as far as it is finished, that is to the death of Montezuma, and it is very fine. There is an epick completeness about the subject, as well as a fiery romance in the details that will make it as taking as a novel. The account of the *noche triste*—the night the Spaniards were driven out of Mexico—is admirable as a piece of eloquent description. It is a thing to dream of after you have read it.[40]

American readers, and nearly simultaneously, British readers, would soon find out. The *History of the Conquest of Mexico* appeared in three volumes in December 1843 to instant success.[41]

Between Romance and History

Prescott's *History of the Conquest of Mexico* follows the steps of Hernán Cortés' campaign against the Aztec empire in the years 1519–1521, with some coverage of his less-than-glorious postconquest life. Based on original manuscript sources, the Bostonian's three-volume work was a triumph of scholarship that, though superseded in many respects by current research, has stood the test of time. The review of the main political and military decisions, the tensions between Crown officials and conquistadors, the study of individuals, and, most importantly, the understanding of Indian divisions, became standard subjects for all the histories that followed.[42] However, what concerns us here is not so much the accuracy of his account (which is by and large high, especially in the context of the documentation available to him) but rather the views of the author, placed in the larger context of American perspectives of the Hispanic world in the middle decades of the nineteenth century. The following are some of the themes that occupied Prescott's attention.

The Hierarchy of Civilizations

Perhaps the central concern of Prescott in his *History* relates to the nature of civilizations, their evolution, characteristics, and reasons for their eventual demise. The book is specifically about the contest between Aztecs and Spaniards in the early sixteenth century. But both the time-span of the coverage, and the statements about older and emerging empires and civilizations, show that Prescott had a more ambitious goal in mind: to present the dynamics of how civilizations evolve, reach their peak, encounter other competing civilizations, and either prevail or collapse. From his perch in the nineteenth century, Prescott offered an evolutionary view of how civilizations, historically, have moved from barbarism to ascending, ever more refined forms of social, political, cultural, and religious life. Thus, the Aztecs could engage in a variety of "barbaric" practices, like human sacrifice and cannibalism, but they were "advanced in civilization far beyond the wandering tribes of North America." Indeed, Prescott stated, "as inferred by their political institutions, [the Aztecs] may be considered, perhaps, not much short of that enjoyed by our Saxon ancestors, under Alfred." Ultimately, however, "they may be better compared with the Egyptians" (44). Still, they could not match the civilization of the Spaniards: "The Aztec had plainly reached that middle station, as far above the rude races of the New World as it was below the cultivated communities of the Old" (441–442). Well aware of Spanish cruelties toward the Aztecs, Prescott concluded from the conquest that "the cause of humanity, indeed has gained. [Mexicans] live under a better system of laws, a more assured tranquility, [and] a purer faith" (45). The Aztecs, Prescott determined, showed traces of refinement, even civilization, but these coexisted with a number of brutal practices. Such a mix could only be explained, he wrote, "as the result of religious superstition; superstition which clouds the moral perception, and perverts even the natural senses, till man, civilized man, is reconciled to the very things which are most revolting to humanity" (119). The Aztecs and their "gloomy superstition," just in case there was any doubt, "were emphatically a fierce and brutal race" (814). Therefore,

> In this state of things [the barbarism of the Aztecs], it was beneficently ordered by Providence that the land should be delivered over to another race, who would rescue it from the brutish superstitions that daily extended wider and wider, with extent of empire. The debasing institutions of the Aztecs furnish the best apology for their conquest. It is true, the conquerors brought along with them the Inquisition. But they also brought Christianity, whose benign radiance would still survive, when the fierce flames of fanaticism should be extinguished; dispelling those dark forms of horror which had so long brooded over the fair regions of Anahuac. (68–69)

Fanaticism, bigotry, and greed, are listed in the *History* among the dismal legacies of the Spaniards. "We may well doubt," wrote Prescott, "which has the strongest claims to civilization, the victor, or the vanquished" (80). Initially, one of the early explorers, Francisco Hernández de Córdoba, was astonished to witness indications of "a civilization far superior to any thing he had before witnessed in the New World" (165), but other Spaniards gradually came to the conclusion, or found it convenient to believe, that this was a civilization so antithetical to the principal pillars of Christianity that it must be subjugated. Prescott implied that Hernán Cortés, more than a clever and opportunistic conquistador, was "the instrument selected by Providence to scatter terror among the barbarian monarchs of the Western World, and lay their empires in the dust" (190). He proceeded with a series of deliberate steps: "The first object of Cortés was to reclaim the natives from their gross idolatry and to substitute a purer form of worship." Perhaps echoing Washington Irving's *Conquest of Granada* (1829), the Boston historian stated that to Cortés the Mexican campaign "was a holy war. He was in arms against the infidel" (196). The conquistador determined that, either through persuasion or force, Indians should "embrace a better faith" (197). Addressing the cacique of Cempoala, for instance, Cortés announced that "he had come to the Aztec shores, to abolish the inhuman worship which prevailed there, and to introduce the knowledge of the true God" (247).

Stepping away from Cortés at one point in the narrative, Prescott reflected that "the light of civilization would be poured on their land. But it would be the light of a consuming fire, before which [the Aztec's] barbaric glory, their institutions, their very existence and name as a nation, would wither and become extinct! Their doom was sealed, when the white man had set his foot on their soil" (252). Prescott also told his readers that the Spanish conquerors "carried with them the sword in one hand and the Bible in the other. They imposed obedience in matters of faith, no less than of government" (291). The conquistadors, moreover, were not troubled by whether it was right or wrong to invade the land, for they "held it to be their 'mission' . . . to conquer and to convert" (467). Before engaging in battle with their enemies, or their own countrymen—as when Cortés rushed from Tenochtitlan to the coast to meet the challenge of Pánfilo de Narváez—Spaniards celebrated mass and made their confessions, prompting Prescott to observe that "the incident is curious, and well illustrates the character of the time—in which war, religion, and rapine were so intimately blended together" (520). The astonishing victory over the Aztec empire, however, remained to be explained, and again Prescott resorted to religious motives: "There can be no doubt, that Cortés, with every other man in his army, felt he was engaged on a holy crusade, and that, independently of personal considerations, he could not serve Heaven better, than by planting the Cross on the blood-stained towers of the heathen metropolis" (722–723). Spaniards under his command carried "the banner of the Cross triumphant over this barbaric empire" (813). That was the driving force, as well as the central reason, for the triumph of the Spaniards. It is, therefore, important to examine how Prescott viewed Catholicism in a larger spectrum of organized religions.

The Hierarchy of Religions

Prescott used the conquest of Mexico to illustrate the strengths and weaknesses of various religions. He intimated that the higher civilizations were those that practiced a milder religion, and applied a more rational and scientific approach to social and political issues. Catholicism was presented as superior to Aztec "superstitions," but quite capable of superstitions of its own. Moreover, Catholicism was also characterized by the bigotry and fanaticism of its priests. Cortés himself is at one point in the narrative tempted to consider the recommendations of an astrologer. "Superstition was the feature of the age, and the Spanish general . . . had a full measure of its bigotry" (587).[43] Prescott noted that the Spaniards often attributed their victories—or escapes—to miracles:

> More than one grave historian refers the preservation of the Spaniards to the watchful care of their patron Apostle, St. James, who, in these desperate conflicts, was beheld careering on his milk-white steed at the head of the Christian squadrons, with his sword flashing lightning, while a lady robed in white—supposed to be the Virgin—was distinctly seen by his side, throwing dust in the eyes of the infidel! (577)

The Virgin appears repeatedly in Prescott's narrative of the conquest, often in the form of prayers, dedication of places, shrines, and images placed in Aztec temples. She also appears quite literally in some events, though often as an invocation by the soldiers, or visions by both Spaniards and Mexicans. But in all cases, there is a sarcastic touch to the historian's description, such as Irving also used in the *Conquest of Granada*. After multiple references to the Virgin during the conquest period, Prescott made it clear that her role was not confined to early Mexico. "The last instance, I believe," Prescott wrote, "of the direct interposition of the Virgin in behalf of the metropolis was in 1833." After explaining that she—or her likeness—had been brought to Mexico City to fight the cholera epidemic, and that she had turned up unexpectedly in another location, Prescott added that "by the mud with which she was plentifully bespattered, that she must have performed the distance—several leagues—through the miry ways on foot!" (604). More than the Virgin, however, it was the Catholic liturgy that most attracted his attention.

From the very beginning of their campaign, Spaniards were surprised to observe some similarities between their own Christian practices and those of the Indians. They quickly saw that Indians possessed images of the cross, were familiar with baptism and confession, understood the ceremony of the Eucharist (because of their ritual cannibalism), and were even receptive to some basic concepts of Christianity.

According to Prescott, the most central commonality was quite helpful to the Catholics,

> The Aztec worship was remarkable for its burdensome ceremonial, and prepared its votaries for the pomp and splendors of the Romish ritual. It was not difficult to pass from the fasts and festivals of the one religion to the fasts and festivals of the other; to transfer their homage from the fantastic idols of their own creation to the beautiful forms in sculpture and in painting which decorated the Christian cathedral. (851)

Nineteenth-century American Protestants, especially Unitarians, believed that the purpose of Catholic rituals was to appeal to the senses rather than to thought. According to this view, shared by the Unitarian Prescott, images of the Virgin, of Christ, and of the Cross were corporeal manifestations that detracted from a firmer and deeper understanding of divinity. Still,

> The Roman Catholic communion has, it must be admitted, some decided advantages over the Protestant, for the purposes of proselytism. The dazzling pomp of its service and its touching appeal to the sensibilities affect the imagination of the rude child of nature much more powerfully than the cold abstractions of Protestantism, which, addressed to the reason, demand a degree of refinement and mental culture in the audience to comprehend them. The respect, moreover, shown by the Catholic for the material representations of Divinity, greatly facilitates the same object. (210)

Thus, Prescott was interested not only in establishing the superiority of Catholic over Aztec beliefs, but also in promoting his own Unitarian brand of Protestantism. He praised Cortés for bringing a higher religion to the hemisphere, but criticized him for his attempts to precipitate, by dint of cruel force or showy displays of ceremony, the conversion of the natives. As he put it, "to the more rational spirit of the present day, enlightened by a *purer Christianity* [my emphasis], it may seem difficult to reconcile gross deviations from morals with such devotion to the cause of religion,"

> but the religion taught in that day was one of form and elaborate ceremony. In the punctilious attention to discipline, the spirit of Christianity was permitted to evaporate. The mind, occupied with forms, thinks little of substance. In a worship that is addressed too exclusively to the senses, it is often the case, that morality becomes divorced from religion, and the measure of righteousness is determined by the creed rather than by the conduct. (913)

Prescott repeatedly returned, in this and other writings, to the contrast between Catholicism and Protestantism to suggest that the latter represented a higher, more sophisticated form of religion:

> "The Protestant missionary seeks to enlighten the understanding of his convert by the pale light of reason," he wrote, "But the bolder Catholic, kindling the spirit by the splendor of the spectacle and by the glowing portrait of an agonized Redeemer, sweeps along his hearers in a tempest of passion, that drowns every thing like reflection. He has secured his convert, however, by the hold on his affections,—an easier and more powerful hold with the untutored savage, than reason." (258)

Catholic success was limited by emphasis on the externalities of ritual and by blatant appeal to the emotions rather than to reason. According to Prescott, the fundamental flaw resided in the "physical temperament," of Catholic nations, "for the warm sun of the South, under which Catholicism prevails, stimulates the sensibilities to the more violent expression of passion" (654). The colder North enjoyed not only religious, but also important political advantages.

The Hierarchy of Political Systems

As a conscientious reader of history and political philosophy, Prescott was familiar with the main discussions on the nature and character of different political systems. I argue here that Prescott's analysis of political institutions relied significantly on Montesquieu's tripartite division of governments: monarchical, republican, and despotic, with its respective principles of honor, virtue, and fear. The Boston historian owned the 1758 edition of the *Oeuvres*, and a separate, 1768 copy of the *Spirit of the Laws*. But he did not follow the French thinker in every respect. For instance, Prescott was more favorable to republics than to monarchies, and in this sense he was closer to Voltaire in equating monarchy with despotism. Yet he followed the main outlines of Montesquieu's characterizations, even if he modified his conclusions.

We have seen how Prescott often compared Aztec civilization with various "oriental" civilizations. In analyzing their political system, he echoed Montesquieu's strictures about "oriental despotism": readers are told that the Aztecs princes "lived in a barbaric pomp, truly Oriental" (28). There was no legislative power, which was exercised solely by the monarch, who also relied on the priesthood for enforcing conformity in the population. "Terror, not love, was the spring of education" (58). Facing the conquerors, Indian chief Cuitlahuac reluctantly made concessions to subject tribes in order to secure their support against the Spaniards, "but he was now to experience the instability of a government which rested not on love, but on fear" (628–629). Again, "fear was the great principle of cohesion which bound together the discordant members of the monarchy" (684). Occasionally, monarchs could behave with a great deal of humility, in line with "similar usages in the Asiatic and Egyptian despotisms, where the sovereign occasionally condescended to stoop from his pride of place" (136). Emperor Moctezuma II, however, expected deference quite beyond his willingness to show humility. He made himself not only feared, but also revered in extravagant ways. Describing the first encounter between Cortés and Moctezuma, Prescott offered the following reflections concerning the ceremonies surrounding the emperor, "Such was the homage paid to the Indian despot, showing that the slavish forms of Oriental adulation were to be found among the rude inhabitants of the Western World" (395–396). Spaniards were astonished to witness the luxury of Moctezuma's palace: they "might well have fancied themselves in the voluptuous precincts of an Eastern harem, instead of threading the halls of a wild barbaric chief in the Western World" (404). After reviewing the various daily practices of Moctezuma's household, Prescott concluded that "we are strongly reminded of the civilization of the East" (435). Perhaps not quite like the Arabs and Persians, but certainly like the Tatars. "It is characteristic of such a people," the historian wrote, "to find a puerile pleasure in a dazzling and ostentatious pageantry; to make show for substance; vain pomp for power; to hedge round the throne itself with a barren and burdensome ceremonial, the counterfeit of real majesty" (435).

Prescott departed again from Montesquieu in the characterization of republics. He exemplified the "republican" form of government with the Tlaxcalans (just as Voltaire had done in *The Philosophical Dictionary*). These were the archenemies of the Aztecs who provided crucial aid to the Spaniards during the march against the Mexican empire. With difficulty, they had resisted the dominance of the Aztecs, and resented their taxes and demands for labor service. Prescott imagined the Tlaxcalans as republican champions of liberty fighting against an odious, despotic, and monarchical power. Perhaps he saw here a parallel with the American Revolution. Surely he had his readers in mind, who may not have fully understood the nature of indigenous rivalries, let alone indigenous political institutions. They would, however, have identified and sympathized with any fighter for independence against an abusive power. Prescott described Tlaxcala as "that valiant little republic, which had so long maintained its independence against the arms of Mexico" (292). These Indians were, no doubt, "a bold and partially civilized people," with a "turbulent temper" (295), but Prescott chose to emphasize those features that most closely resembled American values. In his description of their political institutions, Prescott identified four separate states, "bound by a sort of federal compact," each headed by a chief who coordinated with the others in matters of interest to the "nation" (296). The Tlaxcalan political system also included a Senate, which decided on, among other things, matters of war. Tlaxcalans were above all "sturdy republicans" (299) ready to defend their "uncompromising spirit" of independence (301). They were an agricultural people that also had talents for trade. Prescott's emphasis on agricultural labor reveals the historian's desire to associate the Tlaxcalans with the ancient Romans and the republican Americans,

> . . . the Tlascalan [*sic*] earned his bread—from a soil not ungrateful, it is true—by the sweat of his brow. He led a life of temperance and toil. Cut off by his long wars with the Aztecs from commercial intercourse, he was driven chiefly to agricultural labor, the occupation most propitious to purity of morals and sinewy strength of constitution. His honest breast glowed with the patriotism—or local attachment to the soil, which is the fruit of its diligent culture; while he was elevated by a proud consciousness of independence, the natural birthright of the child of the mountains. (340)

Mountains and an independent spirit do not necessarily add up to an American metaphor, so Prescott decided to call the Tlaxcalans "the Swiss of Anahuac" (349). But the point was still clear to American readers of the 1840s that these rivals of the Aztecs bore a family resemblance to their own revolutionary forebears. Not even the defeat of the Spaniards during the *Noche Triste* episode deterred the Tlaxcalans, for they were "trained in a rough school that made them familiar with hardship and privations" (607).

Prescott did not share Montesquieu's reverence for monarchy in any form. In the *History*, monarchy is represented primarily by the Aztecs, but also by Spain, which, under the Habsburgs, "came to overshadow the inferior orders of the state" (157), by destroying the traditional privileges of the municipal councils. Monarchy, in this context, "was unfavorable to constitutional liberty" (158), and became an imperialistic, interventionist Crown under Charles V. This last monarch was himself distracted by larger European issues, uninterested in purely Spanish concerns, and even less in the developing affairs of the New World. This led Prescott to exclaim, "What a contrast to the policy of his illustrious predecessors, Ferdinand and

Isabella!" (497). When Charles returned to Spain for a short period in 1520, it was basically "to disgust his subjects, and, in a great degree, to alienate their affections" (495). Indeed, as shown in Book VI, Chapter 4, the Crown under his leadership was embarrassed by bureaucracy and confusion, as well as torn between the demands of different councils and influential officials. Bureaucrats issued contradictory orders, improvised policy to get rid of problematic issues, and concentrated on advancing their narrow personal or political interests. In addition, the reins of government were in the hands of Charles's preceptor (and later Pope) Adrian of Utrecht, "a man whose ascetic and studious habits better qualified him to preside over a college of monks" (835), a less than flattering reference to a monarchy closely associated with the Catholic Church. Charles V eventually recognized the accomplishments of Hernán Cortés, and even paid him a visit when he was ill, in Spain: "This was an extraordinary mark of condescension in the haughty court of Castile" (885). At the same time, the monarch was cynically moving to establish his own control over the lands conquered by Cortés. "It was the policy of the Crown to employ one class of its subjects to effect its conquests, and another class to rule over them" (887). Absolutist monarchs, especially one such as Charles V, followed no other principle than their own interest. Cortés would spend the remainder of his life writing useless appeals to a cold-hearted emperor. In Prescott's presentation, the difference between monarchy and oriental despotism was simply one of degree, not substance. Only the republican system emerges as virtuous, though in a most unlikely place, the mountains of central Mexico.

The Burning National Questions

Ultimately, Prescott wanted to derive some lessons from the fall of the Aztec empire to pass on to his American readers. He wanted to illustrate, in particular, how empire building inevitably led to costly wars. He also wanted to alert his readers not to be complacent about the nature of their government, which might easily become removed from the interests of the citizenry. And finally, he wanted to address the issues of slavery and, to a lesser extent, the status of Native Americans.

Prescott's sprawling narrative of the conquest emphasized the cruelties of war, but most importantly, made a direct connection between war and empire. While the Aztecs fought to maintain theirs, the Spaniards fought to expand their own. In either case, the result was the awful, often shocking consequence of armed confrontation and its attendant misery for the larger population. Prescott was not content with mere description, and thus made his message explicit. For instance, in describing one particularly destructive flood caused by the Aztecs, Prescott conveyed his horror of war: "The enemy," he wrote, "had little cause for congratulation; since, independently of the number of slain, they had seen one of their most flourishing cities sacked, and in part, at least, laid in ruins—one of those, too, which in its public works displayed the nearest approach to civilization. *Such are the triumphs of war!*" (680, my emphasis). In assessing the appalling devastation of the city of Tenochtitlan, Prescott blamed neither the defiant Aztecs, who were after all defending their homes, nor the Spaniards, who had no desire to ruin that beautiful city. There were Spanish cruelties, he conceded, but "they were no greater than those inflicted on their own countrymen at home, in many a memorable instance, by the most polished nations, not merely of ancient times, but of our own. *They were the inevitable consequences which follow from war*" (816, my emphasis). Alas, within two years, the United States was at war with Mexico, and Prescott felt bound to protest it. As a member of a rather large opposition to the conflict, he seemed prescient when he wrote,

> [The] fate [of the Aztecs] may serve as a striking proof, that a government, which does not rest on the sympathies of its subjects, cannot long abide; that human institutions, when not connected with human prosperity and progress, must fall—if not before the increasing light of civilization, by the hand of violence; by violence from within, if not from without. And who shall lament their fall? (819)

What is striking about this passage is precisely the contrast between prosperity and war. At least for Prescott, they were in clear contradiction. It was indeed a conviction of his generation, or at least of his New England cohort, that expansionism inevitably led to war. In the United States, expansionism was already in full gear and at the expense of Native Americans.

In such a context, it is quite striking to see that Prescott avoided extended discussions on Native Americans. But they appear often enough to indicate that the question about their place in American society was important to the historian. Prescott told readers from the outset that after reviewing Aztec culture, "we find no resemblance to the other races of North American Indians" (118), perhaps in an effort to present them as peculiar and separate. He made some comparisons, however. Discussing Caribbean Indians, for instance, Prescott stated that their "population wasted away with even more frightful rapidity than did the Aborigines in our own country" (162). Drawing a contrast between Puritan settlers and Spanish invaders, Prescott stated that the former "established their title to the soil by fair purchase of the Aborigines" (368). Here the point seems to be that the traditions of the country thus far speak well of the treatment of the Indians, in contrast to the extreme cruelties of the Spanish conquest.

Again using the Aztecs as a point of reference, Prescott took pains to differentiate them from other Indians. Not precisely in praise of the Aztecs, he stated that their manners were "superior in point of refinement to those of the other Aboriginal tribes of the North American continent" (435). Excessive refinement was, of course, a negative trait in the New England historian's mind. In some cases, Prescott drew similarities, to emphasize that all New World Indians were barbarians: "The battle-cry of the Aztec, like the war-whoop of the North American Indian, was an appalling note . . . in the ears of the Spaniards" (692). More surprisingly, he endowed Cortés with the caution and the "undeviating step," of the North American Indian who, "traversing morass and mountain and the most intricate forests, guided by the instinct of revenge, presses straight towards the mark. And, when he has reached it, springs at once on his unsuspecting victim" (870). Prescott made comparatively few direct references to Native Americans, but his comments indicate that, on a larger scale of civilizations, Indians were below Europeans and were bound to be defeated and displaced. But the issue was too close to home, and Prescott preferred to make his points through the history of a civilization that had already disappeared.

Slavery, on the other hand, received much more attention, and opinion. Prescott was neither an abolitionist nor a defender of slavery. It is, therefore, interesting to observe how he praised the manner in which the Aztecs treated their slaves: "The slave was allowed to have his own family, to hold property, and even other slaves. His children were free. No one could be born to slavery in Mexico." Although not referring directly to the United States, he added that this last characteristic was "an honorable distinction, not known, I believe, in any civilized community where slavery has been sanctioned" (36). The Aztecs were not entirely idealized, however, and through the eyes of the Spaniards Prescott described one public sale of slaves as "a spectacle unhappily not confined to the barbarian markets of Mexico." This is an unmistakable reference to the United States, although what made the practice more horrific among the Aztecs was that some of the Indian slaves were likely to be sacrificed (440). The Spaniards did not scruple to force Indians into slavery: Prescott described how Cortés subjected rebellious Tepeacans, who had previously pledged allegiance to the Crown, to this condition. The Spaniards also enslaved and branded Indians in a punitive expedition against the town of Zoltepec (686). They did so, even though colonial legislation prohibited Indian slavery. The massive importation of African slaves into the mainland was yet to occur, but some conquistadors had brought a few of them as personal attendants (although some slaves became conquistadors in their own right). Late in Cortés's life, the old conqueror, suffering from moral pangs, instructed his son to look deeply into the justice of slavery. That command prompted Prescott to make a more direct reference to the United States. It is worth, therefore, to quote the passage at length,

> Such scruples of conscience, not to have been expected in Cortés, were still less likely to be met with in the Spaniards of a later generation. The state of opinion in respect to the great question of slavery, in the sixteenth century, at the commencement of the system, bears some resemblance to that which exists in our time, when we may hope it is approaching its conclusion. [Bartolomé de] Las Casas and the Dominicans of the former age, the abolitionists of their day, thundered out their uncompromising invectives against the system, on the broad ground of natural equity and the rights of man. The great mass of proprietors troubled their heads little about the question of right, but were satisfied with the expediency of the institution. Others more considerate and conscientious, while they admitted the evil, found an argument for its toleration in the plea of necessity, regarding the constitution of the white man as unequal, in a sultry climate, to the labor of cultivating the soil. In one important respect, the condition of slavery, in the sixteenth century, differed materially from its condition in the nineteenth. In the former, the seeds of the evil, but lately sown, might have been, with comparatively little difficulty, eradicated. But in our time they have struck their roots deep into the social system, and cannot be rudely handled without shaking the very foundations of the political fabric. It is easy to conceive, that a man, who admits all the wretchedness of the institution and its wrong to humanity, may nevertheless hesitate to adopt a remedy, until he is satisfied that the remedy itself is no worse than the disease. That such a remedy will come with time, who can doubt, that has confidence in the ultimate prevalence of the right, and the progressive civilization of his species? (903)

This remarkable statement situates Prescott quite clearly among those who opposed slavery on practical rather than moral grounds. He portrays unflatteringly the moralist Las Casas and other members of the Dominican order, "the abolitionists of their day." Prescott's vague hope for the eventual termination of slavery is characteristic of his overall political position: he might condemn war, imperialism, religious bigotry, and slavery, but having no clear remedies, he wished that these problems, especially slavery, would be solved by some form of evolutionary process.

Prescott clearly preferred to dwell on a more chivalrous past, and from a distance. As he wrote to Fanny Calderón in 1840, "The only journey I shall make in the fair regions of Anahuac will be under the strong escort of some half-thousand Spanish *caballeros*, well preserved in stuffed cotton jacket and mail, with the gallant Cortés at their head."[44]

Spanish Chivalry

Prescott was an admirer of Washington Irving, and though he strove to write an empirical history of the conquest of Mexico, he followed the path first pursued by his compatriot in the *Conquest of Granada*. Prescott also shared the interest of his friends George Ticknor and Henry W. Longfellow in identifying the essence of the Spanish national character. It is thus not entirely surprising that in a book concerning the Spanish conquistadors he would gladly depart from a dry narrative of facts to highlight romantic themes. "The subversion of a great empire by a handful of adventurers," he wrote in the preface, "taken with all its strange and picturesque accompaniments, has the air of romance rather than of sober history; and it is not easy to treat such a theme according to the severe rules prescribed by historical criticism" (5). The conquest of the Aztec empire, he added, was as "adventurous and romantic as any legend devised by Norman or Italian bard of chivalry" (13). And he was determined to prove it.

The discovery of the New World by Columbus fired the imaginations of Spaniards, which were already "warmed by the study of those tales of chivalry which formed the favorite reading of the Spaniards" (161). Prescott did not specify his sources for this statement, but one can safely assume that it is derived from a reading of *Don Quixote*, whose well-endowed library of romances of chivalry induced the hero to fancy himself as a knight-errant. Nurtured by similar readings, Spaniards were prepared to endure the greatest pains for the sake of adventure. "Indeed, the life of the cavalier of that day was romance put into action. The story of his adventures in the New World forms one of the most remarkable pages in the history of man" (161). In the case of Cortés, the reference to Don Quixote is unmistakable, when Prescott described how the conquistador first understood the depth of Indian rivalries. "If he had before scarcely shrunk from attacking the Aztec empire in the true spirit of a knight-errant, with his single arm, as it were, what had he now to fear, when one half of the nation could thus be marshaled against the other?" (249). Although the odds were still considerable, Cortés was quite able to rally his followers, for "he shared in that romantic spirit of adventure which belonged to them" (284).

The test for the conquistadors came soon enough, when they confronted the fiercely independent Tlaxcalans on their ascent to the high Mexican plateau. Prescott provided sufficient detail about the encounters, but in the end, he resorted to a romantic analogy. "In the narrative of these campaigns, there is sometimes but one step—and that a short one—from history to romance." The odds, he added, were "as overwhelming as any recorded by the Spaniards in their own romances, where a handful of knights is arrayed against legions of enemies" (303). A talent for improvisation, defiance of danger, and single-mindedness, are all Quixotic traits, and Prescott deployed them often to enliven his narrative. Thus, a search for a pass through the mountains surrounding the valley of Mexico becomes yet another adventure, as when Diego de Ordaz climbs the Popocatepetl volcano. "The undertaking was eminently characteristic of the bold spirit of the cavalier of that day, who, not content with the dangers that lay in his path, seems to court them from the mere Quixotic love of adventure" (379). Then, to illustrate the reaction of the conquistadors upon the sight of Tenochtitlan,

> a scene so new and wonderful filled their rude hearts with amazement. It seemed like enchantment; and they could find nothing to compare it with, but the magical pictures in the "Amadis de Gaula." Few pictures, indeed, in that or any other legend of chivalry, could surpass the realities of their own experience. The life of the adventurer in the New World was romance put into action. What wonder, then, if the Spaniard of that day, feeding his imagination with dreams of enchantment at home, and with its realities abroad, should have displayed a Quixotic enthusiasm—a romantic exaltation of character, not to be comprehended by the colder spirits of other lands! (388)

Just as Don Quixote contrasted the pedestrian realities of his own age with those of the golden age of chivalry, Prescott employed the same device to characterize the age of the conquistadors. "The period which we are reviewing was still the age of chivalry; that stirring and adventurous age, of which we can form little conception in the present day of sober, practical reality" (715). In Prescott's view adventure, glory, honor, were powerful motivators for the Spaniards: "The New World with its strange and mysterious perils, afforded a noble theater for the exercise of his calling; and the Spaniard entered on it with all the enthusiasm of a paladin of romance" (716). Few could equal Cortés, however, for "he was a knight-errant, in the literal sense of the word . . . there was none more deeply filled with the spirit of romantic enterprise" (907). To the skeptical reader, Prescott addressed his ultimate explanation for the success of the conquistadors,

> It is difficult, in this age of sober sense, to conceive the character of a Castilian cavalier of the sixteenth century, a true counterpart of which it would not have been easy to find in any other nation, even at that time—or anywhere, indeed, save in those tales of chivalry, which, however wild and extravagant they may seem, were much more true to character than to situation. The mere excitement of exploring the strange and the unknown was a sufficient compensation to the Spanish adventurer for all his toils and trials. (871)

Prescott was truly a disciple of Irving. He saw chivalry not only in the Spanish soul, but even in the most unlikely places: in the midst of rapine, bloodshed, and calculated cruelty. But he also departed from Irving in that the exploration of chivalry was not the end, but rather the beginning of the larger question on how to examine and assess evidence, sift through contradictory testimonies, balance information across time and place—in short, how to do history.

"Sober" History

We have seen how Prescott often contrasted romance and history. While the former could be colorful, imaginative, and sometimes defied belief, history was "sober" and had "severe rules" (5). He also suggested that written records were more reliable than oral traditions, but that even written records could be deceptive. He was especially skeptical of "monkish annalists" who thrive on "gossip" (43). But no historian escaped criticism for partiality on religious or ethnic grounds. Thus Prescott found

Francisco Xavier Clavijero's *Storia Antica del Messico* (1780–1781) better than the relevant works of Guillaume-Thomas Raynal or Cornelius de Pauw because the former "has applied sound principles of criticism, of which they were incapable" (47). Prescott was also able to discern the politics behind the accounts, especially when it came to offering specific evidence, for instance, on human sacrifices. The revered Bartolomé de Las Casas, with all good intentions, manipulated numbers just as much as his enemies did. "Probably the good Bishop's arithmetic," Prescott stated, "came more from his heart than his head" (65). Here one finds that Prescott's engagement with evidence made him depart from the usual assumptions of the Black Legend, which had gained currency already by the sixteenth century, and accelerated afterward. "However good the motives of its author," Prescott wrote, "we may regret that the book [*The Devastation of the Indies*] was ever written" (272). By exaggerating the tales of cruelty, Las Casas provided fodder to the enemies of Spain. Prescott himself was no cheerleader for the Spaniards, but here the rules of evidence seem to have inspired his critique: "To produce a more striking effect, [Las Casas] has lent a willing ear to every tale of violence and rapine, and magnified the amount to a degree which borders on the ridiculous." Moreover, "the wild extravagance of his numerical estimates is of itself sufficient to shake confidence in the accuracy of his statements generally" (273). However commendable Las Casas's cause, "his defect as a historian is, that he wrote history, like everything else, under the influence of one dominant idea. He was always pleading the cause of the persecuted native" (276). At Cholula, Las Casas had Cortés presiding over the notorious massacre, reciting an old romance, comparing himself favorably to Nero. Prescott could find no evidence of this event in multiple other chronicles. "The excellent bishop of Chiapa[s]," stated Prescott, "wrote with the avowed object of moving the sympathies of his countrymen in behalf of the oppressed natives; a generous object, certainly, but one that has too often warped his judgment from the strict line of historic impartiality" (366). In short, Las Casas's arguments may have won followers, and even a day in court, but did not help to establish the historical truth.

In addition to politically motivated accounts, Prescott expressed doubts about other types of sources. Referring to the native chronicler Fernando de Alva Ixtlilxochitl, Prescott charged that "he has often lent a too willing ear to traditions and reports which would startle the more skeptical criticism of the present time" (153). More generally, he found "tradition," meaning oral traditions, "a slippery authority" (336). He found the chronicles written by actors in the conquest (especially that of Bernal Díaz del Castillo) quite helpful despite their "indifference to fine writing." He certainly found them more helpful than those of the "monkish chroniclers" who often made "a pedantic display of obsolete erudition" (545). Prescott was much more favorable to the work of Antonio de Solís, whose *Historia de la Conquista de México* (1684) he found to provide a good mix of the factual and the literary. However, just like the historical models of Antiquity that he followed, Solís tended to introduce his own views in the speeches and thoughts of historical figures. Prescott argued that "the practice has something in it unsatisfactory and displeasing. . . . History assumes the air of romance, and the bewildered student wonders about it in an uncertain light, doubtful whether he is treading on fact or fiction" (823). Moreover,

As to the value of the researches made by Solís in the compilation of his work it is not easy to speak, for the page is supported by none of the notes and references which enable us to track the modern author to the quarry whence he has drawn his materials. It was not the usage of the age. The people of that day, and, indeed, of preceding times, were content to take the author's word for his facts. They did not require to know why he affirmed this thing or doubted that; whether he built his story on the authority of a friend, or of a foe, of a writer of good report, or of evil report. In short, they did not demand a reason for their faith. They were content to take it on trust. This was very comfortable to the historian. It saved him a world of trouble in the process, and it prevented the detection of error, or, at least, of negligence. It prevented it with all who did not carefully go over the same ground with himself. They who have occasion to do this with Solís will probably arise from the examination with no very favorable idea of the extent of his researches; they will find, that, though his situation gave him access to the most valuable repositories in the kingdom, he rarely ascends to original documents, but contents himself with the most obvious and accessible; that he rarely discriminates between the contemporary testimony, and that of a later date; in a word, that in all that constitutes the *scientific* value of history, he falls far below his learned predecessor [Antonio de] Herrera—rapid as was the composition of this last. (823–824, emphasis in the original)

True to his objections, Prescott quoted only those remarks that had been recorded in letters, legal documents, or in the accounts of either contemporaries or reliable historians. Prescott's use of original documents—thousands of pages, obtained from a variety of sources, including the archives of the Royal Academy of History in Madrid—was quite remarkable in the context of early nineteenth-century historical writing. So was his caution, "It is seldom safe," he wrote, "to use any thing stronger than *probably* in history" (445). He also asked readers to beware of "applying the standard of the present to measure the actions of the past" (468). In terms of methods, Prescott had clearly advanced the field. It remained to be seen, however, how the work would be received by readers abroad.

Carlos María Bustamante, for one, was eager to praise Prescott and to offer to translate the work into Spanish. "The only excuse I can offer," he said, "for the liberty I have taken to address you, is my earnest desire to impart to my countrymen and the people of South America that valuable information of which they must remain deprived without a Spanish translation."[45] Lucas Alamán was less exultant, but offered criticisms with elaborate courtesy. Writing from Mexico on April 29, 1844, he admitted that he had taken just a quick look at the book, which he had received only three days before. "I have noticed very few things that need correction," he stated, and mentioned as examples that the Archbishop of Toledo had not attended the original funeral of Cortés, as Prescott had implied, and that a later procession did not leave from Texcoco but rather from Cortés's grandson's palace in Mexico City. Overall, however, he was pleased to see that they agreed on the main points, by which he meant that the conquest had to be seen under a different, less accusatory light than that presented by many of his compatriots.[46]

In Spain, historian Martín Fernández de Navarrete, who had extended Prescott an invitation to join the Royal Academy of History in Madrid as corresponding member, expressed a similarly sympathetic opinion. Navarrete received a copy of the book through Washington Irving, then serving as U.S. minister to Spain, and read it with enormous satisfaction, telling Prescott that his satisfaction increased "when I saw the subject treated with the erudition, impartiality, and good taste of a distinguished writer like you." He predicted that the volumes on the conquest of Mexico would be as well received as *Ferdinand and Isabella*.[47] This proved to be an understatement, as sales soared, and translations appeared in several countries and languages. Navarrete did not live to see a Spanish translation; he died on October 8, 1844. But he anticipated a verdict that was confirmed by the great majority of readers in the Hispanic world: What most impressed them about Prescott was his seemingly impartial authority.

Translating Prescott, Retranslating the Conquest

Ángel Calderón had every intention of translating the *Conquest of Mexico*, but was discouraged when he read the following printed article, which he forwarded to Prescott from New York in 1844:

> We see in a published advertisement a translation of Prescott's "Conquest of Mexico" announced by Don Lucas Alamán, who is to revise and correct the original, and annotate upon "those passages in which Mr. Prescott has been led into error by his religious prejudices, or from a want of knowledge of the country or of access to sources of information possessed only by Don Lucas."[48]

Alamán, indeed, had decided to address not only specific points in Prescott's history, but also the historian's cultural and historiographical assumptions. He wrote to Prescott on February 1, 1845 to tell him that two simultaneous translations were being prepared in the country, but did not mention his role in one of them.[49] Prescott, who had already received the announcement from Calderón responded with some humorous concern:

> It is a great satisfaction to me to learn that translations of my History are in progress in your capital, though if a prospectus which I met with in a Cuban paper is carried out, there is some metamorphosis made by the translators in my religious sentiments, and I am to talk like a good son of the Pope! I think in that case I have a right to have my Protestant heresies at least preserved in a Note at the bottom of the page in the original English.[50]

Alamán felt slightly embarrassed by this letter and tried to explain and justify the nature of the changes:

> Where variations were attempted [in your text] it was not to make you state anything other than what you intend to say. Rather, the changes were made to suppress some things that here would be badly received. The omissions and their locations have been indicated. Anything else would be an alteration of the text, which should never be allowed. But not even that was done, and the text preserves its integrity. The notes that are introduced follow a format different from yours, and it is there that matters that are contrary to prevalent religious opinion [in Mexico] are avoided.[51]

The logic of suppressing without altering may have escaped Prescott, but when he had a chance to see the translation by José María González de la Vega, with Alamán's notes, he was not entirely displeased,

> As for your criticism in your notes to Vega's translation of my History, I think they are conducted in a perfectly liberal spirit as regards myself. It is true you think I savour

something of the old Puritan acid in my anti-Catholic strictures. A Roman Catholic Dublin review speaks of it as doubtful from my writings whether I am a Catholic or Protestant. A Baltimore Catholic journal condemns me as a deist. The Madrid translator of *Ferdinand and Isabella* (Rector of the University of Madrid) condemns me for my hostility to the Inquisition. So I think between them all I may pass for a very liberal Christian.[52]

Indeed, Prescott seemed comfortable with criticism from opposite camps, for it assured him that he had achieved the middle ground he wanted. With regard to Alamán personally, he was genuinely grateful for his careful reading and his corrections. These constituted the greatest majority of Alamán's notes, although a few were lengthy and substantial. One of Prescott's statements, for instance, was that "The [Aztec] scheme of election, however defective, argues a more refined and calculating policy than was to have been expected from a barbarous nation" (Book I, Ch. 2). To this, Alamán replied,

The epithet "barbarous" cannot be applied to a nation that had such a complicated government as that described by the author himself, where justice was administered through established laws, and tribunals were organized according to them. Nor can it be applied to a nation that possessed not just the arts necessary for life, but those for refinement as well. Only their religion may have deserved that epithet. The civilization of this people was not similar to that of European nations, with which at any rate it had no communication, and therefore this is not a sufficient reason to call it barbarous.[53]

On religious matters, Alamán took an even sharper tone. He reacted, for instance, to Prescott's discussion of the Eucharist. In Book III, Chapter 9, Prescott commented that Moctezuma "may have, perhaps, thought it was not more monstrous to feed on the flesh of a fellow creature, than on that of the Creator himself." In the accompanying note, Prescott cited Blanco White's acerbic *Letters from Spain* (1822) as evidence to refer to the "ludicrous effect" of the doctrine of transubstantiation in Spain itself up to the present time.[54] Alamán ascribed this comment to Prescott's Protestantism, and expounded on this in a different passage, this time pertaining to Servando Teresa de Mier's famous argument regarding the identity of Quetzalcoatl and St. Thomas, which the Boston historian considered a "startling conjecture." Alamán commented,

The reader may have noticed Mr. Prescott's acrimonious treatment of all missionaries who have written on American topics, even [Mariano Fernández de Echeverría y] Veytia, in those cases where the latter addresses matters related to his pious opinions. Protestant writers do suffer from this defect, especially those of the United States, who still retain the persecuting zeal of their grandparents, even when it has lost its edge among European Protestants. This zealotry can be detected in their continuous chiding of writers of a different creed, never caring to cite their opinions without slapping them with some mocking or offensive epithet.[55]

Alamán also found that Prescott's romantic approach exaggerated the magnitude of events or such details as the abundance of tropical fruits and the elaborate luxury of Aztec banquets. But his tone in this respect was courteous, and he showed great regard for the historian's effort. So did José Fernando Ramírez, who wrote extensive notes for the second Mexican translation of Prescott's *Conquest*.

This new translation of the *Historia de la Conquista de Mexico*, which appeared in three volumes in 1844–1846, was a major collaborative effort. The edition was coordinated by Ignacio Cumplido, and included Prescott's text in the translation of Joaquín Navarro, Ramírez's 124 pages of explanatory text, and a separate volume of illustrations arranged and explained by Isidro Gondra, the Director of the National Museum. Although the translator occasionally introduced his own notes, it was Ramírez who addressed Prescott's views and responded in detail to some of the more debatable assertions. He did not hesitate to describe Prescott's work as "the best we have in the branch of modern history," but pointed to the following flaws: partiality to the Spaniards, and especially to Hernán Cortés; use of Spanish sources over indigenous ones, and tendentious, indeed loaded use of words when describing Indian actions. These flaws, according to Ramírez, gave Prescott's history "a certain tone which, though I would not term hostile, it is certainly not employed to flatter us." He was particularly critical of Prescott's use of literary strategies to exalt the Spaniards and diminish the Aztecs. Whereas the former could "retreat," the later would "flee" after reverses in battle. Among multiple other examples, Ramírez seemed particularly upset by the following: "Mr. Prescott has wielded his pen to write the history of *barbarians*, a term which, in alternation with *savages*, pervades the entire history." For all these reasons, Ramírez announced, he had set out "to defend the authenticity and value of the historical sources of our country, and to vindicate the memory of our Indians."[56]

Ramírez took up ten major issues where in his view Prescott had erred or ignored important documents, particularly indigenous sources. Perhaps the longest one concerned Prescott's assertion in Book I, Chapter 1 of the *History* that little could be known about the Toltec past except through defective oral traditions. Indigenous records were one of Ramírez's central interests, and he was knowledgeable enough to provide a massive refutation of Prescott's statements. In addition, the drawings in volume three provided even stronger evidence of the size and complexity of Indian records. Other issues ranged from the erudite (Aztec arithmetic, calendar, mining, currency) to the controversial (human sacrifice and cannibalism, episodes in the life of Cortés). An example of the latter is Prescott's reference—taken literally from Alamán—to the "patriotic mob" that "prepared to break open the tomb which held the ashes of Cortés." "Yet the men who meditated this outrage," the historian had added, "were not the descendants of Montezuma, avenging the wrongs of their fathers. . . . They were the descendants of the old Conquerors . . ." The clever irony did not amuse Ramírez, who declared the episode entirely false, perhaps noticing Prescott's absence of a source, and called the reference "an ornament."[57] Overall, the tone of his responses was uniformly courteous, but it betrayed an element of wounded national pride. In Ramírez's case, in contrast to Alamán, this national pride was rooted in the indigenous rather than the Spanish past.

Prescott was aware of Ramírez's work but could not acknowledge it until January 18, 1849, due to the disruptions caused by the Mexican American War. In his first brief letter after the conflict, Prescott did not take issue with Ramírez's points, in part because he was mainly interested in forwarding a copy of his recently published *Conquest of Peru*.[58] At any rate, it was with obvious esteem that Ramírez wrote to the historian from Durango, reciprocating Prescott's friendly letter with a presentation copy of his *Procesos de residencia, instruidos contra Pedro de Alvarado y Nuño de Guzmán* (1847).[59] The whirlwind of Mexican politics took Ramírez to

Mexico City, where he was expected to take a seat in the Supreme Court but was soon summoned by the government to serve as minister of foreign relations. Political turmoil eventually drove him out of the country. Passing through New York in February, 1855, Ramírez wrote to Prescott about his hopes for a productive exile in Europe. He wanted to continue his work on the Mexican indigenous past, consult libraries and museums, and perhaps print a manuscript in his possession, Diego Durán's *Historia de las Indias de Nueva España*. Ramírez asked for Prescott's advice and help in the form of letters of introduction. He lamented not seeing Prescott in person, intimating that,

> I wanted to consult with you about an idea that haunts me like a nightmare, making me distrust my own judgment. I fear I am the victim of an illusion which might make me the laughing stock of the literary world, and I hope that even an obscure man like myself can avoid it. I believe I have discovered purely and truly *phonetic* characters in the writing of the Mexicans; that is, characters whose specific function is to reproduce *sounds*, without any other meaning. I believe that I have collected a sufficient number of proofs to present this idea, not as conjecture, but as a fully demonstrable proposition.[60]

In his *History of the Conquest of Mexico*, Prescott had made a strong statement to the contrary, and it is possible that Ramírez felt challenged enough to elaborate on his earlier rebuttal. In Book I, Chapter 4 of the *Conquest*, Prescott had acknowledged the Aztec mastery of hieroglyphics, but considered that of the three different types (figurative, symbolic, and phonetic), "they relied on the figurative infinitely more than on the others," and added a comparative comment regarding the relationship between hieroglyphic writing and civilization—"the Egyptians were at the top of the scale, the Aztecs at the bottom."[61] This did not please Ramírez, who decided to investigate the matter more closely. Prescott himself was intrigued by Ramírez's assertions, and seemed willing to change his opinion, but not without previous consultation. He wrote to Joaquín García Icazbalceta, a young scholar introduced to him by Lucas Alamán, to ask whether he knew anything about Ramírez's project. If Ramírez had indeed determined that phonetic characters existed to such a large extent in the writing of the Aztecs, this "would raise the ancient races an important step in the scale of civilization."[62] García Icazbalceta was perfectly aware of the project and made some consultations of his own, but was equally uncertain about the extent of Ramírez's discovery. The phonetic characters could be confined to some prepositions. Still, he agreed that if there were others, they would substantially change current views on Aztec writing.[63]

Prescott did not wait for García Icazbalceta's reply. He sent letters of introduction to Ángel Calderón, who was in exile in Paris at the time, and to his literary acquaintances Adolphe de Circourt and Manoel Francisco de Barros y Souza, Viscount de Santarem. These friends of Prescott provided Ramírez with additional contacts, but the Mexican researcher soon grew discouraged. He wrote to Prescott in the summer of 1855 that in the end he had found only one person in all continental Europe fully devoted to New World archeology, and that this scholar was "sumamente descontento y desconsolado" [extremely unhappy and disappointed] because no editor or scientific society was interested in publishing his works.

> What then can *I* expect? It is true that I am not looking for any particular sponsorship, but I am beginning to doubt that I will even find an appreciation for my scholarship

among intellectuals here, for research on the writing of the ancient Mexicans is not believed to be worth much. It is true that this is a rather arid field of study, and not one for recreation. But if I am confirmed in this impression, which I hope is wrong, I will pack my works and bring them back to American soil, where they belong, and there I will see how to print them.[64]

This was indeed discouraging, neither the first nor the last time that a Latin American scholar failed to gain access to European intellectual circles. Prescott, who had achieved fame in Europe writing on a similar subject, albeit in a Romantic vein that appealed to European taste, was certainly more sympathetic to Ramírez's interests. There is evidence that he fully intended to incorporate both Ramírez's and Alamán's comments and critiques in a revised edition of his *Conquest of Mexico*. As he wrote to Fanny Calderón shortly before he died,

> I am just occupied with making some notes and corrections for a new edition of the "Conquest of Mexico." I have particularly good materials for this in the two Mexican translations of it, one of them having Alamán's notes and the other those of Ramírez. I know very little about these eminent scholars, though I have somewhere a notice which was sent to me for Alamán, far and away so carefully and so long ago that I doubt if I can lay my hands on it. Could you not give me some little account of these two worthies? Of the offices they held, their social positions and general estimation? Ramírez somewhere remarks that he belongs to the old Mexican race. This explains the differences of his views on some points from Alamán's—who has a true love for the "conquistadores." On the whole it is a severe trial—which few historians have experienced—to be subjected to so severe a criticism, sentence by sentence, of two of the most eminent scholars of their country. Though they have picked many holes in my finery, I cannot deny that they have done it in the best spirit and in the most courtly style.[65]

Prescott, it appears, had not known many of the vicissitudes in the lives of his two main counterparts in Mexico. On occasion, he could even be frivolous in referring to them. To Ángel Calderón, for instance, he said of Alamán: "What a quill-driver he is! He puts such tortoises as me to shame. I suppose he is one of those boiling spirits that must be doing something—making *pronunciamientos* or writing an account of them."[66] Prescott was certainly generous and obliging to Alamán and other correspondents, sending presentation copies of his books and faithfully replying to letters and requests. He secured for Alamán memberships to the Massachusetts Historical Society and the American Philosophical Society, which pleased the Mexican intellectual greatly.[67] But he failed to take full stock of their personalities. Fanny Calderón sought to correct that deficiency,

> I must not forget to answer your questions about Alamán and Ramírez. . . . [Alamán] was a man of great learning—and as you know, besides his Mexican history, wrote various dissertations upon its antiquities—and a celebrated pamphlet in defense of his own administration. No man was ever more respected in his own country than Alamán. We were very intimate with him while we lived in Mexico. He was a perfect *caballero*—his manners very distinguished—of a very gentle and pacific character. He had a large fortune, which he left at his death, which took place a few years ago, to his two children—a son and a daughter. Ramírez, Calderón knew less intimately, but saw a good deal of him in Paris in '54 [1855], when he was making occasional journeys to Rome, in search of M[anuscript]s for his history of Mexico. He was also a Minister of State in his own

country, and negotiated a *convenio* concerning the Spanish claims with the Spanish Minister which was afterwards censured in the Cortes of Mexico, who even wished to impeach him in consequence. He is a man of great learning, intelligence and good sense. [Ramírez] appears about 50 or more, and has a completely Indian countenance. Both he and Alamán have always been upon the side of religion and order in Mexico.[68]

Lucas Alamán died in June, 1853. Joaquín García Icazbalceta informed Prescott of his passing on June 27, 1853. "The country has lost one of its most notable men," he wrote, "the current government has lost its leader, and I, a good friend."[69] Prescott's reaction to the news is not recorded, and his letter to Fanny Calderón in 1858 shows no awareness of Alamán's death. Prescott also lost track of Ramírez. His intention to revise the *Conquest of Mexico*, however, is proof of his respect for the scholars who aided him and occasionally disagreed with him.

The Second Conquest of Mexico

The *History of the Conquest of Mexico* appeared on the eve of the Mexican-American war. It is appropriate, therefore, to examine the book in that particular context. Prescott had a patrician dislike of politics, and shared the Whigs' opposition to expansionism in general, and the annexation of Texas in particular. Because of his interest in Mexico, and because he had a number of active correspondents there, Prescott paid unusual attention to political developments as tensions escalated during 1845. He wrote to Lucas Alamán that "the Texas project is very distasteful to most of the North, and the party to which I belong views it with unqualified detestation."[70] Alamán was pleased to hear this opinion, and replied in late April thus:

> It could not be otherwise that you and the party to which you belong should view the blatant usurpation of Texas with detestation. That party of decent people, who base their opinions on established principles and not on the interests of the moment, that party which considers nations as nations, and not just their power and resources, that party to which you belong and which exists in the enlightened portion of all civilized countries, that is the party that should have the authority. And until it does, we will see in the nineteenth century the usurpations and injustices of the sixteenth, without however the excuses that could be invoked for the latter.[71]

In the postscript of his letter, Alamán added that the Mexican Congress favored discussion with public figures in Texas who opposed annexation. He sounded cautiously optimistic that British and French support for negotiation would contribute to a peaceful settlement. Prescott was not optimistic at all when he responded in June:

> The annexation of Texas seems to be going on swimmingly, as the Texans themselves are disposed to take the matter out of the hands of your government . . . I consider the manner that is likely to be acquired as even more pernicious than the acquisition itself and both together as striking the most serious blow ever yet given to our political fabric.[72]

He was also concerned about the military aspects of the potential confrontation, especially when his friend General William Miller, the experienced British soldier who had fought in the South American wars of independence, said in unequivocal terms that "Mexico appears to me to be one of the most unassailable countries I know of, for an enemy to attack with a view to conquer or to force to submissive terms, however powerful by sea or by land that enemy might be." Miller gave eight detailed reasons why a potential invasion would fail. In December 1845, he insisted to Prescott that "the United States may come off second best if they go to war with that country."[73] On hindsight, he was of course wrong, and he himself admitted later to Prescott that "my predictions have turned out totally erroneous."[74] But at the time, there was room to consider that war would be disastrous politically and militarily for the United States. Prescott, on such grounds, opposed it. He was also apprised by Alamán of the consequences of the Texas crisis for Mexican politics. In December of that same year, Alamán told Prescott that General Mariano Paredes was literally at Mexico City's door, leading his troops against President José Joaquín Herrera whom he soon deposed.[75] War then followed and a weary Alamán told his Boston correspondent that, "I will not say anything about political developments in this country, for in my position I might not judge them with sufficient impartiality. I also assume that you are adequately informed from other sources."[76] A long silence followed.

Prescott was busy at the time writing his *History of the Conquest of Peru*, collecting materials for future projects, and keeping up with an ever-growing correspondence. But he was not oblivious to the escalating crisis. Writing to Pascual de Gayangos, he reported that, "I have excited some indignation by a note of mine on Texas, but I care not a rush. I disapprove of [the administration's] manner of proceeding in reference to Texas."[77] More than the cabinet, however, he blamed the president. As he told his British friend Thomas Jadrell Phillips, "We don't comprehend here the politics of President Polk. It is probable that he doesn't perfectly comprehend them himself."[78] He was less guarded when he wrote to his wife Susan that the president, whom he met on April 3, 1846, was "a mean looking individual enough, who gapes and chews tobacco."[79] Prescott's dislike for Polk was matched by his dislike for the war. Soon after the first military clashes took place, he wrote to George Sumner,

> It would have been sounder policy to have settled definitively with Mexico before taking the Oregon question on our backs. With such an enemy on our borders it is giving a manifest advantage to England in her negotiations with us. But we have a happy confidence in our superiority over every and all the nations of Christendom combined together. The South and West seem to be overrun with a dare-devil war spirit that one might expect to meet with in France, but not in a money-making democracy. Yet this same war spirit has been the bane of more democracies than one, and I fear we are reserved to point a moral, if we do nothing to adorn a tale.[80]

With military victory all but assured by May 1847, Prescott revealed another dimension of his opposition to the war. He was deeply interested in the events of the conquest of New Spain, but had serious misgivings about contemporary Mexico, and those misgivings he only communicated privately. He told his friend Robert Winthrop, then in London, that

> the capital and seaports [of Mexico] seem destined to come to our hands. But what shall we do with them? It will be a heavy drag on our republican car, and the Creole blood will not mix well with the Anglo-Saxon. Then there will be the slavery question, as a firebrand which will keep you hot enough next winter in the Capitol.[81]

The sources of Prescott's opposition to the war are to be found in his perception of how it affected the political and moral fabric of the nation, with its attendant questions about expansion, conquest, and slavery.

And yet, Prescott was far from being a pacifist. He told Pascual de Gayangos that "however mad and unprincipled the war, you will admit I think that our fellows fight well."[82] He was much pleased to learn from the secretary of the Navy that the sailors of the USS Delaware had requested that the *History of the Conquest of Mexico* be included in the ship's library, which was done, and that it was now in every man-of-war in the navy.[83] He must have certainly been pleased when he received a letter from Caleb Cushing, who was serving in the army during the war, providing detailed comment on Prescott's book, which he had been reading as the campaign unfolded:

> The second Conquest affords many points of analogy with the first, which strike the observer on the spot. I am posted with five regiments at San Angel which adjoins Coyoacán, and my rides of duty or recreation in the neighborhood afford me ample opportunity of noticing these analogies among others, the fact that General Scott originally advanced to the City by the causeway of San Antonio, and finally by that of Tacuba, though not certainly because Cortés had done the same.

Cushing pointed to some problems in Prescott's depiction of the Mexican landscape, but said he was "struck with the general accuracy of your local descriptions of the face of the country." He was motivated to further explore the history of Mexico by collecting books and other materials, "but my official duties keep me in San Angel and I am in daily expectation of order to march to the north." Cushing left no doubt that he had been enormously impressed by Prescott's book, even when war occupied his attention.[84] Prescott was delighted, and responded enthusiastically that "you have closed a campaign as brilliant as that of the great conquistador himself," and added "it has been a war most honorable to our arms, as all admit, whatever we may think of the wisdom of the counsels that rushed us into it."[85] Cushing's reference to "the second Conquest" was to endure, as Prescott soon found out.

Although the war had been launched by a Democrat, the Whigs fervently embraced Winfield Scott's victory. A group of them in Pennsylvania determined to promote the writing of a history of the campaign, and recruited the help of John Church Hamilton (the son and biographer of Alexander Hamilton) to approach Prescott. Hamilton wrote a confidential letter to the historian explaining that the name of Washington Irving had been mentioned as a potential author, "but the *true* friends of the General would not for a moment listen to this matter taking such a direction—It is out of the question entirely." Hamilton assured Prescott that he would have all the information he wanted at his disposal, and that he would have "little more to do than to throw the matter into shape," and added that "I cannot conceive a work from which more reputation or profit would be gained with so little labor." Hamilton insisted on this aspect, hinting that most of the work would be done by others, including himself. "I do not mean by this that the work in any sense would be other than yours, but the whole labor as to facts, much of it (if you choose) as to argument, will be prepared for you to put in a beautiful and flowing dress."[86] Hamilton was persistent, and wrote a second letter two days later (April 28) to introduce a Mr. Ditmars from Pennsylvania, who would attempt to persuade the historian personally.[87] Prescott met with Ditmars on that same day and was obviously unconvinced, but waited until May 2 to respond to Hamilton. He said that he had previously considered a similar suggestion from the New York businessman and editor Charles King (1789–1867), but had declined and would do the same this time. He had been putting together a rich collection of materials on the reign of Philip the Second, and was finally about to delve into the subject.[88] The reasoning was sound but Prescott may have had other motivations. It would have been inconsistent, for one, to oppose the war and then write what Hamilton and others expected to be a celebratory account of the victory. In addition, he had a profound dislike for any activity that would bring him too close to partisan politics. He expressed no regrets in declining this invitation and noted in his journal that he would "rather not meddle with heroes who have not been under ground—two centuries at least."[89]

How did the war affect some of Prescott's friends in Mexico? They endured great hardship, which inevitably also affected their scholarship. With American troops poised to enter Mexico City, the government issued directives to cultural institutions to evacuate what records they could. Isidro Gondra, in his capacity as director of the National Museum, entrusted the seven extant volumes of Lord Kingsborough's *Antiquities of Mexico* to José F. Ramírez, who took the collection to Durango. There he spent the duration of the war.[90] Manuel de Nájera did his best to aid Lucas Alamán in his research from Guadalajara, but the disruptions of the war unleashed uncontrollable banditry. Precious documents were lost in one particularly unfortunate incident.[91]

By and large, however, Mexican scholars weathered the storm and resumed their activities as best they could. Prescott's correspondence shows that the end of the conflict quickly returned the flow of letters to previous levels, and that no national animosity poisoned the cordial exchanges he had with Lucas Alamán, José Fernando Ramírez, and Ignacio Cumplido, the last of whom he had met in Boston. Soon, he would begin an extensive correspondence with Joaquín García Icazbalceta (1825–1894), who had fought in the war, and occasional exchange of letters with such notables as Miguel Lerdo de Tejada.[92] When Lucas Alamán wrote to Prescott about his experience in the war, there was no trace of resentment: "I did in fact endure some inconveniences, when soldiers of General [William Jenkins] Worth's division entered my house, stole clothing, and destroyed some pieces of furniture. But the general himself arrived in time to stop the mayhem, and we became good friends."[93] It seems as though historians on both sides of the new border wanted to leave the war behind. Mexico soon had plenty more to endure, as the country plunged into the *Reforma* period, civil war, and suffered yet another foreign occupation.

Pizarro's Bones

Prescott's *History of the Conquest of Peru* (1847) was also a success in terms of acclaim and sales. But there was no equivalent to Mexico in terms of the local reception of the work. In fact, there was a more immediate reaction in Chile than in Peru itself. Moreover, the first Spanish American translation was made and published in Mexico, not Peru, by Joaquín García Icazbalceta.[94] It is not easy to explain this on account of political turmoil, for both Mexico and Peru were suffering similarly tumultuous periods in their history. Historians in Peru, it seems, had even fewer incentives and venues to pursue their work than historians in Mexico or Chile. It was only decades later that Sebastián Lorente and Manuel de Mendiburu made full use of Prescott's work and did justice to his contributions to Peruvian history.[95]

A more contemporary reaction was to be found in Chile, where Andrés Bello published his review of Prescott's new work in 1848. The great Venezuelan intellectual was in the midst of his own efforts to give shape to the emerging field of history, and found in Prescott a model of narrative style to counter the proponents of "philosophical history" in the country.[96] What he underscored in his review, therefore, was the historian's craft (he conveyed a sense of the contents through extensive quotes), to demonstrate that patient documentary work could be reconciled with attractive narrative and impartial judgment. "Although he follows [Edward] Gibbon in his historical approach," Bello stated, "[Prescott] possesses to a superior degree the art of giving individuality to his characters and liveliness to his descriptions."[97] For Bello, who had himself read the main sources of the romantic historical tradition, Prescott's approach was well suited for educational purposes and for encouraging an appreciation of the past, especially at a time when Chile was developing a national historical tradition.[98]

Another reaction came from the young Diego Barros Arana, later to become Chile's premier historian. Having read Prescott's *History of the Conquest of Peru*, he had checked the Santiago *Cabildo* (municipal) archives for new information. He found that there were many papers corroborating the opinions of several historians on Peruvian events, and others helping to clarify some obscure issues. "But I must tell you," he added, "that after the publication of your [book] it would be complete madness to attempt to write another history. All the documents I have consulted confirm that you have not departed, not even once, from historical truth in your monumental work."[99] Barros Arana may have been somewhat too enthusiastic, but his subsequent success as a historian of impeccable accuracy makes this early opinion particularly valuable for understanding his own approach to history. It was Prescott's meticulous citation of sources that impressed him the most, and he became just as thorough in their deployment.[100]

Not all, of course, were so obliging. One American, Ferdinand Coxe, wanted to check Prescott's writing against the physical evidence of some records and events in Peru itself. He found the historian's reference to the death and burial of conquistador Francisco Pizarro "entirely at variance with existing facts." In his typical prose, Prescott had written of Pizarro's "sumptuous coffin," placed under "a monument in a conspicuous part of the Cathedral," and subsequently removed to a new resting place, alongside the remains of the Viceroy Antonio de Mendoza.[101] "Allow me, Sir," wrote Coxe, "to describe to you a visit which in March, 1846, I paid to the suppositious tomb of Francisco Pizarro." After describing a generalized lack of local knowledge about the conquistador or his fate, he related how he was able to gain access to the Cathedral where he was told the remains lay. Greedy priests, he said, charged him an enormous amount of money to see the vaults. Then, after wading through an assortment of broken and rotting items, he encountered what he was told were the remains of Pizarro. "A skeleton was there," he wrote, "thickly coated with clay":

> The earth had crumbled or been scraped, from the head, hands and feet and part of the legs, all of which were gone—they had been sold, as had also the bones of the fingers and toes. It seemed that the Sacristan had found many believers in the identity of the

body and drove a thriving business in relics of Pizarro. He said he would have a tooth to sell me the next day, if I would come again. I had no doubt of it, but did not think the genuineness of the relic was sufficiently vouched for.

As for the remains of Viceroy Mendoza, mentioned by Prescott as being next to Pizarro, the priests seemed to know nothing about it. The box next to the conquistador, they said, contained the remains of an unidentified archbishop. For Coxe, there was nothing to authenticate those remains, and if they *were* the archbishop's, "how disgraceful to the Government which allows them to remain in their present condition." If they *were not* authentic, "how disgraceful to the Ecclesiastical authorities which suffer such a farce to be performed in the vaults of the Cathedral."[102]

Coxe was clearly not an easy man to please, and his unforgiving eye left no one unscathed, including Prescott, for straying so far from the reality of Peruvian conditions. The historian, for his part, felt he had to defend the validity of his account, and wrote to Coxe that it was not at all surprising that such decay as described could be possible after two and a half centuries. The lapse of time may also have turned a viceroy into an archbishop in the minds of common folk, something entirely plausible. Prescott did not care much for the enterprising *Sacristán* who, it seemed "has made the most of his deposit," but the main point was that regarding the condition of the remains, "so far from contradicting my account such a fact seems to be perfectly conformable to it." He also defended his source, Francisco López de Caravantes, who was "a man high in office in the Colonies, a person esteemed for his probity and who seems to have had no motive for misstatement on this occasion."[103] Prescott defended himself by seeking no more than to stand by his sources. Coxe had presented him with a difficult challenge, but one that could be explained. Still, Coxe had not just wanted to denounce the greed and dismal conditions surrounding the bones of Pizarro, but rather to point out the distance between Prescott's style of writing, abounding in adjectives of grandeur, and events more prosaic, if not bloodier and crueler.

British reviewers could also be critical, but they viewed Prescott's work as the author intended: a compelling narrative resting on authentic documents yet laudable for its literary merits. A typical, appreciative review was prepared by historian Henry Hart Milman for the *Quarterly Review*:

> Mr. Prescott's style and manner of composition are adapted with singular felicity to this half-poetic history [the conquest of Peru]. His strong imaginative faculty, heightened by the peculiarity of his situation [his near blindness], delights in the rich and the marvelous, both in nature and in human action; he has acquired a skill of arrangement, and grouping the characters and events, which attests long and patient study of the highest models; while the calmer moral and Christian tone of his judgments by no means deadens his sympathies with the fiercer and more barbarous heroism of ancient days. His narrative presents in general, though not without some exceptions, a happy combination of modern historic philosophy with something of the life and picturesqueness of an ancient chronicle.[104]

Closer to home, a critic in the *North American Review* had much to praise in the historian's new book, though "it seems to us that Mr. Prescott's imagination has been somewhat carried away by the romantic nature of [the conquistadors'] exploits, the grandeur of the scene in which they acted and of the results which they accomplished."

This reviewer (Francis Bowen) had a particularly low opinion of the conquistadors, and thus he viewed Prescott's "record of knight-errantry" as misplaced and danger-ous, because "the reader is hurried along with him, and cheated into admiration of a pack of robbers and murderers."[105] He had a point, albeit a surprising one, for Prescott was unusually critical of Pizarro, whom he viewed as crass and perfidious, far below his counterpart Hernán Cortés.[106] Readers, at any rate, appeared to have no such reservations: 5,000 copies of the American edition sold in 5 months, and the first English edition of 2,500 was soon exhausted. Prescott's reputation was such that no criticism could stunt the circulation of his books.

The price of popularity, however, was a number of unusual offers and requests. Writing from Paris in 1847, after two failed attempts to reach Prescott in Boston, Joaquín Acosta (1800–1852), a former Colombian minister to the United States, asked the historian to take over his project on the history of the Chibcha Indians, "the third center of [New World] civilization." He told Prescott that he had all the pertinent documents and materials, but deferred to the Boston historian for the completion of it. "Since my only object has been to fill a void in our ancient history," Acosta said, "I would gladly abandon my work should the pen [i.e., Prescott's] that wrote on the reign of Isabella the Catholic be willing to take it over." That is, rather in the way John Church Hamilton had tried to persuade Prescott to write the history of Winfield Scott's Mexican campaign, Acosta wanted the historian to lend his considerable narrative talents to the Chibcha project. "I would send you all my documents, and limit myself to the role of translator."[107] Prescott did not need to think too much about it, and declined on August 28 on similar grounds: he was determined to pursue the writing of *Philip the Second*, and at any rate his sight would not permit such new exertions.

Other requests bordered on the impertinent, and demanded more diplomacy and firmness. For instance, during the preparation of *A New History of the Conquest of Mexico* (1859), Robert Anderson Wilson (1812–1872) had written to Prescott to ask for his main documentary sources so that he could write his own version of the conquest of Mexico, "without the fable."[108] Somewhat irritated, Prescott replied that "To take you literally I should say that I have no such authorities, for mine all relate to the conquest *with* the fable."[109] He did, however, offer titles by Clavijero and Solís once Wilson mentioned them. "Your views are certainly entitled to respect," he wrote, "and I shall be happy to do what I can without too much incon-venience to myself to aid you in bringing them before the public."[110] What appeared before the public was a scathing critique of Prescott and other historians for failing to understand the conquest, the nature of Indian wars, and the fanciful inventions of Spanish chroniclers. Prescott and William Robertson, Wilson wrote, had relied too much on the "historical romances they quoted," and failed to see that Cortés was not a "Roman [i.e., Catholic] propagandist" but rather "an adroit leader in Indian War." He added that "Mr. Prescott's non-acquaintance with the Indian character is much to be regretted." In his own book, Wilson said, "Their natural character is restored, and their resistance is shown, not as one of pitched battles but as one of plots and counter plots, night assaults, surprises, and ambuscades, the true Indian system of hostility."[111] It was too late for Prescott to respond, but others did after his death in 1859.[112]

Another type of requests is exemplified by Pedro Félix Vicuña, who asked Prescott to take a position on U.S.-Latin American relations. Vicuña was an ardent

Chilean liberal who, as editor and politician, had opposed the conservative establishment of his country's postindependence period (1830–1860). He was also interested in larger hemispheric matters, and had written an ambitious essay on the major issues confronting the region, titled *El porvenir del hombre* (1858). He sent a presentation copy to Prescott, and in a separate letter he told the Boston historian,

> You are the Homer of the glories of our [Hispanic] race. In your history of Philip the Second you have exposed the causes of social disorder that followed the fanaticism of that reign. You are called upon, therefore, to write a book that will put a stop to the emerging evil [territorial conquest and the notion of racial superiority] which will make the two races [i.e., Anglo-Saxon and Hispanic] of our continent new Romans and Carthaginians with all their endless hatreds and wars. The American Confederation is well organized, has more power and more industry. But it also has slavery, and in it the seeds of its dissolution. . . . Your pen, your experience, your enlightenment can do much to contain this evil, which would deprive America of the glory of being the cradle of human regeneration.[113]

Prescott may not have been entirely clear as to what exactly he was supposed to write against, whether it was expansionism (which he had) or slavery (which he also had, though not as an abolitionist). At any rate, he marked the letter "not answer." Discussions of slavery or any other source of current political confrontation made him uncomfortable. His literary fame had put him in a position of influence, but he was reluctant to use it.

It was Pedro Vicuña's son, Benjamín Vicuña Mackenna, one of Chile's most promising young historians, who actually visited Prescott and wrote perhaps the most detailed account by a Spanish American of their encounter in Boston in April 1853. They met in Prescott's home at 55 Beacon Street in Boston and spoke in a combination of French, English, and Spanish.[114] Apparently, Prescott could be elaborately gracious on such occasions; to Vicuña Mackenna he explained that he had undertaken the history of the conquests of Mexico and Peru, and not that of Chile, because the available documents were fewer in the Chilean case, and also because the country already had "that admirable story of the Araucania," by which he meant the sixteenth-century epic poem by Alonso de Ercilla, *La Araucana*, which told the story of the prolonged Indian-Spanish war. Prescott showed him his noctograph (a writing device for the blind) and also inscribed a volume of his *Miscellanies*—Vicuña diligently observed—without looking at the book.

The Chilean historian was particularly interested in Prescott's now famous infirmity (candidly and movingly addressed in the preface of his *History of the Conquest of Peru*), which Andrés Bello had noticed in his lengthy review in the *Revista de Santiago*. "[Mr. Prescott] is tall and trim," Vicuña Mackenna wrote in his diary, "and his countenance is greatly animated by large green eyes which, despite a debilitating illness, are very bright." He also described the historian's library, and detected his weakness for relics and mementos of royalty,

> The library of Mr. Prescott is a historical Potosí [the rich silver-mining area in the Viceroyalty of Peru]. All his documents on Peru, Mexico, and the reign of Isabella, which have cost him more than a few thousand [dollars] are bound and arranged in an orderly fashion. He also showed me some relics from the heroes popularized by his pen: a piece from Cortés' mortuary cloth, given to him by [Lucas] Alamán of Mexico. There

is a copy, at the library's entrance, of the unique portrait of Pizarro located at the sacristy of the Cathedral of Valladolid, and another of Columbus, copied by Madrazo. He had in a briefcase original letters by Isabella the Catholic and Ferdinand, a letter from Charles V to Emperor Maximilian written at the age of fifteen, and some rough notations by Gonzalo de Córdoba. During the display, a letter written in modern handwriting dropped, showing a golden crown. "*C'est une assez belle écriture pour une reine*!" Mr. Prescott told me, passing along a folded sheet covered with writing on all four sides: it was a letter of congratulation penned by Queen Victoria on the occasion of his last trip to England in 1851 [*sic*].[115]

Vicuña Mackenna was duly impressed by the historian and his fame, yet he could not draw from the interview any hopes that Prescott would write anything else about the New World beyond Mexico and Peru. Prescott had no intention of specializing further in either of those countries, much less in any other area of Spanish America. Indeed, he turned down every request that he do so, and was rather amused that he should receive so much attention from scholars in the hemisphere. For in fact he was most firmly rooted in Spanish history, and digressed into New World territory only because the conquests were a consequence of the reign of Ferdinand and Isabella, and very much a part of the concerns of subsequent Spanish monarchs. He was also interested in those conquests because he believed that everything that pertained to Spain in the New World was very much a part of *American* history. But as soon as he could, he returned to the Spanish topics that had captivated him early on and that would occupy him for the remainder of his life.

Chapter 8

Knights-Errant and Bigots:
Prescott's Writings on Spain

In the heroic days when Ferdinand
And Isabella ruled the Spanish land,
And Torquemada, with his subtle brain,
Ruled them, as Grand Inquisitor of Spain

—Henry W. Longfellow, *Tales of a Wayside Inn*

Since history without truth is a body without life, it is necessary that one try to assert nothing
without a basis of fact, and that gradually one purges history of fables, which have crept into
it. . . . It is also necessary to admit that not all parts of history are equally susceptible to
exactitude, for who could assure us of hidden motives reported in ancient history?

—Gottfried Wilhelm Leibniz to Duke Ernst
Augustus of Brunswick (1692)[1]

With the publication of the *History of the Conquest of Mexico*, and the *History of the Conquest of Peru*, William Hickling Prescott became the most successful and internationally recognized historian of the Spanish empire in the New World. Yet he was only peripherally concerned with the nations to the South. He studied their *colonial* past, and especially the earliest period of conquest, because it represented one of the most important accomplishments of the reign of Ferdinand and Isabella. In addition, the discovery and colonization of the New World—the historian's "own favored quarter of the globe"—had been conducted under the auspices of the Catholic monarchy. But his principal concern was Spain itself, and he approached the history of the country by examining the sequence of reigns from the late fifteenth through the sixteenth century, that is to say those of Ferdinand and Isabella, Charles V, and Philip II. He did so by using massive documentation, and endeavoring consistently to remain impartial. But underneath the copious foot-notes, bibliographical commentary at the end of chapters, and exacting standards of accuracy, there lay themes and assumptions that are the key to understanding American interest in, and understanding of, Spain. Prescott *was* the romantic historian that large numbers of readers—and scholars up to the present—saw and enjoyed, but he revealed, especially in his late writings on Spain, an increasing reliance on primary sources as the ultimate arbiter of historical accounts. Therefore, this chapter is primarily concerned with his methods, but I try not to lose sight of the historian's lingering subjectivity and his desire to strike a receptive cord in his readership. I proceed by looking at Prescott's definition of the Spanish "national character," especially in his *Ferdinand and Isabella*, as well as the reception of this book in Spain in the 1840s. I then trace Prescott's sources for his view of Spanish decline and its relationship to Catholicism. It is in this context that the sharp tension between the historian's religious views and the emerging standards of nineteenth-century historical scholarship most clearly show. Since much of this tension was personified in the figure of Charles V, I describe the international hunt for relevant documents to illuminate the emperor's final days, and Prescott's own changing views on his demise. He devoted so much time to the subject, and wrote so compellingly about it, that he managed to influence the views of a larger audience on Spain and its traditions. Literally tens of thousands read his books, and they eagerly read related writings. They could not get enough of the themes of Spanish Catholicism and despotism.

The Spanish National Character

In *Ferdinand and Isabella*, his first major work, Prescott explored the emergence of Spain as a nation, from its beginnings under Muslim occupation, through the eight-centuries-long *Reconquista*, and through the emergence and consolidation of the monarchy under Ferdinand and Isabella. The Boston historian left no doubt that the latter was the greatest period in Spanish history, albeit one containing the seeds of its own decay, which would become more and more apparent under the reigns of the two succeeding monarchs. How Spain reached such a point of glory and achievement, only to sink into a "paralytic torpor" and find itself by the nineteenth century "abandoned to all the evils of anarchy," was the key question that Prescott explored both chronologically and thematically.[2] Following the historiographical conventions of the nineteenth century, Prescott searched for the fundamental components of the "national character," which he identified, in the case of Spain, as religion and the spirit of chivalry.[3]

That Prescott should focus on religion to define the Spanish national character is not entirely surprising. After all, Christian Spain had been invaded by Muslims, and religion provided a central motivation for the prolonged struggle to regain Iberian territory. "The Holy warfare," Prescott wrote in the introduction to his work, "seemed to require the cooperation of the clergy, to propitiate Heaven in its behalf, to interpret its mysterious omens, and to move all the machinery of miracles, by which the imagination is so powerfully affected in a rude and superstitious age." He determined, however, that early Spain was still "untinctured with the fiercer religious bigotry of later times." Such bigotry, he indicated, eventually "sullied the character of the nation in later ages."[4] Old Spain, despite the pervasiveness of Catholicism, had been relatively free from Rome. "It was comparatively late," he stated, "that the nation submitted its neck to the papal yoke, so closely riveted at a subsequent period."[5] It is an important element of Prescott's writing, one that lends much nuance to his work, that events are rarely sudden or confounding: they always have an origin and a direction, and are structured around organic sequences of birth, maturity, and decline. But decline is never final. Thus, for instance, on the matter of religion, old Spain could wallow in the mire of superstition, but not become entirely bigoted. Once corrupted, and under the grip of Rome, there lurk faint flashes of freedom waiting for a more propitious era. This is the kind of historical explanation that rests on the identification of turning points, which traces advances and reverses, but always assumes a degree of continuity and the possibility of renewal. Within that framework, however, there are also pinnacles of good and evil, although in the case of religion in Spain, more of the latter than the former. The Inquisition is a case in point.

Prescott faced an important dilemma: how to reconcile his positive view of the reign of Ferdinand and Isabella (especially the queen), with their sanctioning of the Inquisition, which he described as "one of the grossest abuses that ever disgraced humanity." The Inquisition, he added, was an institution "which has probably contributed more than any other cause to depress the lofty character of the ancient Spaniard, and which has thrown the gloom of fanaticism over those lovely regions."[6] Isabella, in this context, could only have approved of such disgrace as the actions of the Inquisition against her better judgment. The explanation, for Prescott, lay in her upbringing, which taught her to surrender her conscience on matters of religion to the ministers of the faith. He found the role of Torquemada, her confessor, particularly pernicious, and described him as one of those "who compensate for their abstinence from sensual indulgence, by giving scope to those deadlier vices of the heart, pride, bigotry, and intolerance, which are no less opposed to virtue, and are far more extensively mischievous to society."[7] In the same manner, Cardinal Francisco Jiménez de Cisneros, a more moderate character, used his influence on Isabella to make her subordinate her good common sense to religious piety. Prescott described him as playing a positive role in reforming the religious institutions of the country, both secular and regular, but with grim determination and inflexibility. His Catholicism, just as the Reformation was spreading in Europe, "would seem better assimilated to the constitution of his mind, whose sombre enthusiasm naturally prepared him for the vague and mysterious in the Romish faith."[8] Isabella could not escape this influence, and Prescott struggled to justify her decisions: "It should serve much to mitigate our condemnation of the queen, that she fell into no greater error, in the imperfect light in which she lived, than was common to the greatest minds in a later and far riper period."[9] There would be no resolution to this tension, but the overall balance was overwhelmingly in her favor. Ferdinand fared only slightly less well in Prescott's evaluation.

Another important theme in Prescott's work was that of Iberian chivalry, which acquired the full power of historical explanation, especially regarding the motivations of individuals. Referring to King Alfonso of Portugal, for instance, he declared, "Alfonso's fiery character, in which all the elements of love, chivalry, and religion were blended together, resembled that of some paladin of romance; as the chimerical enterprises, in which he was perpetually engaged, seem rather to belong to the age of knight-errantry, than to the fifteenth century."[10] He insisted, however, that his own endeavor was historical and to show it he drew a comparison with the work of Washington Irving, referring specifically to the latter's *The Conquest of Granada* (1829): "The fictitious and romantic dress of his work has enabled him to make it the medium for reflecting more vividly the floating opinions and chimerical fancies of the age, while he has illuminated the picture with dramatic brilliancy of coloring denied to sober history."[11] Such limitations did not prevent Prescott, however, from adding much coloring of his own, as he did in many memorable passages describing the campaigns of Gonzalo de Córdoba in Italy.[12] Speaking of such military actions, he admitted that, "the chronicler might innocently encroach sometimes on the province of the poet, and the poet occasionally draws the theme of his visions from the pages of the chronicler."[13] Bravery was a virtue shared equally among the contending forces and proved that "the age of chivalry—the chivalry of romance, indeed, had not wholly passed away."[14] Moreover, in a clear allusion to the conquest of the New World, he stated,

> The Spaniard was a knight errant, in its literal sense, roving over seas on which no bark had ever ventured, among islands and continents where no civilized man had ever trodden, and which fancy peopled with all the marvels and drear enchantment of romance; courting danger in every form, combating everywhere, and everywhere victorious . . . and the brilliant destinies to which the meanest adventurer was often called, now carving out with his good sword some "El Dorado" more splendid than fancy had dreamed of, and now overturning some old barbaric dynasty, were full as extraordinary as the wildest chimeras which Ariosto ever sang, or Cervantes satirized.[15]

Chivalry and religion, for Prescott, defined the Spanish national character. Indeed, the peculiar nature of the medieval *Reconquista*, with its strong religious undertones and fighting spirit, would do much to shape Spanish values. "Hence the national character," Prescott stated, "became exalted by a religious fervor, which in later days, alas! settled into a fierce fanaticism. Hence the solicitude for the purity of the faith, the peculiar boast of the Spaniards, and that deep tinge of superstition, for which they have ever been distinguished above the other nations of Europe."[16] But however Christian, and however much the Spaniards considered Muslims their enemies, their interaction during several centuries could not but leave a strong imprint on the national character. "The Spaniard acquired something of the gravity and magnificence of demeanor proper to the Arabian; and the latter relaxed his habitual reserve, and above all, the jealousy and gross sensuality, which characterize the nations of the east."[17] As evidenced by Castilian literature, the influence of the Arabs was profound:

> So far from being confined to the vocabulary, or to external forms of composition, it seems to have penetrated deeply into its spirit, and is plainly discernible in that affectation of stateliness and oriental hyperbole, which characterizes Spanish writers even at the present day; in the subtilties [*sic*] and conceits with which the ancient Castilian verse is so liberally bespangled; and in the relish for proverbs and prudential maxims, which is so general that it may be considered national.[18]

Thus not only religion and chivalry, but an important Arab component, came to define the Spanish character. While Prescott was not alone in this interpretation, and much can be said about the tendency to "orientalize" Spain in the literature of the period, it is important to consider this search for a "national character" on its own terms. In an effort to provide a coherent picture of centuries of Spanish struggles and events, Prescott determined to identify those forces that rendered history intelligible. Thus "national character" provided the vehicle for explaining not only the role of Ferdinand and Isabella, who seemed to have captured it best, but that of subsequent monarchies, who seemed to have done much damage to it. Underlying these considerations, there was a larger transatlantic debate over the role of political institutions in fostering, or stifling, individual and social freedoms. If countries would have, as Voltaire once quipped, as good a leader as they deserved, then what was the role of political institutions vis-à-vis the larger society? Could they be of such good design as to improve the lot of the governed, or were they simply a reflection of it? Closer to home, Prescott had his doubts about the democratic orientation of Jacksonian America, and also about whether the politics and culture of the period reflected the true aspirations of the people after the Revolution. But what was the American "national" character? Spain, in this sense, provided the Boston historian with an opportunity to study the emergence, and the fundamental components, of such character in a land so far, and yet so intimately a part of American history.

The Spanish Reception

William H. Prescott viewed the history of the reign of Ferdinand and Isabella as an example of the heroic emergence of a nation out of the harsh conditions of foreign occupation (although the culture of Muslims and Christians blended over the centuries), as well as internal turmoil and division among the Christian kingdoms. Ferdinand and Isabella not only captured, but they themselves embodied the martial and religious spirit that led the nation out of its morass to secure independence, and to propel the country onto the world stage. The only cloud in this triumphant narrative was presented by the extremes of religious zeal associated with the Inquisition, and the close identification of Crown and Church, which ultimately led the nation astray, and corrupted the solid values of the ancient Iberians. The moral of the story did not escape contemporary Spaniards, who first read it in the translation of the Aragonese scholar Pedro Sabau y Larroya.[19]

The book appeared in four volumes in Madrid in 1845–1846, under the auspices of the *Revista de España, de Indias i del Extrangero*. The editors of this journal wrote a lengthy presentation that reveals the enormous political impact of the work in Spain. They first acknowledged what Prescott knew well, that there was no existing work on the subject, not even in Spain itself. There were some old general histories that made reference to the reign of Ferdinand and Isabella, but not a book exclusively and thoroughly devoted to it. The editors made reference to Diego Clemencín's edition of a volume of the *Memorias de la Real Academia de la Historia* (1821) devoted to the period and to Isabella, a work that Prescott himself had used extensively, but had found lacking in substance.[20] What the Boston historian had done, they stated, was to underscore the singular importance, as well as interest and romance of the period: "The sudden transition from chaos to order, from the middle ages to early modern civilization and culture, from the local to the world stage, which was presided by these illustrious monarchs, are extraordinary deeds, and they seem creations of the imagination rather than plain historical reality"[21] The editors cautioned readers not to look for the glories of the past in the small Iberian kingdoms of the Middle Ages, nor in subsequent ones, meaning especially the Habsburg regimes, but rather in the reign of the Catholic monarchs. Prescott's work had left no doubt about the magnificence of that era.

The editors were interested in Prescott's book for reasons quite beyond the scholarly. Spain in the 1840s had just emerged from the brutal succession struggles following the death of Ferdinand VII in 1833. His teenage daughter, Isabella II, was at the head of a shaky and timidly liberalizing government at the moment when the

Spanish version of Prescott's *Ferdinand and Isabella* appeared. The editors were not particularly subtle in making the following political point:

> We believe that there is no period so analogous to ours than that of the first Isabella. A singular coincidence! That was a period of transition from one system of government to another, just like what we have now. It was preceded by disasters and turmoil, antagonisms and factions, and all the evils they produce; there were wars of succession, calamities, injustices, and countless deaths. Isabella triumphed because of national opinion; she captured and led both the public sentiment and the authorities of the kingdom; she destroyed tyranny and anarchy, and reinstated justice, which is the foundation of society and [effective] government. Once she accomplished all of this, she was able to rapidly elevate the nation to its greatest height. The fate of subsequent kingdoms would have been very different had they followed the same policy. May Heaven help the second Isabella during times no less in need of another transition in Spanish society![22]

The editors unabashedly used Prescott's celebratory account of the Catholic monarchs as a blueprint for the politics of contemporary Spain. They praised the historian's impartiality because it suited their purposes: Isabella was the greatest queen, and her rule the best in Spanish history, all confirmed by a scholar far removed from day-to-day political struggles. But there was something less suitable, and that was Prescott's comments on religious freedom. In closing his preface to the work, the New England scholar had expressed a wish that Spain be restored to the grandeur of Isabella's time: "We may humbly trust," he wrote, "that the same Providence, which guided her reign to so prosperous a termination, may carry the nation safe through its present perils, and secure to it the greatest of earthly blessings, civil and religious liberty."[23] The translator was not pleased, and noted as follows:

> This last statement and wish, so natural given the present state of ideas in the author's country [the United States], is not entirely applicable to ours. It is admissible in the sense that conscience ought to be free from the material coercions employed by the Inquisition, to which the author perhaps alludes. But not so in the many other senses that this word can have.[24]

The translator of the work, as mentioned before, was Pedro Sabau y Larroya. Prescott was aware of his work thanks to the peripatetic Fanny Calderón, then in Spain, who had in turn learned about it from Pascual de Gayangos. "He says Sabau's translation," wrote Fanny, "is not good at all, and that his notes are rather ill-natured, that he considers you too much of a Protestant."[25] Gayangos wrote to Prescott directly to tell him not to expect very much from the translation, either in terms of style, or substance. "The translator himself tells me," he informed Prescott, "that he intends to attack you on your views regarding the popular assemblies of Castile and the establishment of the Inquisition."[26] Prescott was not alarmed, and wrote humorously to Fanny Calderón to say that "if Sabau knocks my religion on the head, and [Antonio] Benavides my politics, I wonder what will remain of me."[27]

Indeed, Sabau had a keen eye for detecting the passages where Prescott revealed his opinions about religious matters. In those instances he added a note, but in some cases he omitted lines or rewrote entire paragraphs. One example is Prescott's statement to the effect that "the policy of the Roman Church, at that time [the establishment of the Inquisition in Spain], was not only shown in its perversity of some of the most obvious principles of morality, but in the discouragement of all free inquiry in its disciples, whom it instructed to rely implicitly in matters of conscience on their spiritual advisers."[28] Sabau noted, "I have freely translated the previous paragraph, avoiding one phrase in the original, which refers to matters of dogma." He removed the key words ". . . in its perversity . . . all free inquiry . . . instructed" and reworked the phrase to read, "The policy of the Roman Church, at that time, allowed not only for the relaxation [*se dejaron relajar*] of some of the most obvious principles of morality, but also favored [*se favoreció*] the abandon and ignorance of individuals. . . ."[29] Thus defanged by the use of passive verbs and milder vocabulary, the paragraph retained a literal sense but lost its major force. He did the same with a passage where Prescott pronounced particularly harsh words against Pope Sixtus IV, who had authorized the introduction of the Holy Office into Castile. Likewise, in the chapter on the Conquest of Málaga, Sabau commented, "I omit in this paragraph a sentence, very typical of Protestants, which is completely unnecessary to this history."[30] This is a reference to Prescott's statement about how the Reformation "opened to mankind the uncorrupted channel of divine truth."[31] Sabau noticed that Prescott's critique of Catholic misdeeds, however just or subtle, showed a bias of its own. For instance, Prescott issued a devastating critique of Pope Alexander VI, whom Sabau himself would not defend, but added the following comment: "His pontificate, however, was not without its use; since that Providence, which still educes good from evil, made the scandal, which it occasioned to the Christian world, a principal spring of the glorious Reformation."[32] The translator noted tersely, "I render the facts, but not the assessment of them, for there can be no agreement between Catholics and Protestants on these points."[33] He did his work thoroughly, but sometimes used short, unexplained sentences such as "the author exaggerates," or "this is not accurate."

Others were less restrained than Sabau. José Güell y Renté, who was just as interested as his liberal compatriots in drawing a parallel between Isabella the Catholic and Isabella II, was considerably more exercised about Prescott's calls for religious liberty.[34] He argued that Spain was rapidly recovering under Isabella II and that great prosperity, and even grandeur, was within reach. "But this prospect," he added, "which will return Spain to what it used to be, will never make us look for that happy blessing cited by Prescott: religious liberty. Our country does not need that disastrous means to achieve greatness. The system that the American historian views as such great good, would be ruinous to Spain" (12–13). Isabella II and the Regency had authorized the massive confiscation of Church property in the 1830s and 1840s, but for political reasons she proclaimed to be a devout Catholic. Güell was, therefore, defending the same line, attacking the institution but retaining the cult. "Freedom of religion," he argued against Prescott, "will turn any nation into a den of immorality and crime" (13). In the end Spain, the confident Güell stated, "Which achieved its nationality through [the Catholic] religion, will never permit freedom of belief" (19).

Prescott was not overly concerned about such disagreements, which at any rate he first read in the more moderate version of Sabau's translation. Gayangos sent a copy to him in December 1845, and the historian was not at all displeased when he read it. Prescott told his Spanish correspondent that,

the translation of [*Ferdinand and Isabella*] appears faithful as far as I have compared it [to the original]. As to its literary execution in other respects, a foreigner cannot decide.

But I wish you would give my thanks to the translator for the pleasure it has given me. His notes on the whole are courteous, though they shew [*sic*] that Señor Sabau has contemplated the ground often from a different point of view from myself. But this is natural, for am I not the child of democracy? Yet not a bigoted one, I assure you. I am no friend to bigotry in politics or religion, and I believe that powers are not so important as the manner in which they are administered.[35]

Prescott elegantly deflected Sabau's critiques, but did not acknowledge the political environment in which the translator and the editors of the *Revista* operated.[36] *Ferdinand and Isabella* allowed these scholars to address the current political situation of the country under the guise of endorsing an erudite work that celebrated the glories of Spain. But they were also concerned about the political implications, in that continued attacks against the Catholic Church could backfire, much as it soon did in Mexico. The editors were by no means militant Catholics, and their preface shows evidence of their support for the typical liberal agenda of the period, most importantly the establishment of the rule of law, a centralist state, and economic development. The issue was too delicate to present in an unaltered version, with such a strong undercurrent of Protestant assumptions, in a country still struggling to define the role of religion in society.[37]

Prescott was not oblivious to the predicament of the nation, and knew much about it through his correspondence with friends. But he also had his own scholarly concerns and commitments, which led him to view the history of Spain as the constant advance of bigoted political and religious institutions, and to deploy various literary strategies to reveal the extent of the damage inflicted on the ancient Spanish culture by the sixteenth-century monarchs. It might be appropriate, then, to take a closer look into his sources, and into his diagnosis of the sad story of Spanish decline.

Spanish Bigotry

When Prescott contemplated his scholarly options in the 1820s, he was quite aware of the work of William Robertson, the great eighteenth-century Scottish historian.[38] So aware, indeed, that he adopted many of the historian's themes, concepts, and sometimes expressions. Prescott shared Robertson's interpretation of Spanish history, especially with regard to the significance of Charles V's reign for both Spain and Europe. Robertson had stated in his 1769 work that "it was during his administration that the powers of Europe were formed into one great political system. . . . The political principles and maxims then established still continue to operate. . . . The age of Charles the Fifth may therefore be considered as the period at which the political state of Europe began to assume a new form."[39] We have seen how Prescott used the same statement, almost verbatim, in his correspondence with Alexander H. Everett. Moreover, in his private journal he wrote that "the age of Ferdinand is most important as containing the germs of the modern system of European politics."[40] Prescott's debt to Robertson in this regard is clear, but he borrowed much more liberally from the Scottish historian's views on religion, and especially his depiction of Catholicism.

In his overview of the state of Europe before the sixteenth century, Robertson emphasized the disproportionate powers of the nobility vis-à-vis the monarchs, the corruption of Christianity into superstition, and the central importance of the values and attitudes of chivalry. The sixteenth century had brought a much welcome change to this state of affairs. Princes were now in firm control of their governments, internal administration had improved, and their ability to wage war had extended their area of operations, making Europe one large theater of conflict, diplomacy, and politics. Spain lagged somewhat behind most European kingdoms, in that still under Charles V, the nobility, the Church, and the survival of the values of chivalry had an enormous influence on both the country and in its dominions. Given his position as Holy Roman Emperor, Charles found himself bound by duty as well as conviction to counter the formidable challenge of the Reformation. Hence, Robertson's *History* is not only informed by, but fully structured around, the themes of religious conflict.[41] It is important, then, to review which episodes he considered most significant, and especially those that would later be echoed by Prescott.

After the fall of the Roman empire, Robertson stated, Christianity had "degenerated . . . into an illiberal superstition."[42] For several centuries afterward, religion "consisted chiefly in believing the legendary history of those saints whose names crowd and disgrace the Romish calendar."[43] Moreover, priests became the objects of "superstitious veneration."[44] Combined with chivalry after the great crusades, religion loomed large in creating an ethos of warlike fanaticism that was particularly apparent in Spain. To illustrate the noxious effects of such a mix, Robertson focused on the doctrine of the immaculate conception of Mary, which enjoyed wide acceptance among the Spaniards even when some monastic orders opposed it, and the Vatican itself was not insistent on the matter. Still, Robertson observed, the military order of Santiago, perhaps destitute of a purpose after the expulsion of the Moors, embraced it wholeheartedly, as did another of the great military orders of Spain, that of Calatrava. Such extravagant choices did not end in the sixteenth century, for much later, in the eighteenth century, Charles III had created a new military order devoted to Mary and to the mystery of her conception. This prompted the following reflection by the Scottish historian:

> To undertake the defence of the Virgin Mary's honor had such a resemblance to that species of refined gallantry which was the original object of chivalry, that the zeal with which the military orders bound themselves, by a solemn vow, to defend it, was worthy of a true knight, in those ages when the spirit of the institution subsisted in full vigor.

However, in his own day, "it must excite some surprise to see the institution of an illustrious order connected with a doctrine so extravagant and destitute of any foundation in Scripture."[45] Religious practices in Spain were not only extravagant, but resilient. If Robertson did not invent the concept of a timeless Spain, he certainly gave it new force.

The Scottish historian was also interested in illustrating the effects of monasticism, especially when combined with political power, on the politics and society of Spain. He chose for this purpose to examine the story of Cardinal Jiménez de Cisneros, to whom Prescott also devoted significant attention. This austere figure elicited some praise from Robertson, but he quickly pointed out that the Cardinal was notorious for "those excesses of superstitious devotion which are the proper characteristics of monastic life."[46] The greed of the priests, the corruption of the clergy due to the misguided policy of celibacy, and the arbitrary behavior of the

Popes provided Robertson with additional examples of Catholic misdeeds. But he devoted particularly detailed attention to the emergence and purposes of the Society of Jesus, which he considered as "the most political and best regulated of all the monastic orders, and from which mankind have derived more advantages, and received greater injury, than from any other of those religious fraternities."[47] The founder of the order, Ignatius Loyola, was "a fanatic distinguished by extravagances in sentiment and conduct, no less incompatible with the maxims of sober reason than repugnant to the spirit of true religion."[48] The order's "large infusion of fanaticism" was to be attributed directly to its founder. As is clear from previous comments, Robertson was no friend of any monastic order, but the difference between the Jesuits and other congregations was crucial. While many of the regular clergy were "dead to the world," living a cloistered life preoccupied with their own salvation, the Jesuits were trained for active service in the world. Their system of government was "a perfect despotism"; they set out into the world to sow intrigue, and stir schemes of persecution, especially against Protestants. The Jesuits, he concluded, may "justly be considered as responsible for most of the pernicious effects arising from that corrupt and dangerous casuistry, from those extravagant tenets concerning ecclesiastical power, and from that intolerant spirit, which have been the disgrace of the Church of Rome throughout the period, and which have brought so many calamities upon civil society."[49]

It is perhaps not surprising that in Robertson's account of the reign of Charles V, only Martin Luther received admiring praise. Luther's opinions presented a formidable challenge to Charles, and "led to that happy reformation in religion which rescued one part of Europe from the papal yoke, mitigated its rigor in the other, and produced a revolution in the sentiments of mankind, the greatest, as well as the most beneficial, that has happened since the publication [i.e., emergence] of Christianity."[50] In Robertson's presentation, Luther was not afraid to question papal authority, and was prepared to confront the Dominicans who threatened him with the rigors of the Inquisition. His persistence, beginning with his unremitting denunciation of the clerical use of indulgences, made the entire Reformation possible: "The doctrines of popery are so closely connected, that the exposing of one error conducted him naturally to the detection of others; and all the parts of that artificial fabric were so united together, that the pulling down of one loosened the foundation of the rest, and rendered it more easy to overturn them."[51] Luther, he leaves no doubt, was "raised up by Providence" to launch the Reformation, but was not free from flaws. However, the flaws needed to be "charged to the manners of the age." Perhaps no other statement would influence Prescott as much as this one: "In passing judgment upon the characters of men, we ought to try them by the principles and maxims of their own age, not by those of another. For although virtue and vice are at all times the same, manners and customs vary continually."[52] Prescott applied this principle consistently, whether in medieval Spain, pre-Columbian Mexico, or Conquest-era Peru.

A less noticed source of Prescott's views, choice of themes, and style, is Joseph Blanco White's *Letters from Spain* (1822).[53] Although Blanco White was not especially profuse in citing his sources, and indeed he made no attempt to write a history of Spain, he derived many of his own themes and views from Robertson's *History.* In many ways, he provides a bridge between the Scottish and the American historian. Prescott owned the princeps edition of the *Letters*, quoted it in his own works, and used his picturesque illustrations as evidence. Blanco White was a former Catholic priest who fled Spain for England during the Napoleonic invasion, converted to Anglicanism in London, and later became a Unitarian. This last conversion made him better known and, indeed, quite well received in Boston Unitarian circles.[54] Blanco White's book was written in the style of Montesquieu's *Persian Letters*, and provided a scathing critique of Spanish Catholicism, its hold and influence on both the government and the larger population.

Like Robertson, and perhaps because of him, Blanco White devoted significant attention to many of the same themes. One example is the Spanish embrace of the doctrine of the immaculate conception of Mary, which Blanco White depicted with sarcastic humor. The Spaniards, he said, with their characteristic gallantry, "stood for the honor of our Lady" and proclaimed it in endless processions continually to the present time. He referred to the same actions of Charles III concerning this peculiarly Spanish belief, but added more editorial comment. His government, Blanco White stated, "shewed the most ludicrous eagerness to have the *sinless purity* of the Virgin Mary added by the Pope to the articles of the Roman Catholic faith."[55] When he succeeded, Charles instituted the military order referred to by Robertson, but Blanco White added that an oath declaring belief in the immaculate conception was required from every individual taking degrees or joining corporations, and "even mechanics."[56] In Blanco White's account, the Jesuits did not fare much better than they did with Robertson, although he chose a different way of illustrating the Order's "despotism": a Jesuit priest in Granada reluctantly but good-naturedly danced a few steps at a party. Years passed and he was considered for an important appointment for which he was eminently qualified. He was denied it because of the ill-timed and certainly not well-appreciated courtesy of the dance.[57] Anecdotes such as this were used to illustrate all manner of political, cultural, and especially religious practices. But the humor had an edge, and the stories were intended to portray a culture entirely corrupted by a superstitious attachment to Catholic practices. As he put it in the opening letter,

> Religion, or, if you please, superstition, is so intimately blended with the whole system of public and domestic life in Spain, that I fear I shall tire you [Blanco White's fictional correspondent] with the perpetual recurrence of that subject. I am already compelled, by an involuntary train of ideas, to enter upon that endless topic. If, however, you wish to become thoroughly acquainted with the national character of my country, you must learn the character of the national religion. The influence of religion in Spain is boundless. It divides the whole population into two comprehensive classes, bigots and dissemblers.[58]

Prescott extracted from Blanco White the confirmation that Spanish religious bigotry extended to the present time, but in terms of style of historical writing, he followed Robertson's themes much more closely. So much so, in fact, that he absorbed the entire text of the *History* into his own set of works, which later became a standard part of his complete works. He added, however, a substantial section on Charles V after his abdication in 1556. Robertson's own treatment of this episode was brief, and thus allowed—perhaps invited—Prescott to substantially expand it. But there was more involved here than filling an obvious gap: the fate of Emperor Charles V had a particular attraction not only for Prescott, but for many others as well, in the United States and in Europe.

The Holy Roman Emperor

Robertson's brief treatment of Charles's twilight shows a tormented figure caught up in the complexities of his time, burdened by his responsibilities, and prisoner to his obstinate beliefs. There is something tragic about his demeanor as he abdicates his throne to live a monastic life in the isolated monastery of Yuste (he mistakenly called it St. Justus) in Old Castile. Robertson's style, generally forceful but quite dry, changes drastically from the narrative of high politics to a more involved biographical account. In seeking to explain Charles's abdication, aged 56 and at the height of his political power, Robertson's answer is on the surface quite simple: Charles's health was broken, and his mind "impaired by the excruciating torments which he endured" because of the gout.[59] Accustomed to supervising every minute aspect of his government, he could not suffer to delegate the responsibilities of his office due to bodily infirmities. Careful, but not always copious in his citation of sources, Robertson departed in this case from his usual economy to discuss competing interpretations of the abdication. He dismissed, in particular, the argument that it had been differences between Charles and his son Philip that led him to resign. The scholar who had made this claim, Dom Lévesque, had consulted the papers of Cardinal Anthony Perrenot de Granvelle, arranged and preserved by the Abbé Boizot at Besançon. But because the papers remained unpublished, Robertson stated, "I cannot determine what degree of credit should be given to this account of Charles' resignation."[60] It is quite possible that Prescott's usual thirst for authentic sources may have motivated him to pursue the subject. This was also the sort of historical mystery that captured his literary imagination. The gap was obvious, the issues were contested, and Charles remained an enigmatic figure.

Robertson himself displayed unusual eloquence in describing the emperor's last journey, using as a main theme the contrast between apparently omnipotent worldly powers, and human flaws and limitations. The Scottish historian depicted Charles's destination, the Hieronymite monastery of Yuste, as a "humble retreat." "He buried there," wrote Robertson, "in solitude and silence, his grandeur, his ambition, together with all those vast projects, which, during almost half a century, had alarmed and agitated Europe, filling every kingdom in it, by turns, with the terror of his arms, and the dread of being subdued by his power."[61] At Yuste, his life could not present a sharper contrast to his previous station: he lived frugally, attended by only a few servants, completely devoted to reading religious books, and prayer. He was also totally oblivious to European political affairs: "He restrained his curiosity even from any inquiry concerning them; and he seemed to view the busy scene which he had abandoned with all the contempt and indifference arising from his thorough experience of its vanity, as well as from the pleasing reflection of having disentangled himself from its cares."[62] While indulging his obsession with watches and other mechanical instruments, he also contemplated the failure of his "vain attempt to bringing mankind to a precise uniformity of sentiment concerning the profound and mysterious doctrines of religion."[63]

Charles did not achieve spiritual peace in the serene environment of Yuste in Extremadura. When gout struck again, "an illiberal and timid superstition depressed his spirit."[64] He resorted to mortification of the flesh with such vengeance that after his death a whip was found "tinged with blood." The climax in Robertson's description, however, was the celebration of Charles's own funeral: "He was laid in his coffin, with much solemnity. The service for the dead was chanted, and Charles joined in the prayers which were offered up for the rest of his soul, mingling his tears with those which his attendants shed, as if they were celebrating a real funeral."[65] He died, a broken man, shortly thereafter. Robertson quickly switched tone after this description; he had not set out, he said, to provide an account of Charles's life, and left the scene of such twisted religiosity with alacrity. The Scottish historian was certainly not guilty of hero worship.

Prescott had been aware of Robertson's work since the 1820s, but a number of developments, especially in the 1840s and early 1850s convinced him to write his nearly two-hundred-page "The Life of Charles the Fifth after his Abdication," which he appended to Robertson's *History* and had it published in 1856. Thanks to his Spanish correspondents, and especially Pascual de Gayangos, he knew that the keeper of the Simancas Archive in Spain, Tomás González, had compiled some records of the last years of the emperor, specifically to contest Robertson's account.[66] The unpublished work, *Estancia y muerte del emperador Carlos Quinto en el monasterio de Yuste*, ended after González's death in the hands of his brother Manuel, who tried to sell it at an exorbitant price. It was finally purchased by the French government and stored at the *Archives des Affaires Étrangères*, then under the direction of the scholar François Mignet.[67]

The manuscript was not destined to gather dust on the shelves. Indeed, an international chase for the work and its sources began in the 1840s, when the British scholar William Stirling (later Stirling-Maxwell) learned about its existence from two sources, Richard Ford's *Handbook of Spain* (1845), and Louis Prosper Gachard's 1845 essay in the *Bulletins* of the Royal Academy of Brussels. Stirling-Maxwell was intrigued enough to visit, in 1849, the monastery at Yuste. There, he determined that not much could be obtained in the way of records, due to the devastations of the Peninsular War, and the plunder that followed it. He wrote an account of his visit, which appeared in the April and May 1851 issues of *Fraser's Magazine*. Soon thereafter, he tracked down the González manuscript in Paris, and found there all the information he needed to write the enormously successful *The Cloister Life of Charles the Fifth* (1852).[68] It was not only a rebuttal of Robertson's account, but a triumph of scholarly persistence. His work stimulated other scholars, who set out not only to investigate the story of Charles V, but also to locate more documents pertaining to the period in various European archives, and especially in the infamously disorganized Simancas repository. Amédée Pichot prepared his account, *Chronique de Charles-Quint* in 1854, and Gachard obtained a commission from the Belgian government to study the records at Simancas. The result was his three-volume *Retraite et Mort de Charles-Quint* (1854–1855). Mignet, who had been less than diligent in making full use of the González manuscript, finally published his *Charles-Quint; son abdication, son Séjour, et sa Mort au Monastère de Yuste* (1854). Rarely has there been so much scholarly interest and productivity, in such a short time, and on such dour a figure as Charles V.

Prescott had started his own pursuit of documents on a related subject (the history of Philip II) soon after he finished his *Ferdinand and Isabella*. Inevitably, he encountered the story of the last days of Charles, and the frustrations of obtaining documents about it. At the suggestion of Ángel Calderón, he wrote directly to Tomás González in 1838, to request access to documents pertaining to the conquests of Mexico and Peru (both had taken place during the reign of Charles V), but González died before he could answer.[69] Prescott then decided to hire a German scholar residing in Spain, Friedrich Wilhelm Lembke, to help him locate documents. It was to Lembke that he communicated one of the earliest indications of his determination to pursue the history of Philip II, "a reign which still remains to be written in English."[70] His German aide, himself a specialist on the history of Spain, did most of his work at the Archives of the Royal Academy of History, where both he and Prescott could count on the friendly and determined support of Martín Fernández de Navarrete. But Simancas was another story. As Lembke put it, now that Tomás González was dead, no one could give him a clear account of the state of the archives. "Some persons state that all the papers are in the greatest confusion." He added that it would be useless to go to Simancas, "as there was no literary man to assist one's researches. Besides I could not ascertain whether the government would grant a permission for copying documents, namely to foreigners, and a permission granted by a minister of today may be revoked by his successor of tomorrow, whom the storm of revolution may bring to power."[71] The secretary of the American Legation in Madrid, Arthur Middleton (a Harvard classmate of Prescott with strong scholarly inclinations), was sorry to confirm Lembke's account, and mentioned another piece of bad news: "The papers are all thrown together without order or index." Under the circumstances, it would not be worth his while "to dive into these waters for the sunken treasure."[72]

Prescott was somewhat dismayed, but did not abandon the hope that either Lembke or someone else would finally gain access to Simancas and ascertain what could be found in the collection. In addition, he was in no great hurry, occupied as he was with the history of the conquest of Mexico and planning to write the related history of the conquest of Peru. He knew from assorted publications that there were important documents at Simancas, and thus he kept insisting. In 1840, he learned from Middleton that the González papers were on sale, but not knowing exactly what was in them he found the price too high to risk a purchase. Most importantly, these papers could not be a substitute for a direct examination of the archival records.[73] Because many of the documents at Simancas had been carried by Napoleon's troops to France, it would be well worth exploring repositories there. In correspondence with Edward Everett, who was the U.S. minister in Paris at the time, he learned of Mignet and got a general sense of the records available at the *Archives*.[74] Meanwhile, Pascual de Gayangos had offered his own research assistance to Prescott, and in an exchange of correspondence mentioned that González's *Estancia y muerte* was still available for purchase. It was Gayangos's estimation that, because the price was so high, the work would most likely remain in Spain.[75] Prescott responded to Gayangos that he would not buy it at the going price of $3,000 because "to a man who wants original documents, it would scarcely be worth as many reals."[76] In the process, the circle of scholars became wider, and knowledge of what was where more precise. Jared Sparks wrote to Prescott from London,

[Henri] Ternaux[-Compans] says that there is a valuable collection of manuscripts in the *Archives des Affaires Étrangères* in Paris, relating to a quarrell between France and Spain in Philip II's time on some point, which you doubtless understand. The papers were brought from Simancas when the French had possession of Spain. They were reclaimed at the Restoration, but could not be found. They are since found, and deposited in the Archives. I said nothing to Mignet about them, because I suppose [Edward] Everett has given you the particulars. If not, this hint will enable you to make further inquiry through Ternaux at the proper time. The papers are undoubtedly important for your purpose.[77]

This sounded like an idea worth pursuing, but Prescott did not give up the search for a way into the documents at Simancas. In his view, such records would have a higher degree of "authenticity" if they could be cited as extant in the country under study. Even though he himself had used copies of Spanish records for his previous books, he would not suffer copies to be made from documents residing elsewhere, or by anyone not directly accountable to him. There might be relevant materials in several European countries, but he gave higher priority to those available—though not exactly accessible—in Spain itself. His big breakthrough came when Gayangos decided to go to Spain, and take on the assignment of consulting the archives.[78] "I think you will find some things of positive value in Simancas," Prescott wrote to Gayangos, and added,

I see it stated that González the old *archivero* has made some very curious and important revelations in his unpublished manuscript respecting the latter days of Charles V, especially when in the cloisters of St. Justus [*sic*]. These particulars were gathered from other accounts of that prince, sent to Juana, sister of Philip II and widow of the Prince of Portugal, by the Emperor's private secretary [Juan Vásquez de] Molina and his Major-Domo [Luis Méndez] Quijada. Also that in the same archives González had availed himself of correspondence between Charles V and his unhappy grandson Don Carlos. All these events will come within my range. I suppose the manuscript of old González is the same that his nephew [*sic*] offered to me for the modest sum of $3,000! But which I would give but a trifle for, since it is the documents on which it rests that I want, and not a modern compilation. I trust you will get access to those papers, though I fear you will encounter some coldness and opposition even, in effecting this.[79]

Prescott was now clearly aware of the significance of González's findings, even though he still considered the reign of Philip II his main subject.[80] "Señor González seems to have found there [Simancas] very curious documents," he wrote to Gayangos, "relating to the latter days of Charles V, which I hope you will get access to, as his latter days fall within my period, and from the novelty of the facts would be valuable."[81] Gayangos arrived in Madrid in October 1843, after a stop in Paris in search of documents and books for Prescott, and soon confirmed all the stories about Simancas and other repositories in Spain. But he did what he could to address the historian's requests. With regard to Prescott's interest in Charles V, Gayangos reported that,

One of the first things I did here was to hunt up [Manuel]González, who as you know owns a work composed by his late brother, the Archivero of Simancas, on the abdication of Charles V and his retirement to the Monastery of [Yuste]. It is established by the original documents cited in it that instead of living a life of devotion, with a few servants, disillusioned with the world and occupied in making watches as Robertson says, he did not relax his attention to politics for an instant but maintained a correspondence with his son and advised him in every difficult question that arose. Instead of living as has been said with few or no followers and reduced to a meager pension which was not paid very regularly he had a retinue of five hundred servants and gentlemen with a large income which was religiously paid, and after the death of their master his followers were without exception placed in lucrative employment or given high rank in the army.[82]

Gayangos's statement cast an entirely new light on the last days of Charles V, and on Robertson's portrayal of the emperor. For more than seven decades, Robertson's version had gone unchallenged, and thus the potential of these documents did not escape Gayangos. He bargained hard, and though Manuel González brought down the price to $2,000, Gayangos resorted to a bluff: because the documents were in a public repository, (theoretically) available for consultation, he would only pay for those copies of original records contained in González's work, or else go directly to Simancas. González did not budge. Go there, he said, and you will find nothing. "This is not improbable," Gayangos wrote ruefully, "as González has friends there among the employees, to whom he would not fail to give instructions to that effect."[83] A month later, González brought the price down substantially, to $300, but it was now Gayangos's turn to refuse the offer. He would go to Simancas the following summer (1844), or sooner if he could obtain the necessary permits. "I realize the impatience with which you must be awaiting the surmounting of this obstacle, as of course you must begin your history with the residence of Charles V in [Yuste], before plunging into the intricate labyrinth of the history of his son's reign."[84]

Prescott was philosophical about it. "*Meliora speremus,*" he wrote to Gayangos. Surely there must be other things to do in alternative repositories in the meantime. With regards to González's manuscript, he said, "I would not give a sixpence for anything but the documents" and would wait as necessary for a visit to Simancas. At the same time, he encouraged Gayangos to keep the doors of negotiation open, for he understood the value of at least some of the materials. "It is a part of Philip's reign you know," he wrote to his Spanish aide, "and it would never do to tell the story of Robertson's latter days of Charles, now that it is proved to be an error."[85] Assure González, he instructed Gayangos, that he would not print any of the documents, or do more than use them as reference. In the end, it was all to no avail. Prescott was now truly disheartened: "The affair is very perplexing and I will not embarrass you more with my suggestions. I leave the whole matter to your much superior judgment and am sure whatever may be your determination it will be the right one."[86] At the same time, he said "I must have these materials, to write the declining days of Charles V."[87] Gayangos, accordingly, waited for the propitious time to visit Simancas, but something totally unexpected happened. He announced to Prescott that,

> A new development several days ago may greatly impede our literary projects. It appears that a certain M. Gachard, who calls himself Director of the Archives of Belgium, and who has been at Simancas for some time securing copies of documents relating to the history of Flanders during its occupation by Spain has recently given cause for complaint or suspicion to the officials there. He probably committed some indiscretion or exceeded his authority; perhaps also the crass ignorance of our officials and literary men simply made them think that some evil could result from allowing him to examine the documents which he wished.

Gayangos's implication was that those seeking the restrictions did not want Spain to be shown in an unfavorable light. Government officials brought the matter to the

Royal Academy of History, which produced regulations that severely restricted access to the archives, especially by foreigners.[88] Gayangos could not tell how much this would prevent the pursuit of research for Prescott's project, but he was certain that it would now be more difficult. "There is no help for it," he wrote to the historian, "I know that you cannot undertake the history of Philip II without having authentic information on the last years of his father, and so I am resolved *coûte que coûte* [at all costs] to ask the Government for the necessary permit to visit Simancas."[89] That was clearly the only option left, as yet another setback occurred when González sold the manuscript to François Mignet for a reported 4,000 francs, a fraction of the original price. Gayangos tried to put a positive spin on the bad news: "This may facilitate our finding the documents cited in it as he can have no further interest in their being hidden."[90] Prescott was not as sanguine. "Pray do not lose time," he wrote to Gayangos, "when you can do so without detriment to your own affairs, in securing copies at Simancas."[91]

At long last, Gayangos announced on June 6 that he was about to depart for the archives. Prescott was giddy with excitement when he pictured Gayangos departing "mounted in Gil Blas fashion, for Simancas."[92] The Spanish scholar reached the archives later in the month and set out to work. But he encountered problems immediately:

> As soon as I got here armed with the necessary royal orders for examining the State Papers relative to the first years of the reign of Philip II and the retirement of the Emperor at the Monastery of St. Gerónimo de Yuste, I found that one of the articles of the barbarous and stupid general regulations of the Archives promulgated by the last Minister Peñaflorida forbids visitors to the Archives to copy, make extracts or notes or even to make a summary of the papers which they examine.

He appealed this regulation and won, but then took the full dimensions of the chaos in the arrangement of the papers: there was no clear organizing principle in the 40,000 or so packets of documents and the staff was of no help. The Archive was open only four hours a day and "in spite of our political revolution," meaning the liberalizing regime of Isabella II, all the saint's days were scrupulously observed. The litany continued, but then Gayangos finally revealed what he had found,

> The letters from the Princess Regent [Juana, daughter of the emperor] to Charles V and his letters to his son are in my humble opinion the most precious documents of this period. From them it is clear that although he was aloof from affairs and decided nothing alone, the Emperor was informed of all the important affairs of the monarchy and was consulted on the most trivial matters of state and government. I have had the most important of these letters also copied.[93]

Here, finally, was the documentary confirmation that Robertson was wrong, or at least deceived by his own limited sources, and perhaps by the logic of his narrative of the Reformation, which required a bigoted and superstitious Charles. Prescott was delighted, but also practical, "I shall look with impatience and anxiety," he wrote, "for the safe arrival of the precious box containing the literary treasures which you speak of sending me before long, I trust before the winter storms set in."[94] When he at last received the records in late 1845, he wrote excitedly to Gayangos that "they are precious documents. The letters from San Gerónimo de

Juste [*sic*] have much interest, and show that Charles V was not as Robertson supposed a retired monk, who resigned the world and all knowledge of it when he resigned his crown."[95] The thrill of discovery, however, would soon yield to some doubts.

While he was waiting for the documents, Prescott received another letter from Simancas. Gayangos had moved on to study other aspects of the reign of Philip II, but mentioned that Gachard and an agent of Mignet (Joseph Melchior Tiran) were both working at the Archives. They had, he said, reached an agreement not to duplicate their efforts, given the fact that the copying needed was massive and the time limited.[96] They were all working on different projects, but there was necessarily a great deal of overlap requiring coordination. Obviously the restrictions on access to the Spanish archives because of the Gachard affair did not stymie the interest in, and in fact contributed to augmenting the historical record on, sixteenth-century Spain. Gayangos triumphantly reported to Prescott from Madrid that since the Spanish government could not prevent Gachard's use of the Simancas materials, it resorted to copying everything that the scholar had copied, "not only to ascertain just what he was procuring but also for the purpose of publishing everything here." Gayangos did not approve of the government's methods, but stated with some glee that "the unlucky Belgian has been doing our work."[97]

Still, Gayangos could not be sure that he had identified all the documents available to *archivero* Tomás González, and thus Prescott decided to pursue Sparks's recommendation to extend his inquiries to France. He wrote to the statesman and occasional scholar Adolphe de Circourt, who had reviewed his *Ferdinand and Isabella* for the *Bibliothèque Universelle de Genève*, asking him for suggestions:

> Among the curious documents which escaped me in Madrid was a collection made by the late *Archivero* of Simancas, named González. His nephew [*sic*] and heir asked for the modest price of 15,000 francs. I declined to give it, and M. Mignet subsequently purchased it for a sum considerably less, I believe for one-third of the price demanded of me. But I am not quite certain of the cost to him. I relied on getting copies of the originals from which this collection was made at Simancas. But my agent after six weeks' researches in that Golgotha, where there is no arrangement or even catalogue of contents, expresses great doubts whether he has got some of the most important papers in the González collection. These packets had particular reference to the last days of Charles V, shewing them in a very different light from that in which they have been exhibited by historians. This falls within my subject and I should be most desirous to have copies of such manuscripts. Now if you can advise me when you next do me the favor to write to me, what you think my best way of proceeding to secure them, I shall be much obliged to you. . . . If Mignet would allow me to inspect the documents and have copies made for me of the manuscripts relating to Charles V's retirement and latter days, the portion I desire, it would be a very important boon to me.[98]

Circourt wasted no time in going directly to Mignet to ask for access to González's work on behalf of Prescott. The news was not good, however, as Mignet would only let the manuscript be seen after he was done with it, which did not appear to be very soon.[99] Mignet was a bit more accommodating when George Sumner (Charles's brother) approached him on behalf of the Boston historian. After many assurances of his desire to help, he still "did not like to resign this manuscript until he had taken its *prémices*." Perhaps in a year or two, the French scholar reportedly said, he might make it available to his American counterpart.[100] Prescott was not entirely discouraged, given his own timetable, contemplating as he was two or three years of work on the history of the conquest of Peru. He responded to Sumner that he was not at all surprised about Mignet's parsimony, because "such manuscripts are a writer's literary capital, and it is expecting too much that it can be surrendered before it has been explored and used by the owner."[101] If he felt any disappointment, it was soon assuaged by the arrival of the manuscripts copied by Gayangos at Simancas. Prescott told him that "I sent word to [Mignet] that I could not blame him for keeping the documents in his own hand. Nor indeed can I. No man likes to encourage poachers on his own preserves. But I doubt not that we can do perfectly well without him."[102]

Prescott began work on his *Philip the Second* in July 1849.[103] He was determined to proceed with the work, but had grown considerably anxious in the last couple of years. "My eyes are in very poor condition," he wrote to Gayangos, "the vision has become dim, almost too dim to use them in reading. Yet I do not fear blindness, only the loss of vision for purposes of literary labour."[104] His work proceeded very slowly, and indeed the first two volumes of his work did not appear until 1855. Meanwhile, the British scholar William Stirling-Maxwell established contact with Prescott. "I have heard it so frequently said that you are engaged in writing the History of Philip II, that I cannot help taking leave to say that I hope the rumour is well founded, and that you have sufficiently recovered from the infirmity of eyesight to enable you to prosecute that great undertaking with ease and satisfaction."[105] Vision problems, various other activities, and a trip to England delayed his work considerably until, in late 1850, he told Ángel Calderón that "I have now returned to my armchair to gnaw upon the dry bones of Philip II."[106] By July 1852, he reported to Pascual de Gayangos that he had begun the second volume of his history.[107] Thus, he had finally confronted the declining days of Charles V during the summer of 1851 and part of 1852. But then he learned that Gayangos had encountered new documents:

> You mention that you have furnished Stirling with the manuscript of Father [Martín de] Angulo [Prior of Yuste] used by [Prudencio de] Sandoval, and that it contains an account of the mock funeral of Charles V. I have treated this as apocryphal in a chapter which I have devoted to the cloistered life of the Emperor. I should be much obliged, therefore, if you could send me in a letter, without waiting for the other manuscripts, that part of Angulo's narrative which relates to the funeral. . . . I only desire what relates to this single subject—which of course will not cover much ground.[108]

That is, Prescott had departed from Robertson by dismissing the account of the funeral, but the Angulo manuscript now seemed to validate the statements of the Scottish historian. As he was waiting for the document, Prescott received, late in the year, a parcel from William Stirling-Maxwell. "Here is my *Cloister Life of Charles V*— a volume which will have some interest for you. . . ."[109] "Interest" was certainly an understatement, for Prescott was completely stunned. He could now see in print the story that he had pursued for so many years. He had procrastinated too long in writing up his account compared to the diligent Stirling-Maxwell, and was still without the Angulo manuscript. Gayangos himself was quite frustrated, for he did not receive Prescott's request until early 1853, and also because, he said, "I have repeatedly reminded Stirling of his promise to forward you the copy of Angulo's relation," obviously to no avail.[110] He thus had another copy made and sent to Prescott, who responded in the summer of 1853: "A fine, legible copy," he stated, "I shall have to rewrite my chapter on the latter days of Charles the Fifth. Plague upon Stirling, who has taken some good things out of my mouth which I was prepared to say! This Cloister Life will be a trite story now."[111]

Despite this momentary dismay, Prescott was determined to forge ahead; the story of the last days of Charles V was just too important. In the opinion of C. Harvey Gardiner, it was upon receipt of Stirling-Maxwell's book that Prescott decided to interrupt his work on Philip II and put together his edition of Robertson's *History* with the addendum mentioned earlier.[112] This is plausible, as Prescott published the first two volumes of *Philip the Second* in 1855, and only a year later the set of Robertson's *History* (one more volume appeared in 1858, but *Philip* remained unfinished) This is how Prescott explained the new project to his British publisher, Richard Bentley:

> Robertson's *History of Charles V* terminates with the account of his reign; at least only two or three pages, and those full of inaccuracies, are devoted to an account of his life after his abdication. This was no fault of his; for he could not get the materials for it, which were to be found in archives in Simancas, and these were not opened until very recently to the scholar. It was from these materials that both Stirling in London and Mignet in Paris made up their accounts of Charles V after his retirement, and from similar materials I wrote a chapter on the same subject in my History of Philip the Second.[113]

Indeed, Prescott related the story of the last days of Charles in the first volume of his *Philip the Second* (Book I, Chapter IX). There he summarized the evolution of the story of the emperor's total withdrawal from worldly affairs, and his religious practices. He told the story of Charles's mock funeral briefly, in a matter-of-fact tone, to conclude that "such is the account of the melancholy farce given us by the Jeronymite chroniclers of the cloister life of Charles the Fifth, and which has since been repeated—losing nothing in the repetition—by every succeeding historian, to the present time." He was referring to William Robertson, as a note to this statement made it clear:

> Robertson, after making the emperor perform in his shroud, lays him in his coffin, where, after joining in the prayers for the rest of his own soul, not yet departed, he is left by the monks to his meditations!—Where Robertson got these particulars it would not be easy to tell; certainly not from the authorities cited at the bottom of this page.

Furthermore, "Nor does there seem to have been any distrust of its correctness till the historical scepticism of our own day had subjected the narrative to a more critical scrutiny. It was then discovered that no mention of the affair was to be discerned in the letters of any one of the emperor's household residing at Yuste."[114]

Prescott's impressive review of the literature on the affair appeared to lead to the inescapable conclusion that it was all a hoax, invented by monks and repeated uncritically by subsequent historians, including Robertson. And yet, in a surprising turn of the argument, Prescott argued that the mock funeral might have indeed happened, and used contemporary chronicles to validate his account. He relied especially on Joseph de Sigüenza's *Historia de la orden de San Gerónimo* (1595–1605), because he was "minute in his notice of the imperial habits and occupation at Yuste,"[115] and had wide access to contemporary sources, including monks of the order who had been with Charles at the monastery. The story, in short, was not a fabrication. Robertson was in the end right, but had built his account on limited and unreliable sources and was thus unable to meet contemporary standards of historical scholarship. One might also expect another related conclusion: that if Robertson relied on insufficient and inaccurate information, then much of the account must have come from his own imagination and prejudices. But that was not Prescott's conclusion. Indeed, he went much further than Robertson in accounting for Charles's "character."

The last days of Charles V were recounted in 60 pages in the relevant section of Prescott's *Philip the Second*. As we have seen, most of the writing of this portion of the book took place in the summer of 1851, when none of the sources by Stirling-Maxwell, Gachard, Pichot, and Mignet had yet appeared in print. As the volume went to press, Prescott was able to add some citations and incorporate some of their findings. But it was only in the nearly two-hundred-page-long addendum to Robertson's *History* that Prescott could present all his evidence, and acknowledge the contributions of other scholars. "It is lucky for your many predecessors in the story of Yuste," Stirling-Maxwell wrote to Prescott upon receiving a copy of the book, "that you told it last—or they would none of them been heard of." The British writer only regretted "the appending of so delightful a piece of history," meaning Prescott's contribution, "to a book so superficial as Robertson's has now become."[116] Indeed, the handful of pages on Charles's last days by Robertson had now become a minutely detailed, impressively researched, and masterfully told story that is yet strikingly simple: Charles V was not solely occupied with mortifying his flesh and mounting ghastly ceremonies to witness his own death in the tears of his attendants and in the chants of the monks. Instead, Charles was shown holding court, receiving numerous visitors, exchanging massive correspondence, issuing orders to stamp out religious dissent, managing Philip II's campaigns in Italy, and, in sum, being very much on top of contemporary European politics. Prescott had successfully mined the correspondence and reports by Charles's secretaries, members of the royal family, visitors, doctors, monks, and, of course, the emperor's own letters, the inventory of his possessions (including his library), and his testament. Prescott had decisively superseded Robertson with regard to scholarship.

And yet, when it came to describing Charles's "character" and other aspects of the emperor's biography, Prescott's account was not very different from that of his Scottish predecessor. "A religious sentiment," wrote the Boston historian, "which unhappily was deeply tinctured with bigotry, lay at the basis of Charles' character, as was shown in the busiest parts of his life, no less that in his retirement."[117] Sounding another Robertsonian theme, Prescott asserted that "Bigotry seems most naturally to belong to feeble and ignorant minds," and the princes of the House of Austria provided a good example, for "more than one member of that dynasty was feeble to the verge of fatuity." Still, Charles was exceptional in that: "no one of his line did so much to fasten the yoke of superstition on the necks of the Spaniards."[118] It should not be surprising, then, that the emperor performed the lugubrious ceremony of his own funeral: the rehearsal fit quite well with Charles's character—it was merely "a piece of extravagance which becomes the more credible when we reflect on the state of unnatural excitement to which his mind may have been brought by dwelling so long on the dreary apparatus of death."[119] But it was not just the proximity of death that elicited such behavior; it was rather the natural consequence of a life of religious fanaticism, and, in short, of his true intolerant and obstinate nature. Furthermore,

> He may be truly said to have stamped his character, not only on his own generation, but on that that followed it. His example and his teachings directed the policies of the piti-less Philip the Second, and through him of the imbecile Philip the Third. His dying words—for his codicil, executed on his death-bed, breathed the same spirit as his let-ters—still lingered in the ears of his posterity, to urge him forward in the path of perse-cution; and thus did he become largely responsible for the woes brought on the land long after he had been laid in the dark chambers of the Escorial.[120]

Prescott succeeded in giving new life to Robertson's basic message. He had improved the scholarly apparatus, illuminated the emperor's last days with much new information, and included a sophisticated historiographical discussion. Prescott's emperor was a Charles V for the present century, when new standards for historical scholarship demanded clearer charts and navigational tools. The ship of history had been outfitted with new rigging, new instruments, and a new captain, but it was still propelled by the same wind.

Conclusion

The nautical metaphor that closes the last chapter brings us to another source centrally, and perhaps most strikingly, concerned with the figure of Charles V: Herman Melville's *Benito Cereno*, which appeared in three installments in *Putnam's Monthly Magazine* in 1855, that is, exactly the same year as Prescott's first version of the last days of the emperor in his *Philip the Second*. The story, it may be recalled, begins when the good-natured but colossally naive captain Amasa Delano encounters by chance, off the coast of Chile, the ship that will launch a harrowing tale of coercion, psychological terror, and murderous violence in the high seas. Melville described the ship as follows:

> Upon gaining a less remote view, the ship, when made signally visible on the verge of the leaden-hued swells, with the shreads of fog here and there raggedly furring her, appeared like a white-washed monastery after a thunder-storm, seen perched upon some dun cliff among the Pyrenees. But it was no purely fanciful resemblance which now, for a moment, almost led Captain Delano to think that nothing less than a ship-load of monks was before him. Peering over the bulwarks were what really seemed, in the hazy distance, throngs of dark cowls; while, fitfully revealed through the open port-holes, other dark moving figures were dimly descried, as of Black Friars pacing the cloisters.[1]

The ship is called the *San Dominick*, a name that evokes the Dominican order and the Inquisition, as well as the island of Santo Domingo, notorious for the bloody slave rebellion that led to the creation of the first independent republic in the Caribbean. The ship has been taken over by mutinous slaves presumably on its way from Buenos Aires to Lima. They have murdered their owner, Alejandro Aranda, and taken captive the commander, Benito Cereno, ordering him to deliver them to Senegal. Badly in disrepair and running out of supplies, the vessel has reached the island of Santa Maria on the Pacific Ocean, where Captain Delano boards it to offer his help. It is then that he encounters the diffident Captain Benito Cereno. The Spanish commander displays impatience and a "contemptuous aversion" to everything around him. His authority is dubious, for the experienced eye of the American sailor has recognized behavior that would be unacceptable in a well-commanded ship. And yet, there are moments when Cereno acts like a cruel despot. The clueless Captain Delano hence describes his manner as "not unlike that which might be supposed to have been his imperial countryman's Charles V., just previous to the anchoritish retirement of that monarch from the throne."[2] Benito Cereno is actually a creole, a native of Chile, who belongs to a distinguished family with Peninsular

Spanish connections. Perhaps because the event is said to take place in 1799, that is, before Spanish American independence, Melville makes no distinction between a Spaniard from the Iberian Peninsula and a creole from the colonies. Therefore, the parallel between Captain Cereno and Charles V relates more to their confinement in cloistered quarters, under the close supervision (if not captivity) of Hieronymite friars in the case of the latter, and "Black Friars" (or slaves) in the case of the former. Cereno's own private quarters in this floating monastery are bare, though it has such items as a "thumbed missal," a "meager crucifix," and some "melancholy old rigging, like a heap of poor friars' girdles." Moreover, there are some "long, sharp-ribbed settees of Malacca cane" which are "uncomfortable to look at as inquisitors' racks."[3]

Cereno's reserved demeanor, haunted looks, and total obliviousness to the disarray in his ship all add to Delano's puzzlement. He gropes for an answer by referring to Cereno's origins: "These Spaniards are an odd set; the very word Spaniard has a curious, conspirator, Guy-Fawkish twang to it."[4] As the American captain finally leaves the ship in frustrated incomprehension, Benito Cereno makes a desperate move to be rescued, which reveals the horror that has entirely escaped the well-meaning but psychologically inept sailor. It turns out that Cereno, in the end, has saved Delano's life by affecting cooperation with his captors. Delano later seizes the runaway ship and takes it to Spanish authorities, first in Chile and subsequently in Peru, seeking to punish the rebels, reinstate Cereno to his command, and secure his own compensation. The Viceregal court in Lima does exonerate Cereno and executes his tormentor Babo, but the Spanish American captain has become so disturbed and demoralized that he relinquishes his command and seeks refuge in a monastery, just like the weary emperor Charles V. The story closes with Melville's memorable words, referring to Cereno's withdrawal from worldly affairs and his ultimate demise, ". . . and across the Rimac bridge [the severed head of Babo] looked towards the monastery, on mount Agonia without; where, three months after being dismissed by the court, Benito Cereno, borne on the bier, did, indeed, follow his leader."[5] A life of despotic yet hollow authority has ended in spiritual torment, cloistered confinement, and a withering death.

Melville's work provides a strong demonstration that the themes of religion and despotism associated with Spain had cut deeply into the American imagination of the nineteenth century, and had projected to it the agonizing fears and moral dilemmas related to slavery. Few pieces of literature involving Hispanic-related topics could match the same level of artistry and complexity, and make such compelling statements about the evils of slavery. But Melville's work is also a demonstration that Robertson had done his work so well that even historians who tried to correct him, like Prescott, ultimately strengthened the very foundations on which he built the prevailing image of Spain: the country remained the place where the unhealthy mixture of religion and politics spawned such fanatical tyrants as Charles V and his equally infamous progeny. The Boston historian did, indeed, follow his leader.

The sinister Charles V did not lose his grip on the American imagination in the four decades after *Benito Cereno* was published. Writing in 1898, Henry Charles Lea, the great historian of the Inquisition in Europe, began his analysis of the decadence of Spain with a reference to the emperor, whose rise to power he described as "an unmitigated misfortune for Spain."[6] Just as U.S. marines were driving the hapless descendants of the powerful monarch off the island of Cuba during the Spanish-American War, Lea felt that the time had come to issue a postmortem report on the fall of the Spanish empire. The causes of decadence, he wrote with lapidary assurance, were three: pride, conservatism, and clericalism.

Spanish pride, Lea thought, was manifested in the Spanish sense of superiority, even as the country sank into the lot of second-rate powers: "It could learn nothing, and forget nothing," he said. Conservatism was reflected in the systematic rejection of innovation, be it technological, commercial, or administrative. The country could simply not compete with other, more energetic nations. Finally, clericalism was responsible for "the ferocious spirit of intolerance" that produced "a fierce and implacable hatred of all faiths outside of Catholicism," which paved the way for the Inquisition. The real significance of the latter office, Lea added, "lay in the isolation to which it condemned the land, and its benumbing influence on the intellectual development of the people."

Pride, conservatism, and clericalism found additional support in the "autocratic absolutism of the form of government," which not coincidentally had been inaugurated by Charles V's suppression of the ancient Castilian liberties, during the uprising of the *Comuneros* in 1520, which marked with blood his ascent to imperial power. Despotism and religious intolerance, in turn, produced a colonial policy that Lea did not hesitate to call "a failure." The Jesuits had been able to build "an independent theocracy" in Paraguay, and the "monastic hypertrophy" of other religious orders had engulfed the New World colonies in their constant bickering and narrow pursuits. No wonder, then, that the final liberation of the region from Spain should be greeted with delight. Liberating oppressed peoples from corrupt priests and despotic monarchs was indeed a cause for celebration.

Henry Charles Lea's autopsy of the Spanish empire might be dismissed as the self-serving rhetoric of military triumph, performed when the U.S. victory over Spain in Cuba was nothing but certain. And yet, the fact that the arguments, the themes, and even the very words can be traced to the pioneer generation of U.S. Hispanists requires some concluding comments. The first is that, despite nearly a century of ever improving research techniques, the field of history had not changed in any fundamental way the basic conception of Spain as a despotic and bigoted country. The assumptions about the Spanish empire proved to be resilient, and remained in place despite the massive documentation that was now standard and commonplace among American historians. In the court of history, Spain was declared guilty in absentia; no mitigating evidence was acceptable.

Second, it is clear that no country, especially a country allegedly as weak as Spain could have possibly imposed its ingrained despotism and religious intolerance over another, much less the United States, separated as it was by a large ocean and protected by a growing military establishment. The threat was perceived as coming from another source, closer to home. Spain, indeed, was but a convenient example to remind Americans that the real threat to U.S. democracy came from internal sources and tensions: the country's expansion had accelerated in the second half of the nineteenth century, raising pertinent questions about the moment when a country ceases to be a nation and becomes an empire. Empires may impose their institutions, but however wonderful these might be, they will be resented by their unwilling beneficiaries. Moreover, the religious panorama of the nineteenth century in the United States, though it had no resemblance to the enforced Catholic orthodoxy of Spain, was still not free from bigotry or violence. Keeping zealotry in check was important, and the insistence on its evil consequences was symptomatic of a certain level of anxiety at home. Had not missionary zeal, combined with imperialism, sent Spain into such a sorry downward spiral? Lessons must be learned, as Washington Irving insisted in the 1820s, and as Henry Charles Lea reiterated at the turn of the twentieth century.

Third, it is also clear that the Hispanic world was enormously fascinating to the pioneering Hispanists and the many Americans who eagerly read their books. Despite their sometimes facile negative comments and stereotypes, or their stern condemnations of certain episodes of Spanish history, American intellectuals of the nineteenth century advanced knowledge about Spain and its New World possessions as no other generation had done before. Some of them traveled to various locations within and outside Spain, and they all engaged Hispanic languages and literatures with unprecedented concentration and interest. Some of them developed meaningful emotional bonds with the people of the Hispanic world, and remained concerned about them, their hopes and their fate, to the very end of their lives. They read Spanish-language poetry and prose with a level of professionalism and depth that elicited the admiration of the international scholarly community. They also agonized over specific events in Spanish history, such as Napoleon's invasion of Spain, and the painful emergence of nations formerly under Spanish imperial rule, when they tried to escape the vindictive rule of Ferdinand VII. Surely, they could have looked into such events simply in search of useful lessons, but the evidence provided by this book reveals a much deeper bond.

Indeed, it is in that bond that one finds the key to explain U.S. interest in the Hispanic world. As Walt Whitman once suggested, perhaps the day would come when "the Spanish element in our nationality" would be discerned. Perhaps he knew that those American intellectuals who have concerned us in this book were engaged in precisely that endeavor. Washington Irving had lingered in Spain longer than he anticipated, and was eager to return, because he was certain that Spanish history held the key to the origins of the United States as a nation. So did William H. Prescott, who in addition made an even more direct connection between Spain and the New World, in a similar effort to understand the historical foundations for the emergence of the United States as a distinct nation. George Ticknor, who had painstakingly pieced together the evolution of Spanish letters, was convinced that the trajectory of Spain from nation to empire had left an enduring record, a fountain of wisdom from which the United States could learn as it followed its own path toward national greatness. Henry Wadsworth Longfellow, who as a young man caught at once the musicality and richness of Spanish poetry, adopted its meter and rhyme for poems that have to this day been regarded as quintessential *American* poems. Mary Mann, who had witnessed the horrors of slavery in Cuba, and had followed the career of ruthless *gauchos* in Argentina, drew the lessons that made her the ultimate translator of the Spanish American experience to American readers. Together they assembled, often in conversation with one another, the most enduring view of the Hispanic world's relevance, indeed centrality, to the United States.

It is not just that this intellectual community appears to have been more international in outlook than previous ones (or than many that would come in the future), but rather that these authors showed a certain eagerness to look specifically into the Hispanic world. Long before there had been a country named the United States, Spain had in the course of eight centuries blended religions, languages, and cultures to give rise to a proud and powerful nation. It had fallen, and that fall had to be explained, if sometimes in excruciating detail. But the original spirit that had formed the nation was still inspiring. The pioneer American Hispanists did their best to capture it, and in the process they left a strong, though problematic legacy of ways to view the Hispanic world. But their search for an understanding of the origins of the United States, and the place of the nation—or any nation—in the wider world, was as poignant then as it is now.

Notes

1 "My King, My Country, and My Faith": Washington Irving's Writings on the Rise and Fall of Spain

1. *The World Displayed, or, A curious collection of voyages and travels, selected from the writers of all nations: in which the conjectures and interpolations of several vain editors and translators are expunged, every relation is made concise and plain, and the division of countries and kingdoms are clearly and distinctly noted: illustrated and embellished with variety* (London: Printed for J. Newbery, at the Bible and Sun, in St. Paul's Church-Yard, 1759).
2. Rolena Adorno, "Washington Irving's Romantic Hispanism and Its Columbian Legacies," in *Spain in America: The Origins of Hispanism in the United States,* edited by Richard L. Kagan (Urbana and Chicago: University of Illinois Press, 2002), pp. 49–105. I am extremely indebted to this and two other essays by Rolena Adorno, "Early Anglo-American Hispanism in the 'Columbian Encounter' of Washington Irving and Martín Fernández de Navarrete," which appeared in the Pre-Actas of the Conference "El hispanismo anglonorteamericano: Aportaciones, problemas y perspectivas sobre Historia, Arte y Literatura españolas (siglos XVI–XVIII)" (Córdoba: Universidad de Córdoba, 1997), pp. 5–40, and the revised version that appeared in the book of the same title, edited by José Manuel de Bernardo Ares (Córdoba: Publicaciones Obra Social y Cultural Cajasur, 2001). Adorno's essay appears on pp. 87–106. See also Stanley T. Williams, *The Life of Washington Irving,* 2 vols. (New York: Oxford University Press, 1935), and *The Spanish Background of American Literature,* 2 vols. (New Haven: Yale University Press, 1955). He discusses Irving's youthful readings in volumes I, pp. 20–21 of the former title, and II, pp. 9–11, of the latter. An insightful treatment of Washington Irving as a traveler is by Pere Gifra-Adroher, *Between History and Romance: Travel Writing on Spain in the Early Nineteenth-Century United States* (Madison: Farleigh Dickinson University Press, 2000), pp. 122–157. The best recent biography is by Andrew Burstein, *The Original Knickerbocker* (New York: Basic Books, 2007).
3. References to Cervantes's *Don Quixote* can be found in Washington Irving's letters to his brother William Irving, Jr., December 28, 1804, in *Letters (1802–1823),* 2 vols., edited by Ralph M. Alderman, Herbert L. Kleinfield, and Jenifer S. Banks (Boston: Twayne Publishers, 1978), I, p. 144. See also a reference to *La Galatea* in a letter to Mary Fairlie, May 2, 1807, *Letters,* I, p. 231.
4. Williams, *Life,* I, p. 284.
5. Washington Irving to Thomas Storrow, Haarlem, July 11, 1822, in *Letters,* I, p. 693. Irving mentioned Everett's invitation in his journal of January 30, 1826, in *Journals and Notebooks,* vol. III (1819–1827), edited by Walter A. Reichart (Madison: The University of Wisconsin Press, 1970), p. 563. Also, in the preface of his *A History of the*

Life and Voyages of Christopher Columbus [1828], in *The Works of Washington Irving*, 15 vols. (New York: P.F. Collier & Son, 1904), VI, p. 7. A letter from Lucretia Orne Everett to her father, dated in Madrid, January 9, 1826, suggests that Alexander Everett had proposed the idea to Irving "the other day" meaning very recently, and that "Irving caught at the proposition immediately." Everett-Peabody family papers, Massachusetts Historical Society.

6. Irving to Storrow, Bordeaux, February 3, 1826, in *Letters (1823–1828)*, II, pp. 171–172. The letters of Irving and Storrow have also been edited by Stanley T. Williams, *Washington Irving and the Storrows: Letters from England and the Continent, 1821–1828* (Cambridge: Harvard University Press, 1933), pp. 64–65.

7. Irving, Journal entry of February 16, 1826, in *The Journals of Washington Irving*, edited by William P. Trent and George S. Hellman, 3 vols. (Boston: The Bibliophile Society), III, p. 9, henceforth JWI. Although covering Irving's Spanish notes, this edition ends abruptly on April 30, 1828, and resumes July 28, 1829. For coverage of the hiatus, see Clara Louisa Penney, ed., *Washington Irving Diary: Spain 1828–1829* (New York: The Hispanic Society of America, 1926). Henceforth cited as WID.

8. Irving, Journal entry of August 9, 1826. JWI, III, p. 36. Demetrio Ramos Pérez has argued that as a Romantic, Irving was drawn into Spain's peculiar medieval history precisely because of its Arab, or "Oriental" component. See his "Washington Irving, el romántico que desencadenó la historiografía colombina," offprint, no publication data. Real Academia de la Historia (Madrid), Biblioteca General, Caja 1–295, No. 33.075.

9. Henry W. Longfellow to Stephen Longfellow, Madrid, March 20, 1827, in *The Letters of Henry Wadsworth Longfellow*, edited by Andrew Hilen, 6 vols. (Cambridge, MA: Harvard University Press, 1966–1982), I, p. 222.

10. Irving, various journal entries in March–April, 1827. JWI, III, pp. 57–62.

11. WI to Thomas W. Storrow, Madrid, October 8, 1827, *Letters*, II, p. 253.

12. Alexander H. Everett secured this permission for Irving from the Spanish Secretary of State. Everett to Manuel Gonzáles Salmón, Madrid, August 19, 1828, in Alexander H. Everett, *Prose Pieces and Correspondence*, edited by Elizabeth Evans (St. Paul, MN: The John Colet Press, 1975), p. 225.

13. Diary entry of July 9, 1828. WID, p. 42.

14. Various diary entries from August 26 to November 1, 1828. WID, pp. 62–77.

15. WI to Johann Nikolas Böhl von Faber, Puerto de Santa María, November 2, 1828, *Letters*, II, pp. 354–355.

16. Diary entries of December 30, 31, 1828; January 2, 1829; February, 28, 1829. WID, pp. 89–90, 91, 104.

17. See her "How German Romanticism Travelled to Spain: The Intellectual Journey of Johann Nikolas Böhl von Faber," *The Publications of the English Goethe Society*, New Series, vol. LXXI (2001), 78–90. For the larger connection between German and Spanish Romanticism, see her *Creating a National Identity: A Comparative Study of German and Spanish Romanticism* (Stuttgart: Verlag Hans-Dieter Heinz, 1997), and also Derek Flitter, *Spanish Romantic Literary Theory and Criticism* (Cambridge: Cambridge University Press, 1992).

18. *Vindicaciones de Calderón y del teatro antiguo contra los afrancesados en la literatura* (Cádiz, 1820) and *Teatro español anterior a Lope de Vega por el editor de la Floresta de Rimas Antiguas Castellanas* (Hamburg: Perthes, 1832).

19. *Floresta de Rimas Antiguas Castellanas ordenado por Don Juan Nicolas Böhl de Faber de la Real Academia Española*, 3 vols. (Hamburg: Perthes y Besser, 1821–1825).

20. WI to John Nicholas [*sic*] Böhl, Esq., New York, April 26, 1833. I thank Ramón Bayo of the Grupo Osborne in Puerto de Santa María, Spain, for sending me a copy of the original manuscript of this letter. It is also included in *Letters*, II, p. 760.

21. WI to Thomas Aspinwall, Cádiz, August 31, 1828, *Letters*, II, p. 331.

22. WI to Alexander H. Everett, Puerto de Santa María, October 21, 1828, *Letters*, II, p. 347.

23. Lucretia Orne Everett to William Peabody, Madrid, 6 November 1828, Everett-Peabody family papers, Massachusetts Historical Society.

24. Irving described his visit in a letter to Henry Breevort, Edinburgh, August 28, 1817. *Letters*, I, pp. 497–498. To his friend Charles Leslie he related how the days he spent with Scott "are counted among the happiest of my life," WI to Charles Leslie, Liverpool, February 8, 1818, *Letters*, I, p. 518. Irving stayed in touch with Scott for many years afterward.

25. Henry W. Longfellow to Stephen Longfellow, Trieste, December 27, 1828, *Letters*, I, p. 288.

26. For the purposes of citation, I use *The Works of Washington Irving*. Volume (in Roman numerals) and page numbers will henceforth be indicated in parentheses in the text.

27. Irving was well acquainted with Blanco White. While in the midst of writing the *Conquest*, Irving also met Blanco's brother Fernando in Seville. "Mr White brother of Blanco White & partner of Mr Beck calls on me." Diary entry of June 1, 1828, WID, p. 32.

28. In a letter from Granada in 1828, Irving indicated that these events were celebrated in a popular drama named "Ave María." He stated that "although it has been acted time out of mind, and the people have seen it repeatedly, it never fails to draw crowds, and so completely engross the feelings of the audience, as to have almost the effect on them of reality," *The Works of Washington Irving*, X, p. 493.

29. On the use of "character" for understanding nations and cultures in nineteenth-century America, see Richard L. Kagan, "From Noah to Moses: The Genesis of Historical Scholarship on Spain in the United States," in *Spain in America*, pp. 21–47.

30. WI to Thomas Aspinwall, Puerto de Santa María, October 22, 1828, *Letters*, II, p. 348. That he had serious doubts about his story is clear from a letter to his brother. The story of Roderick, he stated, "has been so much harped upon by Scott and Southey as not to possess novelty with literary persons." WI to Peter Irving, Seville, March 29, 1829, *Letters*, II, p. 387.

31. On the larger American intellectual attempt to "orientalize" Spain and its people, see María DeGuzmán, *Spain's Long Shadow: The Black Legend, Off-Whiteness, and Anglo-American Empire* (Minneapolis: University of Minnesota Press, 2005).

32. Everett's essay appeared originally in the *North American Review* (January 1829). It is included in Everett's *Prose Pieces*, pp. 50–85.

33. William H. Prescott, "Irving's Conquest of Granada," [1829] in *Biographical and Critical Miscellanies* (Philadelphia: J.B. Lippincott Company, 1895), pp. 82–113. For a summary of other, mostly positive reactions, see Claudia L. Bushman, *America Discovers Columbus: How an Italian Sailor Became an American Hero* (Hanover and London: University Press of New England, 1992), pp. 124–126.

34. William H. Prescott, *History of the Reign of Ferdinand and Isabella, the Catholic*, 3 vols. (Philadelphia: J.B. Lippincott Company, 1895), II, p. 133.

35. Ibid., II, p. 466.

36. Ibid., II, p. 108.

37. George Bancroft, *History of the United States, from the Discovery of the American Continent* [1834], fifteenth edition, vol. 1 (Boston: Little, Brown, and Company, 1854), pp. 6–7.

38. On Wallis and his assessment of Navarrete and Irving, see Kagan, "From Noah to Moses," and Adorno, "Romantic Hispanism," both in *Spain in America*.

39. Severn T. Wallis, "Navarrete on Spain," *Southern Literary Messenger* 7, No. 3 (March 1841), pp. 231–239.

40. Severn T. Wallis, "Spain: Her History, Character and Literature. Vulgar Errors—Their Extent and Sources," *Southern Literary Messenger* 7, No. 7 (July 1841), 441–451.

41. Severn T. Wallis, "Mr. Washington Irving, Mr. Navarrete, and The Knickerbocker," *Southern Literary Messenger* 8, No. 11 (November 1842), 725–735.

42. *Colección de los viages y descubrimientos que hicieron por mar los españoles desde fines del siglo XV, coordinada é ilustrada por Don Martin Fernández de Navarrete*, vol. 3 (Madrid: Imprenta Real, 1829), pp. xiii–xiv. As indicated by Adorno, these less credible sources included the accounts of Hernando Colón, the son and biographer of the Admiral, and Bartolomé de las Casas. See her "Un caso de hispanismo anglonorteamericano temprano," pp. 87–88.

43. Washington Irving to Diego Clemencín, Seville, January 8, 1829, in Expedientes de Miembros, Secretaría, Real Academia de la Historia (henceforth RAH). A manuscript note in the back of the file identifies Irving as "the author of the life of Columbus, and other [works]." Irving's response has been printed in *Letters*, II, pp. 371–372.

44. Irving to Navarrete, London, December 31, 1830, in *Letters*, II, pp. 378–379.

45. RAH, "Censuras de Obras Pedidas por el Consejo de la Real Academia de la Historia, 1817–1833," Legajo 11-8028, No. 42.

46. RAH, Actas, December 3, 1830.

47. José Sabau y Blanco, "Censura de la obra intítula Historia de la Conquista de Granada por Washington [Irving]." RAH. Secretaría, Expedientes de Miembros.

48. RAH, Actas, February 4, 1831.

49. RAH, Actas, April 8, 1831. Many of the translations of Irving's work, and indeed other nineteenth-century American authors, were made from the French. See Juan José Lanero and Secundino Villoria, *Literatura en traducción. Versiones españolas de autores americanos del S. XIX* (León: Secretariado de Publicaciones, Universidad de León, 1996).

50. RAH, Actas, July 15, 1831. This was undoubtedly the translation by J. Cohen, published in Paris in two volumes in 1829, a copy of which is in the RAH library.

51. RAH, Actas, July 22, 1831. Martín Fernández de Navarrete had initially agreed to evaluate the Columbus translation, but he obviously delegated the task to the diligent Sabau.

52. RAH, Actas. January 30, 1832.

53. RAH, Actas, January 7, 1831.

54. RAH, Actas, January 28, 1831.

55. RAH, Actas, May 13, 1832.

56. RAH, Actas, March 29, 1833.

57. *Memorias de la Real Academia de la Historia*, VII (1832), p. xxx. Quoted by Williams, *Life*, I, p. 356.

58. RAH, Actas, September 24, 1841. Sabau's manuscript translation, "Artículo que ha publicado el periódico literario de los Estados Unidos de América acerca del Sr. Dn. Martín Fernández de Navarrete y de su colección de viajes" consists of 37 pages. RAH, Informes, Cartas y Documentos, Legajo 11-8246.

59. José Antonio Pizarro, "Vindicación de D. Martín Fernández de Navarrete sobre la Historia de la vida de Colón y descubrimiento de la América publicada por el Sr. Washington Irven [*sic*]." RAH, Manuscripts. Legajo 9-6270.

60. RAH, Actas, November 18, 1842.

61. RAH, Actas, December 30, 1842.

62. RAH, Actas, January 13, 1843.

63. This period in Irving's career has been covered by Claude G. Bowers, whose scholarly merit is not comparable to that of Stanley Williams, but who as a diplomat himself, had easy access to the legation archives. See his *The Spanish Adventures of Washington Irving* (Boston: Houghton Mifflin Company, 1940) and Williams, *Life*, II, pp. 119–200.

64. Enrique Gil y Carrasco, "De la literatura y de los literatos de los Estados Unidos de América, por Eugenio A. Vail," in *Obras completas de D. Enrique Gil y Carrasco*, edited by Jorge Campos (Madrid: Biblioteca de Autores Españoles, 1954), p. 547.

65. Navarrete to Irving, Madrid, April 1, 1831, manuscript letter reproduced in Adorno, "Romantic Hispanism," p. 74.

66. Modesto Lafuente, *Historia General de España, desde los tiempos primitivos hasta la muerte de Fernando VII*, 30 vols. (Barcelona: Montaner y Simon, Editores, 1922–1933), originally published in 1850–1867. The importance of this work, and its place in Spanish historiography, has been treated by Roberto López-Vela, "De Numancia a Zaragoza. La construcción del pasado nacional en las historias de España del ochocientos," in *La construcción de las historias de España*, edited by Ricardo García Cárcel (Madrid: Marcial Pons Historia, 2004), pp. 195–298, and "Carlos V y España en la obra de Modesto Lafuente. La interpretación liberal de la nación española dentro del imperio de los Austrias," in *Carlos V y la quiebra del humanismo político en Europa (1530–1558)*, vol. 3 (Madrid: Sociedad Estatal para la Conmemoración de los Centenarios de Felipe II y Carlos V, 2001).

67. This agenda was also advanced by other historians, including José Güell y Renté in *Paralelo entre las reinas católicas Doña Isabel I y Doña Isabel II* (Paris: Imprenta de Jules Claye, 1858). For various other examples, see Paloma Cirujano Marín, Teresa Elorriaga Planes, and Juan Sisinio Pérez Garzón, *Historiografía y nacionalismo español, 1834–1868* (Madrid: Consejo Superior de Investigaciones Científicas, 1985).

68. For a lucid interpretation of Lafuente's agenda, see Javier M. Donézar y Díez de Ulzurrun, "El austracismo de los historiadores liberales del siglo XIX," in *El siglo de Carlos V y Felipe II: La construcción de los mitos en el siglo XIX*, edited by José Martínez Millán and Carlos Reyero, 2 vols. (Madrid: Sociedad Estatal para la Conmemoración de los Centenarios de Felipe II y Carlos V, 2000), I, pp. 311–341.

69. Menéndez y Pelayo, quoted and translated by Williams, *Life*, II, p. 307. The original quote is in "De los historiadores de Colón," *Estudios de crítica literaria* (Madrid: Est. Tip. Sucesores de Rivadeneyra, 1895), pp. 270–272.

70. See, in this regard, the incisive work of Julián Juderías, *La leyenda negra: Estudios acerca del concepto de España en el extranjero* (Salamanca: Junta de Castilla y León, 2003). This book was first published in 1914.

2   *Labor Ipse Voluptas*: George Ticknor's History of Spanish Literature

1. Thomas Jefferson to Elisha Ticknor, February 9, 1816, Rare Books and Manuscripts Department, Boston Public Library (henceforth BPL). Also quoted in David B. Tyack, *George Ticknor and the Boston Brahmins* (Cambridge, MA: Harvard University Press, 1967), p. 41. Extracts from Ticknor's journal describing his visit to Monticello are included in *Life, Letters, and Journals of George Ticknor*, 2 vols. (Boston: James R. Osgood and Company, 1876), I, pp. 34–38, henceforth cited as *Life*.

2. Thomas Jefferson to George Ticknor, Poplar Forest, November 25, 1817, in *Life*, I, p. 302. Orie W. Long examined the Jefferson-Ticknor exchanges over the years in his *Thomas Jefferson and George Ticknor: A Chapter in American Scholarship* (Williamstown, MA: The McClelland Press, 1933). Ticknor collected books for Jefferson in Europe, as can be seen in several letters from Elisha Ticknor to Jefferson, Jefferson papers (Reel 8), Massachusetts Historical Society (MHS), especially those of October 22, 1816, November 1 and 16, 1816.

3. In time, Ticknor paid tribute to him and his father in his review of Eliza Buckminster Lee's *Memoirs of the Rev. Joseph Buckminster and the Rev. Joseph Stevens Buckminster* (Cambridge: Metcalf and Company, 1849).

4. George Ticknor to Edmund Flagg, October 23, 1808, BPL. Ticknor wrote several letters to Flagg reporting on "Club" events and people, none of which were included in *Life*. They are very valuable for understanding the activities of Ticknor between 1808 and 1811. Clearly, up to this point his major interests were in Latin and classical Greek.

5. See Orie W. Long, *Literary Pioneers: Early American Explorers of European Culture* (Cambridge, MA: Harvard University Press, 1935).

6. George Ticknor to Edward T. Channing, November 16, 1816, in *Life*, I, p. 119. Deucalion is the figure in Greek mythology who repopulates the earth after Zeus's flood.

7. John Kirkland to George Ticknor, July 26, 1816, Ticknor's Letters, 1816–1828, Harvard University Archives (henceforth HUA). This letter, along with several others concerning the appointment, is in this file. It was a complex affair, as some of the letters were delayed. A brief and insufficient account is "Smith Professorship of the French and Spanish Languages, 1817," in *Harvard University, Directory of Named Chairs*, pp. 491–494.

8. George Ticknor to Elisha Ticknor, November 9, 1816, in *Life*, I, pp. 116–118.

9. George Ticknor to John Kirkland, November 9, 1816, Ticknor's Letters, HUA.

10. William Tudor to George Ticknor, Boston, November 5, 1816, Rauner Special Collections Library, Dartmouth College (henceforth RSCL).

11. Edward Everett to Elisha Ticknor, Hamburg, May 26, 1817, RSCL.

12. John Kirkland to George Ticknor, January 31, 1817, Ticknor's Letters, HUA.

13. George Ticknor to John Kirkland, November 6, 1817, Ticknor Letters, HUA.

14. Elisha Ticknor to George Ticknor, February 8, 1817, in *Life*, II, p. 504.

15. He received a reply via Edward Everett that inquiries would be made to Robert Southey and Lord Holland, both knowledgeable British scholars of Spain. Everett to Ticknor, Göttingen, June 8, 1817, RSCL.

16. George Ticknor, Journal, 9 vols. (1815–1819). This manuscript source is located at RSCL. The volumes do not have page numbers, and sometimes the entries are not dated. The cited passage is in the entry of April 5, 1818, Journal, VII (March–August 1818).

17. See Journal, VII. The Spanish portion of Ticknor's Journal has been edited by George Tyler Northup, *George Ticknor's Travels in Spain* (Toronto: The University Library, Published by the Librarian, 1913), pp. 10–11. It should be noted, however, that this otherwise useful work excludes portions that appeared in *Life*, thus making the reading difficult and confusing. Therefore, the manuscript version remains the most important.

18. Entry of May 11–23, 1818, Journal, VII; Northup, *George Ticknor's Travels in Spain*, p. 17.

19. George Ticknor to Elisha Ticknor, May 23, 1818, in *Life*, I, p. 186.

20. These quotations are in Journal, VII. Some extracts appear in *Life*, I, pp. 191–205.

21. George Ticknor to Mrs. Walter Channing, Madrid, July 25, 1818, in *Life*, I, p. 188.

22. Ticknor, Journal, VII. The reference to *mater dolorosa* is in Luke, II, p. 35. Ticknor included a part of this account under the title "Amusements in Spain," *North American Review* 21, No. 48 (July 1825), 52–78.

23. Ticknor, Journal, VIII (September–December 1818); *Life*, I, p. 242.

24. Actas [Minutes], Real Academia de la Historia (henceforth RAH), September 18 and 25, 1818. Also, Ticknor au Secrétaire de l'Academie Royale de l'Histoire à Madrid, Lisbon, October 18, 1818, RAH, Secretaría. Expedientes de Miembros.

25. George Ticknor to Elisha Ticknor, London, December 2, 1818, in *Life*, I, p. 251.

26. Juan Antonio Llorente provided Ticknor with a list of sources on August 20, 1817, when Ticknor was making plans to go to Spain. This illuminating list is located in the

Ticknor papers at RSCL. It consists of 49 well-chosen titles. It reveals the depth and character of the sources available to Ticknor, who retained a grateful memory of Llorente, formerly a secretary of the Inquisition, and the author of a devastating account of its activities, *A Critical History of the Inquisition of Spain, From the Time of Its Establishment to the Reign of Ferdinand VII* (London: Printed for Geo. B. Whitaker, 1826).

27. Ticknor, Journal, VIII. This entry was most likely composed toward the end of his visit to Paris in January 1819.

28. Alexander Hill Everett to George Ticknor, Brussels, January 3, 1819, RSCL.

29. Joseph Green Cogswell to Edward Everett, Edinburgh, February 15, 1819, BPL.

30. Walter Scott to George Ticknor, March 2, 1819, RSCL. Ticknor's account of his visit with the Scottish writer is in Journal, IX (January–June, 1819).

31. Ticknor, entry of March 18, 1819, Journal, IX; *Life*, I, pp. 285–286.

32. Washington Irving to Henry Breevort, London, April 25, 1819, in Washington Irving, *Letters, vol. I (1802–1823)*, edited by Ralph M. Aderman, Herbert L. Kleinfield and, Jenifer S. Banks (Boston: Twayne Publishers, 1978), p. 546.

33. Lord Holland to Ticknor, Holland House, April 23, 1819; John Allen to Ticknor (undated item No. 001472), RSCL.

34. The entries for the London-Liverpool period in vol. IX of the Journal are not dated, but they all correspond to April 1819. The *Albion* sailed on May 1.

35. This oath was added by Ticknor on August 9, 1819 to the contract approved by the Board of Overseers on July 17, 1817. This document is in Ticknor's Letters at HUA. The professorship of Belles Lettres was nominal, in the sense that it did not carry a salary, and was primarily designed for public lectures.

36. Portions of Ticknor's speech are in *Life*, I, pp. 320–321. The italics are mine.

37. He felt he had to remind Kirkland of this point in a letter of October 19, 1822, Ticknor's Letters, HUA. He wanted to have students who volunteered to study the languages, not forced to do so. But once they began, he expected them to complete a sequence of courses, according to their level of proficiency. See, in this regard, Henry Grattan Doyle, "George Ticknor," *Modern Language Journal* 22, No. 1 (October 1937), 3–18, and Ticknor's own "Lecture on the Best Methods of Teaching the Living Languages," included in the same issue, pp. 19–37. See also Samuel M. Waxman, "George Ticknor, A Pioneer Teacher of Modern Languages," *Hispania* 32 (1949), 426–432.

38. *Syllabus of a Course of Lectures on the History and Criticism of Spanish Literature* (Cambridge: Printed at the University Press, by Hilliard and Metcalf, 1823). This 84-page document, with Ticknor's multiple handwritten notes, is at HUA (HUG 1835).

39. George Ticknor, *History of Belles Lettres*. Mss. Vault, RSCL.

40. It is important to consider that up to this point Ticknor's knowledge of Spanish literature was limited to a few sources by major authors such as Cervantes. Under Bouterwek in 1817 he learned about such authors as Boscan, Garcilaso de la Vega, Bartolomé and Lupercio Argensola, Góngora, Ercilla, Calderón, Hurtado de Mendoza, and many others. References to the "national character" or its decline are numerous.

41. *Spanish*, 3 vols. Rauner Manuscript Codex, RSCL.

42. The manuscript *Lectures on Spanish Literature* at HUA (HUG 1835, Box 3) is bound in three volumes of approximately 657 pages of text. Ticknor numbered sheets (323, without indication of volume numbers) rather than pages, and the numbers are often absent or illegible. I have, therefore, decided to use page numbers as one would normally assign them per page of text, and also volume numbers (in Roman numerals) to facilitate their location.

43. The evolution of Cidian studies is well analyzed by Luis Galván, *El* Poema del Cid *en España, 1779–1936: Recepción, mediación, historia de la filología* (Pamplona: Ediciones Universidad de Navarra, 2001).

44. These statements come from the last, unnumbered pages, of the *Syllabus*, in manuscript.

45. Thomas R. Hart compared the approaches of precisely these three authors, Bouterwek, Sismondi, and Ticknor in his "A History of Spanish Literary History, 1800–1850" (Ph.D. Dissertation, Yale University, 1952). An updated summary, mostly on Ticknor, appears in Richard L. Kagan, ed., *Spain in America: The Origins of Hispanism in the United States* (Urbana and Chicago: University of Illinois Press, 2002), pp. 106–121. Hart has also written "Friedrich Bouterwek, a Pioneer Historian of Spanish Literature," *Comparative Literature* 5, No. 4 (Fall 1953), 351–361.

46. The volume devoted to Spanish literature (vol. III), *Geschichte der Spanischen Poesie und Beredsamkeit,* was published in Göttingen in 1804. There is an English version, *History of Spanish and Portuguese Literature,* 2 vols., translated by Thomasina Ross (London: Boosey and Sons, 1823), where the first volume is devoted to Spanish literature. This quotation is in Vol. I, p. 295. Subsequent quotations are from the English version and are accompanied by page numbers in parenthesis in the text.

47. J[ean].C[harles].L[eonard]. Simonde de Sismondi, *Historical View of the Literature of the South of Europe,* 2 vols., translated by Thomas Roscoe (New York: Harper and Brothers, Publishers [1813] 1848), II, p. 63.

48. Ticknor to Kirkland, May 23, 1823, Ticknor's Letters, HUA.

49. Ticknor was also opposed to the recitation system prevailing at the College. For a review of his proposed reforms under Kirkland, see Samuel Eliot Morison, *Three Centuries of Harvard, 1676–1936* (Cambridge, MA: The Belknap Press of Harvard University Press, 1936), especially Chapter 10, "Expansion and Reform," pp. 222–245.

50. James Russell Lowell, "Cambridge Thirty Years Ago," in *Lowell's Works* (Boston and New York: Houghton, Mifflin and Company, 1892), I, p. 83.

51. Ticknor to Kirkland, April 22, 1825, Ticknor's Letters, HUA.

52. George Ticknor's Report to the College, May 1, 1826, Ticknor's Letters, HUA.

53. George Ticknor Curtis to George S. Hillard (undated, but possibly early 1870s), in *Life,* I, p. 326.

54. Harvard College, Regulations of the Department of Modern Languages, October 1828, Ticknor's Letters, HUA. It is important to note that "department" meant, not an administrative structure, but rather a subject matter, in this case Modern Languages.

55. In 1826, Ticknor reported that there were 117 students: 73 in French, 13 in Spanish, 22 in Italian, and 9 in German, "besides which 51 students attend lectures on the history and criticism of French and Spanish literature five times in each week." George Ticknor to the College, January 10, 1826, Ticknor's Letters, HUA.

56. The edition of *Comedias españolas* included a selection, by Sales, of three plays: Calderón's "El príncipe constante," Lope de Vega's "La estrella de Sevilla," and Moreto's "El desdén con el desdén." This book, which was dedicated to George Ticknor, was published in 1828 and reprinted in 1840, 1844, and 1860. For information on this and other publications by Sales, see Alfred Coester, "Francis Sales—A Forerunner," *Hispania* 19, No. 1 (February 1936), 283–302. Sales taught at Harvard from 1816 to 1854.

57. George Ticknor to Charles S. Daveis, Boston, January 5, 1835, in *Life,* I, p. 400.

58. Josiah Quincy to George Ticknor, Cambridge, November 4, 1834, RSCL.

59. David Tyack examines Ticknor's efforts in the chapter, "The Cause of Sound Learning" in his *George Ticknor,* pp. 85–128.

60. Francis Sales to George Ticknor, Cambridge, April 24, 1835, HUA.

61. George Ticknor to Robert Southey, Liverpool, June 27, 1835, BPL; entry of September 3, 1835, Journal, I (June–September 1835). This is a second set of

manuscript volumes at RSCL, not to be confused with the Journal of the first European trip (1815–1819), which also consists of nine volumes, RSCL; *Life*, I, p. 434.

62. Ticknor, entry of November 29, 1835, in Journal, III (October 1835–May 1836), p. 75. See also *Life*, I, p. 457. On Tieck, see Edwin H. Zeydel, "George Ticknor and Ludwig Tieck," *PMLA* 44, No. 3 (September 1929), 879–891. He saw Tieck several times, and met other Spanish literary scholars such as Baron Edoard von Büllow of Prussia. Entry of December 29, 1835, Journal, III, 79; *Life*, I, p. 462. He also met with Prince John—later King John of Saxony, to read Dante, a lifelong interest of Ticknor's.

63. Ticknor to William H. Prescott, Dresden, February 8, 1836, in *Life*, I, p. 481.

64. Ticknor, entry of June 24, 1836, Journal, IV (May–July 1836), p. 150; *Life*, II, p. 2. Ticknor's emphasis.

65. Ticknor, entry of July 13, 1836, Journal, V (July–December 1836), pp. 31–32; *Life*, II, pp. 31–32.

66. Entries of February 18, 26, March 2, 4, and 20, all in Journal, VI (December 1836–April 1837).

67. Ticknor, entry of December 18, 1837, Journal, VIII (September 1837–March 1838), p. 108; *Life*, II, p. 114.

68. Ticknor to Prescott, Paris, March 5, 1838, in *Life*, II, p. 143. Fauriel acknowledged receipt of Prescott's work and promised to get it reviewed. Fauriel to Ticknor, Paris, March 5, 1838, RSCL.

69. Ticknor, entry of January 17, 1838, Journal, VIII, p. 145; *Life*, II, p. 127.

70. Ticknor, entry of February 15, 1838, Journal, VIII, p. 163; *Life*, II, p. 133.

71. Ticknor, entry of April 1, 1838, in Journal, IX (March–July 1838), pp. 19–20; *Life*, II, pp. 149–150.

72. Ticknor, entry of April 23, 1838, in Journal, IX, pp. 161–162; *Life*, II, pp. 161–162.

73. Ticknor, entry of June 3, 1838, in Journal, IX, pp. 188–189; *Life*, II, pp. 181–182.

74. Ticknor, entry of May 16, 1838, in Journal, IX, p. 144; *Life*, II, p. 169.

75. Ticknor, entry of June 25–30, 1835, Journal, I (June–September 1835), p. 3.

76. Joseph Blanco White to George Ticknor, Liverpool, June 4, 1838, RSCL.

77. Ticknor to Pascual de Gayangos, Boston, June 16, 1841, Hispanic Society of America (henceforth HSA). Ticknor's letters and manuscripts are bound in three volumes. The correspondence is in the first two volumes, 1839–1848, and 1849–1875. The third volume consists of notes for the Spanish translation of the *History of Spanish Literature*. Clara Louisa Penney edited many of these materials in *George Ticknor. Letters to Pascual de Gayangos* (New York: Hispanic Society of America, 1927). I cite letters included in her volume as P.

78. Ticknor to Washington Irving, Boston, March 31, 1842, in *Life*, II, pp. 245–246.

79. George Ticknor to Henry W. Longfellow, November 22, 1841, Longfellow Papers, Houghton Library, Harvard University (bMS Am 1340.2 [5546]).

80. Ticknor to Nicolaus Julius, Boston, January 25, 1846, in *Life*, II, p. 251.

81. Ticknor to Gayangos, Boston, January 27, 1848, Correspondence, I, 1839–1848, HSA; P, pp. 151–155.

82. Prescott to Mary Lyell, February 11, 1848, William Hickling Prescott papers, Massachusetts Historical Society.

83. Prescott to Ticknor, May 19, 1848, in *Life*, II, pp. 252–253.

84. The review appeared in January 1852. It is included in Prescott's *Biographical and Critical Miscellanies* (Philadelphia: J.B. Lippincott Company, 1895), pp. 600–682.

85. Washington Irving to Ticknor, Sunnyside, February 15, 1850, in P, p. 550.

86. *History of Spanish Literature*, 3 vols. (New York: Harper and Brothers, 1849), I, pp. ix–x. My italics.

87. Hart, "Ticknor's History," in Kagan, *Spain in America*, p. 111. Tyack also believes that Ticknor may have felt that he fell short of the Boston ideal of industry in his *George Ticknor*, pp. 190–191.

88. This letter is undated, but it obviously belongs to either late 1849 or early 1850. It is included in *Life*, II, pp. 253–254. Charles Lyell and his wife Mary first visited the United States in 1841, and became good friends of the Ticknors and the Prescotts. See Leonard G. Wilson, *Lyell in America: Transatlantic Geology, 1841–1853* (Baltimore and London: The Johns Hopkins University Press, 1998).

89. In the preface of the third (1863) edition Ticknor himself states that 3,500 copies had been printed in the United States, and the editors of the *Life* (Anna Eliot, Anna Ticknor, and George Hillard) state that an additional 1,500 had been sold since. See *Life*, II, p. 261.

90. Ticknor to Gayangos, Boston, October 14, 1850, Ticknor's Correspondence, 1849–1875, HSA; P, p. 224.

91. Ticknor to Edmund Head, May 26, 1854, in *Life*, II, p. 289. Indeed, his Spanish and Portuguese books were donated to the Boston Public Library, where they can be consulted to this day. See James Lyman Whitney, *Catalogue of the Spanish Library and of the Portuguese Books Bequeathed by George Ticknor to the Boston Public Library* (Boston: Printed by Order of the Trustees, 1879). On the value and richness of the collection, see Jorge Guillén, "George Ticknor, Lover of Culture," *More Books: The Bulletin of the Boston Public Library* 17, No. 8 (October 1942), 359–375.

92. Nathaniel Hawthorne, entry of May 5, 1850 in *American Note-Books by Nathaniel Hawthorne. Based on the Original Manuscripts in the Pierpont Morgan Library*, edited by Randall Stewart (New Haven: Yale University Press, 1932), pp. 246–247.

93. Ticknor to Gayangos, Boston, March 8, 1850, Ticknor Mss, 1849–1875, HSA; P, pp. 287–289.

94. Ticknor published his *Life of William Hickling Prescott* in 1864. He also paid tribute to his memory, along with many others (Robert C. Winthrop, Jared Sparks, John C. Gray, Josiah Quincy, and Edward Everett) shortly after his death. See *Proceedings of the Massachusetts Historical Society in Respect to the Memory of William Hickling Prescott, February 1, 1859* (Boston: Massachusetts Historical Society, 1859).

95. Ticknor to Gayangos, Boston, January 26, 1861, Ticknor Mss, 1849–1875, HSA; P, pp. 320–323.

96. Ticknor to Gayangos, Boston, June 5, 1863, Ticknor Mss, 1849–1875, HSA; P, pp. 329–331. He wrote in a similar vein to Dr. Nicolaus Julius of Hamburg. See the letters of Ticknor to Julius, January 20, 1861, and March 17, 1862, at BPL.

97. Ticknor to Curtis, July 30, 1869, in *Life*, II, p. 485.

98. Ticknor to Gayangos, Boston, November 17, 1869, Ticknor Mss, 1849–1875, HSA; P, pp. 368–370.

3   The Enlightened Foreigner: The Reception of Ticknor's Work in the Hispanic World

1. Ángel de Saavedra to George Ticknor, Madrid, April 6, 1856, Rare Books and Manuscripts Department, Boston Public Library (henceforth BPL). Unless otherwise stated, all translations are my own.

2. See his *Obras Completas*, with an introduction by Enrique Ruiz de la Serna (Madrid: Aguilar, 1956). An examination of the place of the duke of Rivas in the politics and literary history of Spain is by José Álvarez Junco, *Mater Dolorosa: La idea de España en el siglo XIX* (Madrid: Taurus Historia, 2001), passim. Also, Jon Juaristi, "La literatura de la época Isabelina," in *Liberalismo y romanticismo en tiempos de Isabel II* (Madrid: Sociedad Estatal de Conmemoraciones Culturales-Patrimonio Nacional, 2004), pp. 229–243. On the complex politics of the period, see Charles J. Esdaile, *Spain in the Liberal Age. From Constitution to Civil War, 1808–1939* (Oxford: Blackwell Publishers, 2000).

3. See the important works of Derek Flitter, *Spanish Romantic Literary Theory and Criticism* (Cambridge: Cambridge University Press, 1992), and Carol Lisa Tully, *Creating a National Identity: A Comparative Study of Spanish Romanticism with Particular Reference to the Märchen of Ludwig Tieck, the Brothers Grimm, and Clemens Brentano, and the Costumbrismo of Blanco White, Estébanez Calderón, and López Soler* (Stuttgart: Verlag Hans-Dieter Heinz, 1997), as well as her "How German Romanticism Travelled to Spain: The Intellectual Journey of Johann Nikolas Böhl Faber," *The Publications of the English Goethe Society* (New Series) LXXI (2001), 78–90.

4. *Historia de la literatura española*, por M.G. Ticknor, traducida al castellano, con adiciones y notas críticas, por D. Pascual de Gayangos y D. Enrique de Vedia, 4 vols. (Madrid: Imprenta de la Publicidad, a cargo de M. Rivadeneyra, 1851–1856). The Royal Academy of History was well aware of Ticknor's work, having received a copy of the first English edition on September 20, 1850, as recorded in the Actas (minutes) of that date. The Academy also acknowledged receipt of Gayangos's translation in the meeting of May 3, 1851. Receipt of volumes 3 and 4 of the translation was acknowledged in the meeting of April 30, 1858. Both the English and Spanish editions were thus available in the Academy's library to the small but influential circle of Spanish intellectuals.

5. Ticknor published three other editions in 1854, 1863, and 1866, all of which incorporated Gayangos's comments. Gayangos's translation was reviewed in the *North American Review* [*NAR*]. The anonymous reviewer was more interested in highlighting Ticknor's achievement than in acknowledging Gayangos's erudite work, but the essay is still very informative. Also reviewed is Nicolaus Julius's translation of the *History* into German. See "Translations of Ticknor's Spanish Literature," *NAR* 76 (January 1853), 256–260.

6. *Spain: Her Institutions, Politics and Public Men* [1853], in *Writings of Severn Teackle Wallis*, 4 vols. (Baltimore: John Murphy and Co., 1896), IV, 216–217. About Wallis, see Richard L. Kagan, ed., *Spain in America: The Origins of Hispanism in the United States* (Urbana and Chicago: University of Illinois Press, 2002), pp. 36–39.

7. Lady Louisa Tenison, *Castile and Andalucia* (London: Richard Bentley, 1853), p. 333. She also noted as unfortunate that Ticknor's coverage "does not extend beyond the commencement of the present [nineteenth] century," thus making it even harder to find a wider audience.

8. Pascual de Gayangos to William H. Prescott, Madrid, January 1, 1854, William Hickling Prescott papers, Massachusetts Historical Society (MHS-WHP). Italics in the original.

9. *Prospecto: Historia de la literatura española* (Madrid: Imprenta de la Publicidad, 1851). This document, a copy of which I owe to Peter Accardo of the Houghton Library, contains valuable information about distribution: copies could be purchased for about $3.50 (32 *Reales*) in three establishments in Madrid (La Publicidad, Monier, and Bailly-Balliére) as well as in Barcelona, Córdoba, Málaga, and Seville.

10. George Ticknor to Pascual de Gayangos, Boston, June 25, 1851, Ticknor Mss., Hispanic Society of America (henceforth HSA), Correspondence, vol. II (1849–1875). This and other letters are included in Clara Louisa Penney, *George Ticknor. Letters of Pascual de Gayangos* (New York: Printed by the Order of the Trustees, Hispanic Society of America, 1927), henceforth cited as P. This quotation is on p. 242.

11. George Ticknor to Pascual de Gayangos, Boston, September 22, 1851, HSA, Correspondence, vol. II; P, 245. The second revised edition appeared in 1854.

12. For an overview of literary developments in Spain at the time, see Salvador García, *Las Ideas Literarias en España entre 1840 y 1850* (Berkeley, Los Angeles, and London: University of California Press, 1971).

13. Pedro Aullón de Haro, "Juan Andrés: Historiografía, enciclopedia y comparatismo: la creación de la Historia de la Literatura Universal y Comparada," in *Juan Andrés y la teoría comparatista*, edited by Pedro Aullón de Haro, Jesús García Gabaldón, and Santiago Navarro Pastor (Valencia: Biblioteca Valenciana, 2002), pp. 17–25.

14. Alberto Lista, "Discurso sobre la importancia de la historia literaria de España," Real Academia de la Historia, Biblioteca, MS 11-8234, item No. 30. Lista was elected member of the Academy on May 2, 1828. RAH, Expedientes de Miembros, Secretaría. He delivered his induction address on May 30, 1828.

15. "Historia de la literatura española escrita en Alemán por F. Bouterwek y traducida al castellano," Biblioteca, RAH, MS 9-5661. The minutes of the Real Academia de la Historia show that Cortina and Hugalde submitted their translation on April 11, 1828.

16. "Censuras de obras pedidas por el Consejo de la Real Academia de la Historia, años 1817–1833," Biblioteca, RAH, MS 11-8028. The report is dated April 24, 1828.

17. Minutes of April 25, 1828. Actas de la Real Academia de la Historia, Libro XVI.

18. The book was published by the Imprenta de D. Aguado. There is an excellent modern edition by Carmen Valcárcel Rivera and Santiago Navarro Pastor (Madrid: Editorial Verbum, 2002), which adds materials not included in the original translation. The editors have determined that the translation was most likely made not from the original German, but from the French translation.

19. Caleb Cushing, Library of Congress, Caleb Cushing Papers, Box 1. Diary entries of December 14 and December 22, 1829.

20. There is an English version titled *El Buscapié by Miguel de Cervantes; with the illustrative notes of Don Adolfo de Castro*. Translated from the Spanish, with a Life of the Author, and some account of his works, by Thomasina Ross (London: Richard Bentley, 1849).

21. *History of Spanish Literature*, III, pp. 404–415.

22. Ticknor's manuscript response is in Ticknor's Mss., Vol. III, HSA; P, pp. 490–515. It also appears in Gayangos's translation, vol. IV, pp. 218–232.

23. Pedro José Pidal, "Sobre la legitimidad del Centón Epistolario del Bachiller Fernán Gómez de Cibdareal," *Revista Española de Ambos Mundos* 2 (1854), 257–280. He was responding to Appendix C, vol. III, of Ticknor's *History*. The *Centón Epistolario*, which I have consulted at the RAH (9/781 bis), was supposedly printed in Burgos in 1499, but the print type and spelling suggested a later date. The undeterred Adolfo de Castro happily intervened in the discussion with yet another theory in *Sobre el Centón Epistolario del Bachiller Fernán Gómez de Cibdareal y su verdadero autor el Maestro Gil González Dávila* (Sevilla: G. Álvarez y Cia., 1875), a rare piece also consulted at RAH.

24. *Historia*, vol. IV, pp. 408–409.

25. The Cuban scholar Enrique Piñeyro (1839–1911), an exile in New York City at the time of Ticknor's death in 1871, sorted out the various arguments in his "El 'Centón Epistolario' y la crítica Americana," an essay included in his *Hombres y glorias de América* (Paris: Garnier Hermanos, 1903), pp. 333–348, and determined that Ticknor had been correct in his assessment. Definitive evidence exposing the hoax, on philological grounds, came from the gifted Colombian scholar Rufino José Cuervo in the introduction to his *Diccionario de construcción y régimen de la lengua castellana* (1886), included in *Obras*, 2 vols. (Bogotá: Instituto Caro y Cuervo, 1954), I, pp. 1252–1320.

26. "Historia de la literatura española, por M.G. Ticknor," *Revista Española de Ambos Mundos* 4 (1855), 667–686. This journal published four volumes between 1853 and 1855. It can be consulted at BPL.

27. José Amador de los Ríos, *Historia crítica de la literatura española*, 7 vols. (Madrid: Imprenta de José Rodríguez, 1861–1865). In this work, the author acknowledged Canalejas as "nuestro amado discípulo" (my beloved student), III, p. 70.

28. Ríos's review appeared in *La España* (June 1851), and also in *Eco Literario de Europa. Revista Universal* II (1851), pp. 280–304. I quote from the latter journal.

29. William Hickling Prescott to Pascual de Gayangos, June 1, 1853, Letters of William H. Prescott, HSA, vol. II (1845–1860). It is also included in Clara Louisa Penney, ed., *Prescott. Unpublished Letters to Gayangos in the Library of the Hispanic Society of America* (New York: Printed by Order of the Trustees, 1927), pp. 107–112. Penney identified and quoted Lord Byron's poem on p. 196.

30. Ríos, *Historia crítica*, "A S.M. La Reina, Doña Isabel II," in vol. 1, no page number.

31. Ibid., pp. lxxxviii–lxxxix. It is perhaps passages such as this that made Miguel Romera Navarro assert that Ríos work was superior to Ticknor's because of "the philosophical spirit that informs it." See his *El hispanismo en Norte-America: Exposición y crítica de su aspecto literario* (Madrid: Renacimiento, 1917), pp. 50–51.

32. Ticknor, *History*, I, p. 16. The similarity between Ticknor's treatment of the *Poem of the Cid*, and Robert Southey's, has been pointed out by Bruce Graver, "George Ticknor, Robert Southey, and "The Poem of the Cid," *Wordsworth Circle* 32, No. 3 (Summer 2001), 151–154.

33. Ibid., I, p. 17.

34. Ríos discussed the *Poem of the Cid* in Chapters 3 and 4 of volume I of the *Historia crítica*, pp. 115–218.

35. Ticknor to Gayangos, Boston, August 26, 1867, Ticknor Mss., HSA, Correspondence, vol. II; P, p. 345.

36. Ramón de la Sagra, *Cinco meses en los Estados Unidos* (Paris: En la Imprenta de Pablo Renouard, 1836). I have consulted the inscribed copy at the Ticknor Room, Rauner Special Collections Library (RSCL), Dartmouth College. Born in Spain, De la Sagra was also the author of several scientific publications.

37. On the Cuban press of the period, see Larry R. Jensen, *Children of Colonial Despotism: Press, Politics, and Culture in Cuba, 1790–1840* (Tampa: University Presses of Florida, 1988), especially Chapter 5, pp. 97–125.

38. Francisco Guerra Bethencourt to Domingo del Monte, Matanzas, May 1, 1831, in Academia de la Historia de Cuba, *Centón epistolario de Domingo del Monte*, 7 vols. (La Habana: Imprenta "El Siglo XX," 1923–1957), I, pp. 119–120. Henceforth cited as CE, followed by volume number.

39. Domingo del Monte to Antonio Zambrana, November 28, 1832. Houghton Library, Harvard University, José Augusto Escoto Collection (bMS Span 52), box 54, folder 918. The Real Sociedad Patriótica resisted the creation of the Academy, apparently successfully. The great intellectual José Antonio Saco wrote a devastating critique of the Society, a government body, over this incident, and published it with the assistance of Del Monte as "Justa defensa de la Academia de literatura contra los violentos ataques que se le han dado en el Diario de la Habana" in 1834. Francisco Jimeno believed that this piece caused Saco's exile, as he argued in *Diario de Matanzas*, July 17, 1880. HL-Escoto Collection, box 53, folder 892.

40. George Ticknor to Domingo del Monte, Boston, April 24, 1834, in CE, II, pp. 49–50.

41. Henry W. Longfellow saw Everett in Boston in January 1843, recently arrived from Louisiana. He made the observation that "adversity seems to pursue [Everett] wherever he goes." HWL to Stephen Longfellow, Cambridge, February 5, 1843, in Andrew Hilen, ed., *The Letters of Henry Wadsworth Longfellow*, 6 vols. (Cambridge, MA: The Belknap Press of Harvard University Press, 1966–1982), II, pp. 502–503. Jefferson College had recently burned down.

42. Domingo del Monte to George Ticknor, La Habana, May 30, 1837, in *Revista Cubana* 10 (1889), 319–320.

43. Alexander H. Everett alerted Daniel Webster and Caleb Cushing of Del Monte's precarious situation, the "alarming" situation in the Island, and the danger to which

he was exposed. Everett to Caleb Cushing, Boston, January 20, 1843. Library of Congress, Caleb Cushing Papers, box 3 [General Correspondence]. The most complete biography of Del Monte is by Urbano Martínez Carmenate, *Domingo del Monte y su tiempo* (La Habana: Ediciones Unión, 1997). A collection of documents pertaining to his life is at the Cuban Heritage Collection, Otto G. Richter Library, University of Miami. A synopsis of these documents can be found in Enildo A. García, *Indice de los documentos y manuscritos delmontinos en la Biblioteca Otto G. Richter de la Universidad de Miami* (Miami: Ediciones Universal, 1979). On the incident known as "La Escalera," which caused Del Monte's exile, see Robert L. Paquette, *Sugar is Made with Blood: The Conspiracy of La Escalera and the Conflict between Empires over Slavery in Cuba* (Middletown, CT: Wesleyan University Press, 1988), and Manuel Barcia Paz, "Entre amenazas y quejas: un acercamiento al papel jugado por los diplomáticos ingleses en Cuba durante la conspiración de La Escalera, 1844," *Colonial Latin American Historical Review* 10, No. 1 (Winter 2001), 1–23. On the combined literary and political role of Del Monte, see Lorna Valerie Williams, *The Representation of Slavery in Cuban Fiction* (Columbia and London: University of Missouri Press, 1994), passim.

44. Alexander Everett to Domingo del Monte, Boston, January 6, 1843, in CE, V, p. 87. This and several other letters are included in *La correspondance entre Domingo del Monte et Alexander Hill Everett*, Présentée et annotée par Sophie Andioc Torres (Paris: Harmattan, 1994).

45. Everett to Del Monte, Boston, August 15, 1843, in CE, V, p. 121.

46. The article appeared in Madrid in 1848. It was included in *Revista de Ciencias, Literatura y Artes* (Seville) 2 (1856), 754–775, which I have consulted at BPL. The quote appears on p. 758. It also appears in *Escritos de Domingo del Monte*, edited by José Fernández de Castro, 2 vols. (Habana: Cultural S.A., 1929), II, pp. 255–282.

47. Domingo del Monte to George Ticknor, Madrid [no date] 1850, RSCL, Dartmouth College.

48. RAH, Actas, September 7, 1849. The Academy had been supportive of Del Monte's project, but agreed to break up their arrangement after Del Monte withdrew his proposal in response to the government's order. The discussion of the case continued on the meetings of September 14 and December 21, 1849.

49. "Carta sin firmar al Presidente del Consejo de Ministros defendiendo la conducta de Domingo del Monte con motivo de su destierro de la corte," Madrid, November 2, 1852. Domingo del Monte, Documentos (No. 41), Cuban Heritage Collection, Richter Library, University of Miami.

50. Pascual de Gayangos to William H. Prescott, Madrid, January 1, 1854, MHS-WHP.

51. Pedro J. Guiteras to Ticknor, Bristol (R.I.), September 22, 1865, BPL.

52. Nicolás Azcárate to Ticknor, Tremont House [Boston], June 20, 1866, BPL.

53. Quintero eventually joined Jefferson Davis's Confederacy, serving during the Civil War as his confidential agent in Mexico. See James W. Daddysman, "Quintero, José Agustín," *The Handbook of Texas Online*. For an analysis of Quintero's poetry as well as biography, see Kirsten Silva Gruesz, *Ambassadors of Culture: The Transamerican Origins of Latino Writing* (Princeton and Oxford: Princeton University Press, 2002), passim, but especially pp. 152–160.

54. "Lyric Poetry in Cuba," Ticknor Manuscripts (D Mss. 33), item 14, BPL.

55. Quintero, *Apuntes biográficos del mayor jeneral Juan Antonio Quitman* (Nueva Orleans: Sherman, Wharton y comp., 1855). Presentation copy at BPL. Quintero also maintained an active correspondence with Henry Wadsworth Longfellow, which is discussed in chapter 5. For references to Quitman in the context of Cuban exile in the United States, see Rodrigo Lazo, *Writing to Cuba: Filibustering and Cuban Exiles in the United States* (Chapel Hill and London: The University of North Carolina Press, 2005).

56. William Henry Hurlbert, "The Poetry of Spanish America," *NAR* 142 (January 1849), 129–160. A shortened version appeared in his *Gan-Eden: Or, Pictures of Cuba* (Boston: Published by John P. Jewett and Company, 1854), pp. 202–224. A number of Cuban exiles published a collection of poetry in New York titled *El laud del desterrado*, edited by José Elías Hernández (New York: Imprenta de "La Revolución," 1858). There is a modern edition of this work by Matías Montes-Huidobro (Houston, TX: Arte Público Press, 1995).

57. The poem, written in 1824, was translated, at least in part, by William Cullen Bryant. An analysis of the poem and its dissemination is in Gruesz, *Ambassadors of Culture*, pp. 36, 40–48, and passim.

58. Ticknor to Gayangos, Boston, March 8, 1850. Ticknor's Mss. Correspondence, HSA, vol. II; P, p. 204.

59. Antonio José Irisarri, *Cuestiones filológicas sobre algunos puntos de la ortografía, de la gramática y del origen de la lengua castellana, y sobre lo que debe la literatura española a la nobleza de la nación* (New York: Imprenta de Esteban Hallet, 1861), p. 397.

60. Pedro P. Ortiz to Ticknor, New York, June 27, 1853, BPL.

61. Diego Barros Arana to Ticknor, Valparaíso, January 29, 1856, BPL.

62. Matías Romero to Ticknor, Washington, August 19, 1861, BPL.

63. Domingo Faustino Sarmiento to Aurelia Vélez, Boston, October 15, 1865, in *Obras completas*, 53 vols. (Buenos Aires: Universidad Nacional de La Matanza, 2001), XXIX, p. 50. Henceforth cited as OC. Sarmiento had first visited Boston, in 1847, but his main purpose then was to see Horace Mann in West Newton. Sarmiento's diary shows no record of meeting Ticknor during this brief visit to the area. See Michael Aaron Rockland, ed., and trans., *Sarmiento's Travels in the United States in 1847* (Princeton: Princeton University Press, 1970).

64. Sarmiento to José Mármol, October 17, 1865, in OC, XXX, p. 162.

65. "La Doctrina Monroe: Discurso de recepción en la Sociedad Histórica de Rhode Island, Providence, October 27, 1865," in OC, XXI, p. 171. This speech was printed in English, in an unsigned translation by Mary Peabody Mann, as *North and South America* (Providence: Knowles, Anthony & Co., Printers, 1866).

66. Sarmiento's negative views on Spain and its intellectual life are amply recorded in his *Viajes por Europa, Africa y América*, in OC, V.

67. Juan María Gutiérrez to George Ticknor, Buenos Aires, October 29, 1866, BPL. Stuart Cuthbertson has studied the same issue, and concluded that the dearth of materials, rather than lack of interest, discouraged Ticknor. He estimated that with the 168 books pertaining to the continent in his possession, "no adequate treatment of the subject was possible." See his "George Ticknor's Interest in Spanish American Literature," *Hispania* 16, No. 2 (May 1933), 117–226.

68. Ticknor to Gutiérrez, Boston, February 25, 1867, Archivo del Dr. Juan María Gutiérrez, Biblioteca del Congreso de la Nación, Buenos Aires, Argentina. Henceforth AJMG.

69. Gutiérrez's biographical essay, "Don José Antonio Miralla," appeared in *La Revista de Buenos Aires. Historia Americana, Literatura y Derecho* 4, No. 40 (August 1866), 481–522. Other biographical essays, in addition to Miralla's few writings, are in Francisco J. Ponte Domínguez, ed., *José Antonio Miralla y sus trabajos* (La Habana: Publicaciones del Archivo Nacional de Cuba, 1960). A more recent essay is by Edmundo Heredia, "José Antonio Miralla, un discípulo del Deán Funes en la independencia de Cuba," *Estudios: Revista del Centro de Estudios Avanzados de la Universidad Nacional de Córdoba* 11–12 (January–December 1999), 213–222.

70. Ticknor to Gutiérrez, Boston, October 15, 1867, AJMG.

71. Ticknor to Gutiérrez, Boston, May 10, 1869, AJMG. This is a sad letter, where Ticknor apologizes for not answering earlier. "It is simply that I am very old—almost

seventy eight—and quite unable to do the work I could do even two years ago." He died in 1871, some months short of his eightieth birthday.

72. This clipping by Bradford is dated Roxbury, October 21, 1854. It can be seen, along with the translation of Gray's poem, in Ticknor's papers at BPL. Charles F. Bradford (1806–1877) was himself a scholar of Spanish literature, although he pursued his interests rather as an amateur. He prepared a remarkable index to Diego Clemencín's edition of *Don Quixote*, which was published in Spain under the title *Índice de las notas de D. Diego Clemencín en su edición de El ingenioso hidalgo Don Quijote de la Mancha* (Madrid: Imprenta y Fundición de Manuel Tello, 1885). An appreciative note on Bradford and his work by Antonio Flores, Ecuador's Minister to the United States (and later president of his country), appeared in *El Mundo Nuevo* (New York), May 15, 1874. It was also reprinted in the *Boston Daily Advertiser*, June 15, 1874. A bound volume of clippings (including those that refer to Miralla), letters, and documents pertaining to Bradford's Index can be consulted at the Houghton Library, Harvard University, call No. 91–953.

73. For a representative selection of his writings see Iván Jaksić, ed., *Selected Writings of Andrés Bello*, translated by Frances M. López-Morillas (New York and Oxford: Oxford University Press, 1997).

74. Bello's speech to the faculty (one can safely assume that in a version shorter than the 172 pages of printed text) appeared in several installments in *Anales de la Universidad de Chile*, vols. IX (1852), XI (1854), XII (1855), and XV (1858), which are included in the latest version of his *Obras completas*, 26 vols. (Caracas: Fundación La Casa de Bello, 1981–84), VII, 515–516. Bello personally sent reprints of these articles to Ticknor, which can be seen today at the BPL. The quote in this paragraph comes from vol. VII of the *Obras completas*, pp. 515–516. I have discussed some aspects of the Bello-Ticknor debate in my *Andrés Bello: Scholarship and Nation-Building in Nineteenth-Century Latin America* (Cambridge: Cambridge University Press, 2001).

75. George Ticknor to Andrés Bello, Boston, October 1, 1860, in Bello, OC, XVI, p. 394. Juan Bello was a member of the Chilean diplomatic corps, and had been ill with tuberculosis. His passing was widely reported in the U.S. press.

4   The Spanish Student: Henry Wadsworth Longfellow

1. Josiah Stover Little, "The Influence of Government on Literature," MS, George J. Mitchell Department of Special Collections and Archives, Bowdoin College.

2. Henry Wadsworth Longfellow, "Our Native Writers," *Every Other Sunday* I, No. 8 (April 12, 1884). This is a printed version from the original manuscript at Bowdoin College.

3. The most recent biography of Longfellow is by Charles C. Calhoun, *Longfellow: A Rediscovered Life* (Boston: Beacon Press, 2004). A notable analysis of Longfellow's creativity and reception is by Christoph Irmscher, *Longfellow Redux* (Urbana and Chicago: University of Illinois Press, 2006). In addition to manuscript sources available at the Houghton Library, Harvard University, and Bowdoin College, two indispensable sources for the study of Longfellow's life are *The Life of Henry Wadsworth Longfellow, with Extracts from His Journal and Correspondence*, edited by Samuel Longfellow, 3 vols. (Boston and New York: Houghton, Mifflin and Company, 1886), (henceforth referred to as *Life*) a part of Longfellow's complete works, and *The Letters of Henry Wadsworth Longfellow*, edited by Andrew Hilen, 6 vols. (Cambridge, MA: The Belknap Press of Harvard University Press, 1966–1982), henceforth cited as *Letters*. I will use the abbreviation HWL to identify Longfellow as either the sender or recipient of correspondence.

4. Iris Lilian Whitman wrote a notable monograph, *Longfellow and Spain* (New York: Instituto de las Españas en los Estados Unidos, 1927), which reviewed the references to Spain in Longfellow's work, but was more concerned with the poet's sources than with the larger context of the development of American Hispanism. The earlier treatment by Miguel Romera Navarro, *El Hispanismo en Norte-America: Exposición y crítica de su aspecto literario* (Madrid: Renacimiento, 1917), pp. 54–68, addresses the larger context, but briefly and on the basis of printed sources. A more complete treatment can be found in Stanley T. Williams, *The Spanish Background of American Literature*, 2 vols. (New Haven: Yale University Press, 1955), II, 152–179. A discussion on Longfellow as traveler through Spain can be found in Pere Gifra-Adroher, *Between History and Romance: Travel Writing on Spain in the Early Nineteenth-Century United States* (Madison, NJ: Farleigh Dickinson University Press, 2000), pp. 158–186. On Longfellow as translator of cultures and his contacts with Spanish American authors, see Kirsten Silva Gruesz, *Ambassadors of Culture: The Transamerican Origins of Latino Writing* (Princeton: Princeton University Press, 2002).

5. HWL to Stephen Longfellow, March 13, 1824, *Letters*, I, p. 83.

6. HWL to Stephen Longfellow, December 5, 1824, *Letters*, I, p. 94.

7. HWL to Stephen Longfellow, December 31, 1824, *Letters*, I, p. 99. Longfellow published 24 poems in *The United States Literary Gazette* while a student at Bowdoin. See Calhoun, *Longfellow*, p. 37.

8. HWL to Stephen Longfellow, January 24, 1825, *Letters*, I, p. 103.

9. Longfellow had some limited knowledge of French, which he had studied under Charles Nolcini in Portland in 1823, but had no other modern language training. See Carl L. Johnson, "Longfellow's Beginnings in Foreign Languages," *The New England Quarterly* 20 (September 1947), 317–328.

10. HWL to Zilpah Longfellow, May 2, 1826, *Letters*, I, p. 152.

11. HWL to Stephen Longfellow, May 5, 1826, *Letters*, I, p. 153.

12. HWL to Stephen Longfellow, Paris, October 2, 1826, *Letters*, I, pp. 182–185.

13. HWL to Stephen Longfellow, Paris, October 19, 1826, *Letters*, I, p. 187.

14. Stephen Longfellow to HWL, December (3), 1826, *Life*, I, p. 95. It was probably not insensitivity that led Stephen to ignore his son's pleas, but rather the delay in communications across the Atlantic.

15. HWL to Stephen Longfellow, Bordeaux, February 26, 1827, *Letters*, I, pp. 214–215. Many years later, Longfellow told his friend George Washington Greene that it was his conversation with Pierre Irving (Washington Irving's nephew) and David Berdan, whom he saw in Paris as recent arrivals from Spain, that "I think determined me to go there first." HWL to George Washington Greene, Cambridge, September 28, 1880, *Letters*, VI, p. 637.

16. HWL to George Wadsworth Wells, December 18, 1824, *Letters*, I, p. 98. Andrew Hilen has noted that "although a Unitarian in principle, [Longfellow] was fascinated by the richer symbolism of the Catholic Church," *Letters*, V, 3. Calhoun points out that in his old age Longfellow became more of an agnostic. See his *Longfellow*, pp. 278–279.

17. HWL to Zilpah Longfellow, December 25, 1823, *Letters*, I, p. 67.

18. HWL to Stephen Longfellow, Madrid, March 20, 1827, *Letters*, I, pp. 220 and 222.

19. Ibid., p. 216.

20. Alexander Slidell-Mackenzie, *A Year in Spain* (Boston: Gray, Little, and Wilkins, 1829), p. 174. I have consulted Longfellow's copy of this book at the Longfellow National Historic Site (LNHS) in Cambridge, Massachusetts.

21. Lucretia [Orne] Everett to Rev. William Peabody, Madrid, April 8, 1827, Everett-Peabody family papers, Massachusetts Historical Society.

22. For more information on this remarkable family and their descendants, see Eric Beerman, "Spanish Envoy to the United States (1796–1809): Marqués de Casa Irujo

and His Philadelphia Wife Sally McKean," *The Americas* 37, No. 4 (April 1981), 445–456.

23. Caleb Cushing visited Spain in 1829. See Caleb Cushing Papers, Box 1, Library of Congress. Diary entries of September 1, and November 24, 1829. Díaz Cuenca also taught Slidell-Mackenzie and Irving.

24. HWL to Stephen Longfellow, Madrid, July 16, 1827, *Letters*, I, p. 235.

25. Journal in Spain, 1827. Longfellow Papers, Houghton Library, Harvard University, item 172 (henceforth LP-HL [172]). The Longfellow papers at Houghton consist of 227 volumes and boxes. The call number for these manuscripts is MS Am 1340, followed by the specific volume number in parentheses. I cite these documents from here on by reference to the specific volume rather than the full call number. Letters addressed to Longfellow that belong to the collection have a different call number. When citing these sources, I provide the complete call number to facilitate their location.

26. LP-HL (172). This English-language portion of the journal is marked "Journal" and penciled "September 1827."

27. Ibid. This booklet in the box is titled "Brother Jonathan in Spain," and is dated November 11–17, 1827.

28. Ibid. Also cited in *Life*, I, p. 132, but with a slight variation. Other edits—and omissions—are far more extensive. Thus, I rely more heavily on the manuscripts, but will provide the printed citation, where it exists, as well.

29. *Life*, I, p. 134. Samuel's comment must be qualified. Longfellow did make an unsuccessful attempt to obtain an appointment as Legation secretary in the early 1830s. He also had every intention of visiting Spain in 1842, while he was in Germany, but he could not obtain a paid extension of his leave of absence from Harvard.

30. HWL to Zilpah Longfellow, Florence, January 23, 1828. *Letters*, I, p. 255.

31. Irving provided Longfellow with letters to Carl Otto von Löwenstern and Marie-Hippolyte Gueilly in Dresden, George Philips and William Sotheby in London, and Walter Scott in Abbotsford. See Washington Irving, *Letters, 1823–1838*, vol. 2, edited by Ralph M. Aderman, Herbert L. Kleinfield, and Jenifer S. Banks, (Boston: Twayne Publishers, 1979), pp. 247–250.

32. Journal, February 4, 1829, LP-HL (179). Also in *Life*, I, p. 164. This is a reference to Hernando del Castillo's poetry compilation of that title, published in Valencia in 1511. Longfellow took copious notes on this and other sources, transcribing several Romances contained in that book. See LP-HL (176), which also contains various comments on the emergence of national literatures.

33. HWL to Stephen Longfellow, Göttingen, May 15, 1829, *Letters*, I, p. 310.

34. Stephen Longfellow had warned his son that there was a movement afoot to either downgrade the position or redirect the funds of the endowment, a product perhaps of religious factionalism within the College. See Calhoun, *Longfellow*, pp. 58–59 and 69.

35. *Origin and Growth of the Languages of Southern Europe and of Their Literature* (Brunswick: Bowdoin College Library, 1907), pp. 63–64.

36. Ibid., pp. 86–87.

37. Ibid., pp. 87–90. A heavily edited version of this passage appears in *Life*, I, pp. 185–186.

38. HWL to James Berdan, Portland, January 4, 1831, *Letters*, I, p. 351.

39. Journal, December 1, 1832. LP-HL (186). Cortés, who had been a member of the Royal Guards in Spain, also gave him a copy of the fourth edition of the Royal Academy's *Grammar* (1796), which is now at the LNHS.

40. HWL to George Ticknor, Brunswick, June 16, 1834, *Letters*, I, pp. 439–440.

41. George Ticknor to [James McFarlane Matthews], June 18, 1834, LP-HL (bMS Am 1340.2 5546]).

42. "Spanish Devotional and Moral Poetry," *NAR* 34 (April 1832), 277–315; "Spanish Language and Literature," *NAR* 36 (April 1833), 316–345.

43. Longfellow, *Coplas de Don Jorge Manrique. A Translation from the Spanish* (Boston: Allen and Ticknor, 1833).

44. George Ticknor to HWL, Boston, December 6, 1833, LP-HL (bMS Am 1340.2 [5546]).

45. HWL to George Washington Greene, Bowdoin College, March 9, 1833, *Letters*, I, p. 408. *Outre-Mer; A Pilgrimage Beyond the Sea* came out in two parts, I (Boston: Hilliard, Gray & Company, 1833), and II (Boston: Lilly, Wait & Company, 1834). The two-volume set was then published by Harper & Brothers in 1835. For the purposes of citation, I use the following edition: *The Works of Henry Wadsworth Longfellow*, 14 vols. (Boston and New York: Houghton, Mifflin and Company, 1886). *Outre-Mer* appears in volume 7, pp. 9–277. Citations in parentheses in the text correspond to this edition.

46. HWL, "Address on the Death of Washington Irving. Delivered to the Massachusetts Historical Society, December 15, 1859." It is included in J.D. McClatchy, ed., *Longfellow: Poems and Other Writings* (New York: The Library of America, 2000), pp. 800–802. Earlier he had articulated the same thought to a correspondent: "My necromantic book is Irving's 'Sketch Book' which first appeared when I was fourteen, and which has never lost its magic over me!" HWL to Frederick Thomas Brown, Cambridge, December 1, 1855, *Letters*, III, p. 505.

47. Longfellow's address in Madrid is confirmed by Caleb Cushing, "Longfellow succeeded Slidell [Mackenzie] in his own Calle de la Montera near the P[uerta] del Sol." Caleb Cushing Papers, Library of Congress, Box 1, diary entry of December 4, 1829.

48. Longfellow had provided an earlier version of this classification in *Origin*, pp. 90–99. Longfellow's exposure to German Romanticism was limited, but the view of ballads as reflecting the popular national character was present in Walter Scott and, to mention someone very close to him, Washington Irving.

49. Longfellow included one major example of a Moorish ballad, "A Very Mournful Ballad on the Siege and Conquest of Alhama," in the translation of Lord Byron. This is the ballad that closes each stanza with the verse "Woe is me, Alhama!" that became a popular expression among English speakers on both sides of the Atlantic.

50. On the antebellum Protestant views of Catholicism, see Jenny Franchot, *Roads to Rome: The Antebellum Protestant Encounter with Catholicism* (Berkeley, Los Angeles, London: University of California Press, 1994). Franchot provides an insightful coverage of Longfellow's *Evangeline*, which she describes as a "Unitarian romance of Catholic suffering" (p. 208) but, surprisingly, makes no reference to *Outre-Mer* or other Longfellow works with substantial Spanish Catholic content. A more thorough, but less analytical approach can be found in Walter V. Gavigan, "Longfellow and Catholicism," *The Catholic World* 138 (October 1933), 42–50.

51. Josiah Quincy to HWL, Cambridge, December 1, 1834, *Letters*, I, p. 459. On Longfellow's appointment, see Carl L. Johnson, *Professor Longfellow of Harvard* (Eugene: University of Oregon Press, 1944). I am indebted to this source, which reproduces substantial documentation, for the information that follows.

52. Longfellow kept detailed records of his teaching at Harvard, complete with statistics about enrollments in the various language sections, the names of the instructors, and their time commitments. There are records of the examinations, textbook assignments, and Longfellow's courses beyond language instruction. See *Records of Harvard Classes, 1837–1854*, LP-HL (4).

53. Longfellow gave some indication of trouble to George Ticknor, who was still in Europe: "The four-fold team of instructors jogs on its wonted pace—but during y[ou]r absence the harness got very much out of order," HWL to George Ticknor, Cambridge, September 28, 1837, *Letters*, II, p. 41.

54. Pietro Bachi was an accomplished instructor of languages until financial troubles led him to neglect his duties. He authored several important textbooks, including *A Grammar of the Italian Language* (1829 and 1838), *A Comparative View of the Spanish and Portuguese Languages* (1831), and *A Comparative View of the Italian and Spanish Languages* (1832).

55. Journal, October 19, 1840, LP-HL (194).

56. HWL to Stephen Longfellow, Cambridge, October 4, 1840, *Letters*, II, p. 251.

57. Journal, March 28, 1840, LP-HL (195). Also in *Life*, I, p. 362. He had been reading Fernando de Rojas, Lope de Vega, Torres Naharo, and most recently Lope de Rueda. The Journal of that year (1840) has numerous references to Spanish drama.

58. Samuel Ward to HWL, New York, May 23, 1840, LP-HL (bMS Am 1340.2 [5820]).

59. HWL to Samuel Ward, Cambridge, December 18, 1840, *Letters*, II, p. 270. Longfellow and Ward had been exchanging correspondence about Fanny Elssler since the summer.

60. HWL to Stephen Longfellow, Cambridge, December 20, 1840, *Letters*, II, p. 274. In his correspondence, he often referred to this work as "The Student of Alcalá."

61. Samuel Ward to HWL, New York, February 22, 1842, LP-HL (bMS Am 1340.2 5820]).

62. Iris Lilian Whitman has discussed some variations from manuscript to journal publication, to book, in her *Longfellow and Spain*, pp. 175–181. A review of the manuscript shows extensive changes; see LP-HL (76). Part of the reason for the delay in publication was precisely the need for revisions. Several friends, most notably Samuel Ward, encouraged him to make changes. Longfellow grew quite frustrated, "Neither you [Ward], nor Sumner, nor Ticknor, nor Felton likes it; and I am so weary, that I cannot nerve my mind to the task of connecting it. I shall probably throw it into the fire," HWL to Samuel Ward, Cambridge, January 14, 1842, *Letters*, II, p. 376. Fortunately, he did not. *The Spanish Student* is included in Longfellow's *Works*, I, pp. 103–184. The quotations that follow in the text come from this edition.

63. Longfellow noted in his journal that *The Spanish Student* had sold 38,400 copies by 1857, ahead of *Evangeline* (35,850), which would be now considered a canonical work. It was still below the enormously successful *Song of Hiawatha* (50,000 copies), but was fourth in a list of 11 best-selling works. Journal, January 31, 1857, LP-HL (207).

64. Edgar Allan Poe, "The American Drama," *The American Review: A Whig Journal of Politics, Literature, Art, and Science* 2 (August 1845), 117–131. The article was unsigned. This was not the only time that Poe issued a scathing attack against Longfellow and his works, which he found to be overrated. For the larger context of the "Longfellow war," see Calhoun's *Longfellow*, pp. 159–162.

65. Longfellow had lived as a bachelor since his wife Mary died in Europe in 1835. By the late 1830s and early 1840s he had fallen desperately in love with Fanny Appleton, who had rejected his overtures. A story that ended as well as *The Spanish Student* did might well have been what he wanted for himself. Perhaps definitive evidence of this personal wish can be found in a scratched sentence in his Journal, which is, however, readable: "Now I will try to make her laugh," Journal, March 28, 1840, LP-HL (195). His previous publication, with clear references to Fanny, *Hyperion*, did not please her or her family at all. See Calhoun, *Longfellow*, p. 143.

66. Longfellow's work in this regard was not without precedent, however, as shown by the publications of Andrews Norton and Charles Folsom, eds., *Select Journal of Foreign Periodical Literature*, 4 vols. (Boston: Charles Bowen, 1833–1834), and George Ripley, *Specimens of Foreign Standard Literature*, 14 vols. (Boston: Hilliard, Gray, and Company, 1838–1842).

67. Perhaps the most notable example is the meter of *The Song of Hiawatha*. As he explained to a correspondent, "the metre of 'Hiawatha' is the unrhymed trochaic, the

metre of the Spanish drama, and of the popular poetry of Finland," HWL to Apphia Horner Howard, Cambridge, January 7, 1880, *Letters*, VI, p. 549.

68. *The Poets and Poetry of Europe* was first published in 1845. A new edition, revised and enlarged, including 20 additional Spanish and Portuguese poems, appeared in 1871.

69. HWL, ed., *Spain*, 2 vols., in *Poems of Places*, 31 vols. (Boston and New York: Houghton, Mifflin and Company, 1876–1879). The Spanish volumes appeared in 1877. I thank the National Park Service for permission to consult this set at LNHS.

70. HWL to Stephen Longfellow, Cambridge, March 27, 1842, *Letters*, II, p. 394.

71. Journal, March 19, 1844, LP-HL (199).

72. HWL to Alexander Wadsworth Longfellow, Cambridge, June 10, 1846, *Letters*, III, p. 112.

73. HWL to John Forster, Cambridge, December 7, 1851, *Letters*, III, p. 317.

74. HWL to Charles Sumner, Cambridge, February 1, 1871, *Letters*, V, p. 396. Sumner had opposed Grant in a speech pronounced at the Senate on December 21, 1870.

75. HWL to Charles Sumner, Cambridge, November 19, 1873, *Letters*, V, pp. 693–694.

76. Henry Clay, "Petitions for the Abolition of Slavery," in *The Life and Speeches of the Hon. Henry Clay*, edited by Daniel Mallory, Sixth ed., 2 vols. (New York: Van Amringe and Bixby, 1844), II, p. 357.

77. HWL to Stephen Longfellow, Washington, February 9, 1839, *Letters*, II, p. 130.

78. Journal, 1829–1855 (Miscellaneous notes and translations), November 1, 1834, LP-HL (183). Earlier in the year, he also considered writing a drama in three parts about "evil deeds done in the world," where the third part (the others being "The Elixir of Life" and "Witchcraft") was named "The Slave." His notation under this last reads: "The idea of slavery supposed to have been a suggestion of the spirits of evil. Scenes of slavery portrayed," Journal, July 19, 1834, LP-HL (187).

79. Charles Sumner to HWL, May 14–15, 1842, LP-HL (MS Am 1340.2 [5394]). On Sumner's early career, and his friendship with Longfellow, see Anne-Marie Taylor, *Young Charles Sumner and the Legacy of the American Enlightenment, 1811–1851* (Amherst: University of Massachusetts Press, 2001).

80. HWL, "Poems on Slavery," in *Works*, I, p. 97.

81. HWL to Henry Russell Cleveland, Cambridge, November 27, 1842, *Letters*, II, p. 477.

82. HWL to Henry Russell Cleveland, Cambridge, January 1, 1843, *Letters*, II, p. 489.

83. HWL to Henry Russell Cleveland, Cambridge, January 4, 1843, *Letters*, II, p. 491. He was responding to Cleveland's letter of December 13, 1842 from the Cafetal of Santa Marta (continued from Matanzas on December 17), LP-HL (MS Am 1340.2 [1194]).

84. HWL to William Plumer, Cambridge, December 9, 1842; HWL to John Forster, Cambridge, December 15, 1842, *Letters*, II, pp. 480–481.

85. HWL to George Lunt, Cambridge, January 4, 1843, *Letters*, II, p. 494. Italics in the original.

86. HWL to John Greenleaf Whittier, Cambridge, September 6, 1844, *Letters*, III, p. 44.

87. Journal, March 4, 1846, LP-HL (199).

88. Journal, June 26, 1846, LP-HL (200). Henson told the story of how this happened in his autobiography, *The Life of Josiah Henson. Formerly a Slave* (1849). He became the model for Harriet Beecher Stowe's *Uncle Tom's Cabin*.

89. HWL to Charles Sumner, Cambridge, March 13, 1854, *Letters*, III, p. 425.

90. Journal, June 2, 1854, LP-HL (206).

91. HWL to Charles Sumner, Cambridge, May 24, 1856, *Letters*, III, p. 540.

92. HWL to Charles Sumner, Cambridge, May 28, 1856, *Letters*, III, p. 540.

93. HWL to Charles Sumner, Nahant, August 5, 1856, *Letters*, III, p. 549.

94. Arthur Helps, *The Spanish Conquest in America and Its Relation to the History of Slavery and to the Government of Colonies*, 4 vols. (London: John W. Parker and Son,

1855), I, p. vii. In the United States, the introduction of slavery into the New World had been discussed by Washington Irving in *The Life and Voyages of Christopher Columbus* (1828) and by George Bancroft in *History of the United States* (1834), vol. 1, Chapter V.

95. Ibid., IV, p. 449.
96. HWL to Charles Sumner, Cambridge, April 7, 1858, *Letters*, IV, p. 73.
97. Longfellow, *Origin*, p. 44.
98. Ibid., p. 44. The emphasis is mine.
99. Ibid., p. 47.
100. HWL to his Sisters (Elizabeth, Ann, Mary, and Ellen), Rome, September 1, 1828, *Letters*, I, p. 279.
101. Journal, December 5, 1862, LP-HL (209). Also in *Life*, II, p. 18. The story took a heavy toll on Longfellow, himself the father of three daughters, and a widower whose wife had recently (July 1861) died of severe burns. "A week has passed," he wrote, "of deepest gloom and depression. I cannot lift my head out of this darkness," Journal, December 6, 1862, LP-HL (209). The manuscript of the poem shows that he began on November 25, and finished by midnight on December 5, *Tales*, LP-HL (105).
102. Adolfo de Castro, *Historia de los protestantes españoles y de su persecución por Felipe II* (Cádiz: Imprenta, Librería y Litografía de la Revista Médica, 1851). The copy owned by Longfellow, still at LNHS, does indeed show penciled markings in the passages that he used in the poem (pp. 310–311). He followed Castro's account closely, but with some important variations, the main one being the date of the incident, which he located a full century earlier. The book was given to him by Guillermo Picard, who had received two copies from Castro. Picard to HWL (Boston) May 12, 1851, LP-HL (4409).
103. Ibid., p. 311.
104. Longfellow, *Works*, III (*Birds of Passage*), p. 104.

5 *Outre-Mer*: Longfellow's Hispanic Ties

1. Francis Sales, Autograph and Manuscript file, Harvard University Archives (HUG 1763.5). The manuscript autobiography has a notation by his daughter: "Life of my father written by himself in 1853." Sales provided more particulars about his life in a manuscript letter to François Arago, Cambridge, October 5, 1849, in the same file.
2. A listing of Sales's edited works, and its various editions, is in Alfred Coester, "Francis Sales—A Forerunner," *Hispania* 19, No. 1 (February 1936), 283–302. Sales's books, which were auctioned on November 1, 1854, are listed in *Catalogue of the Library of the Late Francis Sales, Esq.* (Cambridge: Metcalf and Company, 1854).
3. Andrew Peabody, quoted by Carl L. Johnson, *Professor Longfellow of Harvard* (Eugene: University of Oregon Press, 1944), p. 63.
4. Henry Wadsworth Longfellow (HWL), Manuscript Journal, November 5, 1846. Longfellow Papers-Houghton Library (LP-HL) MS Am 1340 (200). From now on I will only cite the item or folder number in parenthesis, in the understanding that, unless otherwise indicated, it refers to the same call number.
5. Journal, May 24, 1851, LP-HL (204). Also quoted in Andrew Hilen, ed., *The Letters of Henry Wadsworth Longfellow*, 6 vols. (Cambridge, MA: The Belknap Press of Harvard University Press, 1966–1982), III, p. 295 (henceforth *Letters*, followed by volume number in Roman numerals, and page numbers).
6. Journal, June 15, 1851, LP-HL (204). The original poem by Quevedo uses "caballero," not "señor."

7. Francis Sales to HWL, Cambridge, June 13, 1851, LP-HL (bMS Am 1340.2 [4864]).

8. Francis Sales to HWL, August 18, 1851, LP-HL (4864).

9. Francis Sales to HWL, Cambridge, January 15, 1852, LP-HL (4864).

10. Francis Sales to HWL, January 10, 1853, LP-HL (4864).

11. Journal, February 15, 1854, LP-HL (206). Also quoted in *Letters*, III, p. 412.

12. Charles Sumner to Miss Sales, Washington, August 9, 1854. Francis Sales Autographs and MS Papers, Harvard University Archives.

13. HWL to Stephen Longfellow, Cambridge, December 7, 1836, *Letters*, II, p. 567.

14. HWL to George Washington Greene, Cambridge, October 22, 1838, *Letters*, II, p. 107.

15. HWL to Stephen Longfellow, Cambridge, December 17, 1843, *Letters*, II, p. 556.

16. Journal, January 10 and 26, 1855, LP-HL (206).

17. HWL to William Hickling Prescott, Cambridge, December 13, 1855, *Letters*, III, p. 507.

18. Journal, January 17, 1856, LP-HL (207).

19. HWL to Stephen Longfellow, Cambridge, September 1, 1841, *Letters*, II, p. 325.

20. Longfellow was enthusiastic about Fanny Calderón's publication of *Life in Mexico*, a book he called "a very amusing work." HWL to Henry Russell Cleveland, Cambridge, January 4, 1843, *Letters*, II, p. 493. Fanny reciprocated, conveying her regard for such works as *The Golden Legend*, which she found particularly admirable. Charles Sumner had written to Longfellow to tell him about Fanny Calderón comments on April 13, 1852. See the excerpt in *Letters*, III, p. 341.

21. Journal, August 25, 1851, LP-HL (204).

22. HWL to Charles Sumner, Cambridge, January 30, 1859, *Letters*, IV, p. 118. Prescott died on January 28.

23. For a description of this incident, see Anne-Marie Taylor, *Young Charles Sumner and the Legacy of the American Enlightenment* (Amherst: University of Massachusetts Press, 2001), pp. 149–150 and 226–228. On Ticknor's position, to some extent influenced by Harvard Unitarianism, see Louis Menand. *The Metaphysical Club* (New York: Farrar, Straus and Giroux, 2001), pp. 11–12.

24. George Ticknor to HWL, Boston, January 15, 1844, LP-HL (bMS Am 1340.2 [5546]).

25. Journal, January 26, 1871: "Read in the evening paper the death of Mr. Geo. Ticknor," LP-HP (213).

26. HWL to Charles F. Bradford, Cambridge, February 11, 1875, *Letters*, VI, pp. 20–21. Also, HWL to Bradford, June 8, 1881, *Letters*, VI, p. 720. At Houghton, there is a file LP-HL (692) containing 23 letters from Bradford to Longfellow, 1853–1881, many concerning their respective elections to the Royal Academy. Bradford's work was never printed in English, but it was published in Spanish as *Indice de las notas de D. Diego Clemencín en su edición de El Ingenioso Hidalgo Don Quijote de la Mancha* (Madrid: Imprenta y Fundición de Manuel Tello, 1885).

27. Journal in Spain, 1827, entries of May 20 and May 26. They traveled together to the village of Villanueva del Pardillo in the Guadarrama mountains, LP-HL (172).

28. Florencia González to HWL, Madrid, July 4, 1831, LP-HL (2298).

29. Cortés y Sesti to HWL, Madrid, April 2, 1828, LP-HL (1319).

30. Journal, June 25, 1829, LP-HL (184). The translation of *y cuando me miro en ellos* cannot be literal, for it would have the opposite meaning intended by Longfellow: "when I look at myself in them." He certainly did not intend his heart to flutter when looking at his own image.

31. Cortés y Sesti to HWL, Madrid, April 30, 1829, LP-HL (1319).

32. For what particulars of the courtship and marriage there are, and their sources, see Charles C. Calhoun, *Longfellow: A Rediscovered Life* (Boston: Beacon Press, 2004), pp. 90–91.

33. Cortés y Sesti to HWL, Madrid, June 26, 1831, LP-HL (1319).

34. Cortés y Sesti to HWL, Madrid, May 30, 1830, LP-HL (1319). My italics. Cortés implied that Florencia and her father were dishonest, for they both wanted a marriage for money. Most of the letters from Longfellow to Cortés are unrecovered. We only know about them through Cortés's replies, which sometimes include the dates of Longfellow's letters.

35. Cortés y Sesti to HWL, Écija, June 17, 1838, LP-HL (1319). Longfellow and Fanny Appleton did not marry until 1843.

36. Cortés y Sesti to HWL, Madrid, December 12, 1838, LP-HL (1319).

37. Cortés y Sesti to HWL, Madrid, April 1844, LP-HL (1319). He was responding to a letter by Longfellow dated November 8, 1843.

38. See John De Lancey Ferguson, *American Literature in Spain* (New York: Columbia University Press, 1916), pp. 225–226.

39. Fermín de la Puente Apezechea to Antonio Flores, Madrid, April 18, 1875, LP-HL (4540).

40. Lowell to Longfellow, Madrid, November 17, 1877, LP-HL (3364). HWL to Lowell, Cambridge, January 6, 1878, *Letters*, VI, p. 326.

41. The Archives of the Spanish Royal Academy in Madrid show that Longfellow was nominated by members Cañete, Escosura, and Valera on November 8, 1877. He was unanimously elected on December 13, 1877. Real Academia Española, *Actas*, No. 31, folio 74.

42. Manuel Tamayo y Baus to Charles F. Bradford, Madrid, December 14, 1877, Ms letter pasted to Bradford's *Indice*, Houghton Library, call No. 91–953. Tamayo wrote formally to congratulate Longfellow on the same day, LP-HL (5227). This file has two other letters by Tamayo on Academy business.

43. The book was published in Madrid by the Tipografía de Manuel G. Hernández. The citations in the text correspond to this edition. I use my own translations, but Ferguson translated extensive quotations from Suárez's work in his *American Literature in Spain*, pp. 114–147.

44. Longfellow's *The Spanish Student* appeared in Spanish the same year of Suárez's book, in the translation of Carlos Soler y Arqués (1836–1896). It was published in three installments in the *Revista Contemporánea* (Madrid), 45 (May 1883), 154–175, 45 (June 1883), 281–304, and 46 (July 1883), 32–57. Soler provided an appreciative, elegant translation, but cleansed Longfellow's Act II, Scene II, which depicted the Church officials' voyeuristic examination of Preciosa's dance. Soler wrote that the scene was "somewhat exaggerated and grotesque," on page 55 of the last installment.

45. The culmination of Spanish antimodernism is treated by Lily Litvak, *A Dream of Arcadia: Anti-Industrialism in Spanish Literature, 1895–1905* (Austin and London: University of Texas Press, 1975).

46. HWL to Aubrey Thomas de Vere, Nahant, September 3, 1870, *Letters*, V, p. 371.

47. HWL to Karl Keck, Cambridge, April 18, 1873, *Letters*, V, p. 663.

48. HWL to Romeo Cantagalli, Cambridge, October 23, 1866, *Letters*, V, p. 89. William Dean Howells vividly remembered Longfellow's reasoning and sincerity in *Literary Friends and Acquaintance: A Personal Retrospect of American Authorship* (1900) (Bloomington and London: Indiana University Press, 1968), p. 167.

49. HWL to Angelo Messedaglia, Cambridge, February 15, 1868, *Letters*, V, pp. 211–212. He reiterated his position to Charles Sumner on March 18, 1868, *Letters*, V, p. 221.

50. HWL to Louis Agassiz, Rome, December 31, 1868, *Letters*, V, p. 270.

51. "Cubí's Spanish Grammar," *NAR* 20, No. 47 (April 1825), 450–453.

52. HWL to Stephen Longfellow, Cambridge, May 2, 1840, *Letters*, II, p. 225.

53. "Cubí's *Spanish Grammar*," *NAR* 52 (April 1841), 516–518.

54. Cubí y Soler to HWL, October 8, 1840, LP-HL (1375).

55. Journal, April 22, 1853. LP-HL (205) and Log of Visitors, LNHS. On the visit of Polo and Flores, see Journal, June 21, 1872, LP-HL (213). See also HWL to Charles Sumner, June 22, 1872, *Letters*, V, pp. 557–558. Longfellow's correspondence with Flores was more extensive. The Ecuadorian sent him books, and told him of various literary matters. See letters of July 9, 1872 and June 22, 1874, LP-HL (2011). Flores was the son of President Juan José Flores, and he himself became one when he returned to Ecuador (1888–1892). He was also the author of perhaps the earliest examination of Spanish literary activity in the United States, the rare *Las letras españolas en los Estados Unidos* (Quito: Imprenta del Clero, 1884).

56. Dom Pedro to HWL, May 22 and June 9, 1876, LP-HL (58).

57. HWL to Dom Pedro II, Cambridge, June 1, 1876, *Letters*, VI, pp. 140–141.

58. Journal, June 10, 1876, LP-HL (214). Roderick J. Barman makes a brief reference to this visit in *Citizen Emperor: Pedro II and the Making of Brazil, 1825–91* (Stanford: Stanford University Press, 1999), pp. 279–280. For more details, see "The Emperor and the Poet: Longfellow House's Brazilian Connection," *Longfellow House Bulletin* 4, No. 2 (December 2000), pp. 1 and 4.

59. HWL to George Washington Greene, Cambridge, June 11, 1876, *Letters*, VI, p. 144.

60. HWL to Dom Pedro, Cambridge, (Christmas day) 1877, *Letters*, VI, p. 323.

61. HWL to Dom Pedro, Cambridge, July 12, 1879, *Letters*, VI, p. 498. This letter was in response to Dom Pedro's missive of June 2, 1879.

62. Dom Pedro to HWL, Rio de Janeiro, June 2, 1879, LP-HL (58).

63. Journal, June 10, 1876, LP-HL (214).

64. HWL to Dom Pedro II, Cambridge, November 25, 1864, *Letters*, IV, p. 440.

65. Dom Pedro's translation is at the Instituto Histórico e Geográfico Brasileiro (Case 302, No. 15, 148) in Rio de Janeiro. I thank archivist Jeferson Texeira for securing me a copy of this rare document.

66. HWL to James E. Hewitt, Cambridge, January 27, 1875, *Letters*, VI, p. 15.

67. Miguel Maria Lisbôa, *Romances históricos por um brasileiro*. Nova edição correcta, augmentada e seguida de algumas soltas (Bruxelas: Typographia de A. Lacroix, Verboeckhoven e Cia., 1866). This book is at the Houghton Library (AC85 L8005 Ej8bbl). The translation of "Robert of Sicily" (O conto do Siciliano) is on pp. 188–192.

68. *Evangelina*, poema de Henrique Longfellow traduzido por Miguel Street de Arriaga com duas palabras de introducção sobre a litteratura Americana por Xavier da Cunha (Lisboa: Empreza Horas Romanticas, 1879). Arriaga made contact with Longfellow while he was making the translation to ask for clarification of the meaning of some passages. Arriaga to HWL, Fayal, March 24, 1877, LP-HL (215).

69. *Evangelina*, traduzida do original inglez por Franklin Doria (Rio de Janeiro, 1874). Houghton Library, (AC85 L8605 Ej874d).

70. The literature on Sarmiento is voluminous, but a few representative sources in English include the classic, but somewhat dated biography of Allison Williams Bunkley, *The Life of Sarmiento* (Princeton: Princeton University Press, 1952); William H. Katra, *Sarmiento de Frente y Perfil* (New York: Peter Lang, 1993); and Tulio Halperín Donghi, Iván Jaksić, Gwen Kirkpatrick, and Francine Masiello, eds., *Sarmiento: Author of a Nation* (Berkeley, Los Angeles, and London: University of California Press, 1994).

71. Journal, October 12, 1865, LP-HL (210). Also cited in *Letters*, IV, p. 512.

72. Domingo Faustino Sarmiento to HWL, Buenos Aires, July 10, 1876, LP-HL (4903).

73. A signed copy of *Las Escuelas* ("Mr. Henry W. Longfellow [,] with the highest regard from the author") is at LNHS. A recent version is *Las Escuelas: Base de la prosperidad y de la República en los Estados Unidos*, in *Obras Completas*, 53 vols. (Buenos Aires: Universidad Nacional de la Matanza, 2001), XXX, pp. 148–149. The book was originally published in New York by Appleton.

74. HWL to Sarmiento, Cambridge, March 30, 1866. Museo Histórico Sarmiento (Argentina), Archivo, Carpeta 42, No. 4741. Sarmiento's book, signed "*Al Señor Longfellow [,] homenaje del autor*" [to Mr. Longfellow, as a homage from the author] is at LNHS.

75. HWL to Mary Peabody Mann, Cambridge, April 13, 1867, *Letters*, V, p. 131.

76. HWL to Mary Peabody Mann, Cambridge, April 2, 1868, *Letters*, V, pp. 223–224. In Spanish, this book is better known as *Facundo*, first published in Chile in 1845. It is included in *Obras Completas*, vol. VII.

77. The original bust was made by the American artist Martin Milmore (1844–1883). The replica at the Sarmiento Museum in Buenos Aires was purchased from DeVries, Ibarra & Co. in Boston. I thank Curator María Rosa Codina for allowing me to examine this piece.

78. Benjamin A. Gould to Sarmiento, Córdoba, October 24, 1882. Museo Histórico Sarmiento, Archivo, Carpeta 11, No. 1527. The book is in the Library of the Museum (LH 390). The inscription reads "With kind remembrance & regards of the author. October 10, 1881."

79. Scholar Michael Aaron Rockland uncovered an anonymous obituary of Longfellow in the Argentine Press, which he recognized as authored by Sarmiento. For this and other details of their relationship, see his *Sarmiento's Travels in the United States in 1847* (Princeton: Princeton University Press, 1970), pp. 53–57. See also his "Henry Wadsworth Longfellow and Domingo Faustino Sarmiento," *Journal of Inter-American Studies and World Affairs* 12, No. 2 (April 1970), 271–279.

80. "El poeta Longfellow," May 8, 1882, in *Obras Completas*, XLV, pp. 262–264.

81. "Signs of the Times," *The Harbinger*, No. 21, Saturday, May 1, 1847, Massachusetts Historical Society.

82. She read the journal in October 1834. See Claire Badaracco, *The Cuba Journal, 1833–35 by Sophia Peabody Hawthorne*, edited from the original in the Berg collection with annotations, and an introduction (Ann Arbor, MI: University Microfilms International, 1981), pp. xxxviii and xlv.

83. Journal, April 19, 1847, LP-HL (201). Longfellow erred on the manner of Plácido's execution: he was shot. Heredia was indeed well known to Longfellow. He received a presentation copy of the British judge James Kennedy's *Selections from the Poems of José María Heredia* (Habana: Imprenta de J.M. Eleizegui, 1844) on May 28, 1847, LNHS.

84. Journal, May 1, 1847. LP-HL (201). The diligent Vinageras brought more books to Longfellow in September, as he noted in his Journal entry of September 30, LP-HL (201). Longfellow had in his possession two manuscripts on Cuban poets, one a description of Plácido's end, with some of his poems (five leaves), and the other a tran-scription of two poems by José Jacinto Milanés and Plácido. After comparing the manuscripts with Vinagera's correspondence, I conclude that the handwriting is the same. Longfellow donated these items to the Harvard College Library on January 8, 1861. They are bound with a compilation of Plácido's poems (mostly clippings) by John G.F. Wudermann, the author of *Notes on Cuba* (1844). Houghton Library (SAL 475.1.2).

85. Nicolás Vinageras to HWL, Brook Farm, September 27, 1847, LP-HL (5733). The diligent Cuban sent additional books, as Longfellow noted in his Journal of September 30, 1847, LP-HL (201). A copy of Mendive's *Pasionarias* (1847), signed by Vinageras "to Mr. Henry W. Longfellow with the best regards of Nicolás Vinageras, September 27, 1847" is at the LNHS collection.

86. Nicolás Vinageras to HWL, letters of January 14, 1848; May 23, 1848, and August 19, 1849, LP-HL (5733). Hurlbert's article, "The Poetry of Spanish America" is in *NAR* 68, No. 142 (January 1849), 129–160. Other books presented and signed by

Vinageras at the LNHS collection are Ramón de Palma, *Melodías poéticas* (no publication data) and Narciso de Foxá, *Canto épico sobre el descubrimiento de América por Cristóbal Colón* (Havana, 1846). The last was signed in Matanzas, February 18, 1848.

87. Journal, June 25, 1849, LP-HL (203).

88. Eusebio Guiteras to HWL, Bristol, July 16, 1849, LP-HL (2459).

89. Eusebio Guiteras to HWL, Bristol (R.I.), August 18, 1849, LP-HL (2459).

90. Clippings of Longfellow's poems in translation can be found in the José Augusto Escoto Collection (bMS Span 52), HL, boxes 16 (417), 20 (550), and 22 (607-1). A tribute to his memory, along with references to his poetry, appeared after he died in *Revista de Cuba: Periódico Mensual de Ciencias, Derecho, Literatura y Bellas Artes*, XI (1882), pp. 552–560.

91. José Agustín Quintero to HWL, New Orleans, April 19, 1855, LP-HL (5694).

92. Quintero to HWL, New Orleans, June 21, 1855, LP-HL (5694). In this letter, he mentioned that he was undertaking the translation of *Evangeline*. A thoughtful examination of the Quintero-Longfellow correspondence is by Kirsten Silva Gruesz, *Ambassadors of Culture: The Transamerican Origins of Latino Writing* (Princeton and Oxford: Princeton University Press, 2002), pp. 154–158. On Cuban exiles in the United States and their problematic relationship to the Island, see Rodrigo Lazo, *Writing to Cuba: Filibustering and Cuban Exiles in the United States* (Chapel Hill and London: The University of North Carolina Press, 2005).

93. His main contact on the island was Rafael María Mendive, who edited the *Revista de la Habana, Periódico Quincenal de Ciencias, Literatura, Artes, Modas, Teatros, etc.* Translations of "Excelsior" and "The Arrow and the Song" appeared in vol. IV (November 1854), p. 200. I have consulted this periodical at the Hispanic Society of America in New York.

94. Santiago Cancio Bello to HWL, Boston, March 28, 1870, LP-HL (954). His need was genuine and his personal circumstances difficult as can be seen in a letter from Cancio Bello to Federico Milanés, Boston, April 19, 1870, José Augusto Escoto Collection, HL, box 2 (28).

95. Journal, June 10, 1853, LP-HL (205).

96. Journal, September 7, 1854. LP-HL (206). The entry includes pasted clippings from the *Evening's Transcript* of September 4 and 7, 1854. Luján de Moretto was probably not the man's real name, just as Peru was not likely his country of origin.

97. Pedro [Luján] de Moretto, Boston, September 15, 1854. The file has multiple letters, dated from June 10, 1853 to September 15, 1854, LP-HL (3963).

98. Juan Antonio Pérez Bonalde to HWL, New York, December 1, 1879, LP-HL (4341).

99. HWL to Juan Antonio Pérez Bonalde, Cambridge, December 6, 1879, *Letters*, VI, p. 540.

100. The inscribed copy of *Estrofas* is at the LNHS collection. María de Haro Gad, a member of the Spanish-speaking community in New York, subsequently sent Longfellow the proofs of Pérez Bonalde's "Poema de Niágara." María de Haro Gad to HWL, New York, August 18, 1880, LP-HL (2542).

101. Pérez Bonalde is one of the most frequently anthologized Venezuelan poets. See, e.g., Pedro P. Barnola, ed., *Las cien mejores poesías líricas venezolanas* (Caracas: Lit. y Tip. Casa de Especialidades, 1935), and Joaquín Marta Sosa, *Poetas y poéticas de Venezuela. Antología, 1876–2002* (Madrid: Bartleby Editores, 2003). An examination of the parallels between Longfellow and Pérez Bonalde (among other authors) is in Kirsten Silva Gruesz, "*El Gran Poeta* Longfellow and a Psalm of Exile," *American Literary History* 10, No. 3 (1998), 395–427.

102. José Martí, *Obras Completas*, 28 vols. (La Habana: Editorial Nacional de Cuba, 1963–1973), XVII [*Poesía*], pp. 331–335. A collection of Martí's writings in English

is by Luis A. Baralt, *Martí on the U.S.A.* (Carbondale and Edwardsville: Southern Illinois University Press, 1966). On Martí's life in and reflections on the United States, see Manuel Pedro González, *José Martí, Epic Chronicler of the United States in the Eighties* (Chapel Hill: University of North Carolina Press, 1953), José de Onís, "José Martí, 1853–1895," in *Abroad in America: Visitors to the New Nation, 1776–1914*, edited by Marc Pachter and Frances Wein (Reading, MA: Addison-Wesley Publishing Company, 1976), pp. 218–227, and Julio Ramos, *Divergent Modernities, Culture and Politics in Nineteenth-Century Latin America*, translated by John D. Blanco (Durham and London: Duke University Press, 2001), especially Part II. None, however, discuss Martí's writings on Longfellow.

103. Martí, *Obras*, XIII [*En los Estados Unidos*], pp. 225–228.

104. Ibid., XIII, pp. 228–231.

105. Ibid., XXI [*Cuadernos de Apuntes*], 232–233. For additional Martí references to Longfellow, see Anne Fountain, *José Martí and U.S. Writers* (Gainesville: University Press of Florida, 2003), especially Chapter 6, "Martí and Longfellow," pp. 59–66.

106. José Enrique Rodó, *Ariel*, translated by Margaret Sayers Peden (Austin: University of Texas Press, 1988), pp. 76–77.

107. These and other authors translated such poems as "Psalm of Life," "The Arrow and the Song," "Afternoon in February," and "Sand of the Desert in an Hour-Glass" in the 1870s and 1880s. "Excelsior" was well known enough to be recited in Peruvian schools into the 1930s. See Estuardo Núñez, *Autores ingleses y norteamericanos en el Perú* (Lima: Editorial "Cultura," 1956), pp. 171–174, 182. Márquez lived in the United States between 1857 and 1861, and again between 1872 and 1874. There is a modern edition of his *Recuerdos de un viaje a los Estados Unidos, 1857–1861* [1862] with an introduction by Carmen McEvoy (Lima: UNMSM, Fondo Editorial and COFIDE, 2003).

108. Carlos Morla Vicuña, "El último poema de Longfellow. Ensayo sobre Prometheo en diversas literaturas," *Revista Chilena* 4 (1876), 545–586.

109. *Evangelina. Cuento de la Acadia*, translated by José Toribio Medina (Santiago: Imprenta de la Librería del Mercurio, 1874), and the second edition, with the same title, published in Santiago by the Imprenta Elzeviriana in 1899.

110. On José Toribio Medina, see Maury A. Bromsen, ed., *José Toribio Medina, Humanista de América* (Santiago: Editorial Andrés Bello, 1969). Also, Armando Donoso, "Conversando con Don José Toribio Medina," *Pacific Magazine* (July 31, 1915), 35–48, and *Recuerdos de cincuenta años* (Santiago: Nascimento, 1947), 81–112. On Medina's translation of Longfellow, see Eugenio Pereira Salas, "The American Book in Chile," *Andean Monthly* 3, No. 2 (April 1940), 99–103, and "Las traducciones chilenas de Longfellow," *Andean Quarterly* (Summer 1943–1944), 4–7.

111. See the "Prologue" to the second edition, pp. v–xxvi.

112. *Evangelina. Poema de Henry W. Longfellow*. Traducido en verso castellano por Joaquín D. Casasus, con un prólogo de Ignacio M. Altamirano. Segunda edición (Mexico: Imprenta de Ignacio Escalante, 1901). Casasus dedicated this book to his daughter, perhaps not surprisingly named Evangelina. Medina met Casasus when he visited Mexico in 1903. Casasus's letters to Medina, dated May 27 and June 16, 1904, are at the Sala Medina, Biblioteca Nacional de Chile.

113. For a combined biography and bibliography of Rafael Pombo, see Héctor H. Orjuela, *Biografía y Bibliografía de Rafael Pombo* (Bogotá: Instituto Caro y Cuervo, 1965). On Pombo's residence in New York and his contacts with American writers, see Gruesz, *Ambassadors*, pp. 163–176 and passim. The most important recent biography is by Beatriz Helena Robledo, *Rafael Pombo: La vida de un poeta* (Bogotá: Vergara, 2005).

114. In his diary of February 13, 1856, Pombo mentions the purchase of an unnamed volume by Longfellow. See Mario Germán Romero, ed., *Rafael Pombo en Nueva York* (Bogotá: Editorial Kelly, 1983), p. 130.

115. Rafael Pombo to HWL, New York, January 1, 1868, LP-HL, (bMS Am 1340.2 [4456]). Pombo's translation, "El Salmo de la Vida (de Longfellow)," is attached to the letter. Antonio Flores also registered the influence of Longfellow's translations of Manrique in *Letras españolas*, pp. 30–31.

116. HWL to Rafael Pombo, Cambridge, March 30, 1871, *Letters*, V, pp. 415–416.

117. Rafael Pombo to HWL, New York, January 27, 1872, LP-HL (4456). The poem "Cadena" appears in Antonio Gómez Restrepo, ed., *Poesías de Rafael Pombo*, 2 vols. (Bogotá: Imprenta Nacional, 1917), I, pp. 278–280. Gwen Kirkpatrick has emphasized Pombo's point, stating that nineteenth-century Spanish American poetry "was linked to social practice in a way inconceivable to contemporary readers." She also shows the significant influence of Longfellow on various Spanish American poets in her "Poetic Exchange and Epic Landscapes," in *Literary Cultures of Latin America*, edited by Mario J. Valdés and Djelal Kadir, 3 vols. (New York and Oxford: Oxford University Press, 2004), III, pp. 173–187.

118. HWL to Rafael Pombo, Cambridge, February 6 and 14, 1872, *Letters*, V, pp. 504 and 507–508.

119. HWL to Rafael Pombo, Cambridge, February 14, 1872, *Letters*, V, p. 508. This is the second letter Longfellow wrote to Pombo on that day. The poem "Fonda Libre" is in Pombo, *Poesías*, I, pp. 283–286.

120. HWL to Rafael Pombo, Cambridge, November 27, 1880, *Letters*, VI, p. 655. These poems by Pombo appear in *Poesías*, I, pp. 287–292, and II, pp. 100–103, respectively.

121. Rafael Pombo to HWL, Bogotá, October 18, 1880, LP-HL (4456).

122. These translations are included in Antonio Gómez Restrepo, ed., *Traducciones poéticas de Rafael Pombo* (Bogotá: Imprenta Nacional, 1917).

123. Ibid., p. 48.

124. Samuel Bond to Rafael Pombo, Bogotá, October 6, 1880, LP-HL (bMS Am 1340.3 [22]).

125. Rafael Pombo to HWL, Bogotá, June 18, 1880, LP-HL (4456).

126. *Traducciones poéticas de Longfellow* (1893). The vice president of Colombia, Miguel Antonio Caro, invited Torres Mariño to put together the collection on the occasion of the 400th anniversary of the discovery of America, "as a token of fraternity and affectionate homage to the people of the United States." The book was printed in New York, but it reflected the work and the choices of Spanish Americans. In addition to the Colombians Bond, Caro, José Joaquín Casas, Diego Fallón, Ruperto S. Gómez, Venancio G. Manrique, Manuel and Rafael Pombo, Alejandro Posada, and Torres Mariño, other Spanish Americans included Enrique J. Varona, Francisco Javier Amy, Luis López Méndez, Pedro Santacilia, José Agustín Quintero, Antonio Sellén, Rafael Merchán, and Olegario Andrade.

127. John E. Englekirk, "Notes on Longfellow in Spanish America," *Hispania* 25 (1942), 295–308. A more recent treatment is by Silva Gruesz, "*El Gran Poeta* Longfellow," quoted earlier.

128. Mitre's "El Salmo de la Vida (de Longfellow)" appeared in *El Correo del Domingo. Periódico Literario Ilustrado* (Buenos Aires), No. 7, February 14, 1864.

129. The full meaning is apparent in the previous stanza, "Old legends of the monkish page, / Traditions of the saint and sage, / Tales that have the rime of age, / And chronicles of eld."

130. Rafael Pombo to HWL, Bogotá, July 8, 1880, LP-HL (4456).

6 Mary Peabody Mann and
the Translation of South American Politics

1. Domingo Faustino Sarmiento, *Obras Completas*, 53 volumes (Buenos Aires: Universidad Nacional de La Matanza, 2001), XLV, p. 259. Sarmiento wrote this letter to the editor of *El Nacional* upon learning of the death of Mary Mann in February 1887.

2. Claire M. Badaracco, *The Cuba Journal, 1833–35 by Sophia Peabody Hawthorne*, edited from the original in the Berg Collection with annotations, and an introduction (Ann Arbor, MI: University Microfilms International, 1981). Henceforth cited as *Cuba Journal*. Badaracco is also the author and editor of "'The Cuba Journal' of Sophia Peabody Hawthorne, Volume I; Edited from the Manuscript with an Introduction" (Ph.D. Dissertation, Rutgers University, 1978). The most outstanding recent biography of the Peabody sisters, who also included Elizabeth Palmer Peabody, is by Megan Marshall, *The Peabody Sisters: Three Women Who Ignited American Romanticism* (Boston and New York: Houghton Mifflin Company, 2005). An older biography, though still useful, is by Louise Hall Tharp, *The Peabody Sisters of Salem* (Boston: Little, Brown and Company, 1950).

3. *Cuba Journal*, 21, January 26, 1834.

4. Ibid., 71, April 1, 1834.

5. Ibid., 61, March 21, 1834.

6. Ibid., 131, June 14, 1834.

7. Elizabeth Palmer Peabody to Mary Tyler Peabody, June (n.d.) and September 14, 1834, in *Cuba Journal*, p. 674.

8. The book was originally published by Lothrop Publishers in Boston. It has been recently edited, with a valuable introduction, by Patricia M. Ard (Charlottesville and London: University of Virginia Press, 2000). I use this last edition for the purposes of citation. Page numbers appear in parentheses in the text. Ard's introduction, "Mary Peabody Mann's *Juanita*: A Historical Romance of Antillean Slavery," provides a useful contextualization of the novel's place in nineteenth-century American literature.

9. The *Cuba Journal* provides evidence of discomfort, especially with her host's tolerance of slavery. See the letters of March 25 and 27, 1834, in the *Cuba Journal*, pp. 195, 202, and 205.

10. Marshall, *Peabody Sisters*, p. 274.

11. Abiel Abott, *Letters Written in the Interior of Cuba* (Boston: Bowles and Dearborn, 1829). Abbot was a Unitarian pastor of the First Church in Beverly, Massachusetts. He had gone to Cuba to seek relief from consumption. He died upon his return to the United States in 1828. The book was published posthumously.

12. Nathaniel Hawthorne's "Edward Randolph's Portrait" (1838) was inspired by Sophia's story of how she had cleaned an old painting in Havana, which yielded a beautiful Mary Magdalene that she believed to be an original Murillo masterpiece. Hawthorne set the story in colonial New England, whereby Governor Hutchison confronted the consequences of his intended actions as he witnessed the cleaning of a painting. Mary herself used the story in her *Juanita*. Marshall, *Peabody Sisters*, pp. 364–365; Nathaniel Hawthorne, *Tales and Sketches* (New York: The Library of America, 1982), pp. 640–651.

13. This report became a book titled *Educación popular*, published in Santiago, Chile, in 1849.

14. Patricia M. Ard, "Seeds of Reform: The Letters of Mary Peabody Mann and Domingo F. Sarmiento, 1865–1868" (Ph.D. Dissertation, Rutgers University, 1996), p. 7. Henceforth cited as SOR.

15. Mary Mann to Miss [Dorothea Lynde] Dix, Concord, January 18, 1864. Houghton Library, Dorothea Lynde Dix Papers (b MS Am 1838-450). The emphasis is Mann's. The original of this letter is at Antioch College in Yellow Springs, Ohio.

16. Domingo Faustino Sarmiento to Mary Mann, New York, July 8, 1865, SOR, p. 62.

17. Mary Mann to D.J. [*sic*] Sarmiento, Concord, July 13, 1865, in Barry L. Velleman, *"My Dear Sir:" Mary Mann's Letters to Sarmiento, 1865–1881* (Buenos Aires: Instituto Cultural Argentino Norteamericano, 2001), p. 33. Henceforth cited as MDS.

18. Sarmiento to Mann, New York, September 23, 1865, SOR, p. 82. Original in English.

19. The full title is *Las escuelas, base de la prosperidad y de la República en los Estados Unidos* (1866). It is included in *Obras Completas*, vol. XXX. A portion of the same text, on the life of Horace Mann reappears in vol. XLIII, pp. 219–271.

20. Sarmiento to Mann, New York, July 28, 1865, SOR, p. 73. Original in English. The title of Sarmiento's book, first published in Santiago in 1845, is *Facundo, o civilización y barbarie*. The best modern edition is by Noé Jitrik, annotated by Nora Dottori and Silvia Zanetti, 2nd edition (Caracas: Biblioteca Ayacucho, 1985).

21. Sarmiento to Mann, New York, September 23, 1865, SOR, p. 82. Original in English.

22. Mann to Sarmiento, Concord, September 25, 1865, MDS, p. 45.

23. Sarmiento to Mann, New York, September 28, 1865, SOR, p. 85. Sarmiento went to Concord in mid-October to meet Mary Mann. He wrote about the visit to Aurelia Vélez: "Mary Mann is an old angel! Her heart rules her . . . Mrs. Mann is the victim of a fascination that comes, perhaps, from the excess of maternal love overflowing from her heart, perhaps from finding in me an admirer and continuer of her husband's work. . . . She lives for me, to help me, and to make my work successful," Sarmiento to Aurelia Vélez, Boston, October 15, 1865, in Allison Williams Bunkley, ed., *A Sarmiento Anthology*, translated by Stuart Edgar Grummon (Princeton: Princeton University Press, 1948), pp. 274–275. The full Spanish text is in Domingo Faustino Sarmiento, *Obras Completas*, XXIX, p. 50.

24. Mann to Sarmiento, Concord, October 17, 1865, MDS, p. 57. Emphasis in the original.

25. Mann to Sarmiento (December 1865), MDS, p. 71.

26. Mann to Sarmiento, November 3, 1867, MDS, p. 170. Emphasis in the original. A letter from Mann to Juana Manso suggests that she started to work on the biography about August, 1866. Mann to Manso, Cambridge, August 27, 1866, in *Anales de la Educación Común* (Buenos Aires) 4, No. 41, November 30, 1866, pp. 137–140. Juana Manso was a remarkable Argentine educator, writer, and feminist. See Lidia F. Lewkowicz, *Juana Paula Manso (1819–1875). Una mujer del siglo XXI* (Buenos Aires: Ediciones Corregidor, 2000). Also, Francine Masiello, *Between Civilization and Barbarism: Women, Nation, and Literary Culture in Modern Argentina* (Lincoln and London: University of Nebraska Press, 1992), passim.

27. "Biographical Sketch," *Life in the Argentine Republic in the Days of the Tyrants*, (New York: Hurd and Houghton, 1868), p. 278.

28. Ibid., p. 324. My emphasis. No record of such translation exists. Subsequent references to the "Biographical Sketch" will be provided in parentheses in the text.

29. Sarmiento to Mann, New York, June 30, 1868, SOR, p. 437.

30. Mary Mann to Henry W. Longfellow (undated). Longfellow Papers, Houghton Library (LP-HL), call number bMS Am 1340.2 (3720). Because of the contents, the date of this letter is most likely early 1868.

31. Henry Wadsworth Longfellow to Mary Mann, Cambridge, April 2, 1868, Horace Mann collection, Massachusetts Historical Society (MHS). Also in *The Letters of Henry Wadsworth Longfellow*, edited by Andrew Hilen, 6 vols. (Cambridge, MA: The Belknap Press of Harvard University Press, 1966–1982), V, pp. 223–224.

32. Mary Mann informed Sarmiento of Howells's suggestion on September 9, 1867, MDS, p. 160.

33. See, in particular, Diana Sorensen Goodrich, *"Facundo" and the Construction of Argentine Culture* (Austin: The University of Texas Press, 1996). See also Noël Salomon, *Realidad, ideología y literatura en el "Facundo" de D.F. Sarmiento* (Amsterdam: Editions Rodopi, 1984), and the relevant essays included in Tulio Halperín Donghi, Iván Jaksić, Gwen Kirkpatrick, and Francine Masiello, eds., *Sarmiento: Author of a Nation* (Berkeley, Los Angeles, and London: University of California Press, 1994).

34. Domingo Faustino Sarmiento, *Facundo: Civilization and Barbarism*, translated from the Spanish by Kathleen Ross, with an introduction by Roberto González Echevarría (Berkeley, Los Angeles, and London: University of California Press, 2003). For an assessment of the importance of Mary Mann's translation, see Ilan Stavans's introduction to the Penguin edition of *Facundo* (New York: Penguin Putnam Inc., 1998), pp. vii–xxxii.

35. This part appears in pp. 237–275 of *Life in the Argentine Republic*, from which the quotations that follow have been taken.

36. *The New York Times*, August 17, 1868.

37. "Reviews and Literary Notices," *The Atlantic Monthly* 22, No. 131 (September 1868), 374–377.

38. "Life in the Argentine Republic in the Days of the Tyrants," *The Atlantic Monthly* 22, No. 132 (October 1868), 666–679. The article is unsigned.

39. Sarmiento to Mann, New York, May 31, 1866, SOR, p. 189.

40. Sarmiento to Mann, April 6, 1867, SOR, p. 292.

41. Mary Mann to Henry W. Longfellow, LP-HL (3720). This letter is undated, but it was surely written in March or April 1867.

42. H.W. Longfellow to Mary Mann, Cambridge, April 13, 1867, Horace Mann collection, MHS. Also in *Letters*, V, p. 131.

43. Mann to Sarmiento, April 4 and 9, 1867, MDS, pp. 137 and 139.

44. Mary Mann to Juana Manso, Cambridge, June 29, 1868, Museo Histórico Sarmiento, Buenos Aires, Argentina, Carpeta 1A, doc. 83. I thank Professor Barry Velleman for providing me with a copy of this letter. Sarmiento told Mary Mann that he was surprised by the granting of the degree, as he sat during commencement. Sarmiento to Mann, Ann Arbor, June 24, 1868, SOR, p. 434. For the particulars of this episode, see Allison Bunkley, *The Life of Sarmiento*, pp. 441–442, and Irving A. Leonard, "The Education of a Great South American: Domingo Faustino Sarmiento," in *Portraits and Essays: Historical and Literary Sketches of Early Spanish America*, edited by William C. Bryant (Newark, DE: Juan de la Cuesta-Hispanic Monographs, 1986), pp. 131–141.

45. Mann to Sarmiento, Cambridge, July 21, 1868, MDS, p. 218.

46. Manuel R. García to Mary Mann, Washington, D.C., May 25, 1870, Papers of Mary T.P. Mann, Library of Congress, Manuscript Department. Henceforth cited as LOC-MMP. The underlined words appear in English in the original.

47. Manuel R. García to Mary Mann, Washington, D.C., October 30, 1869, LOC-MMP. Sarmiento wrote to Mary Mann in similar terms, and added more: the province of Corrientes was at the edge of civil war; the Southern frontier was constantly harassed by "savages," and the diplomacy concerning the war was extremely complex. Sarmiento to Mary Mann, Buenos Aires, November 12, 1868, LOC-MMP.

48. Domingo F. Sarmiento to Mary Mann, Buenos Aires, September 2, 1868, LOC-MMP. Original in English.

49. Manuel R. García to Mary Mann, Berkeley Springs, August 24, 1869, LOC-MMP.

50. Manuel R. García to Mary Mann, Washington, D.C., October 19, 1869, LOC-MMP. He repeated his complaints in several other letters. Sarmiento himself did not spare epithets against López, "that ferocious animal," as he called him, adding that "if any

sympathies remain for López it will be necessary to believe that the human mind is capable of inexplicable aberrations." Sarmiento to Mann, Buenos Aires, September 2, 1868, LOC-MMP.

51. Manuel R. García to Mary Mann, Washington, D.C., November 22, 1869, LOC-MMP.

52. Juana Manso to Mary Mann, Buenos Aires, February 12, 1869, LOC-MMP.

53. Juana Manso to Mary Mann, Buenos Aires, August 8, 1870, LOC-MMP.

54. For an examination of Sarmiento's ideas in this regard, and the challenges confronted by the U.S. teachers, see Georgette Magassy Dorn, "Sarmiento, the United States, and Public Education," in *Sarmiento and His Argentina*, edited by Joseph T. Criscenti (Boulder and London: Lynne Rienner Publishers, 1993), pp. 77–89.

55. Juana Manso to Mary Mann, Buenos Aires, November 5, 1870, LOC-MMP. Emphasis in the original.

56. Juana Manso to Mary Mann, Buenos Aires, May 2, 1870, LOC-MMP.

57. Juana Manso to Mary Mann, Buenos Aires, August 8, 1870, LOC-MMP.

58. Juana Manso to Mary Mann, Buenos Aires, September 13, 1872, LOC-MMP.

59. Mann to Sarmiento, Cambridge, August 6, 1870, MDS, 279.

60. Mann to Sarmiento, Cambridge, November 5, 1868, MDS, 228.

61. "Preface," pp. xx–xxi. The emphasis is mine.

62. Mann to Sarmiento, Cambridge, February 4, 1868, MDS, p. 194. Underlined in the original.

63. Sarmiento to Mann, Chicago, February 6, 1868, SOR, pp. 398–399.

64. "Preface," p. xxii.

65. Mann to Sarmiento, Cambridge, November 5, 1868, MDS, p. 228.

7   The "Annals of Barbarians": William H. Prescott and the Conquest of the New World

1. Although there are numerous articles on Prescott, only three biographies of this major nineteenth-century figure exist: George Ticknor's *Life of William Hickling Prescott* (Boston: Ticknor and Fields, 1864); Rollo Ogden's *William Hickling Prescott* (Boston and New York: Houghton, Mifflin and Company, 1904); and C. Harvey Gardiner, *William Hickling Prescott: A Biography* (Austin and London: University of Texas Press, 1969). Ticknor's *Life* is a groundbreaking, but celebratory account of Prescott's life, while Ogden's, as he put it in his preface, "aims only to supplement" Ticknor's work, by adding anecdotes and some unpublished letters. Gardiner's book comes close to a full biography based on unpublished sources, but he missed many records of importance, and said little about the Latin Americans who interacted with the historian. An important collection of essays was published on the occasion of the centenary of Prescott's death in the *Hispanic American Historical Review* (*HAHR*) 39, No. 1 (February 1959). The recent book edited by Richard L. Kagan, *Spain in America: The Origins of Hispanism in the United States* (Urbana and Chicago: University of Illinois Press, 2002), contains many references to Prescott, especially Kagan's own "Prescott's Paradigm: American Historical Scholarship and the Decline of Spain," pp. 247–276, which first appeared in the *American Historical Review* 101 (April 1996), 423–446. There are valuable collections of correspondence and memoranda, including Roger Wolcott, ed., *The Correspondence of William Hickling Prescott, 1833–1847* (Boston and New York: Houghton, Mifflin and Company, 1925), which however limits Prescott's correspondence to those years, is not thorough, and omits portions of letters. There have been two major efforts to add to the published record of correspondence, Clara Louisa Penney, *Prescott. Unpublished Letters to Pascual de*

Gayangos in the Library of the Hispanic Society of America (New York: Hispanic Society of America, 1927), and C. Harvey Gardiner, *The Papers of William Hickling Prescott* (Urbana: University of Illinois Press, 1964). However valuable, these volumes are also incomplete as they reflect the interests of the editors. Gardiner is also the editor of a most valuable source, *The Literary Memoranda of William Hickling Prescott*, 2 vols. (Norman: University of Oklahoma Press, 1961), which includes journal entries, notes on books, business records, and assorted reflections. The main sources for this chapter are the manuscripts of William H. Prescott at the Massachusetts Historical Society (MHS) and the Hispanic Society of America (HSA). While I use the originals I do indicate which documents appear elsewhere in print.

2. On November 20, 1824, he composed a list of "Spanish Authors to be studied" which included well-known writers, but also some who would be known in the United States to only a few specialized scholars such as George Ticknor. See *Literary Memoranda* (henceforth LM), I, pp. 54–55.

3. William Hickling Prescott to William Prescott, August 23 (1811), William Hickling Prescott papers, Massachusetts Historical Society (henceforth MHS-WHP). Also included in *The Papers of William Hickling Prescott*, edited by C. Harvey Gardiner, p. 4. Henceforth GP.

4. WHP to William and Catherine Prescott (young William's mother), March 15, 1816, MHS-WHP. Also GP, pp. 5–12.

5. WHP to William H. Gardiner, March (no day) 1816, in George Ticknor, *Life*, I, p. 39.

6. William Prescott to WHP, June 1, 1817, MHS-WHP.

7. Ticknor, *Life of WHP*, I, p. 44.

8. Ibid., I, p. 66.

9. Journal entry, December 25, 1825, LM, p. 65. He was probably familiar with the related work of Adam Ferguson's *History of the Progress and Termination of the Roman Republic* (1783) as, indeed, most educated Bostonians were. He had a copy of this book in his personal library.

10. Journal entry, January 8, 1826, LM, p. 67.

11. WHP to Alexander H. Everett, Boston, December 10, 1826, MHS-WHP.

12. WHP to Alexander H. Everett, December 26, 1826, MHS-WHP.

13. WHP to Alexander H. Everett, 1827, MHS-WHP. Although the letter is undated, I estimate that it was written some time in April, 1827.

14. WHP to Alexander H. Everett, Ibid.

15. LM, pp. 120, 139–140. Prescott referred specifically to Thierry's *Conquête de l'Angleterre par les Normandes* (1825), and Mably's *Observations sur l'Histoire de France* (1765) as well as *De l'étude de l'Histoire* (1778). He had copies of these titles, in different editions, in his personal library. Prescott was also familiar, and perhaps even more influenced, by the work of Edward Gibbon and William Robertson.

16. Journal entry of February 2, 1830, LM, p. 140. This was probably too neat a division, and he himself doubted it. He noted that the seeds of "degrading vice" and "religious bigotry" were planted during the reign of Charles V, but then asked in parenthesis "were they not before?"

17. In Paris, he distributed copies to several scholars, including François Guizot, Adolphe de Circourt, and Claude Fauriel. He also sent copies to Nicolaus Heinrich Julius and Friedrich von Raumer in Germany. George Ticknor to WHP, March 15, 1838, in *Life, Letters, and Journals of George Ticknor*, 2 vols. (Boston: James R. Osgood and Company, 1876), II, pp. 142–143.

18. Journal entry of April 30, 1838, LM, p. 222.

19. WHP to James Rich, January 20, 1838, in Wolcott, *Correspondence* (henceforth W), pp. 22–23. He wrote in the same vein to Charles Sumner: "We are obliged to write a language which is not spoken around us, are brought before foreign tribunals, tried by

foreign laws, while even the venerable authority of ancient British precedent is over
ruled. We have achieved only half our independence." WHP to Sumner, October 16,
1840, in GP, p. 165.

20. WHP to Martín Fernández de Navarrete, April 21, 1838, MHS-WHP. Also in W,
    pp. 31–32.

21. Stanley Williams has discussed this episode in his *The Life of Washington Irving*, 2 vols.
    (New York: Oxford University Press, 1935), II, pp. 103–105.

22. Journal entry of May 27, 1838, LM, pp. 227 and 229.

23. Ángel Calderón to the Secretary of the Real Academia de la Historia, New York, May 1,
    1838. The Academy elected Prescott on May 17, 1839. He responded with thanks on
    August 13, 1839. Real Academia de la Historia (RAH) (Madrid), Secretaría.
    Expedientes de Miembros.

24. WHP to Pascual de Gayangos, March 20, 1839, Hispanic Society of America, Letters
    of William H. Prescott (HSA, Letters). These manuscript letters are arranged chrono-
    logically, but with some misplaced items, in two volumes corresponding to the years
    1838–1844 and 1845–1860. Some of these letters are also in Penney's *Prescott*
    (henceforth P). It is important to mention that before Gayangos, the German scholar
    Friedrich Wilhelm Lembke provided considerable assistance to Prescott from Spain.

25. WHP to Pascual de Gayangos, April 4, 1840, HSA, Letters, 1838–1844; P, p. 154.

26. WHP to Joel R. Poinsett, January 8, 1839, in GP, pp. 133–134. Prescott addressed
    letters to Count Cortina and Gorostiza on January 25, 1839, and to Manuel de San
    Crisóstomo y Nájera, a Carmelite friar who had studied the indigenous past, on
    April 25, 1839, MHS-WHP. There is no evidence that Nájera ever responded directly
    to Prescott.

27. Poinsett to WHP, January 15, 1839, MHS-WHP.

28. There are several pieces of correspondence from Manning and Marshall (later
    Manning and Mackintosh) in the Prescott papers at the MHS. A larger collection of
    records is at the Benson Latin American Collection, University of Texas at Austin,
    Manning and Mackintosh Papers. Series, Correspondence, 1825–1883. A gap exists,
    however, for the years 1838–1842, which makes the records at the MHS all the more
    valuable.

29. WHP to Poinsett, January 26, 1839, in GP, pp. 134–137. Prescott also felt that he
    could find most of what he needed from archives in Spain. He told Poinsett that the
    previous week he had received permission from the Royal Academy of History in
    Madrid to consult and copy materials from its own collection. Indeed, he received
    thousands of pages of copied documents from their collection. "Was there anything
    more liberal?" a grateful Prescott wrote to Gayangos on April 4, 1840. HSA, Letters,
    1838–1844.

30. Manning and Marshall to WHP, March 27, 1839; April 22, 1839; June 15, 1839; and
    November 11, 1839, MHS-WHP.

31. Ángel Calderón to WHP, Mexico, March 5, 1840. The original Spanish is in MHS-
    WHP. A translation is in W, pp. 111–113. On the appointment and instructions to
    Calderón, see Mark Van Aken, *Pan Hispanism: Its Origins and Development to 1866*
    (Berkeley and Los Angeles: University of California Press, 1959), pp. 37–39.

32. WHP to Fanny Calderón, April 17, 1840, in W, pp. 119–123.

33. This statement invited the following comment from Prescott: "I have long since dis-
    trusted [Bustamante], though Mexican letters are under obligations to his editorial
    activities. But between ourselves he is a sorry ranting bigot, with more tongue than
    brains, I suspect." WHP to Ángel Calderón, June 25, 1840, in W, pp. 136–139. His
    reference to Bustamante's valuable "editorial activities" seems to allude to the
    Mexican historian's edition of Bernardo de Sahagún's *Historia general de las cosas de
    Nueva España*, published in Mexico in 1829. To Fanny Calderón, he stated "Perhaps

I wrong him. He is a bigot at all events, quite worthy of the dark ages and furious against the old Spaniards as if come down straight from Guatimozin." WHP to Fanny Calderón, August 15, 1840, W, pp. 146–151. Prescott, who had a more favorable view of the Spaniards, was increasingly aware of competing views of the Mexican past. The best recent treatment on the subject is by Enrique Krauze, *La Presencia del Pasado* (Mexico and Spain: Tusquets Editores, 2005).

34. Ángel Calderón to WHP, Mexico, May 2, 1840, MHS-WHP. An English translation of the Spanish original is in W, pp. 125–128.

35. The Massachusetts Historical Society has six manuscript letters by Fanny Calderón to WHP written from Mexico, June 5, 1840; October 15, 1840; January 19, 1841; May 20, 1841; September 19, 1841; and October 26, 1841, MHS-WHP. Fifteen additional letters to Prescott were written from various other locations. The Mexico letters, except for the January 19, 1841 letter, are printed in W.

36. Fanny Calderón de la Barca, *Life in Mexico during a Residence of Two Years in that Country* (Boston: Little, Brown & Company, 1843). It was also published in London the same year by Chapman and Hall, through the mediation of Charles Dickens, whom Prescott approached for that purpose. Prescott's review, "Madame Calderon's Life in Mexico," appeared in the *North American Review* (*NAR*) 56 (January 1843), 137–171.

37. Calderón often passed Prescott's inquiries on to Alamán, who responded to the first in letters that Calderón forwarded to Boston. Such letters and reports are at the MHS, dated May 15, 1841, May 31, 1841, and June 9, 1841, MHS-WHP. C. Harvey Gardiner has examined Prescott's contacts in Mexico in his "Prescott's Ties with Mexico," *Journal of Inter-American Studies* 1, No. 1 (January 1959), 11–26.

38. WHP to Lucas Alamán, December (15), 1842, MHS-WHP. Alamán responded to this letter by stating that "the rancor of the Mexicans against the Spaniards is certainly incomprehensible, but as it stems from passion, it will yield to reason when it calms down," or so he wished. Alamán to WHP, Mexico, February 25, 1843, MHS-WHP. Prescott took Alamán by his word and reproduced his comments about the 1823 incident nearly verbatim. Copious in his footnotes, he did not cite his source in this case, probably to protect Alamán. See his *History of the Conquest of Mexico*, vol. III, Book VII, Chapter V, p. 350.

39. Lucas Alamán to WHP, Mexico, February 25, 1843, MHS-WHP. A note by Bustamante dated December 28, 1841, MHS-WHP, speaks of a portrait of Moctezuma as authentic. He traces the origin of the painting to Captain Cristóbal de Olid (but does not rule out Indian painters) and provides a synopsis of its subsequent history. Prescott did include the picture in the second volume of his *History of the Conquest of Mexico*. For a discussion of Mexican views of the Aztec past, and the impact of Prescott's *History*, see Charles A. Hale, *Mexican Liberalism in the Age of Mora, 1821–1853* (New Haven and London: Yale University Press, 1968), pp. 216–220. See also Jorge Cañizares-Esguerra, *How to Write the History of the New World: Historiographies, Epistemologies, and Identities in the Eighteenth-Century Atlantic World* (Stanford: Stanford University Press, 2001). This author concentrates on eighteenth-century figures, but provides helpful background to understand nineteenth-century views of the indigenous past.

40. George Ticknor to Henry W. Longfellow, Woods Hole, August 28, 1842. Houghton Library, Harvard University.

41. The full title of the first American edition is *The History of the Conquest of Mexico, with a Preliminary View of the Ancient Mexican Civilization, and the Life of the Conqueror, Hernando Cortés*, 3 vols. (New York: Harper and Brothers, 1843). I have examined Prescott's autographed presentation copy to the Massachusetts Historical Society, of which he was a member.

42. Appreciative assessments of Prescott's contributions, though far from uncritical, are by Hugh Thomas, *Conquest: Montezuma, Cortés, and the Fall of Old Mexico* (New York: Simon & Schuster, 1993) and James Lockhart's introduction to the Modern Library edition of Prescott's *History* (2001). I use this last edition for the purposes of citation in this section. More critical comments about Prescott's work are by Inga Clendinnen, *Aztecs: An Interpretation* (Cambridge: Cambridge University Press, 1991), and Matthew Restall, *Seven Myths of the Spanish Conquest* (New York: Oxford University Press, 2003). On Prescott's narrative techniques and historiographical conventions see David Levin, *History as Romantic Art: Bancroft, Prescott, Motley, and Parkman* (Stanford: Stanford University Press, 1959); John Ernest, "Reading the Romantic Past: William H. Prescott's *History of the Conquest of Mexico*," *American Literary History* 5, No. 2 (Summer 1993), 231–249; and Eric Wertheimer, *Imagined Empires: Incas, Aztecs, and the New World of American Literature, 1771–1876* (Cambridge: Cambridge University Press, 1999), pp. 91–132.

43. Although referring to the Aztecs, Prescott made clear what he thought of astrology: "The false science of astrology is natural to a state of society partially civilized" (p. 91).

44. WHP to Fanny Calderón, April 17, 1840, W, p. 120.

45. Carlos María Bustamante to WHP, New Brunswick, December 26, 1843, MHS-WHP. The letter was written in English. There is no evidence that Prescott responded. At any rate, Bustamante did not translate the work. Nor did Ángel Calderón, who had the intention to do it.

46. Lucas Alamán to WHP, Mexico, April 29, 1844, MHS-WHP. Alamán was not precise about the various removals of Cortés's remains, but he seemed to refer to that of 1629, in Mexico. For a detailed description of the various exhumations, see Francisco de la Maza, who discusses Alamán, but not Prescott, in his "Los restos de Hernán Cortés," *Cuadernos Americanos* 31, No. 2 (March–April 1947), 153–174.

47. Martín Fernández de Navarrete to WHP, August 27, 1844, MHS-WHP.

48. Ángel Calderón to WHP, New York, November 22, 1844, MHS-WHP.

49. Lucas Alamán to WHP, Mexico, February 1, 1845, MHS-WHP.

50. WHP to Lucas Alamán, March 30, 1845, W, pp. 533–534.

51. Lucas Alamán to WHP, Mexico, April 29, 1845, MHS-WHP.

52. WHP to Lucas Alamán, Boston, March 30, 1846, CONDUMEX, Mexico City (Doc. 17–1385). Also in W, pp. 583–584. I thank Eric Van Young for providing me with a transcription of the original. Alamán responded to this letter on September 28, 1846, MHS-WHP. He stated there that he was much pleased by Prescott's judgment of his notes.

53. *Historia de la conquista de Mejico, con un bosquejo preliminar de la civilización de los antiguos mejicanos, y la vida del conquistador Hernando Cortés*, escritas en inglés por Guillermo H. Prescott, autor de la 'Historia de Fernando e Isabel' traducida del inglés por D. José María de la Vega y anotada por D. Lucas Alamán, 2 vols. (Mexico: Imprenta de V[icente] G[arcía] Torres, 1844), p. 15. I have consulted this source at the Rare Books and Manuscripts Department, Boston Public Library. Prescott's notes are preserved in their original Arabic numerical arrangement. Alamán's notes are added alphabetically, and sometimes refer to the text, sometimes to statements made in the notes. There is a modern edition of this translation by Juan Antonio Ortega y Medina, with Alamán's notes, *Historia de la conquista de México*, 3d ed. (Mexico: Editorial Porrúa, 1985).

54. Prescott, *History*, III, Chapter IX, p. 88.

55. *Historia*, vol. I, Book I, Chapter III, pp. 60–61. Page 34 of the Porrúa edition.

56. José F. Ramírez, "Notas y esclarecimientos a la Historia de la Conquista de México del señor W. Prescott, por José F. Ramírez, ciudadano Mexicano," vol. 2 of *Historia de la Conquista de Mexico, con una ojeada preliminar sobre la antigua civilización de los*

Mexicanos, y con la vida de su conquistador Fernando Cortés, escrita en inglés por W. Prescott y traducida al español por Joaquín Navarro, 3 vols. (México: Impreso por Ignacio Cumplido, 1844–1846), pp. vii–xx and 1–124. On Ramírez's work and trajectory, see Krauze, *La Presencia del Pasado,* pp. 59–74, and passim,

57. Ibid., p. 101. Prescott's text in the Spanish translation appears in Vol. II, p. 368. In the original American edition, it is in Vol. III, Book VII, Chapter 5, pp. 350–351 (pp. 905–906 of the Modern Library edition). Alamán described this event in more detail and provided documentation, such as it was, in his *Disertaciones sobre la historia de la república megicana, desde la época de la conquista que los españoles hicieron a fines del siglo XV y principios del XVI de las islas y continente Americano hasta la independencia,* 3 vols. (Mexico: Imprenta de José Mariano Lara, 1844–1849), II, pp. 58–62. The event, alleged to have happened on September 16, 1823, is also briefly described in the manuscript "Apuntes biográficos de D. Lucas Alamán," dated July 1, 1853. Benson Latin American Collection. Alamán Papers, item No. 358.

58. WHP to José F. Ramírez, January 18, 1849, MHS-WHP.

59. José F. Ramírez to WHP, Durango, April 3, 1849, MHS-WHP.

60. José F. Ramírez to WHP, April 17, 1855, MHS-WHP. Emphasis in the original.

61. Prescott, *History of the Conquest of Mexico,* Vol. I, Chapter, 4, p. 93. In the Appendix he was somewhat more qualified about the Mexican hieroglyphics: "The Palenque writing shows an advanced stage of the art; and, though somewhat clumsy, intimates, by the conventional and arbitrary forms of the hieroglyphics, that it was symbolical, and perhaps phonetic, in its character," Vol. III, Part I, p. 410.

62. WHP to Joaquín García Icazbalceta, April 25, 1855, MHS-WHP.

63. Joaquín García Icazbalceta to WHP, Mexico, May 31, 1855, MHS-WHP .

64. José F. Ramírez to WHP, Paris, August 26, 1855, MHS-WHP. He did publish Diego Durán's *Historia de las indias de Nueva España y islas de tierra firme* in Mexico. He saw the first volume in print (1867), but died (1871) before he could see the publication of the second (1880).

65. WHP to Fanny Calderón, September 7, 1858, MHS-WHP.

66. WHP to Ángel Calderón, December 17, 1850, MHS-WHP.

67. Alamán was elected corresponding member of the MHS on February 28, 1850, and Member of the American Philosophical Society on January 17, 1851. The diplomas are at the Benson Latin American Collection. Alamán Papers, items No. 310 and 322, respectively.

68. Fanny Calderón to WHP, Zaranz, October 19, 1858, MHS-WHP.

69. Joaquín García Icazbalceta to WHP, Mexico, June 27, 1853, MHS-WHP.

70. WHP to Lucas Alamán, March 30, 1845, in W, pp. 530–534.

71. Lucas Alamán to WHP, April 29, 1845, MHS-WHP.

72. WHP to Lucas Alamán, June 5, 1845, MHS-WHP.

73. William Miller to WHP, December 21, 1845, MHS-WHP. Miller's memorandum, titled "rough note, private and confidential" is also in the same box. There is a printed version in W, pp. 568–569. Prescott met Miller in Massachusetts in 1840, after the latter's banishment from Peru in 1839.

74. William Miller to WHP, November 10, 1848, MHS-WHP.

75. Lucas Alamán to WHP, December 25, 1845, MHS-WHP.

76. Lucas Alamán to WHP, September 28, 1846, MHS-WHP.

77. WHP to Pascual de Gayangos, January 20, 1846, HSA, Letters, 1845–1860; W, p. 577. The note was in Prescott's review of George Bancroft's *History of the United States,* which he revised for publication in 1845:

> I was unwilling lo let [the review] go into the world with my name in it, without entering my protest, in common with so many better and wiser in our country, against a measure which every friend of freedom, both at home and

abroad, may justly lament as the most serious shock yet given to the stability of our glorious institutions. (*Biographical and Critical Miscellanies* [Philadelphia: J.B. Lippincott Co., 1895], p. 282)

On the larger opposition to the war, see John H. Schroeder, *Mr. Polk's War: American Opposition and Dissent, 1846–1848* (Madison: University of Wisconsin Press, 1973). Curiously, the author makes no reference to Prescott.

78. WHP to Thomas Jadrell Philips, March 30, 1846, W, p. 586.
79. WHP to Susan Amory Prescott, April 5, 1846, W, p. 590.
80. WHP to George Sumner, May 15, 1846, W, p. 597. What Prescott may have meant by "money-making democracy" is rather unclear, but I suspect that, as a Whig, he placed higher value on commerce and industrial development, than on territorial expansion, which in this case meant agriculture, and the extension of slavery. Prescott's fears on the Oregon question proved unfounded, as the issue was settled peacefully in June 1846. Robert W. Johannsen has argued that despite his opposition to the war, Prescott's *History of the Conquest of Mexico* had done much to promote that same "dare-devil war spirit." See his *To the Halls of the Montezumas: The Mexican War in the American Imagination* (New York and Oxford: Oxford University Press, 1985).
81. WHP to Robert C. Winthrop, May 30, 1847, W, p. 642. A similar opinion is in his letter to Adolphe de Circourt, July 10, 1847. "The question of Slavery," he wrote, "which must arise on the settlement of the new conquests, is a formidable one, more formidable than the war itself," W, p. 656.
82. WHP to Pascual de Gayangos, June 15, 1847, HSA, Letters, 1845–1860; W, p. 648, with omissions.
83. WHP to Susan Amory, April 6, 1846, W, p. 590.
84. Caleb Cushing to WHP, San Angel, January 1, 1848, MHS-WHP.
85. WHP to Caleb Cushing, April 3, 1848, MHS-WHP. Also in Ogden, *William Hickling Prescott*, pp. 205–207.
86. John Church Hamilton to WHP, April 26, 1849, MHS-WHP.
87. John Church Hamilton to WHP, April 28, 1849, MHS-WHP. Also in GP, pp. 268–269.
88. WHP to John Church Hamilton, May 2, 1849, MHS-WHP. Prescott did indeed start to compose his *Philip the Second* on July 19, 1849. The first two volumes appeared in 1855. See GP, p. 275. Johannsen mentions Charles King's approach, which had the approval of Winfield Scott, but does not cover John C. Hamilton's, in his *To the Halls of the Montezumas*, p. 248.
89. July 25, 1848, LM, II, p. 181.
90. José Fernando Ramírez to Luis Cuevas, April 27, 1849. Returning the work was not an easy matter, given the condition of the roads and safety after the war. The correspondence relating to this affair is in Archivo General de la Nación (Mexico)—Gobernación. Sin Sección, Caja 360, E. 13.
91. Manuel de Nájera to Lucas Alamán, Guadalajara, May 8, 1849, Benson Latin American Collection. Alamán Papers. Item No. 290.
92. García Icazbalceta and Prescott exchanged correspondence between 1849 and 1856, much of it related to the transcription of documents from the Boston historian's collection. García Icazbalceta acknowledged Prescott's generous assistance in the first volume of his *Colección de documentos para la historia de México* (1858). This was a burden for Prescott, because the Mexican historian bombarded him with requests for several years. Many of these documents are housed at the Benson Latin American Collection. Joaquín García Icazbalceta Manuscript Collection [1500]–1887. His letters to Prescott are at the MHS, and also in Spanish in C. Harvey Gardiner, "Las cartas de Joaquín García Icazbalceta a William H. Prescott," *Boletín de la Biblioteca*

Nacional (Mexico) 13, No. 4 (October-December 1962), 3–33. For an analysis of his contributions to Mexican historiography, see Manuel Guillermo Martínez, *Don Joaquín García Icazbalceta: His Place in Mexican Historiography* (Washington, D.C.: The Catholic University of America, 1947). Miguel Lerdo de Tejada, one of the leaders of the *Reforma* period, sent him a copy of his *Apuntes históricos de la ciudad de Veracruz.* Lerdo de Tejada to WHP, Mexico, February 26, 1852, MHS-WHP.

93. Lucas Alamán to WHP, March 17, 1849, MHS-WHP.

94. *Historia de la conquista del Perú, precedida de una ojeada sobre la civilización de los Incas,* traducida al castellano por J.G.I. (Mexico: R. Rafael, Editor, 1849). A new version, with an added appendix by García, appeared in 1850. A previous translation appeared in Spain in 2 vols. (Madrid: Establecimiento Tipográfico de D. Ramón Rodríguez de Rivera, 1847–1848), but no translator is named.

95. See Joseph Dager Alva, "La historiografía peruana de la segunda mitad del siglo XIX. Una presentación inicial a través de la obra de José Toribio Polo," *Revista Complutense de Historia de América* 26 (2000), 135–179.

96. The historiographical debates of the 1840s in Chile have been amply covered by Allan Woll, *A Functional Past: The Uses of History in Nineteenth-Century Chile* (Baton Rouge and London: Louisiana State University Press, 1982); Germán Colmenares, *Las convenciones contra la cultura: Ensayos sobre la historiografía hispanoamericana del siglo XIX* (Bogotá: Tercer Mundo Editores, 1987); and Cristián Gazmuri, *La historiografía chilena, 1842–1920.* Vol. 1 (Santiago: Taurus Historia, 2006).

97. Andrés Bello, "Historia de la conquista del Perú por W.H. Prescott," *Obras completas,* 26 vols. (Caracas: Fundación la Casa de Bello, 1981–1984), XIX, p. 265. This essay appeared originally in *Revista de Santiago* in the issues of April and May 1848.

98. Cristián Gazmuri, "Algunas influencias europeas en el método historiográfico de Bello," *Bello y Chile,* 2 tomos (Caracas: La Casa de Bello, 1981), II, pp. 325–338.

99. Diego Barros Arana to WHP, Valparaíso, January 29, 1850, MHS-WHP.

100. Barros Arana became a tireless promoter of Prescott's work and historical approach. In the conclusion of his massive *Historia Jeneral de Chile,* 16 vols. (1884–1902), XVI, p. 358, he recalled how he managed to publish extracts of the *History of the Conquest of Peru* in newspapers in the 1850s. In his *Historia de América* (1865), the most widely used secondary school textbook on the subject, he listed Prescott's books on Mexico and Peru as his principal sources for the conquest period. Similar tributes can be found in the works of Miguel Luis Amunátegui and Benjamín Vicuña Mackenna. See "Prescott en Chile," in Guillermo Feliú Cruz, *El imperio español y los historiadores norteamericanos,* 2 vols. (Santiago: Ediciones de la Universidad de Chile, 1960), II, pp. 101–124. The first translation of Prescott's *Peru* to appear in Chile was based on the Spanish publication of 1847–1848, *Historia de la Conquista del Perú,* 2 vols. (Valparaíso: Imprenta del Comercio, July 1851).

101. William H. Prescott, *History of the Conquest of Peru, with a Preliminary View of the Civilization of the Incas,* 2 vols. (New York: Harper and Brothers, 1847). The reference appears in Book IV, Chapter V, pp. 187–188.

102. Ferdinand Coxe to WHP, Philadelphia, July 2, 1847, W, pp. 652–654.

103. WHP to Ferdinand Coxe, July 12, 1847, W, pp. 658–659. Caravantes was the author of the *Noticia general de las provincias del Pirú, Tierra Firme, y Chile,* a manuscript prepared in the early 1630s.

104. This essay appeared in the *Quarterly Review,* vol. 81 (1847). It is included in *HAHR,* p. 173. Whereas the literary components of Prescott's work have survived the test of time, the historical and archeological have understandably not. See Philip Ainsworth Means, "A Re-Examination of Prescott's Account of Early Peru," *The New England Quarterly* 4 (October 1931), 645–662. Means provides an analysis of

Book I, which is devoted to the civilization of the Incas. See also Guillermo Lohman Villena, "Notes on Prescott's Interpretation of the Conquest of Peru," in *HAHR*, 46–48. Prescott inspired younger scholars who carried research on Peru and the Incas forward. The young Clements R. Markham paid him a visit in Pepperell (MA) in September 1852 and noted the historian's hospitality and impressive command of sources. See Peter Blanchard, ed., *Markham in Peru: The Travels of Clements R. Markham, 1852–1853* (Austin: The University of Texas Press, 1991), pp. 1–2.

105. This essay originally appeared in the *NAR* 65 (1847). It is included, but not identified, in *HAHR*, 173–175.

106. Prescott's reflections on the character of Pizarro, with contrasts to Cortés, are in Book IV, Chapter V, pp. 189–200.

107. Joaquín Acosta to WHP, Paris, July 29, 1847, MHS-WHP. Eventually, Acosta published his *Compendio histórico del descubrimiento y colonización de la Nueva Granada en el siglo décimo sexto* (Paris: Imprenta de Beau, 1848). For an examination of Acosta's views see Robert H. Davis, "Acosta, Caro, and Lleras: Three Essayists and Their Views of New Granada's National Problems, 1832–1853" (Ph.D. Dissertation, Vanderbilt University, 1969).

108. Robert Anderson Wilson to WHP, Rochester, April 4, 1857, MHS-WHP.

109. WHP to Wilson, April 8, 1857, MHS-WHP.

110. WHP to Wilson, April 16, 1857, MHS-WHP.

111. Wilson's letter of June 6, 1858 (MHS-WHP) was actually written on the back of a prospectus of the work. The book's title is *A New History of the Conquest of Mexico* (Philadelphia: James Challen and Son, 1859).

112. See George Ticknor, "Wilson's 'Conquest of Mexico,'" *Proceedings of the Massachusetts Historical Society* 4 (April 1859), 277–283.

113. Pedro Félix Vicuña to WHP, Valparaíso, August 20, 1858, MHS-WHP.

114. The house on 55 Beacon Street in Boston is still standing. It is an impressive one, especially the spacious library (though the books were removed soon after Prescott's death) where the historians met. The house is currently maintained by the National Society of Colonial Dames, mainly as a repository for colonial costumes. I thank Ann Huff for arranging my visits to the house in the Fall of 2002.

115. Benjamín Vicuña Mackenna, *Páginas de mi diario durante tres años de viaje, 1853–1854–1855*, 2 vols. (Santiago: Universidad de Chile, 1936), I, p. 160. The date of Prescott's visit to England is actually 1850.

8   Knights-Errant and Bigots: Prescott's Writings on Spain

1. Quoted by James Westfall Thompson, *A History of Historical Writing*, 2 vols. (New York: The Macmillan Company, 1942), II, p. 100.

2. William H. Prescott, *History of the Reign of Ferdinand and Isabella, the Catholic*, 3 vols. (Boston: American Stationers' Company, 1838), I, pp. xiv and III, 496.

3. See Richard L. Kagan's "Introduction," and "Prescott's Paradigm: American Historical Scholarship and the Decline of Spain," in his edited volume *Spain in America: The Origins of Hispanism in the United States* (Urbana and Chicago: University of Illinois Press, 2002), pp. 1–19 and 247–276. Older but still useful sources on American historiography, with particular reference to Prescott, are David Levin, *History as Romantic Art: Bancroft, Prescott, Motley, and Parkman* (Stanford: Stanford University Press, 1959); Michael Kraus, *A History of American History* (New York: Farrar and Rinehart, 1937); and William Charvat and Michael Kraus, eds., *William Hickling Prescott* (New York: American Book Company, 1943).

4. *History*, the quotations come from the introduction, pp. lxvi, lxx, and xli.

5. Ibid., I, p. 218.
6. Ibid., I, p. 230.
7. Ibid., I, p. 247.
8. Ibid., II, p. 404.
9. Ibid., III, p. 191.
10. Ibid., I, p. 175.
11. Ibid., II, p. 109.
12. They are indeed quite impressive, and readers at the time were captivated. President Manuel Bulnes of Chile (1841–1851) liked it enough to name his son after Gonzalo de Córdoba. Gonzalo Bulnes became a historian, and a great admirer of Prescott. See his interview with Armando Donoso in *Recuerdos de cincuenta años* (Santiago: Editorial Nascimento, 1947), p. 255.
13. *History*, III, p. 136.
14. Ibid., III, p. 158.
15. Ibid., I, p. 490.
16. Ibid., I, p. xl.
17. Ibid., I, p. 294.
18. Ibid., I, p. 310.
19. Sabau was in addition rector of the University of Madrid and a member (since 1835) as well as life-secretary (since 1845) of the Royal Academy of History. He held several important positions during the reign of Isabella II (1843–1868), including senator, government advisor, and director of public instruction. Real Academia de la Historia (henceforth RAH), Secretaría, Expedientes de Miembros.
20. Prescott had much trouble securing a copy of it, but received one in time to add references to his manuscript, especially citations of original documents. Otherwise, Clemencín's "*Elogio*" does not add very much to the historical record. I have consulted a copy of this volume (No. 6) bequeathed to the Boston Public Library by George Ticknor, in the Rare Books and Manuscript Department. Also, the original manuscript at RAH, Biblioteca, Legajo 11–8234, No. 15. The "Elogio" was originally presented to the Academy on April 18, 1806.
21. *Historia del reinado de los reyes católicos D.Fernando y Da. Isabel*, escrita en inglés por William H. Prescott, traducida del original por D. Pedro Sabau y Larroya, 4 vols. Edición de la Revista de España, Indias y del Estranjero (Madrid: Imprenta, Librería y Fundición de M. Rivadeneira y Comp., 1845–1846), I, p. vii.
22. Ibid., I, p. viii. Henceforth Sabau. It soon became commonplace among Spanish historians to establish the same parallel. See Paloma Cirujano Marín, Teresa Elorriaga Planes, and Juan Sisinio Garzón, *Historiografía y nacionalismo Español, 1834–1868* (Madrid: Consejo Superior de Investigaciones Científicas, 1985), pp. 112–117.
23. Prescott, *Ferdinand and Isabella*, I, p. xv.
24. Sabau, I, p. xxi. One review that departed from defensive reactions and which still managed to be both critical and favorable was by Fermín Gonzalo Morón in *Revista de España, de Indias i del Extranjero* 1 (1845), pp. 245–247.
25. Fanny Calderón to William H. Prescott (WHP), Madrid, October 8, 1843, William Hickling Prescott papers, Massachusetts Historical Society (MHS-WHP). Also included in Roger Wolcott, *The Correspondence of William Hickling Prescott, 1833–1847* (W), p. 392. Because Wolcott's selection is partial and incomplete, I first cite the original documents. Other printed collections of letters by Prescott include C. Harvey Gardiner, *The Papers of William Hickling Prescott* (Urbana: The University of Illinois Press, 1964) (GP), and Clara Louisa Penney, ed., *Prescott: Unpublished Letters to Gayangos in the Library of the Hispanic Society of America* (New York: Printed by the Order of the Trustees, 1927) (Henceforth Penney).
26. Pascual de Gayangos to WHP, Madrid, October 10, 1843, MHS-WHP; W, p. 398.

27. WHP to Fanny Calderón, November 15, 1843, MHS-WHP; W, p. 407. Antonio Benavides (1807–1884) was working on a translation of *Ferdinand and Isabella*, but never completed it. A member of the RAH, of which he became director, Benavides was a *moderado* liberal and a professor of law.

28. Prescott, *Ferdinand and Isabella*, I, p. 245.

29. Sabau, I, p. 339.

30. Ibid., II, p. 178.

31. Prescott, *Ferdinand and Isabella*, II, p. 42.

32. Ibid., III, p. 116.

33. Sabau, IV, p. 14.

34. José Güell y Renté, *Paralelo entre las reinas católicas Doña Isabel I y Doña Isabel II* (Paris: Imprenta de Jules Claye, 1858). Citations are given in parenthesis in the text.

35. WHP to Gayangos, August 31, 1846, Hispanic Society of America (HSA), Letters of William Hickling Prescott. These manuscript letters are bound in two volumes, 1838–1844 and 1845–1860. They are far more reliable than those transcribed by Wolcott from the drafts. See W, pp. 610–611, and Penney, pp. 60–62.

36. Even though he does not make a reference to Sabau, the work of José Álvarez Junco, *Mater Dolorosa: La idea de España en el siglo XIX* (Madrid: Taurus Historia, 2001) is indispensable for understanding the period, and the process of national identity formation in Spain.

37. There was a second translation of Prescott's *Ferdinand and Isabella* by Atilano Calvo Iturburu, titled *Historia del Reinado de los Reyes Católicos D. Fernando y Da. Isabel* (Madrid: Imprenta de Gaspar y Roig, Editores, 1855). This is a single volume edition, fully illustrated, whose principal aim was to reach a wider audience. It is not as critical as the first edition, although Calvo Iturburu tended to react to many of the same statements by Prescott. Perhaps the major difference between the two translations, in addition to the thoroughness of the first, is that Calvo reacted more often to matters he deemed offensive to national honor rather than religion. Thus, for instance, he reacted against Prescott's references to, (1) the neglect of manuscripts in Spanish repositories, (2) the insinuation that Isabella was to be blamed to any extent for the excesses of the Inquisition, and (3) the suggestion that the Spaniards were particularly cruel in the treatment of their Muslim enemies during the fall of Granada. His conclusion was that foreigners could not be trusted, not even the best of them, like Prescott, when it came to judging Spanish national events.

38. Prescott noted in his journal that he had read Robertson's *Charles the Fifth* between December 11, 1826 and January 15, 1827. He returned to volume I on September 29, 1828. See *The Literary Memoranda of William Hickling Prescott* (henceforth LM), edited by C. Harvey Gardiner, 2 vols. (Norman: University of Oklahoma Press, 1961), I, pp. 81–82 and 93.

39. William Robertson, *The History of the Reign of the Emperor Charles the Fifth, by William Robertson, D.D., with an Account of the Emperor's Life After His Abdication*, by William H. Prescott, 3 vols. (Boston: Phillips, Sampson, and Company, 1856), I, p. x. Henceforth cited as Robertson's *History*.

40. January 8, 1826, LM, I, p. 67.

41. Ernest F. Henderson, writing in 1903 and comparing Robertson's work to the newly published *The Emperor Charles V* by Edward Armstrong (1902) put it more bluntly: "This is no history of the reign of Charles V; it is a history of the Reformation enlivened by details of Charles' campaigns." See his "Two Lives of Emperor Charles V," *American Historical Review* 9, No. 1 (October 1903), 24. For a more recent treatment of the work of William Robertson, although making no mention of the historian's view of the monarch's "character," see J.G.A. Pocock, *Barbarism and Religion*, 2 vols. (Cambridge: Cambridge University Press, 1999), especially Section IV in

vol. II, "William Robertson and the History of Europe," pp. 258–305. See also Jorge Cañizares-Esguerra, *How to Write the History of the New World: Histories, Epistemologies, and Identities in the Eighteenth-Century Atlantic World* (Stanford: Stanford University Press, 2001), pp. 38–44 and 54, who considers Robertson a moderate and impartial historian. Robertson's influence on Spanish historians, especially Modesto Lafuente, is discussed by Roberto López Vela, "Carlos V y España en la obra de Modesto Lafuente. La interpretación liberal de la nación española dentro del imperio de los Austrias," in *Carlos V y la quiebra del humanismo político en Europa (1530–1558)*, vol. 3 (Madrid: Sociedad Estatal para la Conmemoración de los Centenarios de Felipe II y Carlos V, 2001), pp. 153–259.

42. Robertson's *History*, I, p. 22.
43. Ibid., I, p. 59.
44. Ibid., I, p. 73.
45. Ibid., I, p. 383. In 1760, Charles III made the Immaculate Conception of Virgin Mary the patroness of Spain, after receiving the authorization of Pope Clement XIII. See John Lynch, *Bourbon Spain, 1700–1808* (Oxford: Basil Blackwell, 1989), p. 276. Pope Pius IX proclaimed it a Catholic dogma on December 8, 1854. The impact of the cult on Spanish art is impressively illustrated by the exhibit "Inmaculada: 150 años de la proclamación del dogma," Santa Iglesia Catedral-Sevilla, May–November 2004.
46. Ibid., I, p. 457.
47. Ibid., I, p. 592.
48. Ibid, II, p. 346.
49. Ibid., II, p. 358.
50. Ibid., I, p. 524.
51. Ibid., I, p. 551.
52. Ibid., II, pp. 463–464.
53. The book was published under the pseudonym "Don Leucadio Doblado," (London: Printed for Henry Colburn and Co., 1822). The best biography of Blanco White is by Martin Murphy, *Blanco White, Self-Banished Spaniard* (New Haven and London: Yale University Press, 1989). See also *The Life of the Rev. Joseph Blanco White, written by himself, with portions of his correspondence*, edited by John Hamilton Thom, 3 vols. (London: John Chapman, 1845). Prescott noted in his journal that he had read Blanco White's *Letters* between July 3 and July 10, 1825, LM, I, p. 62.
54. Andrews Norton owned a copy of this book, which I use in this chapter. Blanco corresponded with him and with William Ellery Channing. See Murphy, *Blanco White*, pp. 181–182. For an analysis of the philosophical foundations of American Unitarianism, see Daniel Walker Howe, *The Unitarian Conscience: Harvard Moral Philosophy, 1805–1861* (Cambridge, MA: Harvard University Press, 1970).
55. Blanco White, *Letters from Spain*, p. 24.
56. Ibid., p. 25.
57. Ibid., pp. 474–475.
58. Ibid., pp. 7–8.
59. Robertson's *History*, III, p. 197.
60. Ibid., III, p. 199. Robertson was referring to Lévesque's *Mémoires pour servir à l'Histoire du Card. de Granvelle* (Paris, 1753).
61. Ibid., III, p. 227.
62. Ibid., III, p. 272.
63. Ibid., III, p. 273.
64. Ibid., III, p. 274.
65. Ibid., III, p. 275.
66. Nineteenth-century Spanish views of Robertson, and of Charles V, are treated by Ignacio Peiró Martín, "La fortuna del emperador: La imagen de Carlos V entre los

españoles del siglo XIX," in *El siglo de Carlos V y Felipe II: La construcción de los mitos en el siglo XIX*, edited by José Martínez Millán and Carlos Reyero, 2 vols. (Madrid: Sociedad Estatal para la Conmemoración de los Centenarios de Felipe II y Carlos V, 2000), pp. 153–194.

67. On François Mignet (1796–1884), who played an important role in the transatlantic search for Charles V documents, see Yvonne Knibiehler, *Naissance des sciences humaines: Mignet et l'histoire philosophique au XIXe siècle* (Paris: Flammarion, 1973). On the French historical profession, see Pim den Boer, *History as a Profession: The Study of History in France, 1818–1914*, translated by Arnold J. Pomerans (Princeton: Princeton University Press, 1998).

68. The definitive edition of this work, incorporating all of Stirling-Maxwell's revisions and prefaces, is the fourth (London: John C. Mimmo, 1891).

69. WHP to Tomás González, April 21, 1838, MHS-WHP; W, pp. 24–25.

70. WHP to Lembke, January 18, 1839, MHS-WHP; W, p. 51. An earlier demonstration of interest appeared in a letter to Obadiah Rich (August 13, 1833) in GP, p. 93.

71. Lembke to WHP, Madrid, August 9, 1839, MHS-WHP; W, p. 89.

72. Arthur Middleton to WHP, Madrid, August 10, 1839, MHS-WHP; W, pp. 90–91.

73. WHP to Lembke, September 1, 1840, MHS-WHP; W, p. 156.

74. WHP to Edward Everett, September 28, 1840, MHS-WHP; W, p. 161.

75. Gayangos to WHP, London, October 15, 1840, MHS-WHP; W, p. 167.

76. WHP to Gayangos, November 28, 1840, HSA, Letters, 1838–1844; the version in W, p. 182, is incomplete. A *Real* was one-eighth of a Spanish silver peso, and a peso was roughly equivalent to one American dollar.

77. Jared Sparks to WHP, London, March 9, 1841, MHS-WHP; W, p. 212.

78. Gayangos to WHP, London, September 22, 1841, MHS-WHP; W, p. 255. A series of delays kept Gayangos in England until 1843.

79. WHP to Gayangos, June 15, 1843, HSA, Letters, 1838–1844; W, p. 367.

80. He did not want to write a history of the Charles the Fifth period, he explained, because that monarch's reign "has been handled by Robertson, and I have not the courage yet to venture to tread where he has gone before," WHP to Gayangos, May 30, 1842, HSA, Letters, 1838–1844; W, p. 308.

81. WHP to Gayangos, September 29, 1843, HSA, Letters, 1838–1844; W, p. 389.

82. Gayangos to WHP, Madrid, October 10, 1843, MHS-WHP; W, p. 396.

83. Ibid.

84. Gayangos to WHP, Madrid, November 8, 1843, MHS-WHP; W, p. 404.

85. WHP to Gayangos, November 30, 1843, HSA, Letters, 1838–1844; W, p. 414.

86. WHP to Gayangos, December 31, 1843, HSA, Letters, 1838–1844. This letter has several words missing due to a large tear, but the draft at MHS-WHP is complete; W, p. 428.

87. WHP to Gayangos, January 30, 1844, HSA, Letters, 1838–1844; W, p. 439. Prescott again insisted that "the manuscripts relating to the closing days of Charles V must be had, and I shall not feel assured that I have the corner-stone of the history till you have paid your visit to Simancas and obtained them," WHP to Pascual de Gayangos, May 1, 1844, HSA, Letters, 1838–1844; W, p. 464. Also Penney, pp. 173–174. Later in the month, he stated "it will never do to show my ignorance on the very threshold of the work, and all my present collection will be unavailing without materials for this part of the subject, especially as such misapprehensions respecting it have been made popular through Robertson's work," WHP to Pascual de Gayangos, May 30, 1844, HSA, Letters, 1838–1844; W, p. 468.

88. Actas de la Real Academia de la Historia, February 16, February 23, March 8, 1844. The minutes of the meeting of May 3 show that the Spanish government issued regulations on April 20, 1844.

89. Gayangos to WHP, Madrid, April 13, 1844, MHS-WHP; W, p. 460.
90. Gayangos to WHP, May 17, 1844, MHS-WHP; W, p. 468. Mignet confirmed in the June 1854 preface of his *Charles Quint* that the French government purchased the work for 4,000 francs in 1844. He also explained that González's work consisted of 532 pages of text and a 241-page appendix that included 11 documents, including Charles V's testament and inventory of his possessions.
91. WHP to Gayangos, June 30, 1844, HSA, Letters, 1838–1844; W, p. 481.
92. WHP to Gayangos, July 30, 1844, HSA, Letters, 1838–1844.
93. Gayangos to WHP, Simancas, August 1, 1844; MHS-WHP; W, pp. 488–491.
94. WHP to Gayangos, October 13, 1844; HSA, Letters, 1838–1844; W, p. 508.
95. WHP to Gayangos, November 10, 1845, HSA, Letters, 1838–1844; W, p. 561.
96. Gayangos to WHP, Simancas, August 28, 1844, MHS-WHP; W, pp. 494–496.
97. Gayangos to WHP, Madrid, November 11, 1844, MHS-WHP; W, p. 517.
98. WHP to Adolphe de Circourt, April 30, 1845, MHS-WHP. The date is incorrectly listed as March 30 in W, p. 536.
99. Circourt to WHP, Paris, May 28, 1845, MHS-WHP; W, p. 539.
100. George Sumner to WHP, Paris, June 16, 1845, MHS-WHP; W, p. 545.
101. WHP to George Sumner, August 14, 1845, MHS-WHP; W, p. 549.
102. WHP to Gayangos, December 15, 1845, HSA, Letters, 1845–1860; W, p. 565.
103. He noted in his journal entry of February 15, 1849 that he was committed to "take up the subject—the whole subject—of Philip II," LM, II, p. 184. Then, on July 22, 1849, he noted that he had begun composition of the first chapter the previous Thursday, LM, II, p. 191.
104. WHP to Gayangos, July 30, 1847, HSA, Letters, 1845–1860; W, p. 664.
105. William Stirling-Maxwell to WHP, February 8, 1849, MHS-WHP; GP, p. 267.
106. WHP to Ángel Calderón, December 19, 1850, MHS-WHP; GP, p. 303.
107. WHP to Gayangos, July 11, 1852, HSA, Letters, 1845–1860; GP, p. 314.
108. Ibid. Gayangos, indeed, had written to Prescott that Angulo's *Relación*, "is the same used by Sandoval and [Joseph de] Sigüenza. Accordingly, the Emperor really and truly arranged his own [mock] funeral and honors." He added with a bit of feigned frustration, "well, which way is it?" Gayangos to Prescott, June 9, 1852, MHS-WHP. The Hispanic Society of America in New York has a 1618 copy of Sandoval's *Historia de la vida y los hechos del emperador Carlos V.* There is a modern edition of Sigüenza's *Historia de la orden de San Jerónimo* (Madrid: Bailly-Balliére e hijos, 1907).
109. Stirling-Maxwell to WHP, London, November 8, 1852, MHS-WHP; GP, p. 316. Although Prescott and Stirling were basically competing for the same subject, their relationship was one of mutual respect and friendship. The two scholars met in person in London in 1850, and exchanged significant correspondence. Stirling-Maxwell's 12 letters and notes written to Prescott between 1849 and 1857 are at the MHS. Prescott sent eight letters to Stirling-Maxwell: June 5, 1849; November 7, 1849; November 12, 1850; May 12, 1852; November 28, 1852; June 9, 1854; November 12, 1855; and June 13, 1856. The drafts of these letters are in the MHS-WHP, multiple boxes.
110. Gayangos to WHP, March 31, 1853, MHS-WHP.
111. WHP to Gayangos, June 1, 1853, HSA, Letters, 1845–1860. Also in Penney, pp. 109–110. A manuscript copy of Martín de Angulo's account of Charles V's last days is at BPL. It is not as clear on the mock funeral as Gayangos initially thought, but it confirms the emperor's devotion. Prescott used this source for many of his points, but on the alleged funeral he relied more on Sandoval and Sigüenza.
112. Note by Gardiner in GP, p. 317. Prescott wrote in his journal (May 20, 1855) that he had begun work on the subject "founded on the latest researches at Simancas," LM, II, p. 221.

113. WHP to Richard Bentley, August 4, 1856, MHS-WHP; GP, p. 363. A note in his journal dated June 18, 1856 shows that he had finished his addendum in January of that year; LM, II, p. 224.
114. William H. Prescott, *History of the Reign of Philip the Second, King of Spain*, 3 vols. (Boston: Phillips, Sampson, and Company, 1855–1858), I, p. 328. The work was quickly translated into Spanish by Cayetano Rosell, *Historia del reinado de Felipe Segundo*, 2 vols. (Madrid: Establecimiento Tipográfico de Mellado, 1856–1857). Rosell, a member of the RAH and a respected historian of the Battle of Lepanto, found much to praise in Prescott's work, but he also had objections, especially regarding religious violence on the part of Spaniards on account of their Catholicism. He felt that Prescott relied too heavily on Juan Antonio Llorente's account of the activities of the Inquisition.
115. Ibid., I, p. 311.
116. William Stirling to WHP, February 19, 1857, MHS-WHP.
117. Robertson's *History*, III, p. 405.
118. Ibid., III, pp. 465–466.
119. Ibid., III, pp. 475–476. Prescott, therefore, ignored the arguments of Mignet, who in his *Charles Quint* argued that Charles V could not have performed this ceremony on account of extremely delicate health, absence of reports from his closest aides, and specific Church prohibitions against such practices.
120. Ibid., III, p. 466.

Conclusion

1. Herman Melville, *Benito Cereno* (Barre, MA: The Imprint Society, 1972), p. 44.
2. Ibid., p. 52. H. Bruce Franklin identifies the same reference and is convinced that Melville closely followed William Stirling-Maxwell's *The Cloister Life*. See his essay "Benito Cereno: The Ascetic's Agony," in *Melville's Benito Cereno*, edited by John P. Runden (Boston: D.C. Heath and Company, 1965), pp. 105–117. The most recent biography by Hershel Parker says nothing about the relation between *Benito Cereno* and the story of the last days of the emperor, but the parallels are too strong to ignore. See Parker's *Herman Melville: A Biography*, Vol. 2 (1851–1891) (Baltimore and London: The Johns Hopkins University Press, 2002). He does, however, regard *Benito Cereno* as "formally one of the most nearly perfect things Melville ever did" (p. 242). Very insightful and useful are the analyses of *Benito Cereno* by Jenny Franchot, *Roads to Rome: The Antebellum Protestant Encounter with Catholicism* (Berkeley, Los Angeles, and London: University of California Press, 1994), pp. 171–181; Eric J. Sundquist, "*Benito Cereno* and New World Slavery," in *Reconstructing American Literary History*, edited by Sacvan Bercovitch (Cambridge and London: Harvard University Press, 1986), pp. 93–122, and María DeGuzmán, *Spain's Long Shadow: The Black Legend, Off-Whiteness, and Anglo-American Empire* (Minneapolis and London: University of Minnesota Press, 2005), pp. 47–67.
3. *Benito Cereno*, p. 83.
4. Ibid., 79–80.
5. Ibid., 120.
6. Henry Charles Lea, "The Decadence of Spain," *North American Review* 82, No. 489 (July 1898), 36–46.

Bibliography

Archives and Special Collections

Archivo General de la Nación (Mexico)
Benson Library, University of Texas at Austin
    Latin American Collection
Biblioteca del Congreso de la Nación (Argentina)
    Archivo del Dr. Juan María Gutiérrez
Biblioteca Nacional (Chile)
    Sala José Toribio Medina
Boston Athenaeum
Boston Public Library
    Rare Books and Manuscript Department
Bowdoin College
    George J. Mitchell Department of Special Collections and Archives
Butler Library, Columbia University
    Rare Book and Manuscript Library
Harvard University Archives
Hispanic Society of America (New York)
Houghton Library, Harvard University
Instituto Histórico e Geográfico Brasileiro (Brazil)
Library of Congress
    Manuscript Department
    Hispanic Division
Longfellow National Historic Site
Massachusetts Historical Society
Museo Histórico Sarmiento (Argentina)
New York Historical Society
Rauner Special Collections Library, Dartmouth College
Otto G. Richter Library, University of Miami
    Cuban Heritage Collection
Real Academia de la Historia (Spain)
Real Academia Española (Spain)

Printed Primary Sources

Ard, Patricia M. "Seeds of Reform: The Letters of Mary Peabody Mann and Domingo Faustino Sarmiento, 1865–1868." Ph.D. Dissertation, Rutgers University, 1996.
Bouterwek, Frederick. *History of Spanish and Portuguese Literature*. 2 vols. Translated by Thomasina Ross. London: Boosey and Sons, 1823.

Channing, William Ellery. *The Works of William E. Channing*. 2 vols. 2nd Ed. Boston: James Munroe and Company, 1843.

———. *Selected Writings*. Edited by David Robinson. New York: Paulist Press, 1985.

Cortés, José Domingo. *Prosistas Americanos: Trozos escojidos de literatura*. Paris: Tipografía Lahure, 1873.

Cushing, Caleb. *Reminiscences of Spain, the Country, Its People, History, and Monuments*. 2 vols. Boston: Carter, Hendee and Co., 1833.

Del Monte, Domingo. *Centón Epistolario de Domingo del Monte*. 7 vols. Havana: Imprenta El Siglo XX, 1923–1957.

———. *Escritos de Domingo del Monte*. 2 vols. Edited by José Antonio Fernández de Castro. *Colección de Libros Cubanos*, vols. XII and XIII. Havana: Cultural, S.A., 1929.

Everett, Alexander Hill. *America, or a General Survey of the Political Situation of the Several Powers of the Western Continent, with Conjectures on their Future Prospects*. Philadelphia: H.C. Carey & Lee, 1827.

———. *Critical and Miscellaneous Essays*. Boston, 1845.

———. *Critical and Miscellaneous Essays*. Second Series. Boston, 1846.

———. *Prose Pieces and Correspondence*. Edited by Elizabeth Evans. St. Paul: The John Colet Press, 1975.

Flores, Antonio. *Las Letras Españolas en los Estados Unidos*. Quito: Imprenta del Clero, 1884.

Howells, William Dean . *Familiar Spanish Travels*. New York and London: Harper & Brothers Publishers, 1913.

———. *Literary Friends and Acquaintance: A Personal Retrospect of American Authorship*. Edited by David F. Hiatt and Edwin H. Cady. Bloomington and London: Indiana University Press, 1968.

Hurlbert, William Henry. "The Poetry of Spanish America." *North American Review* 142 (January 1849), 129–160.

———. *Gan-Eden: or, Pictures of Cuba*. Boston: John P. Jewett, 1854.

Irving, Washington. *The Works of Washington Irving*. 15 vols. New York: P.F. Collier & Son, 1904.

———. *Letters from Sunnyside and Spain by Washington Irving*. Edited by Stanley T. Williams. New Haven: Yale University Press, 1928.

———. *Washington Irving and the Storrows: Letters from England and the Continent, 1821–1828*. Edited by Stanley T. Williams. Cambridge, MA: Harvard University Press, 1933.

———. *Journal of Washington Irving (1823–1824)*. Edited by Stanley T. Williams. Hamden, CT: Archon Books, 1968.

———. *Letters*. Volume I (1802–1823) and Volume II (1823–1838). Edited by Ralph M. Aderman, Herbert L. Kleinfield and Jenifer S. Banks. Boston: Twayne Publishers, 1978–1979.

Lea, Henry Charles. "The Decadence of Spain." *North American Review* 82, No. 489 (July 1898), 36–46.

Longfellow, Henry Wadsworth. *Poems of Places*. 2 vols. (Spain and Portugal) Boston: James R. Osgood and Company, 1877.

———. *The Works of Henry Wadsworth Longfellow*. 14 vols. Boston and New York: Houghton, Mifflin, and Company, 1886.

———. *The Letters of Henry Wadsworth Longfellow*. Edited by Andrew Hilen. 6 vols. Cambridge, MA: The Belknap Press of Harvard University Press, 1966–1982.

Lowell, James Russell, "Nationality in Literature." *North American Review* 60, No. 144 (March 1849), 196–215.

———. *Lowell's Works*. 11 vols. Boston and New York: Houghton, Mifflin and Company, 1892.

———. *Letters of James Russell Lowell*. Edited by Charles Eliot Norton. 2 vols. New York: Harper & Brothers Publishers, 1893.

——. *Impressions of Spain.* Compiled by Joseph B. Gilder. Boston and New York: Houghton, Mifflin and Company, 1899.

Mann, Mary Peabody. *Juanita: A Romance of Real Life in Cuba Fifty Years Ago.* Edited with an Introduction by Patricia M. Ard. Charlottesville and London: University Press of Virginia [1887] 2000.

——. *"My Dear Sir." Mary Mann's Letters to Sarmiento (1865–1881).* Edited by Barry L.Velleman. Buenos Aires: Instituto Cultural Argentino Norteamericano, 2001.

Martínez Villergas, Juan. *Juicio Crítico de los Poetas Españoles Contemporáneos.* [1854]. Edited by James A. Dunlop. Lanham, New York, and London: University Press of America, 1995.

Pettigrew, James Johnston. *Notes on Spain and the Spaniards, in the Summer of 1859, with a Glance at Sardinia. By a Carolinian.* Charleston, SC: Presses of Evans & Cogswell, 1861.

Piñeyro, Enrique. *Hombres y glorias de América.* Paris: Garnier Hermanos, 1903.

Pombo, Rafael. *Rafael Pombo en Nueva York.* Edited by Mario Germán Romero. Bogotá: Editorial Kelly, 1983.

Prescott, William Hickling. *The Works of W.H. Prescott.* 16 vols. Philadelphia: J.B. Lippincott Company, 1895.

——. *The Correspondence of William Hickling Prescott, 1833–1847.* Transcribed and edited by Roger Wolcott. Boston and New York: Houghton, Mifflin and Company, 1925.

——. *Prescott. Unpublished Letters to Gayangos in the Library of the Hispanic Society of America.* Edited by Clara Louisa Penney. New York: The Hispanic Society of America, Printed by Order of the Trustees, 1927.

——. *The Literary Memoranda of William Hickling Prescott.* Edited by C. Harvey Gardiner. 2 vols. Norman: University of Oklahoma Press, 1961.

Sarmiento, Domingo Faustino. *Life In The Argentine Republic in the Days of the Tyrants; or, Civilization and Barbarism.* With a biographical sketch of the author, by Mrs. Horace Mann. New York: Hurd and Houghton, 1868.

Sismondi, J.C.L. Simonde de. *Historical View of the Literature of the South of Europe.* Translated by Thomas Roscoe. 2 vols. New York: Harper & Brothers Publishers, 1848.

——. "Fragment on Spanish Literature." *American Register* 2 (1817), 183–200.

Spain. An Account of the Public Festival Given by the Citizens of Boston, at the Exchange Coffee House, January 24, 1809, in Honor of Spanish Valor and Patriotism. Boston: Russell and Cutler, 1809.

Stewart, Randall, Ed. *American Note-Books by Nathaniel Hawthorne. Based on the Original Manuscripts in the Pierpont Morgan Library.* New Haven: Yale University Press, 1932.

Ticknor, George. *Syllabus of a Course of Lectures on the History and Criticism of Spanish Literature.* Cambridge: Printed at the University Press, 1823.

——. *History of Spanish Literature.* 3 vols. New York: Harper and Brothers, 1849.

——. *Historia de la literatura española.* 4 vols. Translated, with additional notes, by Pascual de Gayangos and Enrique de Vedia. Madrid: Imprenta de la Publicidad, 1851–1856.

——. *George Ticknor's Travels in Spain.* Edited by George Tyler Northup. Toronto: The University Library, Published by the Librarian, 1913.

——. *Letters to Pascual de Gayangos, From the Originals in the Collection of the Hispanic Society of America.* Edited by Clara Louisa Penney. New York: The Hispanic Society of America, Printed by Order of the Trustees, 1927.

Wallis, Severn Teackle. *Glimpses of Spain; or Notes of an Unfinished Tour in 1847.* New York: Harper & Brothers, 1849.

——. *Spain: Her Institutions, Politics and Public Men: A Sketch.* Boston: Ticknor, Reed & Fields, 1853.

Webster, Daniel. *The Writings and Speeches of Daniel Webster.* 18 vols. Boston: Little, Brown, and Company, 1903.

Whitney, James Lyman. *Catalogue of the Spanish Libraries and of the Portuguese Books Bequeathed by George Ticknor to the Boston Public Library; Together with the Collection of*

Spanish and Portuguese Literature in the General Library. Boston: Printed by Order of the Trustees, 1879.

Whitten, Arthur Fisher. "An Unpublished Letter in French by George Ticknor." *PMLA* 48 (1933), 164–166.

Secondary Sources

Álvarez Junco, José. *Mater Dolorosa: La Idea de España en el Siglo XIX.* Madrid: Taurus Historia, 2001.

Beerman, Eric. "Spanish Envoy to the United States (1796–1809): Marqués de Casa Irujo and His Philadelphia Wife Sally McKean." *The Americas* (April 1981), 445–456.

———. "Washington Irving en Madrid (1826–28), Cristóbal Colón." *Revista Complutense de Historia de América* No. 18 (1992), 197–217.

Benassar, Bartolomé. *The Spanish Character: Attitudes and Mentalities from the Sixteenth to the Nineteenth Century.* Translated by Benjamin Keen. Berkeley, Los Angeles, and London: University of California Press, 1979.

Bernardo Ares, José Manuel, Ed. *El Hispanismo Anglonorteamericano: Aportaciones, Problemas y Perspectivas sobre Historia, Arte y Literatura Españolas (siglos XVI–XVIII).* 2 vols. Córdoba: Publicaciones Obra Social y Cultural Cajasur, 2001.

Bernstein, Harry. *Origins of Inter-American Interest, 1700–1812.* Philadelphia: University of Pennsylvania Press, 1945.

Bowers, Claude G. *The Spanish Adventures of Washington Irving.* Boston: Houghton, 1940.

Brack, Gene M. *Mexico Views Manifest Destiny, 1821–1846: An Essay on the Origins of the Mexican War.* Albuquerque: University of New Mexico Press, 1975.

Brooks, Van Wyck. *The Flowering of New England.* New York: E.P. Dutton and Company, Inc. [1936], 1952.

———. *The World of Washington Irving.* New York: E.P. Dutton and Company, Inc. [1944], 1950

———. *The Times of Melville and Whitman.* New York: E.P. Dutton and Company, Inc. [1947], 1953.

Buell, Lawrence. *New England Literary Culture: From Revolution to Renaissance.* Cambridge: Cambridge University Press, 1986.

Burns Marañon, Tom. *Hispanomanía.* Barcelona: Plaza & Janés Editores, 2000.

Burstein, Andrew. *The Original Knickerbocker: The Life of Washington Irving.* New York: Basic Books, 2007.

Buscaglia-Salgado, José F. *Undoing Empire: Race and Nation in the Mulatto Caribbean.* Minneapolis and London: University of Minnesota Press, 2003.

Bushman, Claudia L. *America Discovers Columbus: How an Italian Explorer Became an American Hero.* Hanover and London: University Press of New England, 1992.

Caro Baroja, Julio. *El Mito del Carácter Nacional.* Madrid: Editorial Caro Raggio, [1970] 2004.

Chapin, Clara Cutler. "Bryant and Some of His Latin American Friends." *Bulletin of the Pan American Union* 78, No. 11 (November 1944), 609–613.

Chapman, Charles E. *Colonial Hispanic America.* New York: Macmillan Co., 1933.

Charvat, William. *The Origins of American Critical Thought, 1810–1835.* Philadelphia: University of Pennsylvania Press, 1936.

———. *The Profession of Authorship in America, 1800–1870.* Edited by Matthew Bruccoli. New York: Columbia University Press, 1992.

Cirujano Marín, Paloma, Teresa Elorriaga Planes, and Juan Sisinio Pérez Garzón. *Historiografía y Nacionalismo Español, 1834–1868.* Madrid: Consejo Superior de Investigaciones Científicas, 1985.

Clark, Harry Hayden. "Nationalism in American Literature." *The University of Toronto Quarterly* 2, No. 4 (1932–1933), 492–519.

————. "Literary Criticism in the *North American Review*, 1815–1835." *Transactions of the Wisconsin Academy of Sciences, Arts, and Letters* 32 (1940), 299–350.

Coester, Alfred. "Frances Sales—a Forerunner." *Hispania* 19, No. 1 (May 1936), 283–302.

Cummins, Light Townsend. *Spanish Observers and the American Revolution, 1775–1783*. Baton Rouge and London: Louisiana State University Press, 1991.

Cuthbertson, Stuart. "George Ticknor's Interest in Spanish-American Literature." *Hispania* 16, No. 2 (May 1933), 117–226.

Dangerfield, George. *The Awakening of American Nationalism, 1815–1828*. Prospect Heights, IL: Waveland Press [1965] 1994.

DeGuzmán, María. *Spain's Long Shadow: The Black Legend, Off-Whiteness, and Anglo-American Empire*. Minneapolis and London: University of Minnesota Press, 2005.

Delbanco, Andrew. *William Ellery Channing: An Essay on the Liberal Spirit in America*. Cambridge, MA: Harvard University Press, 1981.

Diehl, Carl. *Americans and German Scholarship, 1770–1870*. New Haven: Yale University Press, 1978.

Ellsworth, Clayton. "American Churches and the Mexican War." *American Historical Review* 45 (January 1940), 301–326.

Englekirk, John E. "Notes on Longfellow in Spanish America." *Hispania* 25 (October 1942), 295–308.

————. "El Epistolario Pombo-Longfellow." *Thesaurus: Boletín del Instituto Caro y Cuervo* 10, No. 1, 2, 3 (January–December 1954), 1–58.

Ernest, John. "Reading the Romantic Past: William H. Prescott's *History of the Conquest of Mexico*." *American Literary History* 5, No. 2 (Summer 1993), 231–249.

Esdaile, Charles J. *Spain in the Liberal Age: From Constitution to Civil War, 1808–1939*. Oxford: Blackwell Publishers, 2000.

Feliú Cruz, Guillermo. *El Imperio Español y los Historiadores Norteamericanos*. 2 vols. Santiago: Ediciones de los Anales de la Universidad de Chile, 1960. (On Irving and Prescott.)

Ferguson, John De Lancey. *American Literature in Spain*. New York: Columbia University Press, 1916.

Fitzmaurice-Kelly, James. *A New History of Spanish Literature*. London: Oxford University Press, 1926.

Flitter, Derek. *Spanish Romantic Literary Theory and Criticism*. Cambridge: Cambridge University Press, 1992.

Foletta, Marshall. *Coming to Terms with Democracy: Federalist Intellectuals and the Shaping of an American Culture*. Charlottesville and London: University Press of Virginia, 2001.

Franchot, Jenny. *Roads to Rome: The Antebellum Protestant Encounter with Catholicism*. Berkeley, Los Angeles, London: University of California Press, 1994.

Gardiner, C. Harvey. "Prescott's Ties with Mexico." *Journal of Inter-American Studies* 1, No. 1 (January 1959), 11–26.

————. *William Hickling Prescott: A Biography*. Introduction by Allan Nevins. Austin and London: University of Texas Press, 1969.

Gavigan, Walter V. "Longfellow and Catholicism." *Catholic World* 138 (October 1933), 42–50.

Gazmuri, Cristián. *La historiografía chilena, 1842–1920*. Vol. I. Santiago: Taurus Historia, 2006.

Gifra-Adroher, Pere. *Between History and Romance: Travel Writing on Spain in the Early Nineteenth-Century United States*. Madison, NJ: Fairleigh Dickinson University Press, 2000.

Gómez Restrepo, Antonio. "Rafael Pombo, 1833–1933." *Bulletin of the Pan American Union* 62, No. 11 (November 1933), 835–845.

González Echevarría, Roberto. *Celestina's Brood. Continuities of the Baroque in Spanish and Latin American Literature*. Durham and London: Duke University Press, 1993.

————. *Myth and Archive: A Theory of Latin American Narrative*. Durham and London: Duke University Press, 1998.

Gooch, G.P. *History and Historians in the Nineteenth Century.* London: Longmans, Green & Co., 1935.

Goodrich, Diana Sorensen. *Facundo and the Construction of Argentine Culture.* Austin: The University of Texas Press, 1996.

Graver, Bruce. "George Ticknor, Robert Southey, and *The Poem of the Cid.*" *Wordsworth Circle* 32, No. 3 (Summer 2001), 151–154.

Gruesz, Kirsten Silva. "*El Gran Poeta* Longfellow and a Psalm of Exile." *American Literary History* 10, No. 3 (1998), 395–427.

———. *Ambassadors of Culture: The Transamerican Origins of Latino Writing.* Princeton: Princeton University Press, 2002.

Guillén, Jorge. "George Ticknor, Lover of Culture." *More Books: The Bulletin of the Boston Public Library* 17, No. 8 (October 1942), 359–375.

Hale, Mathew Rainbow. "Many Who Wandered in Darkness." The Contest over American National Identity, 1795–1798." *Early American Studies* 1, No. 1 (Spring 2003), 127–175.

Hämel, Adalbert. "The Spanish Movement in Germany." *The Modern Language Journal* 12, No. 4 (January 1928), 261–271.

Handlin, Lilian. *George Bancroft: The Intellectual as Democrat.* New York: Harper & Row, Publishers, 1984.

Hanke, Lewis U. "The Development of Latin American Studies in the United States." *Americas* 4 (July 1947), 58–60.

Hart, Thomas R., Jr. "A History of Spanish Literary History, 1800–1850." Ph.D. Dissertation, Yale University, 1952.

———. "Friedrich Bouterwek, A Pioneer Historian of Spanish Literature." *Comparative Literature* 5, No. 4 (Fall 1953), 351–361.

———. "George Ticknor's *History of Spanish Literature*: The New England Background." *PMLA* 69 (1954), 76–88.

Heiser, Merrill F. "Cervantes in the United States." *Hispanic Review* 15 (1947), 409–435.

Hellman, Edith F. "Early Interest in Spanish in New England (1815–1835)." *Hispania* 29 (1946), 326–351.

Hespelt, E. Herman. "Ticknor's First Book from Argentina." *Hispania* 32 (1949), 433–435.

Hickey, R.P. *Catholic Influence on Longfellow.* Kirkwood, MO: Maryhurst Normal Press, 1928.

Horsman, Reginald. *Race and Manifest Destiny: The Origins of American Racial Anglo-Saxonism.* Cambridge and London: Harvard University Press, 1981.

Howe, Daniel Walker. *The Unitarian Conscience: Harvard Moral Philosophy, 1805–1861.* Cambridge, MA: Harvard University Press, 1970.

———. *The Political Culture of the American Whigs.* Chicago and London: The University of Chicago Press, 1979.

Humphreys, R.A. *Tradition and Revolt in Latin America and Other Essays.* London: Weidenfeld and Nicolson, 1969. (Essays on William Robertson and Prescott.)

Irmscher, Christoph. *Longfellow Redux.* Urbana and Chicago: University of Illinois Press, 2006.

Jameson, John Franklin. *The History of Historical Writing in America.* New York: Antiquarian Press [1891] 1961.

Jensen, Larry R. *Children of Colonial Despotism. Press, Politics, and Culture in Cuba, 1790–1840.* Tampa: University of South Florida Press, 1988.

Johannsen, Robert W. *To the Halls of the Montezumas: The Mexican War in the American Imagination.* New York and Oxford: Oxford University Press, 1985.

Johnson, Carl L. *Professor Longfellow of Harvard.* Eugene: University of Oregon, Printed at the University Press, 1944.

———. "Longfellow's Beginnings in Foreign Languages." *New England Quarterly* 20 (September 1947), 317–328.

Jones, Howard, and Donald A. Rakestraw. *Prologue to Manifest Destiny. Anglo-American Relations in the 1840s*. Wilmington, DE: Scholarly Resources, 1997.

Juderías, Julián. *La leyenda negra: Estudios Acerca del Concepto de España en el Extranjero*. Salamanca: Junta de Castilla y León [1914] 2003.

Kagan, Richard L. Ed. *Spain in America: The Origins of Hispanism in the United States*. Urbana: University of Illinois Press, 2002.

Kirkpatrick, Gwen. "Poetic Exchange and Epic Landscapes." In *Literary Cultures of Latin America*, edited by Mario J. Valdés and Djelal Kadir, vol. 3, 173–187. New York and Oxford: Oxford University Press, 2004.

Kraus, Michael and Davis D. Joyce. *The Writing of American History*. Revised Edition. Norman: University of Oklahoma Press, 1985.

Krauze, Enrique. *La Presencia del Pasado: La Huella Indígena, Mestiza y Española de México*. Mexico and Spain: Tusquets Editores, 2005.

Lanero, Juan José and Secundino Villoria. *Literatura en Traducción: Versiones Españolas de Autores Americanos del Siglo XIX*. León: Secretariado de Publicaciones de la Universidad de León, 1996.

Lazo, Rodrigo. *Writing to Cuba: Filibustering and Cuban Exiles in the United States*. Chapel Hill and London: The University of North Carolina Press, 2005.

Levin, David. *History as Romantic Art: Bancroft, Prescott, Motley, and Parkman*. Stanford: Stanford University Press, 1959.

Long, Orie W. *Thomas Jefferson and George Ticknor: A Chapter in American Scholarship*. Williamstown, MA: McClelland Press, 1933.

———. *Literary Pioneers. Early American Explorers of European Culture*. Cambridge, MA: Harvard University Press, 1935.

Marshall, Megan. *The Peabody Sisters: Three Women Who Ignited American Romanticism*. Boston and New York: Houghton Mifflin Company, 2005.

Martínez Carmenate, Urbano. *Domingo del Monte y su tiempo*. La Habana: Ediciones Unión, 1997.

Martínez Fernández, Luis. *Torn Between Empires: Economy, Society, and Patterns of Political Thought in the Hispanic Caribbean, 1840–1878*. Athens and London: The University of Georgia Press, 1994.

Martínez Millán, José, and Carlos Reyero, Eds. *El Siglo de Carlos V y Felipe II: La Construcción de los Mitos en el Siglo XIX*. 2 vols. Madrid: Sociedad Estatal para la Conmemoración de los Centenarios de Felipe II y Carlos V, 2000.

Masiello, Francine. *Between Civilization and Barbarism: Women, Nation and Literary Culture in Modern Argentina*. Lincoln and London: University of Nebraska Press, 1992.

Matthews, Jean V. " 'Whig History': The New England Whigs and a Usable Past." *New England Quarterly* 51, No. 2 (June 1978), 193–208.

May, Ernest R. *The Making of the Monroe Doctrine*. Cambridge: Harvard University Press, 1975.

May, Robert E. *The Southern Dream of a Caribbean Empire, 1854–1861*. Gainesville: University Press of Florida, 2002.

McCloskey, John C. "The Campaign of Periodicals after the War of 1812 for National American Literature." *PMLA* 50, No. 1 (March 1935), 262–273.

Menand, Louis. *The Metaphysical Club*. New York: Farrar, Straus and Giroux, 2001.

Morison, Samuel Eliot. *Three Centuries of Harvard, 1636–1936*. Cambridge, MA: The Belknap Press of Harvard University Press, 1936.

Núñez, Estuardo. "Herman Melville en la América Latina." *Cuadernos Americanos* 68 (March–April 1953), 209–221.

———. *Autores Ingleses y Norteamericanos en el Perú*. Lima: Editorial Cultura, 1956.

Onis, José de. *The United States as Seen by Spanish American Writers (1776–1890)*. 2nd ed. New York: Gordian Press, 1975.

Ortega y Medina, Juan Antonio. *México en la Conciencia Anglosajona.* 2 vols. Mexico: Porrúa-Obregón, 1953–1955.

Owsley, Frank Lawrence Jr., and Gene A. Smith. *Filibusters and Expansionists: Jeffersonian Manifest Destiny, 1800–1821.* Tuscaloosa and London: The University of Alabama Press, 1997.

Pachter, Marc, and Frances Wein, Eds. *Abroad in America: Visitors to the New Nation, 1776–1914.* Reading, MA: Addison-Wesley Publishing Company and the National Portrait Gallery, Smithsonian Institution, 1976.

Park, James William. *Latin American Underdevelopment: A History of Perspectives in the United States, 1870–1965.* Baton Rouge and London: Louisiana State University Press, 1995.

Pearce, Charlotte A. "Longfellow and Spanish America." *Hispania* 58 (December 1975), 921–926.

Peers, E. Allison. "Studies in the Influence of Sir Walter Scott in Spain." *Revue Hispanique* 68 (1926), 1–160.

Pérez Firmat, Gustavo, Ed. *Do the Americas Have a Common Literature?* Durham and London: Duke University Press, 1990.

Perry, Lewis. *Boats against the Current: American Culture between Revolution and Modernity, 1820–1860.* New York: Oxford University Press, 1993.

Pike, Frederick B. *The United States and Latin America: Myths and Stereotypes of Civilization and Nature.* Austin: University of Texas Press, 1992.

Portelli, Alessandro. *The Text and the Voice: Writing, Speaking, and Democracy in American Literature.* New York: Columbia University Press, 1994.

Powell, Philip Wayne. *Tree of Hate: Propaganda and Prejudices Affecting United States Relations with the Hispanic World.* New York and London: Basic Books, 1971.

Riley, Arthur J. "Catholicism and the New England Mind." *Publications of the Colonial Society of Massachusetts.* Vol. 34 (Boston: Published by the Society, 1943), 389–399.

Rivers, Elias L. *Quixotic Scriptures: Essays on the Textuality of Hispanic Literature.* Bloomington: Indiana University Press, 1983.

Robledo, Beatriz Helena. *Rafael Pombo: La Vida de un Poeta.* Bogotá: Vergara, 2005.

Romera Navarro, Miguel. *El Hispanismo en Norte-América. Exposición y Crítica de su Aspecto Literario.* Madrid: Renacimiento, 1917.

Ryder, Frank G., "An American View of Germany—1817." *The American-German Review* 25, No. 2 (December 1958–January 1959), 16–19.

———. "George Ticknor on the German Scene." *The American-German Review* 25, No. 4 (April–May 1959), 28–30.

Schevill, Rudolph. *Menéndez y Pelayo y el Estudio de las Culturas Españolas en los Estados Unidos.* Santander: Sociedad de Menéndez y Pelayo, 1919. (Brief reference to George Ticknor.)

Schoultz, Lars. *Beneath the United States: A History of U.S. Policy toward Latin America.* Cambridge and London: Harvard University Press, 1998.

Scudder, Horace Elisha. *James Russell Lowell: A Biography.* 2 vols. Boston and New York: Houghton, Mifflin and Company, 1901.

Shurbutt, T. Ray, Ed. *United States-Latin American Relations, 1800–1850: The Formative Generations.* Tuscaloosa and London: The University of Alabama Press, 1991.

Simpson, Lewis. "The Era of Joseph Stevens Buckminster: Life and Letters in the Boston-Cambridge Community, 1800–1815." Ph.D. Dissertation, University of Texas, 1948.

———. *The Federalist Literary Mind: Selections from the Monthly Anthology and Boston Review, 1802–1811, Including Documents Relating to the Boston Athenaeum.* Baton Rouge: Louisiana State University Press, 1962.

Smith, Joseph. *Illusions of Conflict: Anglo-American Diplomacy toward Latin America, 1865–1896.* Pittsburgh: University of Pittsburgh Press, 1979.

Sommer, Doris. *Foundational Fictions: The National Romances of Latin America.* Berkeley, Los Angeles, and Oxford: University of California Press, 1991.

Spencer, Benjamin T. *The Quest for Nationality: An American Literary Campaign.* Syracuse: Syracuse University Press, 1957.

Stavans, Ilan. *The Hispanic Condition: Reflections on Culture and Identity in America.* New York: HarperCollins Publishers, 1995.

———, Ed. *Mutual Impressions: Writers from the Americas Reading One Another.* Durham and London: Duke University Press, 1999.

Stimson, Frederick Sparks. *Orígenes del Hispanismo Norteamericano.* Mexico: Ediciones de Andrea, 1961.

Sundquist, Eric J. *To Wake the Nations: Race in the Making of American Literature.* Cambridge, MA, and London: The Belknap Press of Harvard University Press, 1993.

Taylor, Anne-Marie. *Young Charles Sumner and the Legacy of the American Enlightenment, 1811–1851.* Amherst: University of Massachusetts Press, 2001.

Thompson, James Westfall. *A History of Historical Writing.* 2 vols. New York: The Macmillan Company, 1942.

Tucker, Norman P. "Obadiah Rich, 1783–1850: Early American Hispanist." Ph.D. Dissertation, Harvard University, 1973.

———. *Americans in Spain: Patriots, Expatriates, and the Early American Hispanists, 1780–1850.* Boston: The Boston Athenaeum, 1980.

Tully, Carol. *Creating a National Identity: A Comparative Study of German and Spanish Romanticism.* Stuttgart: Verlag Hans-Dieter Heinz, 1997.

———. "How German Romanticism Traveled to Spain: The Intellectual Journey of Johann Nikolas Böhl von Faber." *The Publications of the English Goethe Society.* New Series. Vol. LXXI (2001), 78–90.

Turner, James. *The Liberal Education of Charles Eliot Norton.* Baltimore: The Johns Hopkins University Press, 1999.

Tyack, David B. *George Ticknor and the Boston Brahmins.* Cambridge, MA: Harvard University Press, 1967.

Van Aken, Mark J. *Pan-Hispanism: Its Origin and Development to 1866.* Berkeley and Los Angeles: University of California Press, 1959.

Velleman, Barry L. "Esculpiendo el Mito: Sarmiento, Lincoln y la Traducción de un Poema Escocés." *Cuadernos Americanos* 3, No. 87 (May–June 2001), 91–108.

Vilar, Mar. *Docentes, Traductores e Intérpretes de la Lengua Inglesa en la España del Siglo XIX: Juan Calderón, los Hermanos Usoz y Pascual de Gayangos.* Murcia: Universidad de Murcia, 2004.

Waxman, Samuel M. "George Ticknor, A Pioneer Teacher of Modern Languages." *Hispania* 32 (1949), 426–432.

Wertheimer, Eric. *Imagined Empires: Incas, Aztecs, and the New World of American Literature, 1771–1876.* Cambridge: Cambridge University Press, 1999.

Whitman, Iris Lilian. *Longfellow and Spain.* New York: Instituto de las Españas en los Estados Unidos, 1927.

Wilentz, Sean. *The Rise of American Democracy: Jefferson to Lincoln.* New York and London: W.W. Norton and Company, 2005.

Williams, Lorna Valerie. *The Representation of Slavery in Cuban Fiction.* Columbia and London: University of Missouri Press, 1994.

Williams, Stanley T. *The Life of Washington Irving.* 2 vols. New York: Oxford University Press, 1935.

———. *The Spanish Background of American Literature.* 2 vols. New Haven: Yale University Press, 1955.

Woodbridge, Hensley C. "Prescott's Latin American Reputation." *The American Book Collector* 9, No. 10 (June 1959), 7–12.

Wright, Edith A. "Letters and Manuscripts of William H. Prescott." *The Boston Public Library Quarterly* 11 (July 1959), 115–130.

Zeydel, Edwin H. "George Ticknor and Ludwig Tieck." *PMLA* 44, No. 3 (September 1929), 879–891.

Ziff, Larzer. *Literary Democracy: The Declaration of Cultural Independence in America.* New York: The Viking Press, 1981.

———. *Writing in the New Nation: Prose, Print, and Politics in the Early United States.* New Haven and London: Yale University Press, 1991.

Index